Thinking about Reasons

Jonathan Dancy. Photograph by Sarah Dancy.

Thinking about Reasons

Themes from the Philosophy of Jonathan Dancy

EDITED BY

David Bakhurst, Brad Hooker, and
Margaret Olivia Little

OXFORD
UNIVERSITY PRESS

OXFORD
UNIVERSITY PRESS

Great Clarendon Street, Oxford, OX2 6DP,
United Kingdom

Oxford University Press is a department of the University of Oxford.
It furthers the University's objective of excellence in research, scholarship,
and education by publishing worldwide. Oxford is a registered trade mark of
Oxford University Press in the UK and in certain other countries

© The several contributors 2013

The moral rights of the authors have been asserted

First Edition published in 2013

Impression: 1

All rights reserved. No part of this publication may be reproduced, stored in
a retrieval system, or transmitted, in any form or by any means, without the
prior permission in writing of Oxford University Press, or as expressly permitted
by law, by licence or under terms agreed with the appropriate reprographics
rights organization. Enquiries concerning reproduction outside the scope of the
above should be sent to the Rights Department, Oxford University Press, at the
address above

You must not circulate this work in any other form
and you must impose this same condition on any acquirer

British Library Cataloguing in Publication Data

Data available

ISBN 978-0-19-960467-8

Printed and bound in Great Britain by
CPI Group (UK) Ltd, Croydon, CR0 4YY

Contents

Notes on Contributors vii

    Introduction 1
    Brad Hooker

1 Acting in the Light of a Fact 13
   John McDowell

2 Can Action Explanations Ever Be Non-Factive? 29
   Constantine Sandis

3 The Ideal of Orthonomous Action, or the How and Why of Buck-Passing 50
   Michael Smith

4 Dancy on Buck-Passing 76
   Philip Stratton-Lake

5 Are Egoism and Consequentialism Self-Refuting? 97
   Roger Crisp

6 In Defence of Non-Deontic Reasons 112
   Margaret Olivia Little

7 The Deontic Structure of Morality 137
   R. Jay Wallace

8 Morality and Principle 168
   Stephen Darwall

9 Moral Particularism: Ethical Not Metaphysical? 192
   David Bakhurst

10 A Quietist Particularism 218
    A. W. Price

11 Contours of the Practical Landscape 240
    David McNaughton and Piers Rawling

12	Why Holists Should Love Organic Unities *Sean McKeever and Michael Ridge*	265
13	Practical Reasoning and Inference *John Broome*	286
14	Why There Really Are No Irreducibly Normative Properties *Bart Streumer*	310
	Afterword *Jonathan Dancy*	337
Index		341

Notes on Contributors

DAVID BAKHURST is Charlton Professor of Philosophy at Queen's University at Kingston. His research addresses questions in metaethics, metaphysics, philosophy of education, and Russian philosophy and psychology. His publications include *The Formation of Reason* (2011), *Consciousness and Revolution in Soviet Philosophy* (1991), and many articles in books and journals.

JOHN BROOME is White's Professor of Moral Philosophy at the University of Oxford, and a fellow of Corpus Christi College. He writes on normativity, rationality and reasoning, and also on the ethics of climate change.

ROGER CRISP is Uehiro Fellow and Tutor in Philosophy at St Anne's College, Oxford, and Professor of Moral Philosophy at the University of Oxford. He is the author of *Mill on Utilitarianism* (1997) and *Reasons and the Good* (2006). He is currently writing a book on Henry Sidgwick's *The Methods of Ethics*.

STEPHEN DARWALL is Andrew Downey Orrick Professor of Philosophy at Yale University. He has written widely on the foundations and history of ethics and his books include *The Second-Person Standpoint* (2006), *Impartial Reason* (1983), *Philosophical Ethics* (1995), *The British Moralists and the Internal 'Ought'* (1995), and *Welfare and Rational Care* (2002).

BRAD HOOKER is Professor of Philosophy at the University of Reading. He is the author of *Ideal Code, Real World: A Rule-Consequentialist Theory of Morality* (2000) and co-editor with Margaret Olivia Little of *Moral Particularism* (2000).

MARGARET OLIVIA LITTLE is Director of the Kennedy Institute of Ethics and Associate Professor of Philosophy at Georgetown University. She writes on metaethics, normative ethical theory, and bioethics. She is co-editor, with Brad Hooker, of *Moral Particularism* (2000).

JOHN MCDOWELL taught at Oxford between 1966 and 1986; he is Emeritus Fellow and Honorary Fellow of University College. Since 1986 he has been at the University of Pittsburgh, where he is University Professor of Philosophy. He is a fellow of the British Academy and of the American Academy of Arts and Sciences. His books include *Mind and World* (1994) and four collections of articles.

SEAN MCKEEVER is Associate Professor of Philosophy at Davidson College. His research interests are in contemporary moral theory and metaethics. He is author, with Michael Ridge, of *Principled Ethics: Generalism as a Regulative Ideal* (2006).

DAVID MCNAUGHTON is Professor of Philosophy at Florida State University, and Professor Emeritus at Keele University. He is the author of *Moral Vision* (1988), *Forgiveness* (with Eve Garrard) (2010), and a number of papers on ethics, philosophy of religion, and the relations between the two. He is currently writing a book with Piers Rawling on practical reasons.

A. W. PRICE was educated at Winchester and Oxford, and has taught chiefly at York and Birkbeck College, London. He maintains an interest in both current ethical theory and the moral psychology of Greek philosophers, especially Plato and Aristotle. A monograph *Contextuality in Practical Reason* appeared in 2008.

PIERS RAWLING is Professor and Chair of Philosophy at Florida State University. He has wide-ranging interests, and has published papers on decision theory, ethics (with David McNaughton), metaphysics, quantum computing (with Stephen Selesnick), and philosophy of action, language, mind, and science. He is co-editor (with Alfred Mele) of *The Oxford Handbook of Rationality* (2004).

MICHAEL RIDGE is Professor of Moral Philosophy at the University of Edinburgh. His recent work has been primarily in metaethics, defending a new form of expressivism ('Ecumenical Expressivism'). He is completing a book on that subject, entitled *Impassioned Belief*. In previous co-authored works with Sean McKeever he has published extensively on the debate between particularists and generalists.

CONSTANTINE SANDIS is Reader in Philosophy at Oxford Brookes University. He is the author of *The Things We Do and Why We Do Them* (2012) and editor or co-editor of *Human Nature* (2012), *A Companion to the Philosophy of Action* (2010), *Hegel on Action* (2010), and *New Essays on Action Explanation* (2009).

MICHAEL SMITH is McCosh Professor of Philosophy at Princeton University. His research interests include ethics, moral psychology, and the philosophy of mind and action. He is the author of *The Moral Problem* (1994), *Ethics and the A Priori* (2004), and co-author (with Frank Jackson and Philip Pettit) of *Mind, Morality, and Explanation* (2004).

PHILIP STRATTON-LAKE is Professor of Philosophy at the University of Reading. He is the author of *Kant, Duty, and Moral Worth* (2000), and editor of *Ethical Intuitionism: Re-evaluations* (2002), a new edition of W. D. Ross's *The Right and the Good* (2002), and *On What We Owe to each Other* (2004).

BART STREUMER is Reader in Philosophy at the University of Reading. Between 1999 and 2003 he was Jonathan Dancy's PhD student. He is currently writing a book to be titled *Unbelievable Errors*, which will defend an error theory about all normative judgements.

R. JAY WALLACE is Professor of Philosophy at the University of California, Berkeley. He is the author of *Responsibility and the Moral Sentiments* (1994), *Normativity and the Will* (2006), and numerous papers on moral psychology, practical reason, responsibility, and other topics in philosophical ethics.

Introduction

BRAD HOOKER

Jonathan Dancy has published on a wide variety of topics. He wrote an extremely successful textbook on epistemology and a monograph on Berkeley. He edited an edition of Berkeley's *Principles* and co-edited a *Companion to Epistemology*. He has written articles on topics ranging from Proust to political philosophy. His greatest contributions to philosophy, however, have focused on practical reasons.

His arguments have pushed into mainstream discussion (a) the particularist view that moral reasoning can get along well (indeed is better off) without universal principles, (b) the holist view that an act's having a certain property in one context might be a reason in favour of doing the act and yet in another context an act's having that very same property might be no reason to do the act or might even be a reason against doing it, (c) the view that enabling, disabling, intensifying, and attenuating conditions of practical reasons are no part of the content of practical reasons themselves, (d) the idea that some moral reasons entice rather than insist, and (e) the view that what explains intentional action are not the agent's beliefs or desires, but the facts that are the reasons for which the agent acts. Furthermore, his defences of non-naturalistic moral realism have done much to help rehabilitate this metaethical view. In addition, Dancy has influentially attacked the possibility of organic unities, buck-passing accounts of goodness, and the view that Derek Parfit dubbed 'admirable immorality'.

The essays collected in this volume address all the topics of Dancy's major contributions to contemporary theorizing about practical reasons. The collection is offered as an expression of the contributors' affection and esteem for a man who is not only an innovative and incisive philosopher but also an inspiring and courageous person. He and his work deserve to be honoured.

John McDowell's contribution to this volume, 'Acting in the Light of a Fact', considers a position about practical rationality that Dancy sets out in his book *Practical Reality*. Dancy contends that, when agents act in the light of facts that give them reasons, the reasons are the facts themselves rather than the beliefs that the agents have about those facts, or the fact that the agents have those beliefs. This position has provoked attack but also attracted adherents, one of whom is McDowell.

McDowell's chapter starts by explaining what is attractive about Dancy's position and then discusses a modification to it suggested by Jennifer Hornsby. Hornsby points to cases in which an agent's true belief seems to provide her with reasons for action, and yet the belief is held without sufficient warrant. McDowell's discussion considers the lessons of disjunctivism about experiential warrant for belief and mistaken conceptions of fallibism. The conclusion he arrives at is that our ideal of practical rationality cannot be as independent of theoretical rationality as Dancy's position suggests. Rather, the ideal of practical rationality pictures the agent as acting in the light of a fact that provides a reason for action and that the agent not merely believes obtains but knows obtains.

Constantine Sandis, in his contribution 'Can Action Explanations Ever Be Non-Factive?', turns the spotlight to Dancy's account of motivating reasons for action. Starting in the mid-1990s and building to *Practical Reality*, Dancy attacked the belief-desire view of motivating reasons on the ground that motivating explanatory reasons must at least be capable of being normative reasons, and normative reasons are not beliefs and desires, but features of the situation one is in, rather than the agent's mental states. Dancy's own view is 'non-psychologism', according to which *what* the agent believes about the features of the various things she might do constitute the reasons for which she acts.

A prominent objection to Dancy's non-psychologism points to cases where the agent acted for reasons, but her beliefs were false. Jill hits Jack in the face because she believes this will make him hideous, but then his injuries turn out to make him even better looking. In this case, how can we explain Jill's action by pointing to the facts when there was no such fact? What she believed was false, and falsehoods cannot genuinely explain things. Her *belief* in a falsehood might be thought to explain her action, but Dancy's non-psychologism bars this move. So, how can Dancy's non-psychologism about the reasons for which the agent acts provide an explanation of the agent's acts when the agent's beliefs are false?

In response, Sandis argues that we should keep the non-psychologism but dispense with the idea that agents' reasons explain action. Agential reasons are indeed considerations external to the mind, considerations which we typically take to favour actions; but agential reasons themselves do not explain actions. We explain actions instead by claims of the form: 'His reason for joining the investment club was that it would increase his pension.' Such a claim makes reference to agential reasons, but that is not the same as saying that the reasons are what explain the actions. The explanation, properly understood, is the whole statement that his reason for joining the investment club was that it would increase his pension. When we share the agent's beliefs we might say 'she did it because p' but this is a shorthand for the true explanation, made reasonable by the fact that saying so conventionally implies that the agent (a) took it to be the case that p and (b) took this to be a consideration that counted in favour of the action. Sandis concludes by taking up Dancy's suggestion that contrasting English with other languages illuminates this issue, and by commenting on the debate over causalism in the theory of action.

Michael Smith's 'The Ideal of Orthonomous Action, or the How and Why of Buck-Passing' begins by exploring two different ways in which we might explain what makes an action an action. One way is to characterize the ideal action, even though many or all actual instances of the kind do not match the ideal. The other way is to delineate the feature that all instances of actions, whether ideal or not—that is, all approximations to the ideal—have in common.

Smith argues that ideal actions are instances of what he and Philip Pettit have elsewhere called *orthonomous* actions. These are actions that are motivated by an intention an agent forms as a result of exercising his capacity to recognize and respond to such reasons as there are for intending to act in one way rather than another. Moreover, Smith argues, the capacity required for orthonomous action itself decomposes into two distinct capacities. It decomposes into (a) the capacity to recognize and respond to reasons for intrinsically desiring that things be a certain way and (b) the capacity to recognize and respond to reasons for believing that a certain bodily movement available to the agent will cause things to be that way. Given that the capacity required for orthonomous action decomposes into these two distinct capacities, Smith argues that it should be no surprise that what all instances of action have in common is their being caused in the right way by a belief-desire pair, no matter what the genesis of the belief-desire pair.

Smith also argues that this conception of ideal action shows us what is wrong with Jonathan Dancy's objections to buck-passing accounts of goodness. According to the buck-passer, something's goodness consists in its having other properties that give agents reasons for adopting various pro-attitudes towards it. Dancy rejects this view, but he accepts a buck-passing view of rightness, according to which an action's rightness consists in its having other properties that give agents reasons to do the action. But Smith argues that buck-passing views about goodness and rightness form a package deal, in that to endorse the one is to endorse the other.

In closing, Smith argues that the buck-passing view of goodness is compatible both with 'agent-neutral' reasons (reasons necessarily shared by everyone to favour or disfavour various ways the world might be) and with 'agent-relative' reasons (reasons for each person to favour or disfavour various ways the world might be that are particularly connected with that person himself). Smith contends that this makes the idea of agent-relative values much less problematic than Dancy supposes.

Philip Stratton-Lake's 'Dancy on Buck-Passing' starts by explaining how Tim Scanlon's buck-passing account differs from earlier 'fitting-attitude' accounts of goodness, and proceeds to refine Scanlon's account. Scanlon distinguishes between valuing a thing, which is to take oneself to have reason to care about it, and thinking something is valuable, or good, which is to take everyone to have reason to care about it. Scanlon's distinction looks like the distinction between agent-relative and agent-neutral reasons. Stratton-Lake accepts that both kinds of *reasons* exist. However, in contrast to Michael Smith, Stratton-Lake argues against the idea of agent-relative value on the ground that this idea contains a confusing ambiguity.

Then Stratton-Lake turns his attention to Dancy's attacks on buck-passing. Here again Stratton-Lake's chapter intersects with Smith's. Dancy has argued that his keeping a trivial promise he made to his children about which shoelace he ties first is something he has reason to do though it is not something of any value. Smith's view is that this act does have agent-relative value. In contrast, Stratton-Lake, having argued against agent-relative value, thinks that Dancy's keeping his trivial promise is not good unless it has agent-neutral value.

Stratton-Lake next confronts Dancy's claim that the buck-passing view illicitly settles some basic disputes in normative ethics, in particular debates between deontologists and consequentialists. Stratton-Lake argues that buck-passing does not settle these disputes, because proponents of buck-passing are committed neither to the view that any act for which there is a reason for action is good nor to the view that maximizing is always the appropriate response to value. Stratton-Lake ends by attacking Dancy's argument that the buck-passing account implausibly makes something's value or disvalue contingent on the existence of beings who can take pro- or con-attitudes to it.

Roger Crisp's 'Are Egoism and Consequentialism Self-Refuting?' addresses a problem that Dancy found in Parfit's *Reasons and Persons*. That book postulates that egoism gives one the overriding aim of having one's life go as well as possible in self-interested terms, and that impartial consequentialism gives one the overriding aim of having the history of the world go as well as possible impartially considered. But having these aims is self-defeating: the aims are not best achieved by having them.

While not agreeing with every element of Dancy's attack on Parfit, Crisp ends up accepting that Parfit's formulations of egoism and impartial consequentialism are vulnerable to Dancy's attacks. Crisp proposes that, at the most basic level, egoism and impartial consequentialism should be formulated in terms of practical reasons instead of overriding aims. Egoism holds '[o]ne has most reason to act in that way in which one's life goes, for one, as well as possible'. Impartial consequentialism holds that '[o]ne has most reason to act in that way in which the history of the world goes as well as possible'. Crisp goes on to observe that egoism and impartial consequentialism 'will almost always require agents to follow some strategy in living or acting other than the continual application of the theory itself'. Egoism will prescribe, not the overriding aim that one's life go best in self-interested terms, but whatever aims will make one's life go best in self-interested terms. Impartial consequentialism will prescribe, not the overriding aim that the history of the world go best impartially considered, but rather whatever aims will make the history of the world go best impartially considered.

Margaret Little's 'In Defence of Non-Deontic Reasons' aims to redeem the idea, defended by Dancy, that some reasons for action are merely enticing. Such reasons are not, as she puts it, 'in the wrong-making business': they are capable of rendering action intelligible without bringing any deontic vulnerability in their wake. As she puts the point, 'non-deontic reasons... justify one action without unjustifying anything else, whether that be doing nothing, doing exactly what you had been doing before this reason happened by, or pursuing an action that is supported by a different reason. They invite, as it were, rather than tell you what to do.'

Little proceeds by first arguing against a deontically reductive view of reasons: even if all reasons impose deontic vulnerability, they cannot be reduced to such imposition, on pain of an overly thin view of agency. Reasons also carry a commendatory force—an aspect under which the will may intelligibly act even though it would not be wrong not to do so. Some reasons for emotional states (such as anger) justify an emotional state without placing one in need of justifying its absence; likewise, some reasons justify an action without placing one in need of justifying not doing the action. Little goes on to argue that the normative force of some reasons is structurally like the illocutionary force of requests, which can give their recipients a good reason to do what was requested, without going so far as to require their recipients to do what was requested. (Contrast the non-insistence in a request with the insistence in an order.)

R. Jay Wallace's 'The Deontic Structure of Morality', like Little's contribution, is interested in the distinction between 'deontic' reasons for action that make demands on agents and 'aspirational' reasons that determine what the best action in the circumstances would be without going so far as to require it (Wallace's 'aspirational reasons' are what Dancy and Little call 'enticing reasons'). One might suppose that the way to make sense of the distinction is in terms of weight or importance. But Wallace argues that this path is a dead end. Likewise, appeal to Raz's exclusionary reasons is inadequate. The problem is that sometimes deontic reasons are outweighed or trumped by considerations they might be thought to have excluded. More generally, Wallace argues that deontic significance is potentially independent of deliberative importance.

Another way of trying to explain the difference between aspirational and deontic reasons is to point out that deontic reasons have a connection to social sanctions that aspirational reasons do not. But we cannot plausibly hold that deontic reasons are necessarily connected to extant social sanctions. In fact, deontic reasons are not always accompanied by actual threats of sanctions. Nor can we plausibly hold that aspirational reasons are never connected to extant social sanctions.

Rather, what distinguishes deontic reasons from aspirational ones is that an agent's deontic reasons are necessarily relational in a way that aspirational ones are not. For example, if there are deontic reasons for me to do X for you, then you have a *claim* to my doing X for you; and because of your claim on me, I *wrong* you if I fail to give due regard to the deontic reasons for my doing X for you. My failure gives you a reason for resentment that those who have no claim on me do not have. 'The basic idea is that we have a certain latitude to ignore or discount aspirational reasons, of a kind we do not have when it comes to reasons that exhibit deontic structure.'

Wallace goes on to explain the difficulties act-consequentialism has accounting for the difference between deontic and aspirational reasons, and for the 'presumptive connection' between wrongness and negative reactive attitudes on the part of others. Much more promising, according to Wallace, is the contractualist idea that I wrong you if my action is not justifiable to you on grounds that you could not reasonably reject.

Stephen Darwall's 'Morality and Principle' begins by accepting Dancy's holism about practical reasons and Dancy's distinction between reasons and enablers, disablers, intensifiers, and attenuators of reasons. Darwall goes on to argue, however, that there is an attractive rationale for general moral principles that Dancy fails to consider. While Dancy does attack the view that morality is like traffic regulations in being comprised of public rules justified by their benefits, he does not consider the idea that the concepts of moral obligation and demand are conceptually tied to accountability, or the idea that 'agents can intelligibly be held accountable only if there exist general rules and principles that are accessible to all who are morally bound as a matter of common public knowledge'.

Dancy distinguishes between the moral reasons that are strongest in a particular case and reasons that are outweighed or somehow disabled in the case. Darwall contends, however, that we must distinguish between the moral reasons that are strongest in a particular case and reasons that come from moral obligations and demands. Of course moral obligations and demands often do provide the strongest reasons in the particular situation, but in some situations the moral reasons that happen to be strongest do not come from obligations (perhaps because in the situation no obligations come into play). When reasons are supererogatory, for instance, they do not amount to an obligation and do not render the agent accountable. To hold an agent morally accountable for a wrong is to say that the agent's action is an appropriate target of 'reactive attitudes', such as guilt, resentment, indignation, and moral blame. But just as in the law negative sanctions are appropriate only if there is a publicly accessible rule which agents can be required to avoid breaking, in morality people can be morally blamed only for infringing rules that they should have known they had to observe.

David Bakhurst's 'Moral Particularism: Ethical Not Metaphysical?' explores the moral philosophy of David Wiggins in search of resources that might supplement Dancy's contributions to ethics. Dancy focuses on the theory of reasons for action and takes, as his primary test cases, specific situations in which an agent or agents must respond to the reasons in play there. But an acceptable picture of a good moral agent must not only account for her responses in particular situations but also display her character and enduring commitments, which, after all, contour those responses.

Bakhurst finds in Wiggins an account of the lived ethical life, shaped by its standing commitments. At least many of these can quite naturally be expressed as principles. And some of these standing commitments will be absolute in force because to forsake them is inconsistent with anything recognizable as a moral point of view. Nevertheless, Bakhurst argues that the Dancy-supplemented-by-Wiggins position is still particularist, because, in the normal case where conflicting considerations come into play and none is absolute, uncodifable judgement is needed to resolve what to do.

A.W. Price's 'A Quietist Particularism' begins by considering how Dancy places enablers, disablers, intensifiers, and attenuators of reasons outside the content of reasons. Price first points out that, if any of these sit within the very content of reasons themselves, as opposed to merely sitting within the situational context of the reasons, then 'it would become less plausible that *further* information may always cancel, reverse, intensify, or attenuate a given reason'. He goes on to ask whether, even if enablers, disablers, intensifiers, and attenuators are kept out of the content of reasons, there could not be principles articulating the conditions under which these enablers, disablers, intensifiers, and attenuators obtain. Indeed, Price himself shows that morally compelling facts 'often have a wide degree of generality' even if they aren't perfectly general. He also points to side-constraints, where general principles are supposed to exclude or disable any other considerations.

Price then turns to Pekka Väyrynen's contention that moral reasons have a 'normative basis' in 'hedged general principles'. These are principles specifying the explanation of why a fact is sometimes a moral reason and sometimes not. Though people's grasp of such principles will often be inchoate or incomplete, Väyrynen suggests that the underlying reality is systematic and determinate. Price is dubious. Pointing out that 'certain rules (and other things, such as values, and paradigms) *stand firm for us*', he is sceptical that they can be given 'any grounding of which we are more certain than we are certain of these'. When such rules or values conflict, Price suggests, there may be no correct answer about what to do. At any rate, Price uses Väyrynen's arguments to question whether non-realism might fit better with particularism than Dancy's own realism does: 'If we really thought, like the realist, that the moral world has its contours fixed independently of our ability to map them, it would hard to be sure that Väyrynen's programme might not reveal its true topography.... The non-realist is immune to the fantasy of a fixed ethical world waiting to be captured by ethical systematization.'

David McNaughton and Piers Rawling's 'Contours of the Practical Landscape' presents a general account of practical reasons and the relation of the normative to the non-normative. They distinguish between facts that are themselves reasons and facts that certain other facts are reasons. Facts that certain other facts are reasons are always normative: it is a normative fact that the fact that this action would relieve someone's pain is a reason for doing it. Facts that are themselves reasons for action are sometimes normative facts. For example, the fact that an act would cause undeserved harm is a normative fact and a reason not to do that act. McNaughton and Rawling observe that some facts have invariant polarity: that an act would cause undeserved harm always counts against the act. Here we have an example of what McNaughton and Rawling are willing to call a universal reason and a principle.

They go on to systematize reasons as functions of either impersonal value, of benefits to oneself, or of benefits to those with whom one has some special connection. They hold that there are reasons to do an act if, but only if, the act is of benefit or impersonal value. But the reasons one has to benefit oneself or those with whom one has special connections can outstrip the contribution of these benefits to impersonal value. Meanwhile, impersonal value is not purely a function of benefit and harm, since, for one example, it matters whether benefits or harms are deserved. McNaughton and Rawling close by casting doubt on the existence of moral constraints.

Sean McKeever and Michael Ridge's 'Why Holists Should Love Organic Unities' argues that Dancy should accept rather than reject organic unities. The doctrine of organic unities, proposed by G. E. Moore, holds that the value of a whole need not be a mathematical function (e.g. equal to the sum) of the values of all the non-overlapping parts of that whole. As Dancy explains, holism in the theory of value has the same structure as holism in the theory of reasons. Something's having a certain property in one context might be good-making, but in another context something's having that very same property might be not be good-making. One might have thought that Dancy would accept the doctrine of organic unities, since, like Dancy's holism, that doctrine stresses the complexity and variability of relations between reason-constituting or good-making features and their contexts. However, Dancy argues that the doctrine of organic unities is incoherent.

Dancy's argument is that the doctrine is incompatible with the necessary connection between values and reasons. Take a case where a necessary part of a valuable whole supposedly has no value in itself. We have no reason to preserve the part as a part, but reason to preserve the valuable whole, which depends on the necessary part. Dancy argues that, since we have reason to preserve the whole including the part, the part must have value, because of the necessary connection between reasons and values. McKeever and Ridge catalogue a number of objections to this argument. One is that Dancy's argument threatens his own distinction between values and their enabling conditions. For Dancy does not take the fact that enabling conditions of value are worthy of protection to imply that such conditions are themselves valuable. McKeever and Ridge's chapter concludes by offering putative examples both of organic unities and of holism about reasons.

John Broome's 'Practical Reasoning and Inference' engages with Dancy's contention that practical reasoning is not based on inference. Broome begins by laying out a theory of reasoning conceived as a mental process. Taking inference to be a relation between propositions, he explains how theoretical rationality prohibits basing belief A on beliefs B, C, D, etc., unless the content of belief A can be inferred from the contents of beliefs

B, C, D, etc. Theoretical reasoning involves applying (though not necessarily explicitly knowing) an inference rule.

Broome then turns to practical reasoning, or, more specifically, reasoning to an intention. After identifying an instrumental requirement, Broome argues that practical rationality cannot be derived from theoretical rationality, and that keeping practical and theoretical reasoning separate is tricky, because normally an intention to do X is accompanied by a simultaneous belief that one will do X. Finally, he argues that practical reasoning, when conscious, is also a rule-governed operation on conscious propositional attitudes. Broome's conclusion is that, since practical reasoning is a mental process and inference is a relation between propositions, practical reasoning is not, strictly speaking, based on inference; still, practical reasoning does involve applying rules about the permissible basing of intentions on beliefs.

Bart Streumer's 'Are There Really No Irreducibly Normative Properties?' starts by explaining that an irreducibly normative property is one that is not identical with any descriptive property. He then follows Frank Jackson in supposing that normative properties *must* be coextensive with the (perhaps disjunctive) sets of descriptive properties, across all possible worlds, on which the normative properties supervene. Jackson holds that necessarily coextensive properties are really the same property. So he concludes, against Dancy among others, that normative properties are actually reducible to the descriptive properties on which they supervene.

The usual way of attacking Jackson's argument is to reject its premise that necessarily coextensive predicates ascribe the same property. Streumer carefully considers prominent putative counterexamples to Jackson's premise and argues that they are misconceived. Streumer then turns to Jussi Suikkanen's argument against Jackson. Suikkanen points to various higher-order properties that normative properties possess but descriptive properties do not, and thus concludes that normative properties are not identical with descriptive ones. Streumer replies that the apparent difference in higher order properties can be explained in terms of modes of presentation—a normative mode and a descriptive mode—without conceding there is a difference in higher-order properties.

Then Streumer turns to David Enoch's contentions that the belief that there are irreducibly normative properties is indispensible to our deliberation about what to do and that we think normative properties are just too different from descriptive properties to be identical to them. Streumer responds that, even if these contentions about our thinking are true, our thinking might be systematically mistaken.

Our thinking might indeed be systematically mistaken. So we should test our ideas by considering evidence, arguments, and counterarguments in rigorous, fair-minded, and imaginative ways. That is exactly what Jonathan Dancy has done over a distinguished career, with results that have greatly enriched contemporary philosophy.

1

Acting in the Light of a Fact

JOHN McDOWELL

I

One might expect my title phrase to express an idea that would be central in a book called *Practical Reality*. Practical reality should be made up of facts in the light of which agents act, or at any rate would act if their practical rationality was as it should be. And that is in the spirit of the conception Jonathan Dancy elaborates (2000). But Dancy's treatment of reasons for acting does not accommodate a certain natural interpretation of the idea of acting in the light of a fact. And that means he omits something that would need to figure in a complete account of the operation of practical rationality.

I was led to argue for something on these lines—in self-defence, as it were—in my response to Dancy (2006). The format of that exchange did not give him the opportunity for a comeback. In the relevant part of my response, however, I was urging something I took myself to have learned from a talk by Jennifer Hornsby, which included an example that has since appeared in Hornsby (2008); and Dancy has made it clear (2008) that he is not convinced by the proposal of Hornsby's that impressed me. I assume he would have taken the same line if he had responded to my response.

In this chapter I want to try to persuade him that there is something importantly missing from his picture of rationality in action. I mean this as a friendly intervention, and I hope it will seem an appropriate way of honouring a philosopher I greatly admire. I think it would only strengthen Dancy's conception of practical reality if he made room for the missing idea.

In the strictest sense, perhaps, practical reality would consist of facts that would impress themselves on the will of any rational agent who fully appreciated them. For my part, I think we should recognize that it is also possible for facts to weigh with rational agents only contingently on motivational states they happen to be in, though other rational agents might not be; that is how it is when taking an umbrella is acting in the light of the fact that it is raining. Here I am at least close to embracing a picture of practical rationality that Dancy has criticized as unacceptably hybrid (for instance, in Dancy 2006). But in this chapter nothing will turn on that. I want to consider acting in the light of facts in a way that is neutral on the question whether it is sometimes, always, or never the case that, when facts weigh with rational agents, their weighing is contingent on further motivational facts about the agents.

II

One of Dancy's fundamental concerns is to reject a misconstrual of the way belief figures in explanations of actions in terms of reasons.

One can explain someone's doing this or that by specifying something she believes. There is a perennial temptation to suppose that if the relevant belief, schematically that things are thus and so, is false, the person's reason for doing what she is doing cannot be that things are thus and so, but must be her believing that things are thus and so, or (the fact) that she believes that things are thus and so. And once we have persuaded ourselves that that is the right thing to say when the relevant belief is false, we are under pressure to suppose it is right when the belief is true as well. After all, when a belief makes an action intelligible, the truth-value of the belief surely makes no difference to the character of the understanding that the explanation provides (see, e.g., Dancy 2000: 121, citing Bernard Williams; or Dancy 2008: 267–8). So it comes to seem that whether the belief is true or false, the person's reason for acting as she does must be her believing what she does, or (the fact) that she believes it.

Dancy persuasively resists this. He acknowledges that a person's reason for doing something *can* be her believing that things are thus and so, or (the fact) that she believes that things are thus and so. For instance (this is one of his examples), a person's reason for seeking psychiatric help might be his believing there are pink rats in his boots, or (the fact) that he believes that.[1]

---

[1] One might object that seeking psychiatric help shows that he does not *really* believe there are pink rats in his boots. But the point does not depend on this particular example.

But suppose that, instead of seeking psychiatric help, he holds the boots upside down and shakes them vigorously. In that case his reason for doing that, the consideration in the light of which he is acting, is that, as he believes, there are pink rats in his boots—not (the fact) that he believes that or his believing that. An agent's reason for doing what she does is *what* she relevantly believes, not her believing it or (the fact) that she believes it. And that is so even if the relevant belief is false.

So it is wrong to succumb to that perennial temptation, and suppose that at least when the relevant belief is false, the agent's reason for acting as she does must be her believing what she believes or (the fact) that she believes it. And if that is wrong when the relevant belief is false, the argument for extending it to cases in which the relevant belief is true falls to the ground.

III

Now consider a situation in which things *are* as an agent relevantly takes them to be. If they are, the consideration in the light of which she acts, her reason for doing what she does, is something that is the case. And something that is the case is a fact. So the conception Dancy recommends allows that an agent's reason for acting can be a fact—not the fact of her believing what she does, but the fact in virtue of whose obtaining the relevant belief is true.

Dancy makes room, then, for someone's reason for acting to be a fact. And when someone's reason for acting is a fact, surely she acts in the light of that fact. So how can I claim that acting in the light of a fact is missing from Dancy's thinking? Let me explain.

The forms Dancy exploits—'So-and-so's reason for doing such-and-such is that . . .' and variants of that—are, in the interpretation he supplies for them, not factive in respect of the place for a propositional complement that I have marked with an ellipsis. That is essential to the way he resists that misconstrual of the role of belief in the rational understanding of actions. A statement that exemplifies one of those forms, explained as Dancy explains it, can be true even if the relevant belief is false. That is why there is no go in the idea that when the relevant belief is false, the agent's reason cannot be *what* she believes.

The non-factive character of those forms reflects the fact that the ellipsis marks a kind of *oratio obliqua* position. About the use of 'because' in explanations that work by giving the reason for which someone did, or is doing, such-and-such, Dancy proposes that it can be expanded—not to add new content but just to bring out its significance—on these lines: 'He did (or is doing) such-and-such because, as he supposed (or supposes) . . . ' (see 2000: ch. 6; I used this appositive construction in describing one of the cases involving a belief about pink rats). This makes it plausible that, as I suggested in my response to Dancy (2006), the reason-giving 'because', as Dancy understands it, is a good match for the Latin '*quod*' with the subjunctive. '*Quod*' means 'because', and if a clause governed by '*quod*' is in the subjunctive, that marks its content as something that may or may not be true but is believed by the subject.

Now the sense Dancy enables us to make of an idea of acting in the light of a fact is this: if, in a true statement of one of those forms, what figures in the place marked by the ellipsis is something that is the case, the agent's reason for acting in the relevant way is something that is the case; that is, a fact.

Since we are dealing with an *oratio obliqua* construction, that is analogous to saying, surely acceptably, that what someone believes is a fact if her belief is true.

It is sufficient for what someone believes to be a fact if the belief is true; its being true may be no more than a happy accident in relation to the person's cognitive position. Just so, it is sufficient for someone's reason for doing something to be a fact, in the sense Dancy makes room for, if the belief whose content is the person's reason for acting is true; again, its being true may be no more than a happy accident in relation to the person's cognitive position. If we know that someone's reason for acting in a certain way is a fact, in the sense Dancy makes room for, we know that she takes the relevant fact to obtain, and we know that it does obtain. But in knowing only that much, we do not know whether its obtaining is anything but a happy accident in relation to her cognitive position. Dancy's version of the idea of acting in the light of a fact is not sensitive to the difference between cases in which the obtaining of the fact is, and cases in which it is not, a mere happy accident in relation to the agent's cognitive position.

Here, then, is the missing idea. If, but only if, the obtaining of the fact by virtue of whose obtaining the relevant belief is true is *not* a happy accident in relation to the agent's cognitive position, we can say that the fact itself is exerting a rational influence on the agent's will; we can say that in doing what she is doing the agent is responding rationally to the fact itself. If the truth of the relevant belief is merely good luck, cognitively speaking, on the agent's part, the agent's reason for acting is the relevant fact, in the sense Dancy makes room for. But in such a case it would be absurd to say the agent is rationally responding to the fact itself. To be responding to the fact itself, she would need to have the fact itself in her sights, in a sense that is excluded if it is only by luck that her belief is true. Responding to a fact—acting in the light of a fact, on the natural interpretation that, as I said, is missing from Dancy's thinking—requires not just believing, truly of course (since we are presupposing that it is a fact), that the fact obtains, but *knowing* that it does, being non-accidentally correct in one's belief that it does.[2]

IV

Hornsby recommends an idea on those lines with an example. Here is how she presents it (2008: 251):

> The example concerns Edmund who believes that the ice in the middle of the pond is dangerously thin, having been told so by a normally reliable friend, and who accordingly keeps to the edge. But Edmund's friend didn't want Edmund to skate in the middle of the pond (never mind why), so that he told Edmund that the ice there was thin despite having no view about whether or not it actually was thin. Edmund, then, did not keep to the edge *because* the ice in the middle was thin. Suppose, now, that as it happened, the ice in the middle of the pond was thin. This makes no difference. Edmund still didn't keep to the edge *because* the ice was thin. The fact that the ice was thin does not explain Edmund's acting, even though Edmund did believe that it was thin, and even though the fact that it was thin actually was a reason for him to stay at the edge.

And here is how Dancy responds (2008: 276):

---

[2] Dancy's official line is that his non-factive interpretation of the reason-giving locutions is enough, and there is no need for an interpretation that is factive and so knowledge-requiring. But in at least one place his own language reveals the pull of the idea he officially refuses to countenance. Purporting to be just spelling out the thought that something in the light of which one acts must be something one believes, he says 'one cannot act in the light of a fact that one does not *recognize* to obtain' (2008: 269; my emphasis).

> Hornsby's point... is that action on a true belief in a reason-giving fact is not enough for it to be the case that one is acting for that fact as a reason. It is only if one knows that fact that one can be said to be acting for it as a reason. But this seems to me to involve an invalid inference. One cannot argue that Edmund is not keeping to the edge for the reason that the ice is thin from the premise that he is not skating there *because* the ice is thin. In fact, I would say of both scenarios above (the one where the friend is right and the one where he is wrong) that in them Edmund is skating on the edge for the reason that the ice is thin, or that Edmund's reason for skating there is that the ice is thin, or that the reason for which he is skating there is that the ice is thin. I don't see that Hornsby's two scenarios do anything to upset that entirely natural position.

Dancy here insists on the non-factive, and so certainly not knowledge-requiring, interpretation he has explained for 'He is doing such-and-such for the reason that...', or 'His reason for doing such-and-such is that...', or 'The reason for which he is doing such-and-such is that...'.

But this does not engage with Hornsby's point. Dancy insists that Hornsby cannot infer negations of statements with those forms from her denial that Edmund is keeping to the edge *because* the ice is thin. But he does not query the premise of the supposed inferences. And that gives Hornsby everything she needs. Her point is this: there is an intelligible interpretation of the claim that Edmund is keeping to the edge because the ice is thin, on which that claim is not true in her story, because, given that the friend had no view about whether the ice was thin, his saying so to Edmund cannot have provided Edmund with knowledge that the ice was thin, even in the version of the example in which the ice was indeed thin. She has no need to disallow Dancy's explanatory locutions. It does not matter to her point that, as Dancy insists, negations of them do not follow from the negation of the explanatory locution she focuses on. Her point is not to deny that explanatory locutions explained in Dancy's way are true in her story, but to claim that there is *another* form in which propositions like 'the ice is (was) thin' can—sometimes, but not in the case she considers—be brought into explanatory connection with statements about what people are doing or have done.

It is true that Hornsby sometimes appropriates the forms for which Dancy gives his non-factive interpretation, in order to express the idea she says is not available for explaining Edmund's action, even in the version of the example in which what his friend tells him is true. She says, for instance:

'A condition of ϕ-ing for the reason that p, when one believes that p, is that one knows that p' (2008: 251). But the context restricts this remark to what she calls 'acting for (F)-type reasons'; that is, to cases in which someone acts in the light of a fact, in the sense that I am insisting Dancy does not accommodate. Hornsby's remark need not be taken to imply a denial that 'for the reason that...' can *also* be understood in Dancy's way.

Hornsby's Edmund does not know that the ice in the middle of the pond is thin, even in the version of the example in which the ice is indeed thin. Even though it is a fact, in that version of the example, that the ice in the middle of the pond is thin, we cannot explain his keeping to the edge by saying that that fact is weighing with him (see Hornsby 2008: 254), or that in keeping to the edge he is responding to that fact (p. 256). But suppose we change the example to one in which the person who said the ice was thin was expressing knowledge, so that Edmund can count as knowing that by having been told it. Now we can explain his keeping to the edge as his rational response to the fact that the ice is thin. In this variant, it can be the fact itself that weighs with Edmund.

Just because Dancy's forms are not factive, it does not add to the explanatory power of explanations given by using those forms if things are as the agent relevantly takes them to be. If things are that way, that is just an extra fact about the situation; the action would have had the same intelligibility of Dancy's sort if the agent had been wrong in taking things to be that way. That is: its being a fact that the agent is acting in the light of, in the sense Dancy makes room for, is not integral to the understanding we get from an explanation in Dancy's terms.

And now we can put Hornsby's point like this. There is no need to deny that an explanation in one of the forms Dancy countenances can provide some understanding of an action. But if we have only that understanding, we do not yet know the answer to a question that should concern us if we are interested in how the action manifests the agent's practical rationality at work. We do not yet know, and we ought to want to know, whether the action can be understood as a rational response to the fact in question. If it can, we can have an understanding of the action to which its being a fact that the agent is acting in the light of is integral. That is the idea of acting in the light of a fact that is missing from Dancy's thinking.[3]

[3] Officially at any rate: see note 2 in this chapter.

Dancy responds to Hornsby as if she were putting forward something that competes with his non-factive forms for the title of being *the* way to give an agent's reason for acting as she does. But we do not have to choose between non-factive and knowledge-requiring forms, as if each were a candidate for capturing the whole truth about how we understand actions when we see them as the agent's rationality at work. The point is that if, in a case in which things are the way the agent relevantly takes them to be, we know only something we can express in one of the forms Dancy explains, we know some, by all means, but only some of what there is to know about the rational intelligibility of the action we are considering. There is a question about its rational intelligibility that we are not yet in a position to answer: the question whether the agent, in acting as she does, is rationally responding to the fact in virtue of which her relevant belief is true.

Notice that I am not backsliding from Dancy's point about the role of belief in the rational understanding of action. What I am urging is this: there is a difference, which matters for the rational intelligibility of actions, between, on the one hand, acting in the light of a fact, in the sense of responding rationally to the fact, having the fact weigh with one, and, on the other hand, acting in the light of something one takes to be so without knowing it to be so; and there is still that difference even if what one takes to be so without knowing it to be so is in fact so.

Registering that difference does not prevent us from applauding Dancy for his insistence, in connection with the forms he restricts himself to, that it is what the agent relevantly takes to be so, not her taking it to be so, that is her reason for acting as she does.

V

Like Hornsby, I think it can be helpful to consider the kind of intelligibility an action has when it is a rational response to a fact, in the sense that is missing from Dancy's treatment of reasons for acting, in parallel with a disjunctive approach to perceptual experience.

Dancy (2008) contains a sceptical discussion of this suggestion. But I do not believe he gets the suggestion into focus. This is partly because, as I have been urging, he does not have the relevant kind of intelligibility of actions in view. But it is partly because the disjunctive approach to perceptual experience that he considers is not the right one for the parallel.

In general, disjunctive approaches to experience have as their topic the relation between experiences that provide their subject with opportunities for perceptual knowledge (or would do that; we can consider merely possible experiences) and experiences that are (or would be) subjectively indistinguishable from experiences of the first kind but do not afford opportunities for knowledge.[4] What is characteristic of a disjunctive approach is the denial of a commonality between pairs of experiences related in that way.

But what commonality? The disjunctive approach Dancy considers denies that the members of such a pair have *any* 'common features or qualities' (2008: 262). He says that is part of a consensus, and no doubt it is, in some quarters. But the effect is that the point we need if we are to appreciate Hornsby's proposed parallel goes missing.

The denial we should be focusing on is more specific; it is the denial that the members of such a pair are alike in their relevance to the rational warrant for experience-based beliefs about the environment. If subjective indistinguishability implied sameness in relevance to rational warrant for belief, the contribution made by either member of such a pair to the subject's epistemic standing, with respect to a belief that things are as they, for instance, look to be, could be no better than a *highest common factor* of the contributions of both. The 'good' member of a pair could provide no better warrant for the associated belief than the 'bad' member. That would make it problematic how the 'good' member could afford, by itself, an opportunity for knowledge about the environment. Whereas if we reject the highest common factor conception, we can maintain, with common sense, that an experience of the 'good' kind itself reveals to its subject that things in the environment are a certain way, and thereby affords a warrant for believing things to be that way that suffices to certify the belief as knowledgeable. Rejecting the highest common factor conception frees that thought from

---

[4] Note that an experience can be of the second of these kinds even if it is 'veridical'. Where I speak, below, of subjects being misled, the relevant idea is not that they are misled about how things are in the environment, but that they are misled about whether knowledge of how things are in the environment is available to them through their experience; a subject can be misled about that even if her experience does not lead her to false beliefs about the environment.

seeming to be threatened by the fact that there might be an indistinguishable experience that would not have that capacity to warrant belief.

Rejecting the highest common factor conception is consistent with not being party to the consensus Dancy describes; it is consistent with not believing there is *nothing* in common between experiences that belong to one of those pairs. For my part, in fact, I think it is obvious that members of such pairs have common features. In both members of such a pair it, for instance, looks to the subject as if things are thus and so, with some suitable specification replacing that schematic formula. So I do not belong to Dancy's consensus. The disjunctive approach I endorse holds not that there is *no* feature shared between members of such a pair, but that what they share does not include relevance to epistemic standing.

The point of this is to reject a misconception of the epistemological significance of fallibility.

Capacities to acquire knowledge about the environment through experience are undeniably fallible. It is not just that we are liable to haste or inattentiveness. Even with perfect care and attention one can be misled by appearances, and that is a feature of the capacities themselves. It can happen that one takes oneself, not through any fault in one's epistemic conduct, to have an experience that puts one in a position to know something about the environment, in a situation in which the supposed knowledge is not at one's disposal. That is what it comes to that experiences that do not afford opportunities for knowledge can be subjectively indistinguishable from experiences that do.

This indistinguishability can seem to yield an argument that on any occasion on which one takes oneself to have an experience that reveals how things are in one's environment, one is not in a position to know that the present case is not one of the cases in which one would be misled if one took the experience to put knowledge about the environment at one's disposal. If an experience yields a justification for a belief about the environment, one should be in a position to know one has that justification just by having the experience. It would follow that the justification for belief about the environment afforded by an experience can never be stronger than the justification one's experience provides in the cases in which one is misled—cases of a sort that for all one knows the present case belongs to, according to this line of thought.

That is the highest common factor conception of the epistemic significance of experiences. Obviously enough, it poses problems about the possibility of knowledge through experience.

I believe the problems are intractable. To establish that, I would need to work through all the ways philosophers have devised to deal with them.[5] But we can bypass that task by recognizing that the line of thought that seems to pose those problems involves a mistake about fallibility.

It is true that our capacities to get into positions that are opportunities for knowledge are fallible. That is to say that on some occasions on which such a capacity is at work, what results fails to be a case of what the capacity is specified as a capacity for, namely the subject's getting to be in a position to know something. But it is a mistake to infer that that cannot be a correct specification of the capacity: that whatever the capacity really is, its exercise can never put someone who has it in a position to know things. On the occasions on which a subject is not misled, an exercise of such a capacity does what the capacity is specified as a capacity for; it puts the person who has the capacity in a position to know something.[6]

To be in a position to know something through experience is to have an experience that reveals to one that things are the relevant way, and thus provides one with an indefeasible warrant to believe that they are that way, a warrant that excludes any possibility of the belief's being false. And it is to be in a position to know that that is one's position. The capacity to know that one's experience is revealing to one that things are a certain way is just an aspect of the capacity to know through experience that things are that way. Fallibility attaches to the capacity in both its aspects, and fallibility should be accommodated in the same way in both cases. One cannot discriminate cases in which one is misled (of course unknowingly) from cases in which one is not. But it is a form of that same mistake about fallibility to infer that when one is not misled one is not in a position to know that the present case is not one of the cases in which one is misled. One *is* in a position to know that. Being in a position to know one is not misled is the result of a capacity that is fallible. When the capacity stumbles, one is misled but thinks one is not. But when the capacity does not stumble

---

[5] For an important part of this, see the devastating treatment of 'fallibilist' epistemology in chapter 5 of Rödl (2007). I have been helped by Rödl's chapter in writing the present section of this chapter.

[6] Compare the capacity to throw a basketball through the hoop while standing at the free-throw line. No one makes all free throws. It would be absurd to infer that no one has that capacity.

and one is not misled, exercising the capacity puts one in a position to know that one is not misled—to know that one's experience is revealing things to be a certain way, and thereby providing one with an indefeasible warrant to believe that things are that way.

This undermines the argument that seems to make the highest common factor conception compulsory. It preempts the supposed need to construct an epistemology for knowledge through experience around the idea that experience cannot provide indefeasible warrants for beliefs about the environment.

The disjunctive approach to experience that I have been sketching is a way of expressing this rejection of the highest common factor conception. A disjunctive formulation states the point positively: of the experiences whose epistemic significance the highest common factor conception equates, some reveal to their subject how things are in her environment, thus putting her in a position to know that things are that way, and to know she is in such a position, whereas the others only seem to do that.

In that positive formulation, I spoke of the experiences whose epistemic significance the highest common factor conception equates. That specifies the scope of the disjunctive approach, and it bears on another element in Dancy's consensus.

The consensus view Dancy sets out holds that *any* state or occurrence in sensory consciousness is either a perceptual experience (an experience that reveals how things are in the environment) or something its subject would not be able to distinguish from a perceptual experience. As Dancy notes, such a view would be empirically falsified 'if there were some non-perceptual experiences that are distinguishable (by their owner, and in the relevant way) from perceptions' (2008: 263). He makes this vulnerability to empirical falsification one of the marks of a disjunctive view.

But such experiences would not falsify the disjunctive approach I have explained. They would be irrelevant to it. The purpose of the disjunctive approach I have explained is not to say something completely general about goings-on in sensory consciousness, but to reject a mistake about the implications of fallibility. Experiences that do not afford opportunities for knowledge can seem to their subject to be experiences that do afford opportunities for knowledge. The point of the disjunctive approach is to show that that fact does not threaten the possibility of experience-based knowledge. Experiences whose failure to be perceptual their subject can discern just by having the experiences would not even seem to pose the apparent problems that stem from the highest common factor conception. They would not be within the scope of the disjunctive approach I have explained.

VI

Suppose we know that a subject's belief that things are thus and so has the rational intelligibility a belief has when it is a response to an experience in which things appear to be thus and so. If we know only that much, we do not know something we ought to want to know about the belief's character as a manifestation of the subject's rationality. Is the experience one that reveals things to be thus and so? In that case the belief's rational grounding in the experience is of a sort that qualifies it as knowledgeable. Or is the experience one that merely seems to reveal things to be thus and so? If so, the belief, though rational in the light of the experience in this case too, is not knowledgeable. Those two possibilities are the disjuncts in a disjunctive account of the rational significance of experiences in which things appear to be thus and so. And the formulation I have just given brings out the possibility of a helpful parallel with what I have been urging about acting in the light of facts.

Thus, to repeat a way I put things before: suppose we know a subject is acting in a certain way for a reason consisting in something she takes to be so. If we know only that much, we do not know something we ought to want to know about the action's character as a manifestation of the agent's rationality. Is the action a response to a fact? That would require that she does not just believe the relevant thing, but knows it. Or is she acting in the light of something she takes to be so without knowing it to be so? In that case the action has whatever rational intelligibility we find in it when we see it as undertaken in the light of that consideration, but it cannot be understood as a response to a fact, even if the consideration is, as it happens, something that is so. Those two possibilities are the disjuncts in a parallel disjunctive approach to the rational intelligibility of actions undertaken in the light of things that agents take to be so.

Here are some of the respects in which these two disjunctive approaches are parallel.

First, in both it is acknowledged that the kind of rational intelligibility had by an item that conforms to the 'worse' disjunct—a belief grounded in experience in one case, an action undertaken in the light of something the agent takes to be so in the other— is a kind of intelligibility also had by an item that conforms to the 'better' disjunct.

Second, in both the claim is that our resources for rational understanding are not limited to the resources that afford that kind of intelligibility. That is, we are not restricted to the concepts with which we can make sense of an item that conforms to the 'worse' disjunct—which, as the first point acknowledges, we can also exploit in finding some of the intelligibility there is in an item that conforms to the 'better' disjunct. There is also an explanatory concept in terms of which we can give, for the 'better' disjunct, a positive answer to a further question about the character of the item in question as a manifestation of the subject's rationality. When the 'better' disjunct holds, there is not only the kind of intelligibility that there is when the 'worse' disjunct holds, but also a different kind of intelligibility, which is special to the 'better' disjunct.

Third, in both cases the kind of intelligibility that is common to both disjuncts needs to be understood in terms of the kind of intelligibility that is distinctive of the 'better' disjunct. The latter kind of intelligibility is prior in the order of understanding.

This is especially clear in the case of beliefs grounded in experience. If one has an experience in which it appears that things are a certain way, it is, so far as that goes, rational for one to believe that things are that way. But that is because when one has such an experience, one's experience seems to reveal things to be a certain way: that is, one's belief seems to have the kind of rational status that characterizes the 'better' disjunct. The kind of intelligibility that is common to both disjuncts needs to be understood in terms of there seeming to be an instance of the kind of intelligibility that is distinctive of the 'better' disjunct.

And I would make the parallel claim in the other case too. Our grasp of the kind of understanding we have of an action when we know the agent is acting in the light of something she believes is derived from our grasp of the kind of understanding we have of an action when we know the agent is acting in rational response to a fact.

But there are disanalogies between the two approaches also.

In both cases the point of the disjunctive approach is to reject a highest common factor conception, not in the sense of denying that there are common features between the disjuncts, but in the sense of refusing to restrict our resources for rational explanation to those that are available for the 'worse' disjunct. But it is special to the case of beliefs grounded in experience that the temptation towards the highest common factor conception is generated by considerations involving subjective indistinguishability. In the case of reasons for acting, the 'worse' disjunct is not specified in terms that amount to its seeming to the subject that the 'better' disjunct applies.

Dancy (2008: 271) notes that a disjunctive approach to acting for reasons that unifies its subject matter by subjective indistinguishability would be vulnerable to empirical falsification, since it can seem to a subject that her reason for doing something is that things are thus and so when that is not her reason. But there is no risk of such falsification with the disjunctive approach I am recommending. The approach I am recommending concerns only actions for which the agent's reason *is* what she takes to be her reason, something she believes; it divides those actions into cases in which the reason is something the agent knows and cases in which the reason is something she believes without knowing it.[7]

The irrelevance of subjective indistinguishability in the case of reasons for acting is connected with the fact that the aim of undermining an *epistemological* threat is, unsurprisingly, not one that the disjunctive approach to reasons for acting shares with the disjunctive approach to beliefs grounded in experience. The threat posed by the highest common factor conception in the case of experience is that if we restrict our explanatory resources to those in terms of which we can make rational sense of beliefs grounded in *any* experience that belongs to a sort unified by subjective indistinguishability, we preclude ourselves from singling out perceptual experiences as experiences that reveal things to be a certain way and thereby afford opportunities for knowledge. There is no counterpart to that with the highest common factor conception of reasons for acting.

---

[7] The approach also does not apply to actions whose rationality is that of a bet. One acts on something less than a belief when one's reasons for believing fall short of settling a question for one but one is willing to act on an answer to the question. Dancy (2008: 272–3) mentions cases I would describe in such terms, though he seems to treat them as cases of acting in the light of a belief.

That is to say that rejecting the highest common factor conception of reasons for acting does not have an epistemological payoff. So what do we gain by rejecting it?

I think the idea of acting in the light of a fact, understood in the way I have been urging that Dancy does not accommodate, is completely natural, not a mere creature of philosophical theorizing, and that is enough to show that there is a deficiency in a position that does not accommodate that idea. But there is something deeper at stake than just making room for an idea that ought not to seem problematic.

On what sorts of occasion is practical rationality perfectly manifested? If we reject the highest common factor conception, we can say that practical rationality is fully operative when an agent acts in the light of a fact, in the sense I have been defending, the sense that requires the agent to know the fact in question. If we let the highest common factor conception deprive us of that idea of acting in the light of a fact, we will conceive practical rationality as self-contained: we will take it that perfection in practical rationality can be in view even while we abstract from capacities to know how things are, capacities that belong to theoretical rationality. But if the perfect manifestation of practical rationality is acting in the light of a fact in the sense that goes missing in Dancy's treatment, we cannot consider practical rationality in abstraction from cognitive capacities, and we have to recognize that practical rationality is more integrally embedded in rationality at large than the highest common factor conception allows it to be.

References

Dancy, J. (2000) *Practical Reality* (Oxford: Oxford University Press).

———(2006) 'Acting in the Light of the Appearances', in C. Macdonald and G. Macdonald (eds.), *McDowell and His Critics* (Oxford: Blackwell), 121–34.

———(2008) 'On How to Act—Disjunctively', in A. Haddock and F. Macpherson (eds.), *Disjunctivism: Perception, Action, Knowledge* (Oxford: Oxford University Press), 262–79.

Hornsby, J. (2008) 'A Disjunctive Conception of Acting for Reasons', in A. Haddock and F. Macpherson (eds.), *Disjunctivism: Perception, Action, Knowledge* (Oxford: Oxford University Press), 244–61.

Rödl, S. (2007) *Self-Consciousness* (Cambridge, MA: Harvard University Press).

2

Can Action Explanations Ever Be Non-Factive?

CONSTANTINE SANDIS

Jonathan Dancy's rebellious little book, *Practical Reality* (2000), was completed during my first term as a doctoral student under his supervision. Jonathan's ideas seemed to me to be so right that for a long time I struggled to find a distinctive philosophical voice of my own, and would have probably never approximated one were it not for his continuous encouragement. It is with particular pleasure and gratitude, then, that I take this opportunity to comment on what, ten years later, seems to me to be the book's most radical suggestion.

1. Factive reality

Practical Reality opens with the suggestion that the philosophical distinction between 'motivating' and 'normative' reasons as it is standardly conceived is in danger of leading to the awkward doctrine that one can never act for a normative reason.[1] In an earlier article (1995), Dancy had suggested that philosophers might be altogether better off without the concept of the theory of motivation.[2] If so, we should not talk of two distinct *kinds* of reasons, but

---

[1] For the original distinction, see Smith (1992: 329). It is worth noting that Smith has since distinguished between two different senses of 'good reason', contrasting rational grounds (facts) with rational springs (psychological states) (see Smith and Pettit 1997: 297ff.). Dancy's normative constraint is concerned with the former sense. While Smith concedes that we may act upon reasons so conceived, he denies that they have any explanatory power, which he takes to be part of the notion of a 'motivating reason' (see note 15 in this chapter).

[2] Under Dancy's influence, I express a similar sentiment in Sandis (2009b).

of two overlapping sets of reasons that are motivationally and/or normatively *operative* upon us, it being an open question whether the former set is but a sub-set of the latter (cf. Moyar 2010). *Practical Reality* takes a different route (see, e.g., pp. 6–7, 24), adopting a version of the motivating-normative distinction that allows normative reasons to meet the explanatory constraint of being 'capable of contributing to the explanation of an action that is done for that reason' (p. 101) and motivating reasons to meet the converse 'normative constraint' of being 'capable of being among the reasons in favour of so acting' (p. 103).

I here focus on the reasons *for which* we act, or 'agential reasons',[3] using this term as shorthand for the subset of motivationally operative reasons that are the reasons we act upon.[4] Given that normative reasons seem akin to facts or states of affairs, Dancy concludes that agential reasons must share a similar ontology: they are the *things* we believe and/or desire and not beliefs or desires themselves. Dancy inherits this distinction from Alan White and John McDowell, though its philosophical origins lie with Frege and Wittgenstein.[5] It is also explicit in Latin grammar (e.g. '*quod credo*' vs '*neum fidem*'). Dancy dubs his externalist view 'non-psychologism' because it denies that the reasons for which a person acts are psychological states of the agent. In what follows I shall assume that Dancy's cognitivist version of non-psychologism is by and large true, without quibbling about the differences between facts, truths, and states of affairs.[6]

Agential reasons, at least in so far as these are held to be *motivating* reasons, are commonly thought to be capable of explaining action (for a recent example of this assumption, see Setiya 2007: 23). This outlook, to which Dancy adheres, renders non-psychologism vulnerable to an objection from the possibility of false belief. The trouble is that things are not always as they appear to be to the agent. Dancy rejects the disjunctivist account of agential

---

[3] I borrow the term from Hacker (2009). A subset of agential reasons so understood form what John Skorupski (2010: ch. 3.1) describes as reasons that we act *from*, in a self-determining sense requiring the capacity to recognize and assess reasons as such.

[4] The remaining subset is that of 'defeated motivators' (Dancy 2000: 4), also a subset of the reasons that we *don't* act upon ('con-reasons', to use David-Hillel Ruben's terminology (2009: 63–4)).

[5] See Wittgenstein (1921: §1 and 1953: §§95 and 429); Frege (1956); White (1972); McDowell (1994: 27); Hornsby (1997); and Dancy (2009b). The distinction is decent as far as it goes but in the final section I call for further refinement.

[6] As will become apparent, I also side with Dancy in rejecting the view that one can only act for the reason that *p* if it is indeed true that *p*. For the opposite view, that acting for the reason that *p* is the exercise of the ability that is knowledge that *p*, see Hyman (1999 and 2010; cf. Dancy 2011).

reasons as being external only when our beliefs about what is the case are true, suggesting instead that in cases where what the agent believes is false, her actions may be explained by a falsehood, viz. the agential reason in question.[7] In his own terminology, action explanations which cite agential reasons are *non-factive* in the sense that what the agent believes (the agent's reason, or AR) can explain her action (A) even if it (AR) is false. If this sort of non-factivism is true then we cannot infer both A and AR from a correct explanation of the form 'the reason why it is the case that A is AR' (see Dancy 2000: 131).

It is more natural, however, to think that only *truths* are capable of genuinely explaining anything.[8] We do, of course, use the term 'explanation' in ways which do not imply that the explanation given is true, and accordingly speak of people offering 'poor explanations'.[9] However, such explanations are generally thought to be putative, not genuine: they do not *actually* explain anything but merely purport to. A poor explanation of action will at best correctly point to why someone *might* have done something, without offering any true information about why they *actually* did so: it can render action intelligible without genuinely explaining it (Strawson 1986: 35–6 [2010: 30–1]). Dancy's claim that AR can explain A even if AR is false thus stands in provocative contrast to the standard outlook.

If falsehoods were capable of providing real (one is tempted to say *true*) explanations we would care a lot less about the truth of our beliefs than we actually do. The debate between creationists and evolutionists, for instance, would be inconsequential if we were happy to grant genuine explanatory

---

[7] As Dancy notes, there is 'more than one way in which things can go wrong. The agent can be wrong about whether *p*, or wrong about whether if it were the case that *p*, that would be a reason for acting' (2008: 267; cf. 2000: 140 and Parfit 2011: vol. 1, 150–64). I do not concern myself with the second way here, though my suggestions are compatible with its possibility. Mele (2007) argues that non-psychologists such as Dancy should take the possibility of agents performing actions which they mistakenly think of as being 'objectively favoured' to show that not all 'intentional, deliberate, purposeful' actions are performed for reasons, unless the concept of a reason geared towards action explanation is different from that geared towards evaluation (Mele's own view is that such conceptual matters should be experimentally informed).

[8] This is not to side with realists such as Boghossian (2006) and Peacocke (2008) against pragmatists such as Rorty (1998) and Dummett (2006), but merely to note that we frequently use 'explanation' as shorthand for 'true explanation'. This is so whatever the precise relation of truth to justification, meaning, and belief. Indeed, I am here agreeing with Rorty that 'the resolution of these debates will have no bearing on practice' (Rorty and Engel 2007: 34).

[9] Ruben (2003: 185–6) points out that 'poor' may also be used as a relative term, both objectively and subjectively.

power to falsehoods. This thought should not be confused with an argument from the *metaphysical obscurity* of 'how invoking a putative fact that does not obtain can do explanatory work' (Lenman 2009: §6). My complaint, rather, is that it is a basic *truism* that to have a genuine explanation of anything, the *explanandum* must in some sense, however loose, result *because* of the *explanans*; and this can only happen if the latter is actually the case.[10]

James Lenman puts the problem as follows:

> The biggest headache for anti-psychologists such as Dancy however is furnished by cases where the agent's belief is *false*. The fact of Angus's being fired is naturally adduced to explain his punching his boss in cases where he has indeed been fired. But in cases where Angus punches his boss, believing mistakenly that he has been fired, it seems quite wrong to say he so acts because he has been fired. In such a case we surely must retreat to a psychologized explanation if we are to have a credible motivating reason explanation at all. (2009: §6)

I agree with Dancy's opponents that we should resist non-factivism. We would be throwing the baby out with the bathwater, however, if we took this to be a decisive objection against non-psychologism. Both Dancy and his critics have supposed that his accounts of non-factive explanation and agential reasons must stand or fall together. But it is not at all obvious that we must sacrifice non-psychologism in order to reject non-factivism.

The possibility of rejecting (a) non-factivism whilst holding on to (b) non-psychologism becomes apparent once we realize that (a) results from a *conjunction* of premises which include (b) but are not reducible to it:

(i) Agential reasons are considerations external to the mind (non-psychologism).
(ii) What we consider to be the case may be false (cognitivism).
(iii) Agential reasons are capable of explaining action (agentialism).

---

[10] Marc Lance pointed out to me that Dancy is not committed to the view that *theoretical* explanation can be non-factive. This renders his stance less counter-intuitive than it might initially appear to be. Be that as it may, I see no reason to limit the thought that all genuine explanations are factive to the theoretical domain. If it is false that JD likes to shop for leather trousers, then the statement 'JD went to the Milan conference because he likes to shop for leather trousers' cannot explain why JD went to the Milan conference (even if he ended up buying several pairs during his visit). The same applies to teleological explanation: if it is false that he intended to purchase any leather trousers, then we cannot explain his going to Milan by stating that he went there *in order* to do so.

My own view is that we should hold on to (i) and (ii) but reject (iii). Indeed the problem of false belief may itself be taken to confirm that (iii) is false, though I think that we also have independent grounds against this premise. None of this is to say that agential reasons may not *feature* in action explanations (regardless of the truth of our beliefs), but only that their role within them is not that of an *explanans*. Much of this chapter is geared at developing the above line of reasoning.

Dancy explains that all he 'was doing in maintaining that reasons-explanation is not factive' was to deny the first premise of an 'apparently sound argument' that 'has a false conclusion' (Dancy 2003b: 469), conceding that this approach might lead one, as Aristotle warned, to say 'things that nobody would say unless defending a theory' (Dancy 2008: 267). While he admits that 'it is odd to suppose that on occasion a nothing (something that is not the case) can explain a something (an action that was done)', Dancy concludes that 'we can live with this oddity. Or rather that it is not as odd as people make out' (Dancy 2003a: 427). I suspect, however, that he would welcome less counter-intuitive ways of resisting the psychologistic conclusion.

Though critical of Dancy's account of action explanation, my contribution is thus intended as a defence of his non-psychologistic view of agential reasons. The overall account which emerges is one that I take to cohere with Dancy's aforementioned paper 'Why There is Really No Such Thing as the Theory of Motivation'. I fear, however, that Dancy may see my gesture as a Greek gift harbouring all stripes of philosophical danger. With this in mind, in the final section I propose an alternative approach to which he may be more receptive, one that involves a deflationist attitude to the metaphysics of reasons that parallels his own deflationist approach to action theory (see Dancy 2009a).

2. As Dancy believes

Wayne Davis recommends an approach that is similar in spirit to that which I have been pursuing:

> We need to distinguish the claim that actions can be explained by reference to reasons from the claim that the reasons are what explain the actions. The former

is true, the latter false. The statement that my reason for saving was that my son will need money for college does explain why I saved. But it does not follow, and is not true, that my reason explains my action. For my reason was that my son will need money for college. That something will be true in the future cannot explain the fact that I did something in the past. Moreover, my action would have the same explanation even if I were wrong in thinking that my son will be going to college. (Davis 2003: 455)

Dancy (2003b: 480) has responded that Davis's 'nice distinction between saying that actions can be explained by reference to reasons and saying that the reasons are what explain the action' is not one of which he, Dancy, can make any use. The trouble, as Dancy sees it, is that statements of the form 'her reason for A-ing was AR' cannot *in their entirety* be the *explanans* of her A-ing, for they contain the *explanandum* (her A-ing) as a part. Dancy continues, '[a]fter all, "his reason for ϕ-ing was that p" is equivalent to "he ϕ-ed for the reason that p", which contains his ϕ-ing as a part. If so, it appears that the *explanans* must be the reason for which he ϕ-ed and that alone' (p. 481). Dancy takes it as obvious that the *explanandum* is the action itself. Yet it is as contentious to presuppose that the *explananda* in question are actions as it is to assert that their *explanantia* are agential reasons. In claiming that the statement 'he ϕ-ed for the reason that p' already contains the *explanandum*, Dancy in fact begs the question against some plausible accounts of the relata of explanations.

Hempel and Oppenheim (1948), for example, famously argue that we would do best to conceive of all *explananda* and *explanantia* as sentences and classes of sentences, respectively,[11] whilst Peter Achinstein builds a case for the superiority of 'ordered pair' and 'no product' views, according to which 'we must begin with the concept of an illocutionary act of explaining and characterize explanations, by reference to this, rather than conversely' (Achinstein 1983: 102). If we follow Achinstein's advice, *explanantia* are best understood as statements of fact whose *explananda* are neither sentences nor phenomena but rather *reperienda* or 'discoverables', viz. the things we seek to find out (*why* the bridge exploded when it did, as opposed to the

---

[11] Dancy (2011: 350) claims that 'if we take the whole sentence to be the explanans, then of course all explanation is factive, but trivially so'. But we might equally complain that reasons-explanation is trivially non-factive if we take *reasons* to be the *explanantia*. In what follows I argue that we should not even think they form a *part* of any given *explanans*.

actual explosion of the bridge or a sentence describing it). The approach serves to highlight the proximity between *explanandum* and *explanans*, for in wishing to explain why the bridge exploded as and when it did we are after the *reason* it did so thus. This reason, which we seek to discover, informs us of the very thing we want to explain. The reason cannot be specified independently of any understanding of the thing to be explained, and vice versa,[12] which is not to say that either forms a part of the other.

Put another way, 'he φ-ed' is arguably not an *explanandum*, for to identify an action under a particular description is not yet to identify what it is about it that is to be explained. Depending on our interests, we may ask all sorts of different things about the occurrence of an action, each giving rise to a different *explanadum*: why or how he φ-ed, or perhaps why or how he φ-ed in such and such a way, at a certain time rather than another, for this or that reason, given his character or motivational set, and so on. As Achinstein has pointed out, unless we specify what question it is that we are asking of any given phenomenon we will have failed to fix a specific *explanadum* or 'object of explanation' (Achinstein 1975: 11–18; see Sandis 2012a: 11ff. and 2012b).[13]

Explanantia are not contained in statements of the form 'he φ-ed for the reason that *p*' as these are statements about the agent's reason for acting. As such, they explicitly state what the agent's reason was, but they are not statements *of* the reason nor, *per impossibile*, of the action. This would explain why any implicatures relating to the truth of the agent's belief may be easily cancelled without loss of meaning.

Dancy's non-factive view, by contrast, is that in sentences such as 'his reason for doing it was that, as he believed, *p*', the phrase 'he believed' should be taken appositionally:

> [T]he point of this rephrasing of things is that it removes any suggestion that the explainer is committed to its being the case that *p*. This helps with my second difficulty, which is how 'that *p*' can explain anything when it is not the case that *p*.

---

[12] Hence Elizabeth Anscombe's characterization of intentional actions as 'those to which a certain sense of the question "Why?" is given application' (1957: §5).

[13] For complications relating to emphasis and illocutionary force, see Achinstein (1983: 76–81). The similar but considerably weaker thesis that an *explanandum* is only fixed under sentential representation is briefly discussed by Kim (1989: 275–6), who attributes the view to Hempel (1965: 421–2), with reference to Dretske's related suggestion that we may refer to 'alomorphs' that are akin to *aspects* of whatever it is we seek to explain (1977).

> A familiar form of argument threatens. Where the agent's belief is false, his reason must be that he believed that *p*. But he will not be acting for a *different* reason just because he is in the right on the matter. So even when he is right, his reason must still be that he believes that *p*, not just that *p*. I try to undercut this argument... by denying that explanation in terms of reasons is factive, i.e. that the *explanans* in such cases must itself be the case. First, it is not required for the purposes of the sort of light that reasons-explanations cast on action that things should be as the agent supposed. Second, it seems perfectly possible to continue at least some forms of reasons-explanation with a denial of the contained clause, thus: his reason for doing it was that *p*, a matter about which he was sadly mistaken. (Dancy 2003a: 427)

He claims further that the explanatory statement 'his reason for doing it was that it would increase his pension' is not factive, because we can add that 'he was quite wrong' to think that it would do so, without this affecting the explanation in any way: 'If reasons-explanations were themselves factive, as causal explanations are supposed to be, such a continuation would lead to incoherence or contradiction. But no such result emerges' (p. 427).

What we infer from the above-mentioned explanatory statement, however, is not 'that *p*', but that the agent thought or supposed that *p*.[14] Dancy claims that the whole statement can be true even if what he calls a 'contained part' might not be. But the phrase 'that it would increase...' is not a part of what is being *stated*, let alone 'the thing that does the explaining' (2000: 134). After all, we may cancel any implicature that this is being stated with no explanatory loss. We do not deny its truth while still requiring its presence as a falsehood with explanatory work to do. Rather, when we say such things, we strictly imply that the agent took things to be a certain way and acted accordingly. This is central to our explanation of the action. Since the claim is not itself an agential reason, we must conclude that agential reasons do not explain our actions.

We are now in a position to resist the thought that 'a thing believed that is not the case can still explain action' (2000: 137) without abandoning non-psychologism. What explains the action is the whole statement. More accurately, it is people who explain actions by *citing* one or more agential reasons, thereby implying strictly that (a) the agent took

---

[14] This contrasts sharply with the knowledge case that Dancy claims is analogous. For in the knowledge case what is false is the very thing that is being put forth as a truth/knowledge/fact, whereas here the truth claim/assertion is not 'that *p*' but 'that his reason was that *p*' (2000: 131–2).

p and/or q to count in favour of her action and (b) acted accordingly. But the explanation is not done by the reason cited. What is stated (implicitly or otherwise) is not the thing that the agent believed but, rather, the purported fact that the person acted upon that belief. If this statement turns out to be false then it would fail to provide us with a genuine explanation. Even in cases where we mistakenly agree with the agent's belief at the time of acting and therefore (successfully) explain her action with a simple 'she did it because p' what does the explaining is not the falsehood 'that p' but the implied truth that she acted upon the belief that it was. The explanation is only non-factive in the weak sense that a falsehood can feature in an explanatory statement that is true. The reason cited does not itself even contribute to the explanation. Just as the statement 'this was her cat' can, if true, explain why the animal followed her without the cat being an *explanans*, so the statement 'this was her reason' can explain why she did something, without the reason functioning as an *explanans*.

3. Enabling to imply

In a more recent article, Dancy defines 'non-factive' explanations as ones whose correctness does not require 'that what is offered as an *explanans* in fact be the case' (2004: 25). But the *explanans* on offer is not identical to the agential reason, only to a statement *about* it. The explanation does not require things to be as the agent took them to be because what the agent took to be the case (regardless of whether she was right or wrong to do so) does not explain her action. Dancy (p. 25) is right to say that 'the fact that he is wrong about whether p should not persuade us that his reason was something else, something that he was not wrong about'; but this is compatible with the *explanans* not being an agential reason, but a fact about one.

Consider Dancy's own example of a 'perfectly correct explanation':

(a) His reason for doing it was that it would increase his pension (p. 26).

If all it took to make an explanation non-factive is the *attribution* of potentially false beliefs, then the above explanation would certainly fit the bill. But (a) itself may well be a *true* statement about his reason. Consequently, it cannot be said to explain via a falsehood, the very property which Dancy identifies as the mark of non-factive explanations (2000: 132–7).

It is perhaps possible to distinguish between an explanation and an *explanans*, the latter being only a *part* of the former, namely the part that does the explaining. Dancy seems to suggest something like this in writing that 'the whole can be true as an *explanation*, though the contained part, the thing doing the explaining, is not' (p. 134). I have already questioned the extent to which reasons cited may even count as *explanatory parts* of statements. To this we might add the worry that if only part of an explanation does the explaining, it is unclear what function the rest of it has.

There is an obvious objection to my line of argument so far, namely that when asked to explain our actions we tend to simply state the considerations we (take ourselves to have) acted upon. Similarly, when we explain the acts of others we frequently do so by directly stating their reasons, as follows:

(b) He did it because it would increase his pension.

Are these not instances of explaining an action by stating the reason itself and not through some further statement about what one's reasons are? Not if (b) is elliptical for (a) as John Hyman supposes when he writes: '[T]he canonical form of a sentence stating or giving a reason for doing or believing something is "A F-ed because p" or B believes that q because p' (Hyman 1999: 443). Dancy (2011) acknowledges the 'factive pressure of the word "because", but denies that this factive way of giving a reasons-explanation exhausts the possibilities, rightly complaining that 'the selection of one rather than another way of giving a reasons-explanation as canonical seems [to be] arbitrary and tendentious'. But the fact that no one form is canonical does not entitle us simply to ignore the form given above, for it is not a question of *favouring* the factive form over the teleological (or vice-versa). Rather, all reasons-statements must be translatable (without change of meaning) to any of the standard forms of explanation, on pain of failing to qualify as explanatory.

Explanatory statements which cite agential reasons, then, conventionally imply that the agent did indeed act upon the reason cited. This in turn implies (also strictly) that the agent had the relevant beliefs, all of which supports the view that agential explanation consists of statements *citing* our reasons (or facts related to such statements).

These statements form no part of our agential reasons, but are made implicitly whenever agential reasons are cited. To mention the consideration one acted upon, in response to a request for an explanation of one's action, is to strictly imply that it was the case; by contrast, to say that one acted for this or that reason, involves no more than a *conversational* implicature about what was the case, and conversational implicatures, it is commonly acknowledged, are easily cancellable without loss in meaning. The statement that this was his reason for doing it is altogether different from the statement that it would increase his pension and the truth of either one is independent of the truth of the other. Only the truth of the former is required for either statement (a) or (b) to explain his action.

I follow Dancy in allowing 'that someone's acting intentionally is always explained partly by her believing something, or that her believing as she does is always at least relevant to the explanation'; I also follow him in denying that we can infer from this that 'the agent's so believing was any part of the reason she had for acting as she did' (Dancy 2008: 274). Facts about the agent play a crucial explanatory role in statements which cite agential reasons without being identical to either the statements or the reasons cited. Dancy argues further that the *phrase* 'A's reason for ϕ-ing is that p' is not factive because 'A can act for the reason that p even where A is mistaken about whether p' (p. 270). But this is only true, it seems to me, if non-facticity amounts to no more than the truth of the explanatory statement *as-a-whole* being independent from whether or not it is the case that p.

It is worth undertaking some further Gricean litmus tests by way of comparison. Consider the following statement:

(c) I missed the lecture because I overslept, but this was not a consideration I acted upon.

In the above scenario, the explanation is non-contentiously factive: if it is false that I overslept then the attempted explanation is not a genuine one. In stating that I missed the lecture because I overslept, I am implying that my sleeping is a reason that is explanatorily relevant. This implication is strict, it being far from clear what it would mean to state:

(d) I missed the lecture because I overslept, but my oversleeping was not a reason why I missed the lecture.

The reason in question is not an agential one, in that it is not a consideration I acted upon. Thus it can be perfectly true that:

(e) I missed the lecture because I overslept, although I had no idea that I had done so.

By contrast we would need to tell a seriously complicated story in order for the following to make sense:

(f) I took an umbrella because it was raining, although I had no idea that it was raining.

This is because 'it was raining', in umbrella-taking contexts, typically functions as an *agential* reason. *Eo ipso*, the following statements also make little sense outside of extraordinary explanatory contexts:

(g) I took an umbrella because it was raining, but this was not my reason for taking one.
(h) I took an umbrella because it was raining, but I did not believe that it was raining.

In so far as I am citing the consideration I acted upon, to cite it is to strictly imply that (i) I acted upon this consideration and therefore (ii) took it to be the case. Such examples stand in stark contrast to Dancy's illustrations of non-factive explanations, which have the following form:

(i) My reason for taking the umbrella was that (as I thought) it was raining, but it was not raining.

I have already conceded to Dancy that it can be true that 'that p' was my reason for acting even if it is not the case that p. Thus we may say:

(j) She took the umbrella because it was raining, or so she supposed.

Statements such as (j) are factive in that what they assert is not to be identified with what the featured agent believes. They are statements about agential reasons and, *inter alia*, agential beliefs. To simply say (in looser language) that she took the umbrella because it was raining would only imply *conversationally* that she took it for the reason that it was raining. The wording in (j) transforms such (weak) implicatures into conventional ones. In mentioning a supposition of the agent, the statement conventionally implies that (i) she believed it was raining and (ii) acted accordingly. The statement is factive insofar as it only works as an explanation if both (i) and (ii) are true (see Davis 2003: 458; Smith 2010: 155–6).

For similar reasons (here echoing Moore's Paradox) statements such as the following make little sense:

(k) The (purported) rain motivated her to take an umbrella, but she did not take one for the reason that it was raining.
(l) Her reason for taking an umbrella was that it was raining, but she did not believe that it was raining.

Michael Smith (1998: 158) has appealed to related counterfactuals with the aim of demonstrating that 'while an explanation in terms of a fact presupposes the availability of a Humean belief/desire explanation, the reverse is not true'. This must be right, but it would be an empty victory to infer that agential reasons are psychological states. Once we abandon the notion that agential reasons are capable of explaining action, the debate between Dancy and Smith evaporates, for neither side would any longer be entitled to place an explanatory constraint on the notion of an agential reason. Yet it is such constraints that lead to both Dancy's claim that falsehoods can explain and Smith's suggestion that agential reasons are more closely associated with psychological states that Dancy supposes.[15]

Smith's observations alone cannot persuade Dancy that psychological facts (including facts about our perceptions of where our reasons lie) form even *part* of action explanations in terms of agential reasons. This is because of Dancy's neat distinction between reasons and those conditions which *enable* certain considerations to count as reasons (viz. things without which reasons could not themselves do the explaining they do). In his own words:

> There is a difference between a consideration that is a proper part of an explanation, and a consideration that is required for the explanation to go through, but which is not itself a part of that explanation. I call the latter 'enabling conditions'. (2000: 127)

With this distinction in place, Dancy can claim that what is required for an explanation to make sense cannot be part of the explanation itself. In the case in point, facts about the agent's psychology etc. need to be in place in order for the consideration(s) she acted upon to explain why she acted as

---

[15] See Sandis (2012a: 71–81). According to Dancy, Smith's line of argument lends no support to psychologism, but only to the 'new theory' that motivating reasons are facts *about* our psychological states, and not the states themselves (Dancy 2000: 121ff.; cf. 2003b: 469). Smith, by contrast, sees no great tension, taking 'motivating reasons' to be explanatory (2004: 152) and arguing that all explanations of intentional action appeal to psychological states (Smith 1998: esp. 155–8; cf. Mele 2013).

she did, but these facts do not themselves form part of the explanation being provided (the one in terms of agential reasons):

> The suggestion is therefore that the believing, conceived traditionally as a psychological state, is an enabling condition for an explanation which explains the action in terms of the reasons for (that is in favor of—the good reasons for) doing it. This condition is required for that explanation to go through. That is, in the absence of the believing, what in fact explains the action would not then explain it, either because the action would not then have been done at all, or because, if it had, it would have been done for another reason and so have been explained in another way. But the believing does not contribute directly to the explanation. (2000: 127)

While the distinction between enablers and reasons is a solid one, it is unclear that an analogous distinction is available between enablers and explanatory statements. This is because, as we have already seen, what is stated when one offers an explanation in terms of agential reasons is not the consideration that the agent acted upon (which, as Dancy concedes, the explainer need not commit herself to), but *that* she acted upon such a consideration. This is not merely an enabling condition of the statement being explanatory, but the core of the very statement itself. That it forms no part of the agent's reason lends further support to the view that agential reasons do not themselves explain action.

I agree with Dancy that we can 'explain action by laying out the considerations in the light of which an agent acted, without committing ourselves to things being as the agent conceived them to be' (2000: 131). The 'laying out', however, crucially involves numerous implicatures which the explanation is reliant upon. And whilst implicatures about what the agent believes are cancellable, statements that cite agential reasons conventionally imply that the agent acted upon certain beliefs. This implicature is no mere enabling condition but a core part of the explanation that cites agential reasons: cancel it and you have no such explanation at all.

To say that agential reasons do not explain action is not to say that we cannot explain action by citing such reasons. But conceiving that p is neither a necessary nor a sufficient condition for understanding why A acted as she did when she acted for the reason that p. Merely understanding that p is not sufficient: one must understand *that* she acted upon this reason. This brings us to the vexed question of the very nature of agential reasons. In the next and final section, I argue that Dancy's insistence that action explanation need not be factive is ultimately founded on the misguided idea that locutions of the form 'that p' refer to certain entities, specifically ones that can in certain contexts be termed 'reasons'.

4. Ontological concerns[16]

Wayne Davis has objected that the suggestion that motivating reasons are things that explain actions is 'undermined by the fact that motivating reasons are intentional objects'. Davis argues that to think of reasons as explanatory is to treat instances of the locution 'that p' as referential, viz. as 'occupying the position of a quantificational variable', when in truth such locutions are 'no more referential' than 'to ϕ':

> Motivating reasons are intentional objects. Instances of 'A's reason for ϕ-ing was that p' may be true, and we can explain their truth conditions. But it is misguided to ask 'What sort of thing is the referent of "that p"' therein. It does not have a referent ... We get the same sort of false antimony if we wonder how someone thinking of the perfect husband can be thinking of anything, given that what she is thinking of does not exist. (Davis 2003: 454–5)

Dancy responded as follows:

> Davis ... appeals ... to his view that in 'his reason for ϕ-ing was that p' the 'that p' is not referential. I allow this, taking it to mean that it need not be the case. But I still want to say that something that is the case can explain an action, by standing as the reason for which it was done. (Dancy 2003b: 481)

In a more recent publication Dancy expands on this view, suggesting that '"that p" also names an "intentional object", viz. the sort of thing picked out by the expression "what we believe"' and could thereby qualify as a motivating reason (2009b: 289). Yet this is exactly what Davis is denying. His point is not simply that 'that p' is not referential in the sense of 'need not be the case' (as in the misleading analogy with the perfect husband). Davis's point is that when one states that x ϕ-ed for the reason that p, the that-clause no more refers to something that is not the case than to something

---

[16] I am grateful to David Dolby for ongoing conversations on the matters which follow, upon which we have come to share so many interrelated thoughts over the years that it is no longer possible to individuate them on any basis of original ownership.

that is. (This worry, that is, is not about the non-actuality of referents but about the actuality of non-referrers.) This is not to suggest that questions such as 'what am I thinking?' have no true answer, or to deny sense to phrases such as 'I am referring to the belief that *p*'; but merely to point out that the accusative here is a possible feature of people's psychology and not some mysterious entity 'that *p*' which may be variously described as a belief, a consideration one acts upon, a fact, a reason, etc.

'That *p*' it is not the name of some object, actual or otherwise, about which it is possible to have various so-called attitudes or states, e.g. of accepting, considering, dreaming, fearing, forgetting, regretting, rejecting, supposing, wishing, and so on. Nor is it a possible object we could be related to through processes or events such as those of acting upon one's thought, announcing, informing one, maintaining, signaling, writing, etc. If it were, there would be one thing (a *type*, if you like) called 'that *p*' which A suggests, B predicts, and C suspects. And yet it would not follow from the fact that A suggested that *p*, B predicted that *p*, and C suspected that *p* that C suspected the *thing* that A suggested and B predicted, but only that he suspected that things would be as A suggested and B predicted. Likewise, if A says something silly—say, that fatty foods are healthier than fruit, what is silly is not that fatty foods are healthier than fruit. Nor can the account be that it is silly of A to say this, for in certain contexts it may be very clever of A to say such a silly thing. There is no end to the number of examples one could provide here. Suppose that A accepts that it will rain, B hopes that it will rain, C acts upon the consideration that it will rain. It would be a mistake to conclude from all this that A accepts what B hopes, namely the same consideration that C acts upon. For the meaning of 'that *p*' qua thing believed is different to that of 'that *p*' qua consideration (or indeed qua fact or qua reason). As Alan White has put it, what is said is not an object to which one does something called 'saying'; and what is translated, filled, or interrupted is not an object to which one does something called 'translating', 'filling', or 'interrupting' (1970: 16).[17] Hans-Johann Glock (1997: 98) similarly argues that the word 'what' in the expression 'what I said' does not introduce the name of a thing

---

[17] Despite certain parallels in their conclusions, White's argument should be distinguished from W. V. O. Quine and A. N. Prior's suggestion (later also taken up by Davidson) that we should parse sentences of the form 'Arthur said that it was raining' as 'Arthur said that/it was raining' rather than 'Arthur said/that it was raining' (Quine 1960: 216; Prior 1963 and 1971: 16–22; cf. Davidson 1968). Anthony Kenny comes closer to White in responding to Prior with the added suggestion that expressions

but a propositional clause. *Pari passu*, what was said (that the cake was delicious) is not analogous to what was eaten (the cake).

White (1972) distinguishes between two different senses of the term 'belief': the belie*ving* and the thing belie*ved*, the former being something a person can be said to *have* and the latter something they believe: viz. that *p* (cf. Bennett and Hacker 2003: 172ff., 268). If what I have been suggesting is right, we should be distinguishing not between two but between *three* different things: the belie*ving*, the belie*f*, and the thing belie*ved*. More importantly, for our purposes, it would seem that 'that *p*' cannot be identified with the *reason* that *p* any more than it can with the *reasoning* that *p*. We may, of course, elucidate the concept of an agential reason by describing it as a consideration which we may wrongly take to (a) be the case and (b) count in favour of an action, but we should not infer from this that agential reasons are at times identical to facts, truths, or states of affairs.

It is helpful to look at Latin grammar here,[18] since it highlights the clear distinction between the use of the word 'that' as a verbal clause (as in '*vereor ut*') and as a noun clause (as in '*vereor quod*'). This is also true of ancient and modern Greek (e.g. '$\pi\iota\sigma\tau\epsilon\acute{\upsilon}\omega \; \pi\omega\varsigma$' or '$\pi\iota\sigma\tau\epsilon\acute{\upsilon}\omega \; \acute{o}\tau\iota$' vs '$\pi\iota\sigma\tau\epsilon\acute{\upsilon}\omega \; \alpha\upsilon\tau\acute{o}$', in the modern) and French ('*je pense que*' vs '*ce que je pense*'); the second construction in each pair is demonstrative in the sense that we could say 'I believe *precisely* that', whereas the first is not. By contrast, the English language does not explicitly discriminate between a conjunction in a verbal clause and a relative pronoun, thus making it all too easy to conflate the two through amphiboly. These and other translation exercises confirm that it is a mistake to think that clauses of the form 'that *p*' are typically nominal as opposed to verbal. A fortiori, such clauses do not necessarily pick out referents (be they existing or hypothetical), let alone name reasons in doing so. In philosophy it has become commonplace to think of them as demonstratives. It is, for example, the assumed starting point of Davidson's highly influential paper 'On Saying That'.[19] But it is telling that the

---

of the form 'it was raining' are not names either (Kenny 1963: 127). For objections to the Quine-Prior thesis, see White (1972: 80); Rundle (1979: 286–7); and Künne (2003: 68–9).

[18] Dancy himself encourages such considerations (e.g. 2009b: 286).
[19] Davidson briefly looks into French usage but with an altogether different aim. In doing so, however, he tellingly misreads the '*que*' in '*dit que*' as a demonstrative (1968: 98–9).

examples focused on are of locutions such as 'that p' as opposed to 'whether p'[20] or 'to ϕ'.

Even if it were true that agential reasons can explain our actions, it would not follow that our actions are sometimes explained by falsehoods. The mischaracterization of reasons as being true or false is not aided here by the supposition that the clause in phrases such as 'my reason is that p' is a demonstrative one. No matter what the explanatory power of agential reasons, then, no genuine explanation in terms of agential reasons can be non-factive in the sense in which the *explanans* is 'something that may or may not be the case' (Dancy 2000: 147).

A corollary of this outcome is that we must reject Dancy's argument against causalist interpretations of explanations that cite agential reasons, for it relies on the thought that the former are factive but the latter are not (cf. Dancy 2003a: 427; Schroeder 2010: 559ff.). Ironically, philosophers on different sides of the reasons/causes dispute are united in their assumption that agential reasons are alone capable of explaining *why* we act.[21] Until this common assumption is abandoned, all progress in the theory of action explanation will be compromised.[22]

References

Achinstein, P. (1975) 'The Object of Explanation', in S. Körner (ed.), *Explanation* (Oxford: Blackwell), 1–45.

—— (1983) *The Nature of Explanation* (New York: Oxford University Press).

Anscombe, G. E. M. (1957) *Intention* (Oxford: Blackwell).

Bennett, M. R. and Hacker, P. M. S. (2003) *Philosophical Foundations of Neuroscience* (Oxford: Blackwell).

---

[20] I owe this example to Arto Laitinen.

[21] A refreshing exception is Alfred Mele (2013) who argues that 'even if all reasons for action are true propositions and true propositions can cause nothing, it cannot be inferred from this that causalism about action explanation is false'.

[22] For extremely helpful comments on previous drafts I would like to thank David Bakhurst, David Dolby, Geoffrey Ferrari, and Maggie Little. Thanks also to Arto Laitinen and Mark Lance. An earlier version of section 3 was presented as part of a talk on 'The Role of Agential Reasons in Action Explanation' at the University of Reading's *Philosophy Society*, 13 November 2007. I am grateful to all those who asked questions, particularly John Cottingham, Jonathan Dancy (who pressed me further on the drive back to Oxford), Max de Gaynesford, Brad Hooker, Chris Pulman, Severin Schroeder, and Galen Strawson.

Boghossian, P. (2006) *Fear of Knowledge: Against Relativism and Constructivism* (Oxford: Oxford University Press).
Dancy, J. (1995) 'Why There is Really No Such Thing as the Theory of Motivation', *Proceedings of the Aristotelian Society*, 95: 1–18.
—— (2000) *Practical Reality* (Oxford: Oxford University Press).
—— (2003a) 'A Précis of *Practical Reality*', *Philosophy and Phenomenological Research*, 67(2): 423.
—— (2003b) 'Replies', *Philosophy and Phenomenological Research*, 67(2): 468–90.
—— (2004) 'Two Ways of Explaining Actions', in J. Hyman and H. Steward (eds.), *Action and Agency* (Oxford: Oxford University Press), 25–42.
—— (2008) 'On How to Act Disjunctively', in A. Haddock and F. Macpherson (eds.), *Disjunctivism: Perception, Action, Knowledge* (Oxford: Oxford University Press), 262–80.
—— (2009a) 'Action in Moral Metaphysics', in Sandis (2009a: 398–417).
—— (2009b) 'Action, Content and Inference', in H-J. Glock and J. Hyman (eds.), *Wittgenstein and Analytic Philosophy: Essays in Honour of P. M. S. Hacker* (Oxford: Oxford University Press), 278–98.
—— (2011) 'Acting in Ignorance', *Frontiers of Philosophy in China*, vol. 6, no. 3, 345–57.
Davidson, D. (1968) 'On Saying That', in his *Inquiries into Truth and Interpretation* (Oxford University Press, 1984/2001), 93–108.
Davis, W. A. (2003) 'Psychologism and Humeanism', *Philosophy and Phenomenological Research*, 67(2): 452–59.
Dretske, F. (1977) 'Referring to Events', in *Midwest Studies in Philosophy*, 2: 90–9.
Dummett, M. (2004) *Truth and the Past* (New York: Columbia University Press).
—— (2006) *Thought and Reality* (Oxford: Oxford University Press).
Frege, G. (1956) 'The Thought: A Logical Inquiry', *Mind*, 65: 289–311.
Glock, H-J. (1997) 'Truth Without People?', *Philosophy*, 72: 85–104.
Hacker, P. M. S. (2009) 'Agential Reasons and the Explanation of Human Behaviour', in Sandis (2009a: 75–93).
Hempel, C. G. (1965) *Aspects of Scientific Explanation and Other Essays in the Philosophy of Science* (New York: Free Press).
—— and Oppenheim, P. (1948) 'Studies in the Logic of Explanation', *Philosophy of Science*, XV: 135–75.
Hornsby, J. (1997) 'Thinkables', in M. Sainsbury (ed.), *Thought and Ontology* (Milan: Franco Angeli), 63–80.
Hyman, J. (1999) 'How Knowledge Works', *Philosophical Quarterly*, 49(197): 433–51.
—— (2010) 'The Road to Larissa', *Ratio*, 23: 393–414.
Kenny, A. J. P. (1963) 'Oratio Obliqua', *Proceedings of the Aristotelian Society*, supp. vol. xxxvii, 127–46.

Kim, J. (1989) 'Mechanism, Purpose, and Explanatory Exclusion', in Mele (1997: 256–82). Originally published in *Philosophical Perspectives*, 3: 77–108.
Künne, W. (2003) *Conceptions of Truth* (Oxford: Clarendon Press).
Lenman, J. (2009) 'Reasons for Action: Justification vs. Explanation', *Stanford Encyclopedia of Philosophy*, <http://plato.stanford.edu/entries/reasons-just-vs-expl/>.
McDowell, J. (1994) *Mind and World* (Cambridge, MA: Harvard University Press).
Mele, A. R. (ed.) (1997) *The Philosophy of Action* (Oxford: Oxford University Press).
—— (2007) 'Reasonology and False Beliefs', *Philosophical Papers*, 36(1): 91–118.
—— (2013) 'Actions, Explanations, and Causes', in G. D'Oro and C. Sandis (eds.), *Reasons and Causes: Causalism and Anti-Causalism in the Philosophy of Action* (Basingstoke: Palgrave Macmillan).
Moyar, D. (2010) 'Hegel and Agent-Relative Reasons', in A. Laitinen and C. Sandis (eds.), *Hegel on Action* (Basingstoke: Palgrave Macmillan), 260–80.
O'Connor, T. and Sandis, C. (2010) *A Companion to the Philosophy of Action* (Oxford: Wiley-Blackwell).
Parfit, D. (2011) *On What Matters*, 2 vols. (Oxford: Oxford University Press).
Peacocke, C. (2008) *Truly Understood* (Oxford: Oxford University Press).
Prior, A. N. (1963) 'Oratio Obliqua', *Proceedings of the Aristotelian Society*, supp. vol. xxxvii: 115–26.
—— (1971) *The Objects of Thought*, ed. P. T. Geach and A. J. P. Kenny (Oxford: Oxford University Press).
Quine, W. V. O. (1960) *Word and Object* (Cambridge, MA: MIT Press).
Rorty, R. (1998) *Truth and Progress: Philosophical Papers Volume 3* (Cambridge: Cambridge University Press).
Rorty, R. and Engel, P. (2007) *What's the Use of Truth?* (New York: Columbia University Press).
Ruben, D-H. (2003) *Action and its Explanation* (Oxford: Clarendon Press).
—— (2009) 'Con-reasons as Causes', in Sandis (2009a: 62–74).
Rundle, B. (1979) *Grammar in Philosophy* (Oxford: Clarendon Press).
Sandis, C. (ed.) (2009a) *New Essays on the Explanation of Action* (Basingstoke: Palgrave Macmillan).
—— (2009b) 'Hume and the Debate on Motivating Reasons', in C. Pigden (ed.), *Hume on Motivation and Virtue* (Basingstoke: Palgrave Macmillan), 142–54.
—— (2012a) *The Things We Do and Why We Do Them* (Basingstoke: Palgrave Macmillan).
—— (2012b) 'The Objects of Action Explanation', *Ratio*, 25: 326–44.
Schroeder, S. J. (2010) 'Wittgenstein', in O'Connor and Sandis (2010: 554–61).

Setiya, K. (2007) *Reasons Without Rationalism* (Princeton, NJ: Princeton University Press).

Skorupski, J. (2010) *The Domain of Reasons* (Oxford: Oxford University Press).

Smith, M. (1992) 'Valuing: Desiring or Believing?', in D. Charles and K. Lennon (eds.), *Reduction, Explanation, and Realism* (Oxford: Oxford University Press), 323–60.

—— (1998) 'The Possibility of Philosophy of Action', in J. Bransen and S. Cuyper (eds.), *Human Action, Deliberation and Causation* (Dordrecht: Kluwer Academic Publishers), 17–41. Reprinted in Smith 2004: 155–77.

—— (2004) *Ethics and the A Priori: Selected Essays on Moral Psychology and Meta-Ethics* (Cambridge: Cambridge University Press).

—— (2010) 'Humeanism About Motivation', in O'Connor and Sandis (2010: 153–8).

—— and Pettit, P. (1997) 'Parfit's "P"', in J. Dancy (ed.), *Reading Parfit* (Oxford: Blackwell), 71–95.

Strawson, G. (1986) *Freedom and Belief* (Oxford: Clarendon Press), 2nd revised edn 2010.

White, A. R. (1970) *Truth* (London: Macmillan & Co).

—— (1972) 'What We Believe', in N. Rescher (ed.), *Studies in the Philosophy of Mind*, APQ monograph series no. 6 (Oxford: Blackwell), 69–84.

Wittgenstein, L. (1921/1961) *Tractatus Logico-Philosophicus*, revised trans. D. F. Pears and B. F. McGuiness (London: Routledge).

—— (1953/2009) *Philosophical Investigations*, 4th edn, tr. G. E. M. Anscombe, P. M. S. Hacker, and J. Schulte (Oxford: Wiley-Blackwell).

3

The Ideal of Orthonomous Action, or the How and Why of Buck-Passing

MICHAEL SMITH

1. Two approaches

Imagine trying to explain to a group of people what a philosopher is. There are at least two approaches you could take. One would be to describe what an ideal philosopher does: the sorts of questions he thinks about, the methods he uses in answering them, the level of detail and precision he demands of his answers, how he deals with those who disagree with him, and so on. Having fixed the ideal, you could explain that non-ideal philosophers are approximations to the ideal. The other, much more flat-footed, approach would be to describe what all philosophers, ideal and non-ideal alike, have in common, and how they differ from non-philosophers.

Some might wonder whether there is any difference between these two approaches. If the only way to say what all and only philosophers have in common is to describe them as approximations—some more perfect, others less perfect—to the ideal, then this is indeed the case. However, if approximations to the ideal are such in virtue of their possession of some further (possibly disjunctive) lowest-common-denominator property then the two approaches are genuinely different. Moreover, if the two approaches are genuinely different, then, though both could be pursued in good conscience, a good question to ask is whether there are reasons to prefer one rather than the other, at least in certain circumstances.

The answer is that there may well be. Suppose, for example, that your task is to explain to some group of people what a philosopher is, but that you know in advance that you will disagree with them about some crucial feature of the ideal philosopher. Perhaps the ideal philosopher thinks about interesting problems, but their conception of which problems are of interest is very different to yours. In these circumstances, there would be at least one reason to take the lowest-common-denominator approach, as that approach wouldn't require you to take a stand on which problems are interesting. The lowest-common-denominator approach allows you to dodge this particularly thorny normative question.

This is not to say that the lowest-common-denominator approach allows you to dodge every normative question. For example, it might require you to specify how bad at doing philosophy one would have to be in order not to count as a philosopher at all. But since this is a question to which you would need an answer even if you took the idealization approach, the mere fact that the lowest-common-denominator approach embroils you in this normative controversy doesn't count against it. The earlier problem with the idealization approach thus wasn't that it makes you confront thorny normative issues, whereas the lowest-common-denominator approach doesn't; the problem was rather that it embroils you in all of the normative controversies in which the lowest-common-denominator approach embroils you plus more.

With this in mind, let's now ask a more familiar philosophical question, the question that sets the scene for this chapter. What is an action? According to the best-known version of the so-called 'standard story of action', a story we have inherited from David Hume via Donald Davidson, a subject's actions are those of his bodily movements that are done because he wants certain things and because he believes that he can achieve those things by moving his body in the ways he does (Hume 1777; Davidson 1963, 1971). According to a slightly less well known, but in my view much more plausible, version of the same story, which we owe to Carl G. Hempel (1961), a subject's actions are those of his bodily movements that are done because he wants certain things, because he believes that he can achieve those things by moving his body in the ways he does, and because he exercises his capacity to be instrumentally rational, so deriving an instrumental desire to move his body in the ways he does.

Any fully spelled out version of the standard story of action owes us an account of belief, desire, and the capacity to be instrumentally rational. The most plausible such accounts also derive from Hume. What makes a psychological state a belief, or a desire, or the capacity to be instrumentally rational, is its distinctive functional role. As Robert Stalnaker puts it, in perhaps the pithiest formulation:

> Belief and desire ... are correlative dispositional states of a potentially rational agent. To desire that P is to be disposed to act in ways that would tend to bring it about that P in a world in which one's beliefs, whatever they are, were true. To believe that P is to be disposed to act in ways that would tend to satisfy one's desires, whatever they are, in a world in which P (together with one's other beliefs) were true. (1984: 15)

An agent who acts is thus one in whom these two behavioral dispositions interact in a manner that makes it appropriate to describe him as having exercised his capacity to be instrumentally rational (for more on this, see Smith 2003a). The concepts of belief, desire, rational capacity, and action are therefore all inter-defined. What marks them out are the distinctive ways they each relate to each other and the world.

Does the standard story of action take a lowest-common-denominator approach or an idealization approach to explaining what an action is? As I understand it, the standard story takes a lowest-common-denominator approach. In doing so, the standard story, much like the lowest-common-denominator approach to explaining what a philosopher is, requires us to take a stand on certain thorny normative and non-normative issues. For example, Hempel's version of the standard story commits us to the view that there is a norm of instrumental rationality; to the view that that norm governs relations between an agent's non-instrumental desires and means-end beliefs; to the view that, whenever there are actions, the agent in question possesses the capacity to be instrumentally rational to some degree; and to the view that, whenever there are actions, the agents of those actions exercise their capacity to be instrumentally rational, putting their non-instrumental desires and means-end beliefs together so as to derive instrumental desires to act in the ways in which they do. This last is what approximations to the ideal all have in common, or so the standard story tells us.

But though Hempel's version of the standard story of action takes a stand on these thorny normative issues, it remains non-committal on a whole host of others. Since these are issues on which someone who takes the idealization approach must commit himself, this is the standard story's advantage. For example, someone who takes the idealization approach is committed to telling us which non-instrumental desires and means-end beliefs an agent acts on if he performs the ideal action—which dispositions he ought to have—something about which those who tell the standard story can remain totally silent. Indeed, those who tell the standard story needn't commit themselves to there being any norms at all governing an agent's non-instrumental desires, still less to specifying what the content of those norms is. The reverse is not true, however. Someone who takes the idealization approach, at least when he tries to identify what approximations to the ideal are, has no choice but to take a stand on the sorts of normative issues on which those who tell the standard story take a stand. When explaining what an action is to an audience with whom you have profound normative disagreements, it might therefore be more productive to tell the standard story.

Some might think that the standard story is plagued by problems of its own. Whereas the idealization approach signals that the border between actions and non-actions might be a vague matter—what counts as an approximation is, after all, often a vague matter—the standard story might seem committed to denying such indeterminacy. The whole idea behind the standard story, it might be thought, is to identify a bright line dividing actions from non-actions. But on a charitable reading, the standard story is not committed to there being a bright line. When an agent moves his body not because of anything he believes, but because he is in the belief-like state of vividly imagining something, then he should count as doing something that is at least a borderline case of action even by the lights of the standard story. The same is true when an agent moves his body because of some belief-mediated urge, rather than an ordinary desire. Borderline cases of action are thus predicted by the standard story, not counterexamples to it.

The upshot is that there are two approaches we might take to explaining what an action is and that these two approaches are also complementary. In earlier work, I have defended a version of the standard story. My reason for doing so has in part been the hope that we might get agreement on what an action is without confronting the difficult normative issues raised by the idealization approach. In this chapter, however, I wish to switch tack and say a little about how we might take the alternative and complementary idealization approach instead. The idea I wish to explore is that actions, as identified by the standard story, are approximations to what Philip Pettit and I have elsewhere called *fully orthonomous* actions: that is, they are approximations to actions that are performed by agents who are under the rule of what's correct, as opposed to what's incorrect (Pettit and Smith 1996, Smith 2004). After briefly explaining this idea, I will zoom in and clarify some key aspects of orthonomous actions, so understood. Doing so will provide a background against which I can explain some misgivings I have concerning what Jonathan Dancy has to say about buck-passing conceptions of both rightness and values (2000).

2. Orthonomous agents are ruled by what's correct in which respect?

Fully orthonomous actions are those performed by agents who are themselves fully orthonomous, where agents are orthonomous to the extent that they are ruled by what's correct, as opposed to what's incorrect. An agent's being ruled by what's correct is thus a matter of his being sensitive, in his actions, to the way things are. He does what he does because of his appreciation of the way things are, not because of ignorance or error. This is why what he does counts as an idealized form of action.

An initial difficulty with stating this idea more precisely is that agents can be sensitive, in their actions, to the ways things are in many different respects. We must therefore be clear which respects we have in mind. Consider the following possibilities. There are agents who act in the light of their full sensitivity to all of the reasons that there are, both the moral reasons, if there are any such reasons, and the non-moral reasons too, that have any bearing at all on what they are to do; there are those who act in the light of their full exercise of their rational capacities, where this may or may not be a matter of their being fully sensitive to all of the reasons that there are; there are those who act in the light of a full sensitivity to specifically moral considerations, where this may or may not be a matter of their being fully sensitive to all of the reasons that there are and fully exercising their rational capacities; there are those who act in the light of a full sensitivity to the legal code; others who act in the light of a full sensitivity to considerations of style; yet others who act in the light of a full sensitivity to considerations of humour; and so we could go on. When we describe a fully orthonomous action, and suppose that such an action is one that is performed by an agent who is ruled by what's correct, as opposed to what's incorrect, it follows that we have to make a choice about the relevant criteria of correctness. Correctness in which respect(s)?

One suggestion would be that we are supposed to describe those actions whose agents are ruled by what's correct in every respect. But this isn't a very promising suggestion, as it is not the case that, for every situation in which an ideal agent might find himself, there is an action that is correct in every respect. Humour and style, on the one hand, and morality, on the other, all too often pull in opposite directions from each other. Another possibility is that we are supposed to describe those actions whose agents are ruled by the exemplary mix of features that define what it is to be ruled by what's correct along all of the different dimensions. But this isn't a very promising suggestion either, as the idea of an exemplary mix makes dubious sense. Along which dimension is the mix supposed to be exemplary? Every dimension? Obviously not. But in that case, which? The agent who is moved by the mix that is exemplary as judged from a standpoint of sensitivity to all of the reasons that there are is presumably just the agent who is fully sensitive to all the reasons that there are; the agent who is moved by the mix that is morally exemplary is presumably just the agent who is fully sensitive to moral considerations; and so on.

It seems that we therefore have no alternative but to privilege some of these ideals over the others. In one sense, though, this makes the choice much easier. Since we cannot imagine individuals acting at all who are totally insensitive to reasons and who lack all rational capacities—people who act must display some degree of differential sensitivity to evidence that their environment is one way rather than another—we should suppose that ideal actions are, by their very nature, the sorts of things that are done by agents who are fully sensitive to all the reasons that there are and who fully exercise their rational capacities. Actions are not, in this same sense, defined by reference to the sorts of things done by those who are sensitive to considerations of style or humour, as we seem to have no problem at all imagining agents who have no sense of style or humour, and many insist that the same is true of agents who are insensitive to moral and legal considerations. Of course, this doesn't show that ideal actions, or certain ideal actions, won't be stylish, or humorous, or morally or legally exemplary. But it does suggest that, if they are, then that will be because being stylish, or humorous, or morally or legally exemplary, is itself at bottom a matter of being sensitive to reasons and exercising rational capacities.

Here, then, is a preliminary attempt to describe what a fully orthonomous action is like:

| facts about what there is most reason to do in circumstances C and facts about being in C | ?→ | available evidence about what there is most reason to do in C and about being in C | → | beliefs about what there is most reason to do in C and about being in C | → | intentions in C to do the things that there is most reason to do in C | → | doings in C of the things that there is most reason to do in C |

Figure 1 Fully orthonomous actions—1st try.

For agents to be ruled by what's correct, there must be facts about the various things that there is reason for them to do in their circumstances, and those facts must somehow combine to fix what there is most reason for them to do in their circumstances; there must be evidence of what those facts are when they are in those circumstances, and that evidence must be available to them; and they must exercise their capacities and actually access that evidence. How exactly we should conceive of the circumstances that are relevant to what agents have reason to do, and hence what's required for agents to access evidence that they are in those circumstances, will be a matter for further discussion presently. This is why, for the time being, the '?→' in figure 1 signals no commitment on that issue.

Having accessed this evidence, agents who are ruled by what's correct must respond to that evidence by forming judgements to the effect that the reasons that there are in their circumstances are those supported by the evidence—the '→' in figure 1 signals the exercise of rational capacities that's required for this transition between accessing evidence and judgements to be made—and they must go on to intend to do, and then to do, what they judge themselves to have most reason to do in their circumstances, once again by exercising their rational capacities. How we should conceive of reasons for action, and hence what's required for agents to access evidence that there are facts about reasons, will also be a matter for further discussion presently.

3. What are the circumstances in which fully orthonomous actions are performed?

If an agent is to act orthonomously, then non-normative facts about his circumstances—these are what's referred to in figure 1 as 'circumstances C'—must be available to him via evidence and he must access that evidence. But how exactly should we conceive of the circumstances that are relevant to what an agent has reason to do?

Consider a doctor with a patient who has a debilitating but non-fatal disease (compare Jackson 1991). Suppose that the best medical science tells him that either drug A or drug B will cure his patient completely, but that it doesn't tell him which will do the trick; imagine that it also tells him that whichever doesn't do the trick will kill him. Suppose further that the drug that will in fact cure his patient is drug A, and that there is a further drug, C, which though it won't cure his patient, is well known to ameliorate his disease's symptoms significantly. Given all of these non-normative facts about the doctor's circumstances, which drug does he have most reason to give? Cases like this force us to ask whether agents' circumstances, in the sense relevant to what they have reason to do, are fixed by the way the world is, or whether they are instead fixed by the way that they should believe the world is, given the available evidence.

If agents' circumstances are fixed by the way the world is, never mind what the available evidence suggests, then this suggests that the doctor has most reason to give drug A. If we think of agents' circumstances in this way, then there would always be a potential gap between agents' being in certain circumstances and its being available to them that they are in those circumstances. Even agents who respond perfectly rationally to the evidence available to them may fail to know what their circumstances are, as the available evidence might mislead. Their non-culpable ignorance would constitute some sort of excuse. Since a distinctive feature of orthonomous agents is that they know what their circumstances are, we would therefore need to signal the fact that they are not non-culpably ignorant in this way in figure 1. The '?→' would have to be replaced with a 'K→' which would tell us that the world has conspired to make the facts about the orthonomous agent's circumstances available to him in a manner suitable for knowledge.

If, on the other hand, agents' circumstances are fixed by the available evidence, then that would suggest that the doctor has most reason to give drug C. Though the available evidence might mislead agents about how things actually are in the world in which they act, it could not mislead them about their circumstances in the sense relevant to what they have reason to do, as there would be no gap between the circumstances in which agents find themselves, in this sense, and the availability of evidence that they are in those circumstances. Agents who respond perfectly rationally to the available evidence, as orthonomous agents do, could not fail to know what their circumstances are; there could be no non-culpable ignorance of circumstances. We would need to signal this fact in figure 1 by replacing the '?→' with '=' which would represent the constitutive relationship between agents' circumstances, in the relevant sense, and the evidence available to them about their circumstances.

Which of these is the correct way to think about agents' circumstances? Though I am not absolutely certain, my inclination is to think that agents' circumstances are fixed by the way the world is, not by the way that the available evidence suggests that it is. My reason for thinking this is that I cannot see how we could justify taking an asymmetrical attitude towards the non-normative circumstances in which agents act, on the one hand, and the facts about what there is reason for them to do in those circumstances, on the other (see also Smith 2009a). If we should suppose that one of these is epistemically constrained, then we should suppose that the other is epistemically constrained too. But if the world itself has a normative nature, then it seems plain that it is, *inter alia*, that normative nature that fixes what agents have reason to do, not the possibly misleading evidence agents might have about that normative nature. Similarly, it seems to me that we must suppose that the non-normative circumstances in which agents find themselves are fixed, *inter alia*, by the non-normative nature of the world, not by the possibly misleading evidence agents might have about the world's non-normative nature.

So, at any rate, I am inclined to think. But since nothing in what follows will turn on this, I will say no more about it. The rest of the picture of orthonomous action I go on to sketch could easily be reconceived in terms of the alternative conception of agents' circumstances if it turns out that I am wrong and an asymmetrical attitude can be justified.

4. Reasons for action or reasons for intention?

If an agent is to act orthonomously then, however we should conceive of the circumstances in which he finds himself, there must also be facts about what there is most reason to do in various circumstances, including the circumstances in which the agent finds himself, and these facts about reasons for action must also be available to him via evidence that he accesses. Given that figure 1 is supposed to be portraying the structure of orthonomous action, it therefore represents facts about what there is reason to do in various circumstances as themselves the basic normative facts to which agents respond.

In order to test the plausibility of this, consider a case in which we might suppose that there are reasons for agents to act in certain ways, and let's ask whether it is plausible to suppose that facts about such reasons are basic. People like me who have children have a reason to make sure that their children are safe and well, or so I will assume. But is it a basic normative fact that people like me have such reasons, or is this reason for action explained by something more basic? Thomas M. Scanlon provides what seems to me to be a compelling reason for supposing that such reasons are not basic. He points out that among the mental states that people possess, there is a distinctive class of what he calls *judgement-sensitive attitudes*. Judgment-sensitive attitudes are those

> that an ideally rational person would come to have whenever that person judged there to be sufficient reasons for them, and that would, in an ideally rational person, 'extinguish' when that person judged them not to be supported by reasons of the appropriate kind. (Scanlon 1998: 20)

The reasons to which judgment-sensitive attitudes are sensitive are what he calls reasons in the 'standard normative sense', the paradigmatic examples of which are considerations that support the truth of our beliefs, but other examples include intention, desire, hope, fear, admiration, respect, contempt, indignation, and so on (pp. 20–1).

What is important about the various judgment-sensitive attitudes, according to Scanlon, is that they 'constitute the class of things for which reasons in the standard normative sense can be asked or offered' (p. 20). Among mental states, the judgement-sensitive attitudes thus contrast with states like being in pain, or feeling dizzy, for which reasons in the standard normative sense cannot be given. (It is worth comparing judgement-sensitive attitudes, as Scanlon characterizes them, with what Judith Jarvis Thomson calls the distinctive class of mental states with 'correctness conditions' (Thomson 2008: 132).) But judgement-sensitive attitudes also contrast with actions, and this may seem more problematic. For though actions are not attitudes, and so are not judgement-sensitive attitudes, they are the sorts of things for which reasons in the standard normative sense can be given. So do they constitute a counterexample to Scanlon's suggestion that judgement-sensitive attitudes constitute the class of things for which reasons in the standard normative sense can be given?

Scanlon (1998: 21) thinks not. As he puts it:

> Actions are the kinds of things for which normative reasons can be given only insofar as they are intentional, that is, are the expression of judgement-sensitive attitudes. Against this, it might be pointed out that (at least in normal cases) in order to intend to do something I must take myself to have a reason for *doing* that thing. So it might seem that reasons for action are, after all, primary, and reasons for intending are dependent upon them. But there is no real disagreement here. A reason for doing something is almost always a reason for doing it intentionally, so 'reason for action' is not to be contrasted with 'reason for intending'. The connection to action, which is essential to intentions, determines the kinds of reasons that are appropriate for them, but it is the connection with judgment-sensitive attitudes that makes events actions, and hence the kind of things for which reasons can sensibly be asked for and offered at all.

As Scanlon sees things, reasons for actions are thus nothing over and above reasons for intentions (I will say something about the exceptions Scanlon mentions in passing in a moment). There are therefore reasons for action in the standard normative sense only because there are reasons for intentions.

Assuming that Scanlon is right about this, as I think he is, it follows that we should revise figure 1. Given that our aim is to describe the structure of orthonomous action, we should replace all mention of *reasons for action* with talk of *reasons for intention*:

facts about what what there is most reason to intend to do in circumstances C and facts about being in C → K → available evidence about what there is most reason to intend to do in C and about being in C → beliefs about what there is most reason to intend to do in C and about being in C → intentions in C to do the things that there is most reason to intend to do in C → doings in C of the things that there is most reason to intend to do in C

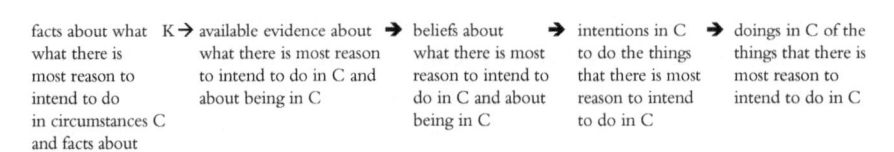

Figure 2 Fully orthonomous agency—2nd try.

Note that facts about reasons for actions are not explicitly mentioned in figure 2 at all. In order to interpret figure 2 as a representation of the way in which fully orthonomous agents respond to facts about reasons for actions, we have bring to it our knowledge that reasons for action decompose into reasons for intention.

5. Reasons for intention or reasons for desire?

But is it any more plausible to suppose that reasons for intention are basic normative facts, as suggested by figure 2, than it is to suppose that reasons for action are basic normative facts? In order to test this idea, consider once again our example.

If people have a reason to make sure that their children are safe and well, and if reasons for action decompose into reasons for intentions, then it follows that people have a reason to intend to make sure that their children are safe and well. Let's now imagine a situation in which my children are already safe and well, and robustly so, but let's suppose further that their being safe and well had, and has, nothing whatsoever to do with me. Their being safe and well is like manna from heaven. What should my reaction be? Would there be something for me to regret about this situation? The answer, I think, is that there would be nothing to regret. I should be delighted that my children are robustly safe and well, as their being safe and well is all that matters. It provides all of the relevant reasons that there are in the circumstances. Insofar as there is a reason for the intention to make my children safe and well, that reason thus seems itself to be explained by the reason for the desire I have that they be safe and well, a desire whose satisfaction brings with it, or perhaps constitutes, my being delighted.

How exactly would that explanation go? The explanation would go something like this: the world could be such that my children are safe and well; I have a reason to non-instrumentally desire that the world is such that my children are safe and well; given that one of the ways in which the world could be such that my children are safe and well is by my taking certain steps to make it that way, I have a reason to instrumentally desire that I take those steps to make it that way; and given that I can take those steps, I have a reason to intend to do so. Facts about reasons for non-instrumentally desiring the world to be a certain way are in this respect seen to be more basic normative facts than facts about reasons for intentions. Indeed, we might well wonder whether reasons for intentions, any more than reasons for action, need to be mentioned explicitly in our description of fully orthonomous action at all. For there seems to be no real difference between reasons for instrumentally desiring to take certain steps, where those steps are ones that can be taken, and reasons for intending to take those steps.

It might be thought that this line of reasoning leads to a limited conclusion at best. Notwithstanding the fact that there would be much to be glad about, it might be thought that there would be something to regret if my children's being safe and well was like manna from heaven. After all, if my children's being safe and well was like manna from heaven, then it would not be possible for me to express my concern for them by making sure that they are safe and well. But, the thought might be, there plainly are reasons for me to engage in such expressive acts, reasons that are quite independent of the fact that one consequence of such acts is that my children are safe and well. Facts about reasons to intend to perform these expressive acts should themselves therefore be thought of as basic normative facts, facts that are not reducible to facts about reasons to non-instrumentally desire the world to be a way that it could be without my intending to do anything.

However this line of thought isn't really convincing. For one thing, though we do often say that we have reasons to perform expressive acts, it isn't entirely clear that the fact that we say such things should be taken at face value. Certain expressive acts, like acts of spontaneous affection for example, don't seem to be acts that we could succeed in performing at all if we did them with the intention of expressing spontaneous affection. These are presumably some of the exceptions Scanlon had in mind when he said that 'a reason for doing something is *almost always* a reason for doing it intentionally' (my emphasis). The upshot is that if we have reasons to perform acts of spontaneous affection, then these are not reasons to perform such acts intentionally. So should we suppose that they are reasons to perform such acts *unintentionally*? What on earth would a reason like that be?

When we say that there are reasons to perform acts of spontaneous affection, what we really have in mind, or so it seems to me, is one of two quite different things. One possibility is that we are saying that there are reasons to perform acts of spontaneous affection under some other description. There is a reason to, say, buy a gift, or plant a kiss, or whatever else it is that we do intentionally when we act spontaneously. But if this is what we have in mind, then it is clear that the example isn't probative, as the reasons to buy a gift, or plant a kiss, or whatever, could well be reasons to intend to buy a gift, or plant a kiss, or whatever. But the other thing that we might really have in mind when we say that there are reasons to perform acts of spontaneous affection is that there are reasons to *desire* that we perform such acts under that very description, and this is probative.

What's peculiar about reasons to desire that we do things like perform acts of spontaneous affection, unlike reasons to desire things like my children's being safe and well, is that there is no way for our sensitivity to such reasons to lead us to acquire the desire for which they are reasons and then to act so as to satisfy the desire. Such reasons thus cannot be reasons for corresponding intentions. In order to perform acts of spontaneous affection I have to *act spontaneously*, not in the light of my appreciation of the reasons for desiring that I so act. Reasons for desiring that I perform acts of spontaneous affection cannot be converted into reasons to intend to act spontaneously because, in the circumstances in which I appreciate those reasons, my very appreciation of those reasons ensures that there are no ways in which the desire could lead me to act so as to satisfy the desire for which they are reasons.

Reasons for other expressive acts are different. Consider the reason I have to express my concern for my children. This is presumably one and the same as the reasons I have to want the world to be one in which my children know that I love them and would be willing to make all sorts of sacrifices to ensure that they are safe and well. To be sure, in the world as it actually is, my children's main source of evidence about such things lies in the actions I perform. Moreover, I could perform those acts fully cognizant of the reasons for so desiring. It therefore seems that, in the world as it actually is, I do have reasons to intend to perform those acts in order to convey that knowledge. But there is nothing necessary about any of this. It is logically possible for there to be a world in which my children know how much I love them, and the sacrifices that I would make for them, without my doing anything to convey that knowledge to them, and indeed without anyone else's doing anything to make that happen either. It seems that we should therefore suppose that the reasons I have to intend to perform such expressive acts are explained by the reasons I have for wanting the world to be a certain way, where this is a way that the world could be without my acting at all. The reasons to intend to perform such expressive acts are not themselves basic.

This is in turn significant. For it suggests is that, quite generally, reasons for action are explained by reasons to non-instrumentally desire the world to be a certain way, where it is left entirely open whether it could in principle get to be that way by agents' being sensitive to those reasons and, as a result, by their taking steps to make it that way. That will depend entirely on the way that there is reason to want it to be. In many cases, the world could be the way that there is reason to want it to be without those who have such reasons being sensitive to those reasons and, as a result, doing something to make it that way. But in other cases this may not be possible. Perhaps there are some ways that we have reason to non-instrumentally desire the world to be where it could only get to be that way if those who have such reasons were sensitive to those reasons and, as a result, do something to make it that way.

Once we acknowledge that this is so, it follows that our conception of orthonomous action must sharply separate out the role played by facts about the steps that an agent could take in his circumstances—ultimately, the movements he makes with his body—to make it the way that he has reason to non-instrumentally desire it to be. When the world is already the way that there is reason to non-instrumentally desire it to be, there won't be any facts about what the agent could do in his circumstances to make it that way. This is a corollary of what we learned by thinking about the reasons that there are for desiring that my children be safe and well when their being safe and well is like manna from heaven. And even when there are such facts, these facts may not be able to play the role that they have to play in action. This is a corollary of what we learned by thinking about the reasons for desiring that we perform acts of spontaneous affection.

When an agent acts orthonomously, he therefore has to be sensitive both to facts about the ways there is reason to non-instrumentally desire the world to be and to facts about the steps that he could take in his circumstances to make it these ways. He must acquire corresponding non-instrumental desires and beliefs; he must put his resultant non-instrumental desires and beliefs together to form instrumental desires; and he must act on those instrumental desires. We must therefore abandon the conception of orthonomous action represented in figure 2 and suppose that orthonomous actions are more properly represented by a two-track process as follows:

THE IDEAL OF ORTHONOMOUS ACTION   65

facts about   K→ available   → beliefs about ways
things one   evidence   one could move
could do in   about things   one's body in C
circumstances   one could do   that would make
C that would   in C that   the world certain
make the   would make   ways
world certain   the world
ways   certain ways

                                            → instrumental desires   → bodily   → the world's being
                                                to move one's body   movements   the ways that it is
                                                in the ways that   non-instrumentally
                                                make the world the   desired to be/there
                                                ways that there is   is most reason to
                                                most reason to   non-instrumentally
                                                non-instrumentally   desire it to be
                                                desire it to be

                                            non-instrumental
                                            desires that the
                                            world be those
                                            ways in those
                                            circumstances

                                                    ↑

facts about   K→ available   → beliefs about
the ways there   evidence about   the ways there is
is most reason   the ways there   most reason to
to non-   is most reason   non-instrumentally
instrumentally   to non-   desire the world to
desire the world   instrumentally   be in various
to be in various   desire the   circumstances
circumstances   world to be
                        in various
                        circumstances

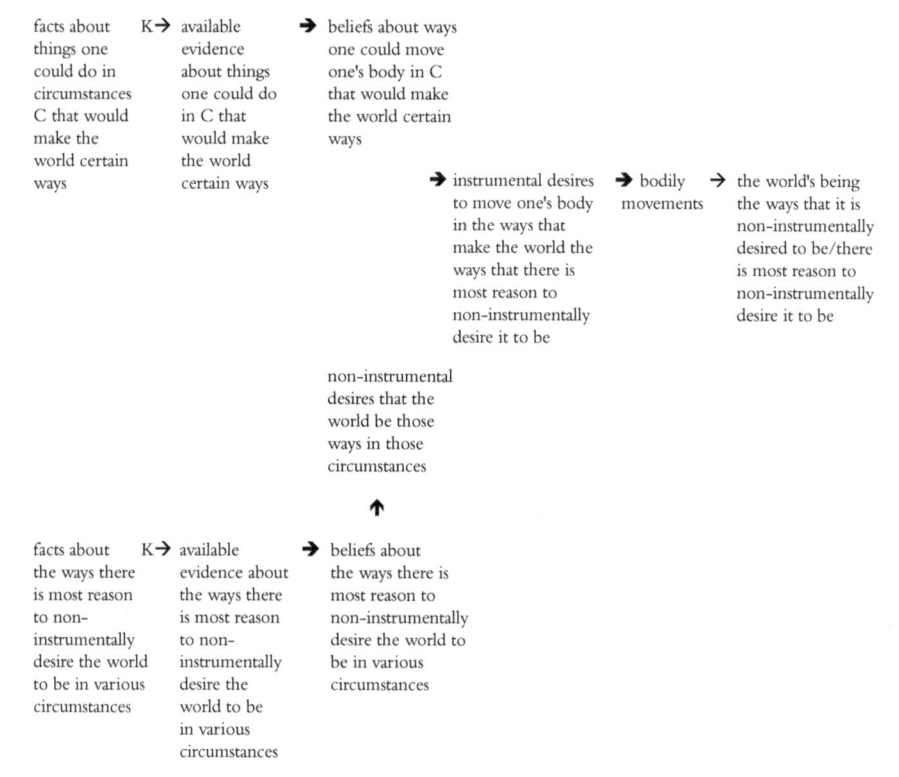

Figure 3 Fully orthonomous action—3rd try.

Though neither reasons for actions nor reasons for intentions are mentioned explicitly in this representation of orthonomous action, both are implicit. We see that figure 3 represents an orthonomous agent's sensitivity to reasons for intentions when we remember that reasons for intentions are nothing over and above reasons for instrumentally desiring, where the instrumental desires in question are desires about steps that can be taken by the orthonomous agent in his circumstances to satisfy the relevant non-instrumental desire for which there are reasons. And it represents an orthonomous agent's sensitivity to reasons for action because, as Scanlon points out, reasons for action are nothing over and above reasons for intention.

Let me sum up. Though we might initially have thought that orthonomous agents are at bottom sensitive to reasons for performing certain actions, we have seen that this is not so. The reasons for action to which orthonomous agents are sensitive decompose into reasons for intention, and these reasons in turn decompose into reasons to desire that the world be certain ways and into reasons to believe that there are things that orthonomous agents can do in their circumstances to make the world those ways. Though these reasons may decompose further, this is decomposition enough for us to see the attractions of the standard account of action.

The standard account, remember, is supposed to be an account of the feature shared by non-ideal actions in virtue of which they are approximations to the ideal. According to figure 3, actions are non-ideal for many different reasons. They might be non-ideal because the facts to which orthonomous agents are sensitive are not available to non-orthonomous agents. Or they might be non-ideal because, though these facts are available to them, non-orthonomous agents do not form their beliefs in the light of the available evidence. Or they might be non-ideal because, though non-orthonomous agents form their beliefs in the light of that evidence, they do not form their non-instrumental desires in the light of these beliefs, and so the non-instrumental desires on which they act are not those for which they believe that there is most reason. And, of course, actions might also be non-ideal because of every possible combination of these various forms of dysfunction.

So do non-ideal actions all share a feature in virtue of which they are approximations to ideal actions? They do indeed. Look again at the various nodes in figure 3 where we might find dysfunction. Non-ideal actions all share the feature of being the product of what their agents non-instrumentally desire to be the case and what they believe they can do to satisfy their non-instrumental desires in their circumstances. This is just the standard account of action. Note, however, that we have arrived at this account not by identifying its requirements as the lowest common denominator shared by ideal and non-ideal actions alike, but rather by independently describing ideal actions and then identifying its requirements as the feature shared by approximations to the ideal. To my mind, this underscores the plausibility of the standard account.

6. Dancy on buck-passing

With this account of ideal actions before us, we are in a position to describe some problems for what Jonathan Dancy has to say about buck-passing views of goodness and rightness. It might initially seem that these two topics have little to do with each other, but, as we shall see, this is far from being so.

Dancy writes:

> To claim that something is good is to claim, according to the buck-passing view, that it has features that give us (*pro tanto*) reasons to take certain attitudes to it. Similarly, we might say, to claim that some action is right is to claim that it has features that give us overall reasons to do it. This is a buck-passing view because it holds that the normative force of a claim that something is right or wrong is inherited from that of the reasons which it asserts to be present. (2000: 166–7)

Though Dancy thinks that a consistent buck-passer would pass both bucks—he would pass the goodness buck to reasons for *attitudes* and the rightness buck to reasons for *actions*—he also insists that there is good reason not to be a consistent buck-passer. An action's being right is a function of the reasons in favour of doing it, according to Dancy, but something's being good is not just a matter of the reasons in favour of taking certain attitudes towards it.

Let me begin with a quibble. Dancy's official argument for, and statement of, the buck-passing view about rightness turns on his suggestion that judgements of rightness are verdictive in the following sense.

> In deciding whether an action is right, we are trying to determine how the balance of reasons lies. Our conclusion may be that there is more reason (or more reason of a certain sort, perhaps) to do it than not to do it, and we express this by saying that it is therefore the right thing to do. The rightness-judgement is verdictive; it expresses our verdict on the question how the reasons lie. It is incoherent, in this light, to suppose that the rightness can add to the reasons on which judgement is passed, thus, as one might say, increasing the sense in which, or the degree to which, it is true. And the same is true of wrongness. (Dancy 2000: 166)

When Dancy says that the same is true of wrongness, I take it he means that wrongness is verdictive in the very same sense. In deciding whether an action is wrong, we are trying to determine whether there is more reason (or more reason of a certain sort) not to do it than to do it, and we express this by saying that it is wrong.

But if an action's not being right entails that it is wrong, and if an action's not being wrong entails that it is right, then Dancy's statement of the buck-passing view of rightness is misleading. When we say that an act is right, we would have to be expressing the negation of the thought we express when we say an act is wrong (compare Wedgwood 2008). In other words, our thought would have to be that it is not the case that there is more reason not to do the act in question than to do it. (Given Dancy's parenthetical remark, it might be better to say that our thought would have to be that it is not the case that the action is of a certain kind, and, among acts of that kind, it is not the case that there is more reason not to do it than to do it. From here on, I will ignore this complication.)

What's important about this way of formulating the buck-passing view of rightness is that it allows that there may be no such thing as *the* right thing to do in a situation—note that this is what Dancy is in fact analysing in the passage quoted—as a number of different acts could equally be right. If, say, I am obliged to ensure that my children are safe and well, and I could do this either by taking out an insurance policy or by investing in stocks and bonds, then there is more than one right thing to do. I act rightly whether I take out the insurance policy or invest in stocks and bonds because it isn't the case that there is more reason not to perform these acts than to do so. But neither act is such that there is more reason to do it than not to do it, so neither satisfies Dancy's criterion of rightness.

With this quibble on the table, I will ignore it in what follows. For if the buck-passing view of rightness just described is correct, then though an act's being right isn't a matter of there being more reason to do it than not to do it, an act's being *the* right act—that is, the one and only right act—will indeed be a matter of there being more reason to do it than not to do it. So let's now focus on that suggestion and Dancy's arguments for it and the correlative view of wrongness. Dancy thinks that an act's being the right act is a matter of the balance of reasons favouring doing it. In other words, remembering now the initial discussion of figure 1, it is a matter of there being most reason to so act. But as the subsequent discussion and revisions of figure 1 make clear, once we pass the rightness buck to what there is most reason to do, we are led ineluctably to pass it much further. The rightness buck passes next to reasons for intention, as in figure 2, and then to reasons for non-instrumental desires and means-end beliefs as in figure 3.

This casts Dancy's initial discussion of consistent buck-passing in a very different light. The consistent buck-passer wouldn't just pass the rightness buck to reasons for action and the goodness buck to reasons for attitudes, he would pass both the goodness buck and the rightness buck all the way to reasons for attitudes, and, moreover, to reasons for the very same attitudes. Being good and being right would both be a matter of there being reasons for non-instrumental desiring. This is somewhat obscured in Dancy's discussion, as he follows Ewing in emphasizing, against Ross, that if we suppose that goodness is the property of having some feature that provides reasons for attitudes, then we should think that that set of attitudes includes all of

> choice, desire, liking, pursuit, approval, admiration... When something is intrinsically good, it is (other things being equal) something that on its own account we ought to welcome, rejoice in if it exists, seek to produce if it does not exist. We ought to approve its attainment, count its loss a depravation, hope for and not dread its coming if this is likely, avoid what hinders its production, etc.
> (Ewing 1947: 149)

But while all of this is true, and while Dancy is surely right that the diversity of attitudes undermines Ross's reasons for not being a buck-passer about goodness, we have also seen that there is a specific attitude that is in play when acts are right, namely, the attitude of intrinsic desiring.

The upshot is that since rightness reduces to reasons for action, and since reasons for action reduce to reasons for non-instrumental desiring, and since this is *inter alia* what goodness consists in, so rightness reduces to goodness. Consistent buck-passing thus entails that the debate between consequentialism and deontology is resolved decisively in favour of consequentialism, a point that Dancy himself notes and to which we will return below. Those attracted to deontology should therefore give up their opposition to reducing rightness to goodness and insist, instead, that there are more goods than those allowed by typical consequentialists. In particular, they should insist that there are goods that underwrite the various deontological duties (Sen 1982, 1988; Broome 1991; Dreier 1998; Smith 2003b, 2009).

However, as noted earlier, Dancy doesn't think that we should be consistent buck-passers. As I understand it, Dancy is opposed to consistent buck-passing because he thinks that there is a more plausible view about goodness in the offing. Instead of supposing that goodness is the property of having some feature that provides us with a reason to have some pro-attitude, he thinks that goodness may be a distinct property, albeit one which is grounded in the very same feature that provides us with a reason to have some pro-attitude. As he puts it, the alternative view that needs to be ruled out before we embrace consistent buck-passing is that 'reasons and values are distinct but may have the same grounds' (2000: 165).

It might be thought that this view could be ruled out on grounds of parsimony—or, to use Dancy's preferred term, on grounds of 'theoretical neatness' (p. 165)—as it allows that goodness and the property of having some feature that provides us with a reason to have some pro-attitude are necessarily co-extensive. But I take it that, at least as Dancy sees things, the two properties are not co-extensive.

> The real point, I think, is one about the polyadicity of rightness and of goodness—and this is a point that translates into thoughts about the polyadicity of reasons. Let us allow, without asking why for the moment, that rightness is a many-place relation. The point will then be that even if goodness is also a many-place relation, it has fewer places than rightness does and fewer than reasons do. Now if this is true, it cannot be correct to define goodness as the presence of reason-giving features. For the presence of reason-giving features will have more places in it, so to speak, than the goodness has.
>
> The reason for supposing that goodness is less polyadic than reasons is that reasons belong to, and are for, individuals. There are no reasons hanging around waiting for someone to have them. If the situation generates a reason for action, it must allot that reason to someone... But goodness is not like this. Something can be good or bad without specification of an agent. The desolation or destitution of someone is bad even if there is nobody around to do anything about it, nobody who has any opportunity to do anything about it, and so nobody who can be said to have a reason to do something about it. Someone's destitution, then, has features that would ground reasons for any agent suitably situated, but it does not follow that those features already ground reasons. And if it does not, we can be sure that to have value or disvalue is not itself to have reason-giving features.
>
> (pp. 170–1)

There may therefore be goodness and badness in circumstances in which the feature that would have grounded reasons, had circumstances been slightly different, doesn't ground any reasons. So, at any rate, Dancy argues. How should we respond?

The first response is that Dancy seems to misunderstand what buck-passing about goodness requires. According to the buck-passer, someone's destitution is bad just in case it has features that provide anyone with a reason to *be averse* to someone's being in a condition like that. And destitution may indeed have such a feature, despite what he says, for what it is like to be destitute may provide anyone with a reason to be averse to someone's being in a state like that, whether or not anyone can do anything about it. Of course, for this feature to provide people with a reason *for action*, there would have to be something that they could do about it in their circumstances. This was why figure 3 depicts orthonomous action as a two-track process. On one track there are reasons for the orthonomous agent to non-instrumentally desire that things be a certain way, where it is left open whether or not there is anything that can be done to make them that way, and on the other track there are reasons for the orthonomous agent to believe that there is something that he can do to make things that way in the circumstances in which he finds himself. Dancy is therefore right that someone's being destitute may be bad, even though no one has a reason to do anything about it, but he is wrong that this counts against the truth of being a buck-passer about the badness of his destitution.

A second response is required, however. For it might be thought that Dancy's real objection has nothing to do with supposing that the reasons in question are reasons for action, rather than reasons for aversion. His real objection is that the buck-passer is committed to there being reasons 'hanging around waiting for someone to have them'. If a situation generates a reason for aversion, then it must allot that reason to someone. But in the imagined situation, Dancy might say, this condition isn't satisfied. For no one is around to be allotted the reasons for aversion to destitution that the buck-passer postulates.

But is this right? I don't think so. According to the buck-passer, *everyone* has a reason to be averse to anyone's being destitute. Of course, some people may not know that a particular destitute person is destitute, and so they may not know that they have a reason to be averse to that particular person's being in the state that he is in. But this is hardly an objection to the buck-passing view, as the buck-passing view doesn't require that people have such knowledge of the destitution of particular people. And though it is presumably a priori knowable that everyone has a reason to be averse to anyone's being destitute, the buck-passer can also allow that some people lack this knowledge too. For even though a priori knowable, the buck-passer isn't committed to the empirical thesis that everyone does in fact know this particular a priori knowable truth. He can therefore allow that everyone has a reason to be averse to anyone's being destitute even though some people do not know that this is so. Dancy's objection to buck-passing on the basis of the different polyadicity of reasons and values therefore fails to convince. We have been given no reason to suppose that reasons and values do differ in their polyadicity.

This connects with another of Dancy's objections:

> An action can be one's duty even though doing it has no value and its being done generates nothing of value. Standard examples here are of trivial duties. Suppose that I promise my children that I will tie my right shoelaces before my left shoelaces on alternative days of the week if they will do their homework without fuss. One can imagine arguing that though I ought to tie my right shoelaces before my left shoelaces today, since I did the opposite yesterday, my doing so has no value of any form. The buck-passing view rules this out in advance. To have value is to have reason-giving features, we are told, and since this is an identity statement it goes both ways. So to have reason-giving features is to be of value. So the deontological view expressed above is ruled out in advance of any significant debate.   (Dancy 2000: 168)

But while this is so, as we have already noted, the real question is whether it's being so constitutes an objection to buck-passing, or merely a surprising consequence of it.

Let's begin by fixing on what it is about keeping even trivial promises, like the one Dancy imagines, that provides everyone with a reason to keep even them. According to one plausible view, which I will simply assume to be correct in what follows, even trivial promises create reasonable expectations, so, since what everyone has a reason to desire is that the reasonable expectations they create are met rather than unmet, it follows that even trivial promises create reasons (compare Scanlon 1998, Smith 2011). Of course, if this is right, then it follows that the value of a kept trivial promise is agent-relative, rather than agent-neutral. The value is agent-relative because, in specifying what it is that everyone has reason to desire, ineliminable reference is made to the agent himself: everyone has a reason to desire that the reasonable expectations that *he himself* creates are met rather than unmet. This means that there is a contrast with the disvalue of destitution, as just discussed. For in characterizing what it is that everyone has reason to be averse to, as regards destitution, no reference at all needed to be made to those who stand in a certain relation to that destitution. Everyone has a reason to be averse to destitution no matter what relation they stand in to that destitution. The disvalue of destitution is therefore agent-neutral.

When Dancy says that an 'action can be one's duty even though doing it has no value and its being done generates nothing of value', we should therefore reply that this assumes that the only value is agent-neutral value. Keeping a trivial promise can indeed be one's duty, even though its being done generates nothing of agent-neutral value. But since there is a reason to keep a trivial promise, it follows that keeping it does produce something of agent-relative value, in particular, the meeting of the reasonable expectation that the person who made that trivial promise created.

Moreover, now going on the offensive, it might further be replied that, absent the creation of something of value, whether agent-neutral or agent-relative—that is, absent the existence of a reason to desire or be averse to something or other, whether the thing in question has to be characterized with or without reference to an agent who bears some sort of special relation to that thing—there can be no obligation, because obligations entail reasons for action, and reasons for action reduce to reasons for intention, which in turn reduce to reasons for desire and aversion. The deontological view Dancy imagines is therefore best recast as a view about the existence of obligations grounded in agent-relative values, not as a view about the existence of obligations that aren't grounded in values.

Dancy in effect notes that a reply of this kind is available, but he rejects it:

> There is, however, a possible way out of this difficulty. It involves the introduction of agent-relative value.... Now I don't want here to go into the details of how this might be done, if indeed it can be done at all. My point at this juncture is going to be merely that, if we are to try to prevent the adoption of the buck-passing view from undermining a significant aspect of deontology by introducing a conception of agent-relative value, this is a considerable theoretical cost, and it is a cost, once again, that we have committed ourselves to paying just for the sake of theoretical neatness. What is more, many people doubt the coherence of the notion of agent-relative value in the first place. If the buck-passing view can only be sustained by introducing a piece of dubious philosophy, it is looking much less attractive.   (Dancy 2000: 169–70)

The trouble with this response, however, is that it gets things the wrong way around.

Even Dancy can and should agree that there may be reasons for all of us to be averse to anyone's being destitute, no matter what relation we stand in to that destitution. And even he can and should agree that there may be reasons for all of us to desire to meet not just any old reasonable expectations, no matter what relation we stand in to those expectations, but specifically the reasonable expectations that we ourselves create. There is no incoherence or theoretical cost involved in supposing that reasons of each of these kinds exist. All that the buck-passing view of value does is parlay this view about reasons for attitudes into a view about values. It tells us that agent-neutral values consist in reasons of the former kind and that agent-relative values consist in reasons of the latter kind. The buck-passing view thus shows not just why there is no incoherence in the concept of agent-relative value, but also why there is no theoretical cost involved in supposing that such value exists alongside agent-neutral value.

References

Broome, J. (1991) *Weighing Goods* (Oxford: Blackwell).
Dancy, J. (2000) 'Should We Pass the Buck?' in A. O'Hear (ed.), *Philosophy, the Good, the True, and the Beautiful*, Royal Institute of Philosophy Supplement, 47: 159–74.
Davidson, D. (1963) 'Actions, Reasons, and Causes', in his *Essays on Actions and Events* (Oxford: Oxford University Press, 1980), 3–20.
—— (1971) 'Agency', in his *Essays on Actions and Events* (Oxford: Oxford University Press, 1980), 43–62.
Dreier, J. (1993) 'Structures of Normative Theories', *The Monist*, 76: 22–40.
Ewing, A. C. (1947) *The Definition of Good* (London: Macmillan).
Jackson, F. (1991) 'Decision Theoretic Consequentialism and the Nearest and Dearest Objection', *Ethics*, 101: 461–82.
Hempel, C. (1961) 'Rational Action', in N. Care and C. Landesman (eds.), *Readings in the Theory of Action* (Bloomington, IN: Indiana University Press, 1968), 285–6.
Hume, D. (1777) *Enquiries Concerning Human Understanding and Concerning the Principles of Morals* (Oxford: Clarendon Press, 1975).
Pettit, P. and Smith, M. (1996) 'Freedom in Belief and Desire', *Journal of Philosophy*, 93: 429–49.

Scanlon, T. M. (1998) *What We Owe to Each Other* (Cambridge, MA: Harvard University Press).
Sen, A. (1982) 'Rights and Agency', *Philosophy and Public Affairs*, 11: 3–39.
—— (1988) 'Evaluator Relativity and Consequential Evaluation', *Philosophy and Public Affairs*, 12: 113–32.
Smith, M. (2003a) 'Rational Capacities', in S. Stroud and C. Tappolet (eds.), *Weakness of Will and Varieties of Practical Irrationality* (Oxford: Oxford University Press), 17–38.
—— (2003b) 'Neutral and Relative Value after Moore' *Ethics*, 113 (Centenary Symposium on G. E. Moore's *Principia Ethica*): 576–98.
—— (2004) 'The Structure of Orthonomy', in J. Hyman and H. Steward (eds.), *Action and Agency*, Royal Institute of Philosophy Supplement 55: 165–93.
—— (2009a) 'Consequentialism and the Nearest and Dearest Objection', in I. Ravenscroft (ed.), *Minds, Ethics, and Conditionals: Themes from the Philosophy of Frank Jackson* (Oxford: Oxford University Press), 237–66.
—— (2009b) 'Two Kinds of Consequentialism', *Philosophical Issues*, 19 (Metaethics): 257–72.
—— (2011) 'The Value of Making and Keeping Promises', in H. Sheinman (ed.), *Promises and Agreements: Philosophical Essays* (New York: Oxford University Press), 198–216.
Stalnaker, R. (1984) *Inquiry* (Cambridge, MA: MIT Press).
Thomson, J. (2008) *Normativity* (Chicago: Open Court).
Wedgwood, R. (2008) 'A Puzzle about "Right" and "Wrong"', *PEA Soup*, 11 May, <http://peasoup.typepad.com/peasoup/2008/05/a-puzzle-about.html>. Last accessed November 2012.

4

Dancy on Buck-Passing

PHILIP STRATTON-LAKE

There is a way of analysing the concept of goodness or value,[1] which can be traced back to Brentano, according to which it is understood in terms of a pro-attitude and some deontic notion, such as rightness, fittingness, or meritedness. According to Brentano to be good is to be the object of a love that is right,[2] for A. C. Ewing (1947: 152), it is to be the fitting object of a pro-attitude, and for John McDowell it is to merit approval.[3]

The latest version of this Brentano-style of analysis is T. M. Scanlon's 'buck-passing' account (BPA) (1998: 95–100). In his 'Should we Pass the Buck?', Jonathan Dancy raises two types of objection to BPA. The first criticizes Scanlon's argument for the view. The second criticizes the view itself. I have already replied to Dancy's objections to Scanlon's argument (in Stratton-Lake 2006, co-authored with Brad Hooker), so here I shall deal only with Dancy's arguments against BPA itself. But before I turn to these I need to state what BPA is.

BPA may be split into a positive and a negative thesis:

Positive thesis—for X to be good is for X to have properties that give us reason to have a certain pro-attitude towards X (Scanlon 1998: 11 and 95).

Negative thesis—goodness itself is never reason-providing—that is, the fact that X is good is never a reason to care about X (p. 11).

---

[1] For the purposes of this chapter, I make no distinction between being good and being of value, so the term value is used in the restricted sense to mean 'good' only. I also make no distinction between thin deontic concepts, such as right, ought, should, required, etc.

[2] 'Wir nennen etwas gut, wenn die darauf bezügliche Liebe richtig ist' (Brentano 2010: 19).

[3] 'A virtue, say, is conceived to be not merely such as to elicit the appropriate "attitude" (as colour is merely such as to cause the appropriate experiences), but rather such as to *merit* it' (McDowell 1985: 118). McDowell does not state what the appropriate attitude is. Dancy suggests 'approval' understood as an attitude of the will. McDowell also denies that what he offers is an analysis of the concept 'value'.

In much of the literature on buck-passing the phrase 'have a pro-attitude towards X' is replaced with the more concise 'favour X'.[4] But because I agree with Scanlon that for F to be a reason to have a pro-attitude towards X is for F to count in favour of, or to favour, that attitude, it would be confusing if I used this terminology. The terminology would be confusing because it would apply 'favour' both to the normative relation of being a reason for, and to one of the terms related in that way. So in what follows I shall talk of reasons to *care* about X, rather than of reasons to have a pro-attitude towards X, or to favour X. This is just a terminological change in the interest of conciseness, and 'care about X' should be understood as synonymous with 'have a pro-attitude towards X'.[5]

Scanlon maintained, plausibly in my view, that the negative thesis follows from the positive thesis. The fact that X has properties that give us reason to care about X can never be one of the reasons we have to care about X. These reasons are provided by other properties of X. That these other properties provide a reason to care cannot be a further reason to care.[6] Dancy does not dispute the negative thesis, so in this piece I shall focus on the positive thesis, and Dancy's criticism of it.

Scanlon devotes only a few pages of *What We Owe to Each Other* to BPA, and as a result leaves a number of aspects of it unclear or unstated. Furthermore, little has been said in discussions of BPA to clarify the view under consideration. So it will be useful to spend time clarifying certain aspects of the account before we consider whether we should accept or reject it.

1. The intentional object constraint

In much of the discussion of BPA, BPA is characterized as identifying the fact that X is good with the fact that there is reason to care about X. This

---

[4] See, for instance, Rabinowicz and Rønnow-Rasmussen (2004); Crisp (2008); and Bykvist (2009).

[5] The disadvantage of this terminology is that there is no natural opposite to use in relation to bad things, whereas the terms 'pro-attitude' and 'favour' do have suitable opposites ('anti-attitude' and 'disfavour'). But since I will mostly be talking about goodness, this will not cause a problem here. Where I talk of badness I shall use the term 'anti-attitude'.

[6] Parfit (2011) and Schroeder (2009) deny that the negative thesis follows from the positive thesis. The existential fact that we have reason to care about X can, they maintain, be a reason to care about X. It is, however, a derivative reason, and so it does not add weight to the reasons from which it is derived. My view is that there is little sense to be given to the notion of a derivative reason as Parfit and Schroeder use it. I will not, however, defend this view here.

characterization misses out an important aspect of BPA that is an improvement on previous fitting-attitude accounts of goodness. According to BPA the fact that X is good is not just the fact that *there is* reason to care about it, but is the fact that X *has properties* that provide these reasons.[7] Previous fitting-attitude accounts state simply that we ought to care about certain things, or that caring about them is fitting, or right (*richtig*). These accounts recommend simply that we care about certain things, but say nothing about *what* recommends this attitude and include no constraint on what must make these recommendations if the object of care is good.

BPA does not tell us what it is about good things that give us reason to care about them—it does not tell us what recommends this attitude—but it does state that whatever gives us such reasons is a property of the good thing. This is an improvement on previous fitting-attitude accounts, as it helps to avoid false positives. The fact that a trusted friend advises you to admire John gives you a reason to admire John, let us assume. So if you have been advised by a trusted friend to admire John, then you *have* reason to admire him (and if this reason is sufficient and not outweighed by other reasons, it will follow that you *ought* to admire John). But it would not follow from the fact that you have reason to admire John that he is good, according to BPA. This is because your friend's advice is not a property of, or fact about, John.[8] It would only follow that John is good, according to BPA, if the reason you have to admire John is provided by some property of, or fact about, John. So according to BPA, the reason to care must be provided by some feature of the intentional object of the caring if that object is good. Call this the 'intentional object constraint'.

Another way in which BPA differs from previous fitting-attitude accounts of goodness is that it includes reasons *to act* in the definition of goodness. Previous fitting-attitude accounts define value in terms of pro-attitudes we ought to take towards the good. But on Scanlon's fitting-attitude account, X's goodness is identified with X's having properties that

---

[7] Actually it is not the properties of X that provide the reasons, but facts about X. But since I understand such facts as the instantiation of a certain property in X, my switching between talk of properties and facts providing these reasons should not cause any confusion.

[8] I appreciate that there may be difficulties specifying what counts as being a property of X, and that there will be difficult cases, especially when relational properties are involved. Also, one can always come up with gerrymandered properties as Rabinowicz and Rønnow-Rasmussen do (2004: 407). But this is not the place to address this tricky issue.

give us *reason to act* in certain ways in regard to it (as well as having properties that give us reason to care about X).[9] According to BPA, then, something must provide reasons to act as well as reasons to care if it is to be good.

For a number of reasons this addition seems to me to weaken BPA, and so is best removed. First, thinking that something has features that give us all reason to have certain pro-attitudes towards it seems sufficient by itself to commit us to thinking that that thing is in some way good. This is, presumably, why all previous fitting attitude accounts defined goodness solely in terms of appropriate attitudes. If something's having features that give us reason to care about it is sufficient for it to be good, then we do not need to incorporate the fact that it has features that give us reason to *act* into BPA.

Second, unlike reasons to care, reasons to act cannot be bound by the intentional object constraint, since actions do not have intentional objects. Consequently the advantage that BPA has over previous fitting-attitude accounts of value is diluted if reasons to act are included in the analysis.

It might be said that there is something like an intentional object of actions, which is the thing upon which one acts, or that with regard to which one acts, and that this can play the role the intentional object does with regard to the attitudes that figure in BPA. One might then claim that, for X to be good is, in part, for properties of the things on which, or towards which, one acts to provide reasons to act on, or towards, those things.

But this modification of BPA will be too restrictive. People from the distant past had good characters, but we cannot act towards them in any way (though we could of course admire or approve of them in virtue of their characters). Similarly, certain acts, such as heroic or saintly acts, are good, but it makes little sense to say that we can act towards, or on, these acts. We might try to emulate them, but it is not clear to me that that is acting *towards* the original heroic acts. It is, at best, acting towards the types of which they were tokens; and even then this seems somewhat stretched.

---

[9] For example, Scanlon writes that 'to value something is to take oneself to have reasons for holding certain positive attitudes towards it and for acting in certain ways in regard to it' (1998: 95). Later he claims that 'to call something valuable is to say that it has... properties that provide reasons for behaving in certain ways with regard to it' (p. 96). He sometimes expresses this point disjunctively. For example, when he writes that 'judgements about what is good or valuable generally express practical conclusions about what would, at least under the right conditions, be reasons for acting or responding in a certain way' (p. 96; see also p. 97).

Another way of trying to apply the intentional object constraint to reasons for action might be to distinguish the doing of some act from the thing done, and maintain that the thing done is the object of the doing. But if the thing done is regarded as the object of the doing then the only things that could be intrinsically good would be acts, if reasons to act were an essential component of BPA. This is because the only thing that could be the object of the doing is an act—that is, the thing done. But things other than acts can be good. So having properties that give us reasons to *act* in certain ways cannot be part of what it is for something to be good if we try to meet the intentional object constraint in this way.

Since (a) X's having properties that give us reason to care about X seems sufficient for X's being good, (b) reasons for actions dilute the advantage BPA has over previous fitting-attitude accounts of goodness, because they cannot meet the intentional object constraint, and (c) things can be good even though it makes no sense to talk of our having reasons to act with regard to them in certain ways, BPA is better if the reference to reasons to act is removed. I propose, therefore, that the only reasons that should figure in BPA are reasons to care—that is, to have certain pro-attitudes. This is not of course to deny that if something is good, then we often, or even standardly, have reason to act in certain ways towards it. All I am claiming is that such practical reasons are not part of what it is for something to be good. That is quite compatible with good things typically having features that give us reason to act towards them in certain ways.

2. The universality constraint

Scanlon introduces BPA by distinguishing between what it is to value something and what it is for something to be of value, or to be valuable:

> To value something is to take oneself to have reasons for holding certain positive attitudes towards it and for acting in certain ways in regard to it. Exactly what these reasons are, and what actions and attitudes they support, will be different in different cases. They generally include, as a common core, reasons for admiring the thing and for respecting it, although 'respecting' can involve quite different things in different cases. (1998: 95)

If I value something, say a possession that has certain associations, then I will think I have reason to care about it. To think that I have reason to care about it is what it is to value that thing, according to Scanlon.[10] But *to value* something in this way is not yet to think that it *has value*, or *is valuable*; it is not yet to think that it is good. To think that it is good I must also think that others[11] have reason to care about it *as I do* (p. 95).

So the distinction between something's being appropriately valued by someone, and its being of value, is determined by the scope of the reasons to care. If some object is good (rather than just appropriately valued by you), then the feature of the object that gives you a reason to care about it must also give everyone else a reason to care about it in the same way (as you do). Call this the 'universality constraint'.

The distinction between valuing something (or its being appropriately valued by someone) and thinking it valuable is a useful one. As Scanlon points out, 'it is natural to say, and would be odd to deny, that I value my children; but it would be odd for me to put this by saying that they are valuable (except in the sense that everyone is)' (p. 95). This point is brought out more strongly in comparative evaluative judgements. We value our own children more than other people's children, but we do not think that our children are more valuable than any other children. Similarly, we might value our children more just because they are ours, but we do not think that they are more valuable just in virtue of their being ours.

But given how Scanlon defines valuing something, judging that something has value cannot be understood as judging that others also have reason to value it as you do.[12] For then, judging that something is of value would turn out to be judging that others have reason to judge that they have reason to care about it, and that is not quite what Scanlon means to say.

What he should have said, and, I believe, what he meant to say, is that for you to judge that X is good is for you to judge that you *and others* have reason to care about X (e.g. to desire or admire X). For you to judge that X is good is *not* for you to judge that everyone has reason *to judge* that they have reason to care about X. Put more succinctly, the idea is that for A to be

---

[10] On the objective side, we may expand this to claim that for something to be an appropriate object of being valued by someone is for it to have properties that give that person reason to care about it.

[11] It is unclear whether Scanlon means all others. All he says is that things that are good are things that 'merit being valued generally' and refers to this as an impersonal quality of goodness (1998: 95).

[12] Dancy makes a similar point (2000: 162).

good is for *everyone* to have reason to *care* about A as you do.[13] This is what I have called the universality constraint.[14]

3. Agent-relative value

On the face of it, Scanlon's distinction between being (appropriately) valued and being of value may seem to be a verbal variant of the distinction between agent-relative and agent-neutral value. If this is right then Scanlon's distinction will pick out different ways of being of value, rather than a difference between being of value and something else (being an appropriate object of someone's care). I think a buck-passer can go either way on this, but when the universality constraint is not met, it is better to say that the fact that X has features that give someone (but not everyone) reason to care about it does not entail that X is good in an agent-relative sense.

If we did regard such reasons to care as establishing agent-relative value, then this form of value would be defined in terms of agent-relative reasons. For X to be good (in the agent-relative sense of good) would be for X to have properties that give someone agent-relative reason to care about X. Because agent-relative goodness would be defined in terms of agent-relative reasons, the agent-relativity of the agent-relative goodness would be built in to this evaluative property, and there would be no need to qualify agent-relative goodness as '*for someone*' or '*from someone's point of view*'. Rather, the term 'good' would be unqualified, and would be ambiguous between 'something's having properties that give everyone reason to care about it' and 'something's having properties that give me, or you (but not everyone), a reason to care about it'.

This ambiguity would mean that it would, after all, be correct to say that my children are better than other people's children. It may seem as though I have said something false, as one would think that I have used the

---

[13] An ability condition should be added here. To be good is to have properties that give everyone who is *able to have reasons* a reason to care about it.

[14] More needs to be said about this constraint. In particular we need to know whether 'everyone' means 'all rational agents', and whether all rational agents means all *actual* or all *possible* rational agents, and whether we need to add a clause limiting the scope to those who think about the particular event or thing that is good. Since my primary aim here is to defend BPA from certain objections, it would take me too far afield to answer all of these questions in detail.

comparative of 'good' in the universal sense, rather than in the agent-relative sense. But in the agent-relative sense of 'good' this would be true, and would not need any qualification.

But although I think there is reason for me to care about my children more than others', I do not think that there is any sense in which my children are better than others', or at least, not simply in virtue of being mine. So I think that Scanlon's distinction between valuing X and X's being of value should not be identified with the agent-relative and agent-neutral value distinction, although buck-passers may go either way on this issue. For buck-passers who agree with me on this point, the universality constraint must apply for something to be good according to BPA.

Much of what I have said so far needs further clarification, defence from objections, and development if the point is to offer a fully detailed account of a buck-passing account of value. But my aim here is simply to highlight certain aspects of BPA which are relevant to Dancy's objections to the view, and I think I have said enough to achieve this end. So I now turn to his objections.

4. Resolving substantive questions by definition

Dancy's first objection to BPA is that it resolves certain substantive debates in moral theory simply by its definition of one of the key terms of that debate. One such issue is that between deontologists and consequentialists. Deontologists, such as Prichard and Ross, argue that certain acts may be right even though they are in no way good, so their rightness cannot be grounded in their goodness. Dancy thinks that BPA loads things in favour of consequentialism on this issue:

> Deontologists have suggested in one way or another that there are duties, and so reasons, that are not value-involving. An action can be one's duty even though doing it has no value and its being done generates nothing of value. Standard examples here were of trivial duties. Suppose that I promise my children that I will tie my right shoe lace before my left shoe lace on alternate days of the week if they will do their homework without fuss. One can imagine arguing that though I ought to tie my right shoe lace before my left shoe lace today, since I did the opposite yesterday, my doing so has no value of any form. The buck-passing view rules this out in advance. To have value is to have reason-giving

> features, we are told, and since this is an identity statement it goes both ways. So to have reason-giving features is to be of value. So the deontological view expressed above is ruled out in advance of any significant debate. (2000: 168)

Dancy claims that when certain reasons to act are present, it follows from BPA that the object is good. Dancy mentions only reasons to act. I suggested that it is better to remove these reasons from the buck-passing analysis, but even if they are left, they are not sufficient to ground value. Even on Scanlon's original formulation, reasons (of the right sort)[15] to care about something, as well as reasons to act in certain ways towards that thing, must be present if that thing is to be good. On the original formulation (a) X's having properties that give us reason to care about X, and (b) X's having properties that give us reason to act in certain ways with regard to X, are each necessary and jointly sufficient for X to be good. There must also be reason to care about the relevant thing, those reasons must be provided by properties of the intentional object of the caring, and they must be universally valid.

But perhaps these conditions are met. In the case Dancy mentions he has good reason to tie his right shoe lace before his left shoe lace, and (although he does not mention this) we may assume that he has reason to want himself to tie his right shoe lace first, and to approve of his doing this, because he would then be doing what he had promised to do. Indeed, since he promised his children that he would do this, it would seem that everyone has reason to want him to tie his right shoe lace first, and to approve of his doing this if he does it. So, one might argue, the universality constraint is met in relation to the reasons to care. It is not, however, met with regard to the reasons to act, as it is not the case that everyone has reason to tie their right shoe lace first. But on my revised version of BPA (which removes reference to practical reasons) that would not spoil Dancy's argument, so long as the universal reason *to care* about his doing this act satisfies the intentional object constraint and the universality constraint, and it may plausibly be argued that it does. For the reason he has to approve of his doing this act is provided by a feature of the act—the fact that it would be the keeping of a promise, and everyone has reason to approve of his doing this. So it may, after all, seem that BPA is committed to saying that this act is in some way good.

---

[15] Where being of the right sort means satisfying the intentional object constraint and the universality constraint.

Does that settle a substantive issue between deontologists and consequentialists, or at least bias the debate in favour of consequentialism? I do not see that it does. If it turns out that we all have reason to approve of Dancy keeping his promise, and this reason is provided by a feature of his promise-keeping, then his keeping it is good, according to BPA. But the debate between deontologists and consequentialists is not about whether such acts are good in some sense, but about whether it is their goodness, or the goodness connected with them, which makes them right. The relevant reasons here are reasons to do the act, not reasons to approve of it. These reasons may be provided by the same fact, but they need not be. I have reason to approve of Dancy doing this act (because he would then be doing something he ought to do, given his promise), but *I* have no reason to do it, as I didn't make such a promise.

BPA has not even settled the question of what feature of the act gives me reason to approve of it. This is something over which deontologists and consequentialists may have substantive disagreements. Deontologists like Ross may claim that this reason is provided by the fact that this act constitutes the keeping of a promise, or that it is worthy of approval because it is the doing of an obligatory act. Consequentialists, on the other hand, may argue that the reason we have to approve of this act is provided by the fact that it is such as to produce the intrinsically best outcome.

Dancy acknowledges some of this, but makes a further claim. He says that BPA still inappropriately rules out a substantive view in moral philosophy—namely the view that what is right is never good and what is good is never right:

> But there would still be one position on this issue that is ruled out in advance, namely that of Ross (and also that of Prichard, one might say). For Ross would not accept that actions that are right are made right by their intrinsic value, or by the features that give them that value. As I briefly pointed out at the beginning of this paper, his view was that no duty has value of any sort, and that nothing that has value is a duty. And he had independent philosophical reasons for the two parts of this view. Can it be right to say that we know his view to be false because of the attractions of the buck-passing view, when those only amount to theoretical neatness? (2000: 169)

As I have said, BPA has said nothing about whether this action, or any other for that matter, is made right by its intrinsic value, or by the features that give it that value. This is because the relevant reasons are reasons to have some pro-attitude towards the act, not reasons to do it, and although these reason-giving features may often go together (the reasons to care about the act may often be reasons to do the act), they need not. This is the case when the act is in the past, or is one that someone else ought to do.

Furthermore, it is not clear to me that this act would be intrinsically good, according to BPA, for it is not clear that the feature that makes it good, and which gives everyone reason to approve of it, is an intrinsic feature of the act. Whether it is or not will depend on a substantive debate about what provides that reason, and BPA does not settle that issue. It just says that something must have features that provide universal reasons to care about it. It does not say what those features are, and thus whether they are intrinsic or not. That is a substantive issue in normative moral theory, and is left open by BPA. BPA does not, therefore, close off this particular substantive debate. Rather, we have to form a view on this before we can form a view about what sort of value the act has.

But however we go on that point, there is the separate objection that BPA rules out Ross's view that whatever is our duty is not good, and whatever is good is not our duty. If it does this, then, Dancy maintains, it rules out a possible view for which Ross has decent arguments. Such a view should not be ruled out in advance by a definition of goodness.

But does BPA even rule out this position? Whether it does or not seems to depend on the outcome of a substantive question about the scope of the reasons we have to care about right acts. It may be that they do not have universal scope—that certain right acts are not such that they provide *everyone* with reason to approve of them. I think it is more plausible to suppose that everyone does have such reason, and it does, I think, follow from this that the object of approval is good. My own view is, then, that if you are obligated to ϕ, then the features that give you reason to ϕ will also give you and others reason to approve of your ϕ-ing. And if everyone has reason to approve of your ϕ-ing, then your ϕ-ing must be good in some way.[16] This is because the attitude of approval is only ever appropriate when it is directed at things that are good, as Ross himself recognized. Ross thought that this is because it is the fact that A is good that *makes* approval

---

[16] Ross would certainly not deny that if others have reason to approve of something, then that thing is good (1939: 261).

an appropriate response (1939: 261). This makes Ross look like a buck-stopper, for it looks as though he thinks that the reason we have to approve of certain acts is that those acts are good. However, one need not agree with Ross about that. One might just as plausibly maintain that approval is appropriate only towards things that are good because what makes the attitude of approval appropriate is what makes its object good.[17] In any case, if everyone has reason to approve of your ϕ-ing then your ϕ-ing must, I think, be good in some way.

Dancy might deny that *everyone* has reason to approve of his tying his right shoelace first, even though this is something he promised to do, and which he is obligated to do. He may think that this act is just too insignificant to warrant approval, even though it is the right thing to do. If he were to argue this point, then we would be arguing about whether such acts are good, given BPA. If this is something about which we can seriously, and intelligibly disagree—which I think it is—then BPA does not even resolve the issue of whether all right acts are good, including the particular example Dancy gives. What makes Dancy think that BPA does resolve this debate is that he has reason to tie his right shoe lace first. I have tried to show that that does not settle the issue of whether such acts are good according to BPA.

5. Agent-relative value and maximizing

Another concern Dancy has with BPA is that it has the potential to undermine the distinction between two sorts of moral rules. Some rules take a maximizing form. They locate some value, and instruct us to produce as much of that value as possible, or minimize instances of disvalue. Sometimes conforming to this rule may involve doing the bad thing in order to minimize its instances. Dancy writes:

> To take an example that I think I owe to Philippa Foot: there is the rule 'do not shout' and there is the rule 'see to it that as little shouting as possible takes place'. The first of these is a deontological rule; it is addressed to the agent, saying, as it

---

[17] My view is that we do not approve of certain things because they are good. Rather, we approve of different things for different reasons. We approve of good things because of their good-making features. We admire good acts because they are heroic, or brave, or selfless, etc., not because they are good (though we cannot approve of them unless we think they are good).

were 'don't shout—this means you' or 'don't be a shouter'; and we break that rule if we shout. The second rule is quite different. We do not necessarily break this rule by shouting; indeed, we would possibly only be able to keep the rule by shouting, as when we need to shout in order to shut everyone else up. In this sense, deontological rules are not maximising rules. You should not shout even if, by shouting, you can minimise the incidence of shouting. A maximising rule is not the sort of rule that deontologists take themselves to be talking about. But if we introduce a link between reasons and values, we undermine this deontological picture of rules (obviously, and especially, of moral rules). For we reintroduce the possibility that the value at issue in keeping the rule is best served by breaking it. (2000: 169)

I'm not quite sure how deontological rules are undermined just by introducing the *possibility* that the value at issue in keeping the rule is best served by breaking it. That it introduces this possibility is such a weak claim that it is hard to see how it might resolve any debate in normative moral theory. Furthermore, it is not obvious (to me at least) why we should accept even this weak claim, and Dancy offers no support for it.

So perhaps Dancy means something stronger than the mere possibility of this sort of maximizing. Perhaps the idea is that it will be hard to resist the idea that the value at issue is best served by maximizing it. But why should we think that a link between certain reasons and value will make it harder to resist the idea that the value at issue is best served by maximizing it? One possible argument runs as follows: Take a deontological rule, such as 'keep your promises'.

1. If you ought to keep your promises, then you have reason to keep your promises.
2. If BPA is true, then the fact that you have reason to keep your promises will imply that promise keeping is good.
3. If such acts are good, then it will be hard (or at least harder) to resist the view that you ought to produce as many promise-keepings as possible.

But then,

4. The deontological rule: 'keep your promises', will be transformed into the very different maximizing rule: 'ensure as many promises as possible are kept'.

Although one transgresses the deontological rule by breaking a promise, one might be acting in accordance with the maximizing rule by doing this, and what started off as a distinctively deontological view will no longer be recognizable.

I have already argued that BPA does not licence a move from 'A has reason to ϕ' to 'ϕ-ing is good'. Such an inference applies only on the condition that the relevant reasons satisfy the intentional object and universality constraints. But the reason to keep your promise satisfies neither constraint. It makes no sense to say that the reason is provided by a property of the intentional object of the action, for unlike attitudes, actions do not have intentional objects, and this reason is not one that applies to everyone. You have reason to ϕ because you promised to ϕ. I do not have reason to ϕ as I made no such promise. So (2) is false.

But even if we allow (2), it seems to me that we would not be committed to convert the deontological rule into a maximizing rule, because we may reject (3). (3) seems to work under the assumption that the only appropriate response to value is to produce as much of it as possible. It is because of this assumption that it is hard to resist the maximizing conversion of the rule once value is introduced. But this assumption may be questioned. It may be, as Scanlon (1998: 78–94) argues, that maximization is not the only way to respond to value, and in fact maximization is often rather peripheral to our valuing something appropriately.

So a strong case linking the connection between practical reasons and value, on the one hand, and a maximizing conception of moral rules, on the other hand, has not yet been shown. First the argument for this link assumes falsely that the presence of a reason to act is sufficient to make that act good, according to BPA. And even if we put this point aside, a link between BPA and maximizing rules is established on the contestable assumption that the only appropriate response to value is maximization.

6. Polyadicity

Dancy objects to BPA on the ground that goodness is a simpler property than the buck-passing analysis represents it as being. He begins with a reference to Ross's claim that goodness could not be a relation. He focuses on his discussion of a fitting-attitude account of goodness in the *Foundations of Ethics*, but Ross has a simpler argument for this claim in *The Right and the Good*. He writes:

> [M]ost theories of value can be divided up into those which treat it as a quality and those which treat it as a relation between that which has value and something else—which is usually but not always said to be some state of mind, such as that of being pleased by the object or desiring it or approving of it or finding its desire satisfied by it. And it seems clear that any view which treats goodness as a relation between that which is good and something else denies that anything is intrinsically good, since by calling a thing intrinsically good we mean that it would be good even if nothing else existed. (2002: 75)

This is Ross's main argument for denying that goodness is a relation, which is supposed to apply to all relational accounts. The arguments in the *Foundations* focus on a specific type of relational account, whereas *The Right and the Good* argument concludes that goodness could not be any type of relation at all. But the argument in *The Right and the Good* is not one of Ross's best arguments.

It is not at all clear that 'intrinsically good' means 'good even if nothing else existed', for many of the things that may be good might not be able to exist if nothing else existed. For instance, pleasure may be intrinsically good, but it makes little sense to say that a particular pleasure could exist even if nothing else existed, including the person whose pleasure it is. The same is true of beauty. It makes perfect sense to maintain that beauty is something that is intrinsically good, but beauty could not exist if nothing else did, for beauty is a property that other properties have, and could not be instantiated if no other properties were instantiated.

A better definition of intrinsic goodness is a variant of G. E. Moore's definition in 'The Conception of Intrinsic Value' (1993). According to this definition, for X to be intrinsically good is for X to be good solely in virtue of its intrinsic properties. On this definition there could be intrinsic goodness even if goodness is a relation; indeed, even if it is the simple relation of causing pleasure in us. There would be intrinsic goodness on this relational account if the properties that caused pleasure in us, and thus made the object of pleasure good, are intrinsic properties of the thing in question.

But Dancy does not rest his argument on Ross's actual arguments, so we need not labour these points here. Dancy writes:

Let us allow, without asking why for the moment, that rightness is a many place relation. The point will then be that even if goodness is also a many place relation, it has fewer places than rightness does and fewer than reasons do. Now if this is true, it cannot be correct to define goodness as the presence of reason-giving features. For the presence of reason-giving features will have more places in it, so to speak, than the goodness has. (2000: 170)

The first thing to note in response to this claim is that Scanlon does not claim that goodness is a relation. Although the property some property has of being a reason for someone to respond in a certain way is a relation of a certain sort, the property an object has of having that property is not a relation. The property of having properties that stand in a normative relation to certain individuals does not itself stand in that normative relation to those individuals, or in any other relation to something other than itself.[18] So Scanlon does not represent goodness as a relation. It is a higher-order property of certain objects, events, and actions, and that higher-order property is not a relational property.

Nonetheless, Dancy's worry can be restated in a way that retains its force, for although the property of being good is not a relation according to BPA, it is a property that depends on a relation, and the concern is that this relation makes the goodness of objects depend upon the presence of certain things in an implausible way. The reasons that figure in BPA necessarily include a reference to some agent or other (or, as I have claimed, to all agents). But the goodness of something seems to have no reference to agents. Dancy writes:

The reason for supposing that goodness is less polyadic than reasons is that reasons belong to, are *for* individuals. There are no reasons hanging around waiting for someone to have them. If the situation generates a reason for action, it must allot that reason to someone. (I don't mean to suggest that this is always or often difficult.) (p. 170)[19]

Dancy supports his view that goodness is less polyadic by arguing that something can be good or bad even if no one is around to respond in the

---

[18] In Stratton-Lake (2009) I argue that BPA should not be understood as claiming that goodness is a property at all, as this has certain implausible implications. But all that need be postulated for evaluative statements to be true is that certain things provide reasons of a certain sort. We need not assume that in addition to this they have a property of *having* those reasons.

[19] In the extended, unpublished version of this paper he goes on to add: 'Perhaps the same reason is allotted to everyone (all have the same reason to avoid extreme pain); but there is still an empty place in the specification of that reason, which is filled in this case by a universally quantified variable.'

appropriate way. Since no one can respond in the appropriate way, there could be no such reason. But something could be good or bad, nonetheless. So goodness (or badness) cannot be understood in terms of reasons.

> Something can be good or bad without specification of an agent. The desolation or destitution of someone is bad even if there is nobody around to do anything about it, nobody who has any opportunity to do anything about it, and so nobody who can be said to have a reason to do something about it. Someone's destitution, then, has features that *would* ground reasons for any agent suitably situated, but it does not follow that those features already ground reasons. And if it does not, we can be sure that to have value or disvalue is not itself to have reason-giving features.
>
> One might reply that there are surely reasons for the destitute person, created by his destitution. In that case, a better example might be the lonely and sudden death of someone without friends or relatives, far from any possible help. We could say that this is bad, even if there is nobody who has reasons to grieve or indeed reasons of any other sort. (pp. 170–1)

The example he gives is of something bad rather than of something good, but this doesn't make any difference to his point. The point is that something could be bad (or good) even if there are no reasons to respond in the appropriate way because no one is around who could respond in that way.

Dancy considers a possible response to this problem by Parfit, who suggested modifying the definition so that X's goodness or badness is identified with its having features that are *potential* reasons (p. 171). Dancy accepts that this would deal with the initial problem, but would do so only by giving rise to another difficulty—namely, that it may make evaluatively indifferent things good. 'Something that has no value at all might well have features that would, in certain circumstances, ground reasons' (p. 171). The same could, presumably, be said if we replace 'having features that are potential reasons' with 'having features that are disposed to be reasons'.

But we do not need to modify BPA in this way to deal with this sort of objection. The first step is to clarify the sort of reasons that figure in BPA. I argued earlier that these reasons should not include reasons to act, but only reasons to have a certain pro-attitude towards (to care about) the object that has those reason-giving properties, if the object is good, or an anti-attitude if it is bad. So the fact that there is no one around to help the desolate person Dancy describes, does not mean that his condition is not bad according to BPA, so long as his condition has features that give everyone reason to have an anti-attitude towards it. That there is no one around to help, and so no one who is able to help, in no way means that the desolate person's condition cannot have features that provide *these* reasons. People on the other side of the world cannot help, but still have reason to regret this poor man's condition. Nothing Dancy says casts doubt on the view that everyone has reason to have such an anti-attitude towards the man's condition, or that those reasons are provided by features of his condition. So the scenario he outlines does nothing to show that this man's condition is not bad, according to BPA.

There is, however, a version of Dancy's scenario that does seem to cause a problem for BPA. Consider the agonizing death of a non-rational animal in a possible world (W1) which contains no rational agents at all.[20] Since there are no rational agents in W1 who could respond to the animal's agony with regret, there could, it may be argued, be no reason for anyone to feel regret at the poor creature's condition. But then it would follow from BPA that the creature's agony is in no way bad. But the badness of the animal's condition seems to depend only on features of its suffering, and does not depend on the existence of rational creatures. This is essentially Dancy's point. It is not as if the creature's agony is any less painful in a world in which there are no rational creatures, so why should we think that it is not bad in such a world? So if BPA meant that the animal's suffering is not bad, this looks like a false negative.

But, we may ask, does the presence of reasons to respond with regret depend upon the presence of rational creatures who could respond in the appropriate way to the creature's condition? Reasons to respond in a certain way do seem to be relations. They seem to be relations between a property of, or more precisely, a fact about, something, and a certain attitude—the attitude favoured by the reason-giving fact. But reasons are unlike most other relations in that they do not require both terms of the relation to exist in order for the relation to exist. Features of your character might have properties that give me reason to admire you, even if I do not admire you. So we cannot think of these reasons as constituting a relation between features of your character and my admiration.

---

[20] I raised this problem for BPA myself in a paper given at a workshop on Reasons and Values at Reading in 1999.

Dancy acknowledges this when commenting on Ross's discussion of a fitting-attitude account of goodness. He writes:

> It is worth pausing to note what Ross means by a relation here.[21] It is not what we would ordinarily mean, because we would ordinarily think that for a relation to obtain, there must be at least two relata and both must, in the relevant sense, exist. But in suggesting (even if only to reject the idea) that goodness might be a relation, Ross is clearly not thinking of relations in this way. For something can be worthy of approval even if no approval and no approver is forthcoming. (2000: 160–1)

The deontic relation of fittingness can obtain even if the attitude that is fittingly related to some feature of its object is not present. A career in medicine may be a fitting or worthy object of desire, even if no one who is suitably talented to pursue such a career desires it, and Socrates' questioning attitude may be a fitting, or worthy object of admiration, even if no one around at the time admired it.

Dancy thinks that reasons belong to the same family of deontic concepts as rightness and fittingness (p. 163). So, we may ask, if the features of something can make it the case that a certain attitude is fitting (is fittingly related to the right-making features), when that pro-attitude is not present, why couldn't something have features that give us reason to care about that thing even when no such caring is present? If deontic relations are odd in that they do not require the existence of one of the relata to exist for the relation to obtain, why couldn't there be reasons to regret a creature's agonising death even in the extreme case where there is no one in W1 who could regret his condition? Presumably the creature's condition in such a world is still a fitting object of regret. If so, why isn't its condition such that it gives everyone (anyone) reason to regret his condition in such a world? Why couldn't there be reasons to regret the creature's condition in a world in which there are no rational agents? Given the peculiarity of deontic relations mentioned above, I do not see that an answer to these questions has been provided.

---

[21] I think Dancy is wrong in how he interprets Ross. Ross thought that all relations, including deontic ones, presuppose that the terms related exist, as is shown by his argument that intrinsic goodness is not a relation in *The Right and the Good* (2002: 75). I agree with Dancy's view about deontic relations and their terms, I just do not think that Ross would.

7. Conclusion

I conclude therefore, that Dancy has not shown that BPA has implausible or unacceptable implications. Some of his objections are generated by the inclusion of reasons to act in BPA itself, which I have argued should be removed. Others stem from the fact that he treats the reasons relation as one that requires both terms of the relation to exist, although he acknowledges that this is not the case for the deontic family of concepts of which he claims reasons are a member.

In this chapter I have not addressed Dancy's arguments to the effect that Scanlon offers no good argument for BPA. But I have (with Hooker: 2006) addressed these arguments elsewhere. Of course there are many other objections to BPA that I have not addressed here. One might, for instance, think that it is vulnerable to the wrong kind of reasons objection, and that it makes goodness a mere Cambridge property.[22] Alternatively, one might think that the notion of a pro-attitude is unacceptably vague. So there still remains plenty of work for buck-passers to do. But I am not persuaded that Dancy has told us why we should not pass the buck.

References

Brentano, F. (2010) *Vom Ursprung Sittlicher Erkenntnis* (Charleston, SC: Nabu Press).
Bykvist, K. (2009) 'No Good Fit: Why the Fitting Attitude Analysis of Value Fails', *Mind*, 118(469): 1–30.
Crisp, R. (2008) 'Goodness and Reasons: Accentuating the Negative', *Mind*, 117 (466): 257–65.
Dancy, J. (2000) 'Should we Pass the Buck?', in A. O'Hear (ed.), *Philosophy, the Good, the True and the Beautiful*, Royal Institute of Philosophy Supplement, 47: 159–173.
Ewing, A. C. (1947) *The Definition of Good* (London: Routledge and Kegan Paul).
McDowell, J. (1985) 'Values and Secondary Qualities', in T. Honderich (ed.), *Morality and Objectivity* (London: Routledge and Kegan Paul), 110–29.
Moore, G. E. (1993) 'The Conception of Intrinsic Value', in his *Principia Ethica*. Revised edn, ed. T. Baldwin (Cambridge: Cambridge University Press), 280–98.
Parfit, D. (2011) *On What Matters*, 2 vols. (Oxford: Oxford University Press).

---

[22] I have addressed these issues in Stratton-Lake (2005) and (2009), respectively.

Rabinowicz, W. and Rønnow-Rasmussen, T. (2004) 'The Strike of the Demon: On Fitting Pro-Attitudes and Value', *Ethics*, 114: 391–423.

Ross, W. D. (1939) *Foundations of Ethics* (Oxford: Clarendon Press).

—— (2002) *The Right and the Good* (Oxford: Clarendon Press).

Scanlon, T. M. (1998) *What We Owe to Each Other* (Cambridge, MA: Harvard University Press).

Schroeder, M. (2009) 'Buck-Passers' Negative Thesis', *Philosophical Explorations*, 12(3): 341–7.

Stratton-Lake, P. (2005) 'How to Deal with Evil Demons: Comment on Rabinowicz and Rønnow-Rasmussen', *Ethics*, 115: 788–98.

—— (2009) 'Roger Crisp on Goodness and Reasons', *Mind*, 118(472): 1081–94.

—— and Hooker, B. (2006) 'Scanlon versus Moore on Goodness', in T. Horgan and M. Timmons (eds.), *Metaethics After Moore* (Oxford: Oxford University Press), 149–68.

5

Are Egoism and Consequentialism Self-Refuting?

ROGER CRISP

Jonathan Dancy has made many remarkable and interesting claims about ethics, the most well known and widely discussed being of course that we can do without moral principles. In previous work, I have said a little in response to that. Here I would like to focus on another noteworthy suggestion—that normative egoism and consequentialism are self-refuting (Dancy 1997, 1993: ch. 12). Since I believe that the most plausible ethical theory is, in a sense, a combination of normative egoism and consequentialism, I am especially keen to answer Dancy's arguments.

I

Dancy makes these claims in the context of a discussion of the first chapter of Derek Parfit's *Reasons and Persons* (1984). He first considers what Parfit says about normative egoism, which Parfit calls 'the Self-interest Theory' ('S'). S's central claim, according to Parfit, is:

(S1) For each person, there is one supremely rational ultimate aim: that his life go, for him, as well as possible (Parfit 1984: 4).

Dancy goes on to explain two different distinctions relevant to S. The first is that between objective and subjective rationality. Since Dancy believes this distinction plays no role in Parfit's argument, we can put it aside. The second is that between act and agent, which Dancy (1997: 2) puts as follows, elucidating Parfit's S:

(D1) An act is... rational if no available alternative would be better for the agent.

(D2) An agent is... rational (here)[1] if his motive is a member of an S-approved set of motives.

According to Parfit (1984: 5), S is indirectly self-defeating. That is to say, if someone tries to achieve the aims given to her by S, these aims will be, on the whole, worse achieved. S gives a person the aim of making her life go, for her, as well as possible; but if she tries to achieve that aim, by never doing what would be worse for her in S's own terms, the outcome will be worse for her. The standard example here is the so-called 'paradox of hedonism' (p. 6). If I try as hard as I can to be happy, I shall be less happy than if I allow myself to become engaged in certain activities, such as playing a game in which I aim at goals internal to the game rather than at my own happiness. Dancy (1997: 4) suggests that, since it seems as if S is giving each of us a *rational* aim (that our lives go, for each of us, as well as possible) which it would be *irrational* to aim at, it might be thought that the problem for S is worse than indirect self-defeat.

Now, as Dancy notes, it might seem that there really is no special difficulty for S here. The situation may be likened to that of an archer's aiming an arrow off-target to compensate for the effects of the wind. But, Dancy suggests, the analogy fails, since in this case we have a distinction between outcome and aim: the outcome desired is to hit the target, while the aim is off-target. S, however, concerns aims, not outcomes:

> The difference between the derived aim of the archer and the motives of which S can approve is that if the archer hits what he is (for derivative reasons) aiming at, he will be (and should be) disappointed, But if we achieve the outcomes which S can approve our aiming for, we should by S's lights be satisfied, even though we will not even have been aiming at the target which S, in specifying a single supremely rational ultimate aim, sets us. (Dancy 1997: 5)

Now there is indeed a disanalogy between the archer case and that of an agent under assessment by S. In the archer case, the target itself and the target aimed at (say, a tree to the left of the target itself) are in different locations, so it is not possible for the archer to hit both. That is why he is

---

[1] 'Here' means 'in the case of any particular action'.

disappointed if he hits the tree. But in the case of the agent, the 'ultimate' aim and the 'derivative' aim are compatible: the agent might both win the game and bring it about that her life goes, for her, as well as possible. Nevertheless, they can of course come apart, in which case the agent will be as disappointed as the archer if, say, she wins the game, but the fruits of victory turn to ashes in her mouth.

Further, I see no reason for drawing an outcome/aim distinction in the case of the archer which cannot be carried across to the case of the agent. Dancy (p. 5) claims of S:

> It does not say: 'Here is an outcome you (should) want and you will best achieve it if you aim off a little.' It says: 'Here is an outcome you (should) want and you will best achieve it if you do not want it.'

In fact, S can be understood as making both of these claims, though the second is somewhat elliptical. On the face of it, it sounds contradictory: you should want ϕ; the best means to achieving ϕ is not to want ϕ; so you should not want ϕ. But the wants in question play quite different roles in our desiderative economy. If we distinguish between general, background desires, and particular, foregrounded, felt desires, then we have no contradiction here: one of your general, background desires (or 'ultimate aims') should be ϕ; the best means to achieving ϕ is not to have a particular desire for ϕ (that is, ϕ should not be a derivative aim); rather, the best way to achieve ϕ is to have a particular desire for ψ.[2]

Nevertheless, isn't there something odd about S? If I seek always to follow S, I shall be what Parfit calls 'never self-denying' (1984: 6). That is, I will never do what I believe to be worse for me. But, even if I succeed in never doing what would be worse for me, it may still be that I would have been better off with some *other* disposition, such as to do what makes someone else happy rather than me. This is one way, indeed, in which S is indirectly self-defeating. Now, according to S:

(S3) It is irrational for anyone to do what he believes will be worse for himself (Parfit 1984: 8).

---

[2] Cf. Kappel (1999: 195, 206). I am in sympathy with much of Kappel's argument throughout his paper.

This has the upshot that S tells agents to be disposed to act in a way that S *itself* claims to be irrational. Is that a reason to reject S?

Parfit's response to this question is *Schelling's Answer to Armed Robbery* (p. 12). In this example, an armed robber threatens my children unless I open my safe. I know that he is quite likely to kill us all anyway, even if I open the safe. So I take a drug I happen to have handy which makes me, for a short time, very irrational. I end up saying things like, 'Go ahead. I love my children. So please kill them.' All the armed robber can now do is try to escape before the police arrive. Since this seems to be a case in which it is clearly rational to make oneself do things that are irrational, the fact that S requires this is no objection to it.

Dancy is unhappy with Parfit's use of this case (1997: 5–8). According to Dancy, I am in fact *rational* in S's terms after taking the drug (since my motives are 'S-approved') and my acts are rational also, since '[a]cts are rational in S's terms if no available alternative would be better for the agent (i.e. would more effectively promote the agent's S-given aims)'.[3] Parfit's argument equivocates on the notion of rationality, appealing to an 'intuitive' sense to justify the idea that after taking the drug I act irrationally—a sense which S cannot accept.

I accept that in general Parfit's conception of rationality could have been clearer in *Reasons and Persons*. But I cannot see that he is guilty of equivocation here. He may well be using a common-sense conception of rationality (let's call it 'C-rationality'), but his point is that, since we have here a case in which it is clearly C-rational to cause oneself to act in a clearly C-irrational way, we should not be overly concerned to find the same phenomenon arising with S.[4]

Parfit also claims that the armed robbery case shows that the following claim is false:

---

[3] In fact, S's conception of rationality is given by (S3), which Dancy himself cites (at p. 2).

[4] Dancy suggests that the Schelling case is not appropriate to resolve the problem Dancy himself has raised, since it does not give us a *single* action which is both irrational and such that the agent doing it is rational (p. 7). Now Parfit himself does not employ it for that purpose, since his concern in the relevant section is: 'Could it be rational to cause oneself to act irrationally?' But in the intuitive sense, the actions after I take the drug *are* both rational and irrational (and that is part of what Parfit wants to say). It is true that, once I've taken the drug, '[w]e could not describe me as acting irrationally on purpose because that is the wisest choice in the circumstances' (p. 7). But this conception of rationality is not C-rationality. My C-irrational actions are C-rational because they are the result of a C-rational decision; they do not have to be governed by rationality in their performance.

(G1) If there is some motive that it would be both (a) rational for someone to cause himself to have, and (b) irrational for him to cause himself to lose, then (c) it cannot be irrational for this person to act upon this motive.

Dancy sees (c) (which Parfit claims to be false in the armed robbery case) as ambiguous (p. 7). It could mean:

(c1) acts done on this motive cannot be irrational, or
(c2) a person who acts on that motive cannot be irrational, or
(c3) it cannot be irrational to cause oneself to act on that motive.

He goes on to suggest that none of these will work for Parfit. First, in S's terms my acts are rational while I'm under the influence of the drug. Second, my motives are ones which, in S's terms, it is rational of me to acquire and irrational of me to cause myself to lose. Third, as Parfit himself admits, it is rational of me to cause myself to act in this way.

As far as I can see, (c) can mean only (c1). 'It is irrational for P to ϕ' cannot mean or even imply 'P is irrational'. For it is quite consistent to claim both that P's ϕ-ing is irrational and that P is rational. And (c) says nothing about causation. Causation is covered in (a) and (b). And again, as far as (c1) is concerned, the same sort of point I made above applies. Parfit does not analyse the armed robbery case using S; as Dancy himself points out, he is using the notion of C-rationality. My actions after taking the drug are clearly irrational in an 'intuitive' sense, and (a) and (b) are likewise true in terms of C-rationality. So, as Parfit suggests, the example does show that (G1) is false.

Dancy recognizes that the armed robbery case concerns the question whether it can be rational to cause oneself to become irrational, suggesting that Parfit's case of *Kate* (1984: 6–7) is more relevant to the issue of rational irrationality in the sense Dancy has in mind. Kate is a writer whose strongest desire is that her books be as good as possible. This makes her work very hard, and she sometimes suffers bouts of severe depression. If she were to work less hard, she could avoid this depression and hence be happier, and her books would be only slightly worse. But she would work less hard only if her desire that her books be as good as possible were much weaker. This would be even worse for her, since she would find her work boring. So this is another case in which S is indirectly self-defeating, since it would be worse for Kate if she were never self-denying.

According to Parfit, Kate's action is irrational. Dancy (1997: 7–10) doubts this, because he believes the nearest possible world in which Kate works less hard is that in which she becomes bored (cf. Kappel 1999: 201–2). This approach, he says,

> starts from here, including the story of Kate's present motivational structure, and asks whether in the nearest world in which Kate works less hard she is happier. It turns out that the nearest world in which, with something like that pattern, she can get herself to work less hard is one in which she gets very bored and unhappy. So what she actually does is rational. (Dancy 1997: 9–10)

Dancy is surely right to think that, in so far as Kate's motivational structure remains the same in this possible world, it is nearer to the actual world than a world in which her motivational structure changes. But Parfit's point is that, in *that* world, she will *not* become bored and unhappy, because her desire that her books be as good as possible remains in place. That is why her action in the actual world of never being self-denying is *irrational*: her well-being in that possible world is higher. But, Parfit suggests, were she to seek to bring that world about by working less hard, she would succeed in working less hard *only* if that desire were to become less strong. And if her desire were to become less strong, then she would become bored and hence worse off than she now is. So in this respect her continuing to work at her present pace is *rational*. But the well-being she adds, through her hard work, in the actual world is the result of the disposition she has, *not* her action.

Nevertheless, I am inclined to agree with Dancy that there is something odd about Parfit's case. It is not so much a problem with choosing possible worlds with which to compare the actual world, however, as a problem with restricting oneself only to possible worlds and not the future of the actual world. One might agree with Parfit (even if only for the sake of argument) that the nearest possible world is that in which Kate works less hard and is happier. But what *will* happen if she seeks to change her situation is that *either* she will fail and things will remain as they are, *or* she will weaken her desire that her books be as good as possible, work less hard, and become bored and less happy. So it does strike me as somewhat peculiar to focus on the comparison of Kate's present strategy with any possible world. If she tries to improve her life, she will fail; so in that respect her present strategy is rational. But one can still view the case of Kate as one of indirect self-defeatingness of the kind we have already discussed: she does not aim at making her own life as good as possible (she aims 'off target'), but in doing that she makes her life as good as possible.[5]

II

The theory Parfit calls 'Consequentialism' (C) includes the following central claim (1984: 24):

(C1) There is one ultimate moral aim: that outcomes be as good as possible.

This claim, of course, mirrors the central claim of the Self-interest Theory ((S1) above), and Parfit argues that C, like S, is also indirectly self-defeating. If our only motive is to make outcomes as good as possible, we will become 'pure do-gooders' (p. 27) and this might well make the overall outcome worse. It would be better, for example, if we had some other set of motives, including, say, partial concern for our friends and relatives. Dancy believes that this results in its running into the same sorts of problems with self-contradiction that Dancy finds in S: 'We have here a moral aim which in some sense it would be immoral to aim at, since there is available to us a better alternative practice' (1997: 12).

Parfit's notion of 'blameless wrongdoing' (1984: 31–5) might be thought to provide a framework for making sense of the apparent contradiction to which Dancy draws our attention. His first illustrative example is that of *Clare* (p. 32). Clare loves her child very much. She could benefit her child in some way, or give much greater benefits to a stranger. According to Consequentialism, then, it might seem that, if she does benefit her child, Clare is open to serious criticism, since she fails to produce an outcome significantly better than the one she does bring about. But, Parfit suggests, Clare can defend herself in the same sort of way as Kate can defend herself when charged with irrationality:

> I act wrongly because I love my child. But it would be wrong for me to cause myself to lose this love. That I make the outcome worse is a bad effect. But this is

---

[5] And it is this distinction which, I suggest, lies behind Parfit's distinction between formal and substantive aims (1984: 1, 9), criticized by Dancy (at 1997: 10–11).

part of a set of effects that are, on the whole, one of the best possible sets. It would therefore be wrong for me to change my motives so that I would not in future act wrongly in this kind of way. Since this is so, when I do act wrongly in this way, I need not regard *myself* as morally bad. (1984: 32)

The reason this wrongdoing is blameless, Parfit suggests, is that, though the *act* here is immoral, the *agent* is blameless.

As we have seen, Dancy reads Parfit's use of *Schelling's Answer to Armed Robbery* as prefatory to the case of *Kate*. He sees Parfit's case of *My Moral Corruption* (1984: 38) as bearing the same relation to that of *Clare*. In *My Moral Corruption*, we imagine that I have a public career which would be ruined were I involved in a scandal. An enemy of mine (sincerely) threatens to kill my children unless I act in an obscene way, which he will film. This film could later be used to end my career. Once he has the film, he will threaten to send the film to a newspaper unless I help him commit certain minor crimes. My character, as I know, is such that I will help him commit these crimes to save my career. So this is a case in which it could be right to cause oneself to act wrongly.

Dancy suggests that Parfit may be intending to use the case of my moral corruption to support the view that, though Clare is someone who is told by C to do acts which are wrong in C's terms, this is no objection to C. But it cannot do this, Dancy continues, because there is no *single* action here which is both wrong and such that I am right (blameless) in doing it.

Now the role of the case of my moral corruption is indeed analogous to that of the armed robbery case. Recall that the latter was to show the falsity of (G1). *My Moral Corruption* is intended to show the falsity of:

(G4) If someone acts on a motive that he ought to cause himself to have, and that it would be wrong for him to cause himself to lose, he cannot be acting wrongly. (p. 35; see also p. 39)

The case is intended to show also that one cannot object to C on the ground that it tells us to cause ourselves to do what C itself claims to be wrong (p. 38). It is not clear whether Parfit thinks that someone might refer to the case of Clare to illustrate such a phenomenon. But it does seem that they might, since Clare does continue acting in such a way that she brings it about that she does what, according to Parfit, is wrong by C's lights. So one cannot object to the moral corruption case on the ground that it does not focus on a single action that is both wrong and such that one is blameless in doing it. It concerns the action of causing oneself to do further actions that are wrong, and is intended to show that that causing is blameless.

Dancy's objection to the case of Clare itself is analogous to his objection to the case of Kate. He suggests that Clare's defence of herself can be seen as a defence of her *act*, on the ground that outcomes would be worse were she to act differently. He again uses the language of possible worlds to explicate Clare's position (1997: 15):

> In the nearest group of worlds in which she does the alternative act, her motives are not her actual set Ma, but a different set M1.
>
> The nearest group of worlds in which her set of motives is M1 are worse in C's terms, contain worse outcomes, than the nearest group of worlds in which her set of motives is Ma.
>
> So the nearest group of worlds in which she does the alternative act is a group in which outcomes are worse in C's terms.
>
> So (unpacking the possible worlds metaphor) if she were to do the alternative act, outcomes would be worse in C's terms.
>
> So this alternative act, at least, is not one which would lead to an improvement in outcomes.
>
> So her act of benefiting her child in preference to the stranger is not shown to be wrong in C's terms by the existence of this 'available alternative'.

Again, however, questions arise here about how to judge the distance of worlds. On the face of it, we should say that a world is nearer to the actual world the more similar it is to the actual world. So the nearest group of worlds in which Clare does the alternative act should not be understood as worlds in which her *motives* are also different. Rather they will be the worlds in which she does the alternative action (so she helps the stranger), but her motives remain in place (so she continues to benefit her child on other occasions). It may be that Dancy is judging nearness here by the criterion of probability or likelihood of occurrence. But there is no reason why a nearby possible world should not be a highly improbable one.

Once again, however, I do agree with Dancy that there is something odd about blameless wrongdoing and the case of Clare. As Dancy goes on to say, instead of Parfit's criterion of rightness for acts:

(1) An act is right if its outcome is better than that of any available alternative;

we might prefer:

> (2) An act is right if outcomes would be better if it was done than if any alternative were done.

And, like Dancy, I do prefer (2). But note that this is a separate objection to Parfit's conception of C than the objection that it is self-refuting. Cases like Clare's could still be used to illustrate how C can give us apparently conflicting aims—that outcomes be as good as possible, and that, say, we should benefit our own children in preference to strangers—without this resulting in C's refuting itself.

III

Dancy closes his paper with some concerns about the act/agent distinction which Parfit makes so much use of. He begins by noting that the distinction is controversial in itself, and points to 'the oddity of allowing that there is a good sense in which the Pharisee is doing what he ought' (p. 17).[6] Dancy believes that the value of the Pharisee's motives 'infect' the value of what is done in the sense that the motive is 'part of' the action. If the motive had been different, it would have been a different action.

This is a little too quick. At least since Aristotle composed *EN* 2.4, it has been quite standard to distinguish the notion of the right action from that of an action's being done rightly. So imagine a Pharisee who honours his father and mother, but merely with the intention of appearing a paragon of filial piety. There is a clear sense in which he does the right action, and hence a sense in which he does what he ought—viz., he does what a morally virtuous person would do in his position. But he does not of course act rightly. Now one might prefer to redescribe his action as that of 'honouring his father and mother with the wrong motives', and that act is clearly different from that of the virtuous person described as 'honouring his father and mother with the right motives'. But just because there is this alternative description of the Pharisee's action available does not throw into doubt the

---

[6] In fact Pharisees tend to have been thought not to do what they ought; rather they told other people what they ought to do and then failed to do it themselves (Matthew 23.2–7).

original description of it as the right action. Any *action* is multiply describable—that is, as we might put it, it instantiates a multiplicity of *acts*.[7]

Dancy goes on to outline various reasons why one might want to draw the act/agent distinction, Parfit's reason being to separate motives from aims and so avoid any problem of self-contradiction in the theory. Dancy suggests that we should focus our moral evaluation on the 'agent-in-acting' in such a way that neither the act/agent distinction, nor the outcome/motive distinction, can get a grip:

> The qualities of the doer in the case must coincide with the qualities of the thing done, in a way that leaves no room for talk of blameless wrongdoing or blameworthy rightdoing. The relevant qualities of the action, conceived as an object of *moral* assessment, are the same as those of the agent in doing it. (p. 18)

I have already agreed with Dancy in doubting the coherence of the notion of blameless wrongdoing (and I would say the same about the idea of blameworthy rightdoing), as construed by Parfit. But any doubt should not rest on the notion that moral evaluation must focus on, and only on, the 'agent-in-acting'. Moral evaluation should be permitted to focus on whatever is appropriate, and acts and agents, understood somewhat independently of one another, seem—if common sense is to be our guide—to be as suitable for assessment as agents-in-acting.

IV

Dancy ends his paper (pp. 18–21) by seeking to explain why his arguments have not removed the very possibility that S and C are indirectly self-defeating. As he points out, this would be quite damaging to his project, since he wishes to claim that they are not only indirectly self-defeating, but self-refuting. He returns again to the case of Kate, and reiterates that he does not see this is as a case of indirect self-defeat. For Kate is, in a sense, never self-denying, and is doing the act of all available alternatives which is making her happiest.

But, Dancy points out, Parfit has another example, that of the driver in the desert (1984: 7). In this case, I am driving at midnight through a desert.

---
[7] I owe this use of the act/action distinction to David Wiggins.

My car breaks down, and you are the only other driver in the desert. I offer you a large sum if you will drive me home. Because I am transparent, it is entirely obvious when I am lying. If I am never self-denying, and know myself to be such, I know that I will not keep my promise to pay you once we get to my home. That means you know I am lying, so you leave me in the desert. It would have been better for me had I been trustworthy, and so disposed to keep my promises even when doing so will be worse for me.

Dancy objects that Parfit has not allowed the driver the option of choosing, in accordance with S, the 'long-term' action of asking for a lift for which he pays later, and is hence imposing on S a very short-term or 'atomistic' conception of an action. Why should there not be such extended, or conjunctive, actions? Further, on this atomistic conception, I cannot now decide to perform a 'delayed' action, such as deciding to go to the library, or indeed engage in any kind of long-term planning.

From the metaphysical point of view, however, I cannot see that Parfit is imposing any particular conception of action, whether short- or long-term, on S. In the desert, I am entitled to consider whether I should adopt the long-term strategy and choose the action of asking-for-a-lift-for-which-I-will-pay-later. Indeed I surely will consider this strategy, even if not under quite the description Dancy suggests for it. The problem is that I will know that I will end up not keeping to my strategy. That option, though one I can consider, is not one that I can sincerely adopt. For I know that, once I am at home, I will not pay you. Now this does mean that, as Dancy says, S is 'deeply flawed', in that it 'cannot capture the rationality of long-term planning'. But that is really just to agree with Parfit.

V

It is part of Dancy's conclusion, then, that Parfit is right to say that S (and presumably C) are indirectly self-defeating. I agree with them that this is so if we define S and C as Parfit does. But in fact, by defining S and C in a different way, one that I think should be acceptable to Parfit, we can avoid the whole issue of indirect self-defeatingness.[8]

---

[8] Cf. Kappel (1999: 195).

Recall that Parfit defines the theories as follows:

(S1) For each person, there is one supremely rational ultimate aim: that his life go, for him, as well as possible (1984: 8).

(C1) There is one ultimate moral aim: that outcomes be as good as possible (p. 24).

The problem of indirect self-defeat arises from the idea that a theory can give us 'aims'. A theory is indirectly self-defeating when it is true that, if someone tries to achieve the aims given to them by that theory, these aims will be, on the whole, worse achieved (p. 5). I suggest, however, that S and C are best not understood most fundamentally in terms of aims. A more basic question in ethics is the Socratic one 'How should one live?', which, as Bernard Williams says, is equivalent to 'How has one most reason to live?' (Williams 1985: 19).[9] So we might understand the egoistic and consequentialist answer to this question as:

(S*) One has most reason to live in that way in which one's life goes, for one, as well as possible.

(C*) One has most reason to live in that way in which the history of the world goes as well as possible.

Now the Socratic question is about one's life as a whole. I believe any adequate first-order normative theory should address itself to this question. But an important part of life consists in the actions one performs, and we are of course entitled to ask the question 'How should one act?', which, translated according to Williams, is equivalent to 'How has one most reason to act?'. And once again we can provide versions of S and C which answer this question straightforwardly, with no reference to aims:

(S**) One has most reason to act in that way in which one's life goes, for one, as well as possible.

(C**) One has most reason to act in that way in which the history of the world goes as well as possible.

Why do I say that these versions of S and C will be acceptable to Parfit? Because of the third and fourth sentences of *Reasons and Persons*: 'We know that there are reasons for acting, and that some reasons are better or stronger

---

[9] For Socrates' question, see Plato, *Gorgias* 500c3–4.

than others. One of the main subjects of this book is a set of questions about what we have reasons to do.' He might prefer not to broaden the focus to life as a whole, and I myself would not find that particularly problematic. It is reasons for action that are especially important to us, since we may be able to make decisions that enable us to act on the reasons that we have. Any such decisions that we make about reasons for living will have to be filtered anyway through our deciding to act.[10] So, in a sense, properly thinking about reasons for action will include reflection upon reasons for living in a particular way in so far as we can do anything about it. Ethics, that is to say, is primarily a practical matter, a matter of *praxis* or action.

How will these restated versions of S and C deal with the various cases Parfit describes? There is no doubt that they will almost always require agents to follow some strategy in living or acting other than the continual application of the theory itself. So according to S**, Kate has reason to concentrate on her work and not always be attempting to maximize her own good, and those who drive in deserts would do well to bring it about, as far as they can, that they have a disposition to be trustworthy. And according to C**, we all have reasons in certain cases to consider and advance the happiness of those who are close to us rather than seeking always to bring about the best history of the world. But this does not make these theories self-defeating, since, as you will recall, a theory is indirectly self-defeating when it is true that, if someone tries to achieve the aims given to her by that theory, these aims will be, on the whole, worse achieved. But what aims *do* S** and C** give us? A proponent of either view might see this as a 'When did you stop beating your wife?' question, and reject talk of aims as unnecessary. There are just acts, and our reasons for them. But this response is perhaps rather churlish. For many of our actions, or doings, can plausibly be described as 'aimings', and in that sense S** and C** can assess them. S** and C** then appear to imply:

(S***) One has most reason to aim in that way in which one's life goes, for one, as well as possible.

(C***) One has most reason to aim in that way in which the history of the world goes as well as possible.

---

[10] I am grateful to discussion with Michael Smith which enabled me to see this.

Take S***. It is not telling the agent to aim at making her life as good as possible. If it was, it would indeed be indirectly self-defeating. Rather, it is telling her to have whichever aims will result in her life going as well as possible. If she aims in that way, her life will not go worse for her. It will go as well as possible. So there is here no self-defeat. And the same will be true, *mutatis mutandis*, for C***.

Parfit's formulations of S and C do not incorporate the distinction that has become known in ethics as that between 'criterion and decision-procedure' (see Bales 1971) and it is this that allows the phenomenon of self-defeat to emerge. My reformulations above concern 'criteria' alone, and those 'decision-procedures' (including aimings) that meet the criteria will not be self-defeating. Nor should it worry egoists and consequentialists that, according to their theories, we have reason, sometimes, at least, not to seek to apply the theory in question directly. For any plausible theory of practical reasons must allow for that.

To conclude: not only are egoism and consequentialism not self-refuting; they are not self-defeating either.

References

Bales, R. E. (1971) 'Act-Utilitarianism: Account of Right-Making Characteristics or Decision-Making Procedure?', *American Philosophical Quarterly*, 7: 257–65.

Dancy, J. (1993) *Moral Reasons* (Oxford: Blackwell).

——(1997) 'Parfit and Indirectly Self-defeating Theories', in J. Dancy (ed.), *Reading Parfit* (Oxford: Blackwell), 1–23.

Kappel, K. (1999) 'Has Dancy Shown a Problem in Consequentialism?', *Theoria*, 65: 193–211.

Parfit, D. (1984) *Reasons and Persons* (Oxford: Clarendon Press).

Williams, B. (1985) *Ethics and the Limits of Philosophy* (London: Fontana).

6

In Defence of Non-Deontic Reasons

MARGARET OLIVIA LITTLE

1. Introduction

On a certain classical picture, reasons, by their very nature, are deontic. If one faces a reason in favour of an action, then one would be *wrong* not to follow its lead, absent sufficient counter-veiling justification. Depending on the type of reason, the wrong in question may be the wrong of immorality, or imprudence, or just the generic wrong of practical reason (what I will refer to in this chapter as 'irrationality' or 'impermissibility'). And of course, counter-veiling justification one may well have. Still, to understand something as a practical reason necessarily brings with it a kind of deontic vulnerability: one who faces such a reason now stands in need of adequate justification to do other than it directs, on pain of going wrong.

Indeed, for many the idea is virtually definitional of a practical reason. It is found, *inter alia*, in the view that it is wrong not to act on the 'balance of reasons', though it is not limited to a particular view of weightings. It is explicit in the accounts of theorists as diverse as Shelley Kagan (1989) and Joseph Raz (1999), and implicit in many more. Reasons for actions are normative entities inherently on their way toward being all things considered deontic oughts. Call this the deontic view of reasons.

In his essay 'Enticing Reasons', Jonathan Dancy (2004) argues against this view. Taking up a suggestion raised by Raz (1999: ch. 5), who rejects it in favour of a picture based on incommensurability, Dancy argues that some reasons favour actions in a gentler fashion. It is not just that they survive the scrum of deontic competition and emerge as reasons on which one may permissibly act: they never place you in need of justification to decline in the first place. To paraphrase him, not all reasons are in the wrong-making business. Instead, we should distinguish between two different types of favouring relations: what he calls 'enticing' and 'peremptory' (p. 94). Some reasons serve to commend an action without placing one in any deontic danger.

I think this is exactly right; and in the present article, my aim is to refine and redeem the claim. More specifically, my aim is to isolate and defend the cogency of what I take to be the important core of Dancy's claim: that considerations can asymmetrically provide justification for ϕ-ing without placing one in need of justification not to ϕ. I'll argue that the idea is far less mysterious, and objections to it far less compelling, than is usually thought by those who theorize about practical reasons.

In the first half of this article, I consider a strong, reductive version of the deontic view; in the second half, a more moderate, non-reductive one. Neither, I will argue, offers a compelling case against the idea of non-deontic reasons for action. At the end of the day, one might decide that all reasons in favour of actions are inherently deontic; but defending it would take much more substantive argument than is usually offered. Such an essay may be a case of bringing coals to Newcastle—or Austin, as the case may be. But it is offered as a gesture of gratitude for a friendship, and in deep admiration for Dancy's insightful work on the nature of reasons.

2. Recovering the commendatory

I want to begin by taking on a particularly strong version of the deontic picture of reasons. On what we might call a deontically reductive account of reasons, reasons in favour of acting are always deontic because they are only deontic. Let's take a look.

As suits discussions about highly abstract concepts, discussions of reasons for action often begin with invocation of metaphors, and the metaphors invoked tend to sound quite friendly. Reasons for action, it is said, *speak in favour* of an action (Scanlon 1998: 19); they *recommend* a course of action; they exert an *attraction* or a *pull* (Hampton 1998: 91–2).[1] Yet when theorists

---

[1] This chapter focuses on reasons for action, but it should be emphasized that this includes reasons for actions whose conditions are best understood as intentional avoidances (see section 5 below). The

set out to unpack these metaphors in favour of something more formal, talk often enters a more censorious neighborhood. Reasons, it will be said, are the sort of thing one can be wrong not to follow. The wrong in question need not be the wrong of immorality, though it can be; it may be the wrong of imprudence, or simply the wrong of practical reason, but wrong, understood as the primitive mark of the deontic, is the word to use. If discussions of reasons for action usually begin with talk of reasons as friendly, they often quickly shift focus to what we might call their peremptory nature—their imposition of deontic vulnerability.

And for some, this is not just the start of the analysis: it is also the end. The favouring force of reasons turns out to be exhausted by their propensity to render an agent wrong not to act as they direct. When we say that a reason recommends a course of action, all we are really saying is that the reason places one in need of a certain amount of justification not to act as it directs on pain of going wrong—what we might call 'exculpatory' justification.[2] One finds the favouring function of a reason for action, as it were, in its negative footprint.

This is an implication, for instance, of a crude (but for all that influential) version of the balancing view of reasons. As promiscuously as the balancing metaphor is used, and as harmless as it is when used as shorthand for 'juxtaposing considerations for purposes of finding comparative guidance' (a big tent notion if there ever were one), it isn't uncommon to find philosophers who take the model of a balance more literally in the following way. Picturing the normative force of reasons as akin to the force that weighted objects exert on a two-armed fulcrum, the account sees reasons as players on a justificatory see-saw. Just as a weight placed on one side of a balance functions, not only to push its side down, but to push the other side up a commensurate amount, so too a reason in favour of an action functions

---

analysis provided here would extend to what are traditionally called reasons against action just in case one believes that all such reasons are in fact reasons in favour of adopting a commitment to intentional avoidance, a claim about which I am here agnostic.

[2] The term 'exculpatory' here is meant to mark two things. First, the term indicates that the justification in question here is justification in the defensive sense: defending against or disabling a negative charge that would otherwise obtain. Such justification might consist of a stronger competing reason to do otherwise, but it might be something else, such as possession of consent, that isn't itself a reason *to* do anything. Second, the term is meant to indicate that the negative charge against which one is defending is the charge of 'wrong', rather than some species of 'bad'. As this chapter is concerned with the deontic life of reasons, it leaves aside issues about evaluative statuses, important and interesting as they are.

not only to push the action in question toward justification, but to push its non-performance away from justification by a commensurate amount. Invoked as an exhaustive model for practical reasons, the only normative function that reasons play is contributing their relative weights on a balance whose fulcrum ensures that the measure to which they commend an action is equivalent to the distance its non-performance is displaced from being permissible. What might at first have been thought to be two functions—pushing one arm up and the other arm down—turn out to be one and the same.

This has the interesting implication that the favouring force of reasons is functionally equivalent to peremptory force. All we really need to talk about, when discussing what it means for a consideration to support an action to some degree, is the degree of deontic vulnerability the consideration imposes on *not* doing so.

The very first thing to say is that this would be surprising. It certainly seems like reasons can render actions intelligible in ways other than by setting up the irrationality of declining them. Take a classic case of heroic supererogation: one could save three lives by giving up one's own. Here, for sure, there is a deontic stick in the offing: if I were in the position of being able to jump in to rescue three people and there were literally no burden or cost to my helping, I would be wrong (indeed, in this case, morally wrong) not to do so. Of course, given the original example, justification for not doing so is ready to hand—that it would cost my life. On a standard (and in my opinion correct) view, the charge is now met: I would not be wrong to forebear.

All that having been said, I might well decide to go ahead and save them. I might decide to jump in, that is, for the very reason that it would save three lives. That reason is still very much in view, *as* a reason—as something that can itself rationalize or render reasonable a decision to act. The fact that its deontic challenge has been met does not mean the reason is thereby rendered normatively inert; it seems to survive as a perfectly intelligible basis on which to act, able to provide a perfectly respectable rational *explicans* if I do, bringing my movement under the umbrella of rational action.

There certainly *seems* to be another element to reasons for action, an aspect of their personality beyond their deontic footprint, that can serve as a rational *explicans* for action. Even if one believes that all reasons impose a deontic challenge, their favouring isn't used up in that imposition. For that challenge might be met, yet one can nonetheless meaningfully act on their basis.

Indeed, this seems to be a defining difference between reasons, understood as substantive merits, and rules. The mode in which rules favour a course of action seems very much exhausted by their deontic push. It's not as though one gets extra credit for following a rule when one has successfully countered its challenge. One may have other reasons to act in conformity with the action it concerns (one wants, say, to show one's support for the authorities that penned the rule, or one is impressed with the merits at the basis of its formation), but the normative force of the rule itself no longer directs.[3] Rules, in the first instance, are nothing *but* peremptory.

Reasons are different. Even if we agree that reasons bring with them a deontic threat—even, indeed, if we thought this intrinsic to their nature as reasons, they are also able to serve as a rational *explicans* when that threat is absent. Favouring reasons can render an action robustly intelligible even when they don't back you into a deontic corner. Over and above any peremptory aspect of reasons for action, they also possess what we might call a *commendatory* aspect—the capacity to render certain actions intelligible, and *pro tanto* consistent with what a well-functioning agent could decide to do, independent of the deontic status of doing so.

3. The rationalist picture of agency

Intuitive as the above will be to many, it is denied by an influential picture of rational explanation and agency. The above states that a reason can serve as a rational *explicans* of action even if one wouldn't have been wrong not

---

[3] Most will concur that rules have some strong intrinsic connection to merits: we might agree, for instance, that the content and enforcement of rules must be holistically constrained by these merits in order to count as authoritative for us. All of this notwithstanding, rules, like demands and orders, are pieces of imperatival force, and the mark of imperatival force is that its legitimate determinations do not follow lockstep with the local economy of merits.

A rule from which you are excused, note, might still constitute an intelligibility ticket for your action if the excuse is understood as changing your status as blameworthy, rather than the action's status as not wrong for you to do. In my view, it is precisely because one might decide not to 'trade on' an excuse and perform the action anyway that indicates that excuses are different from true permission conditions, which extinguish the deontically wrong status of the action.

to act on its basis. On a certain picture of rational explanation and agency, however, this can't be right. In the example above, there was by stipulation a good reason for both options—saving their lives, protecting my own; and neither option, by stipulation, would be irrational to reject. If both are justified and neither is irrational, it will be said, this is the statement of a tie, not a decision. If I decide to sacrifice myself as more than an expression of indifference between options (something that is possible, but unlikely), there must have been something else—a prior commitment, say—in virtue of which I decided to do so. Either this further consideration also leaves open a deontically permissible alternative and the question repeats itself; or we finally come to a resting spot, with a consideration in virtue of which it would have been irrational for me to do otherwise.

The time-honoured way of recovering the reductive deontic view of reasons is to multiply psychological entities against which one's choice becomes normatively necessary (see, e.g., Kagan 1989: 380). If one supererogated, one must have had a stronger desire to help others than to live; in the face of such a desire, it would have been irrational not to sacrifice oneself in order to save them. It would have been, not immoral, now, but the wrong of practical rationality, *not* to sacrifice oneself. Whatever the details, though, the claim is that reasons really do support an action only by their imposition of deontic pressure; for until we reach that deontic bedrock, we do not yet have a terminus to rational explanation.

Here we have arrived at what Raz (1999: 47–9) calls the rationalist conception of agency. On this view, agency is about responding to the determinations of reasons, and reasons don't determine until they necessitate. If we find pockets of latitude in life, it is only where those necessities can be equally well satisfied by different options, like the two piles of hay facing Buridan's ass that would equally satisfy the need for food. But of course, in such cases, the reasons are indifferent over which of those options one takes; and since the will is just about translating the direction of reasons, the will is indifferent as well.

To say that the will is indifferent is not to say that it cannot thereby move. Most such theorists still agree that agency is able to act in the space of optionality—it is able rationally to proceed along grooves other than 'wrong not to'; but given the deontic silence, its movement here has the weak form of intelligibility known as 'picking' rather than 'choosing', randomizing or using some other rule of thumb to break the deadlock and move things along. Strong intelligibility runs out when deontic threat does; the only other mode of explanation is the more modest intelligibility achieved when selecting from options that equally fulfil that necessitating element.[4]

It is, of course, a possible view. It is also a costly one, highly revisionist to pre-philosophical understanding of agency and action. Certainly it is phenomenologically awkward. It would be fun to go to the movies. On the other hand, it would be cozy to stay in. Intuitively, I would not be wrong to decline either, even as it would be intelligible to choose either one, and were I to choose one it needn't be on the basis of a metaphorical coin flip. According to the rationalist conception, though, something can count as rational action only if it would have been irrational to do anything else over which one was utterly indifferent.

Agency, in turn, gets reduced to something remarkably thin. On the rationalist conception, agency turns out to be nothing more than the capacity to translate into causal space the normative necessity presented by reasons, together with the ability to intentionally plump in the face of indifference. Independent of ideological reasons (e.g. remnants of causal models of normativity), it is not clear why one would think that agency is like this. It seems just as paradigmatic to agency that we make fully intelligible decisions that are neither necessitated by reasons nor reflections of indifference. Standing before my easel, I contemplate whether to dip my brush in the

---

[4] Notice that, even for those who agree that the will can move within indifference, indifference is not itself a basis of intelligibility: that one is indifferent between two actions is not itself a reason to do either one. Instead, the intelligibility of picking must be parasitic on the intelligibility provided by a traditional first-order normative reason. Indifference, as it were, cantilevers the reach of other bases of intelligence.

The ability to select across indifference is important. Virtually all actions involve a level of determinateness that goes beyond the level of granularity supplied by the element cited in or constituting the rational *explicans*. All actions taken have near siblings that would equally well have satisfied the rationalizing element—one's hand could have described a slightly different arc in reaching out to the needed cup of coffee. Usually found at the level of automaticity, these normative equivalents can also involve more macro differences that engage us consciously and 'open the question' for us about which option to take. Trying to deliberate, we find, like Buridan's ass, that there are no pros or cons to deliberate about. The intelligibility provided by the rational *explicans*—in this case, that it would be yummy and nutritious hay—distributes to each token that equally fulfils it.

Theorists offer different models of what such 'picking' consists in. On the dominant theory, one invokes a higher-order procedural reason of how to decide, returning us to a standard action at a higher-order level; on another, the will simply closes the decision by letting automaticity, as it were, return within the scope of that selection. For the rationalist, notice, both accounts retain a purely deontic criteron of intelligibility. For higher-order reason accounts, one cannot decide until one finds a higher-order reason it would be wrong not to deploy; having deployed it, one would be wrong not to follow the option its application points to. For accounts that return selection to automaticity, we have reached the boundary of intentional action once the reach of deontic criteria ends.

chartreuse or russet for the next brushstroke. I decide on the chartreuse, citing as my reason how it adds a nice moment of energy to counterbalance the painting's otherwise calm. In citing that reason, though, I don't mean thereby that I would have been wrong not to do so, as though there were some independent premise against which choosing the russet would have been irrational.

Sometimes, to be sure, reasons 'make up our minds for us'. Gazing at the salient considerations, there is only one path forward that a well-functioning agent would take. Anything else would be wrong, and wrong is a line in the sand that such an agent—someone with full discernment, accurate judgement, and no weak will—by definition does not cross. And sometimes, we pick from amongst things to which we are indifferent, selecting from amongst options that would each satisfy the operative desiderata as well as any other. But for broad swathes of paradigmatic agency, meaningful choice seems to include acting under the guise of a feature that makes the action reasonable to do rather than wrong not to. There is robust intelligibility even after deontic debate runs out.

All of which is to say that we might think the model of explanation that undergirds the rationalist conception is itself overly narrow. Rational explanations are explanations that allow us to see the action as intelligible to self and others in the right way. In the right way, one might have thought, includes being able to see it as action, rather than behaviour; as intentional, rather than automatic; and as something that is reasonable—that is, consistent with what a well-functioning agent could choose. The extent to which no such guise is forthcoming is the degree to which we will press whether the movement really counted as behaviour rather than action; and the extent to which a guise seems inadequate to the ambitions of the action taken under its aegis will press whether the action was a function of weak will, confusion, or both. But just in case one accurately depicts the conception under which one in fact performed self-movement, the conception is appropriate to the kind of effort expended on its behalf, and the choice is one that a well-functioning agent could make in that circumstance, then one's job in providing a rational explanation is finished.

Having made that decision, it is of course true that we can *ascribe* to the agent a desire or preference for the option chosen. But as Thomas Nagel (1970) pointed out long ago, this does not demonstrate support for the rationalist conception of agency. When we universally ascribe desires in this way, we are using 'desire' in the thin or attributive sense in which having a desire for ϕ follows tautologously from deciding to ϕ. Desires in this sense, as Raz (1999: 109–12) puts it, are simply the mark of the intentional. They are not prior, independent desires that carry weight in a rational explanation of why one acted as one did, that serve as a premise against which one made one's decision, and about which one could have reasoned well or poorly, or responded with strong or weak will. They are not reasons for action; they are simply a signal that intentional action occurred.

If asked why a given conception was more appealing to you than the other, there may be a further normative reason, but there may not (compare Dancy 2004: 92). To think that such a regress is forced upon us—as opposed to acknowledging that further questions will be apt if the proffered explanation does not satisfy the criteron above—is just an iteration of the claim that intelligibility in action is found only in avoidance of wrong or of randomizing over permissible indifference, not an argument for it.[5]

On this view, the will is not just the capacity to follow the grooves of deontic necessity or to break ties between options to which reasons and it are alike indifferent. The will is the capacity for reasoned self-movement, and this includes the capacity to make decisions in light of non-necessitating reasons. Rational explanation is not always a matter of finding normatively necessitating conditions (any more than physical explanation is always about citing causally necessitating conditions); it is to give the conception under which you exercised your capacity for self-movement in a way consistent with what a well-functioning agent could choose in that context (compare Raz 1999: ch. 3).

If this is right, then there are *two* ways in which reasons for action can show up as rational *explicans*. First, they can do so in virtue of their peremptory force. Peremptory force functions to place one in need of adequate exculpatory justification not to act as it directs; the strength of the force determines how much exculpatory justification is needed to preclude a verdict of wrong. Absent such justification, performing the action is made intelligible by the very good fact that it would have been wrong not to do so. Second, reasons can do so by virtue of their commendatory force. Commendatory force functions to provide a basis of intelligibility

---

[5] Another way a regress might be seen to threaten is the temptation to construe decisions, or exercises of the will, as themselves actions based on reasons. This is a mistake; see, e.g. Velleman (1996).

sufficient to bring a self-movement under the umbrella of intentional action, and intentional action that is *pro tanto* consistent with what a well-functioning agent could choose, without placing one in need of exculpatory justification not to so act. If peremptory force renders actions intelligible by rendering them wrong not to do, commendatory force renders actions intelligible by rendering them reasonable to do.[6]

4. Non-reductive deontic views

I have argued that we should not reduce the normative force of reasons to their deontic function on pain of an overly blunt theory of agency. Even if all reasons are deontic, they are not *only* deontic.

I want now to turn to a more moderate, because non-reductive, version of the deontic view of reasons. Adherents of this more moderate camp agree that reasons can normatively support actions and serve as an intelligible basis of action other than by setting up the impermissibility of declining them. In our parlance, they agree that reasons for action carry commendatory force. Still, they believe that reasons for action always impose deontic vulnerability. If reasons for action carry more than peremptory force, carry such force they do.

---

[6] One might put the point by saying that commendatory force makes reasonable while peremptory force *pro tanto requires*. Dancy objects to applying the language of requirement to reasons, stating that requirement is not something that occurs at the level of the contributory (or *pro tanto*). If 'required' is instead meant simply as a stand-in for 'wrong not to'—as the mark of deontic necessity, the lack of latitude or optionality, then reasons can be said to *pro tanto* require, since a reason can make something *pro tanto* wrong not to do. I prefer not to use 'require' in this way, but only because it carries the connotation of imperatival force—deontic force that has an embedded exclusionary structure, which is something I do not believe reasons, even peremptory ones, can carry (see note 14 in this chapter).

As a separate matter, let me note there are important questions about whether to apply, and how to understand, the concept of strength as applied to commendatory force (something the above definition sidesteps). While he does not put it in quite these terms, this is one of the major agendas of Dancy's paper: one of Dancy's central aims there is to defend the possibility of choosing the 'lesser enticing' or again the 'worse' action, which implies that enticing admits of degrees and can normatively order options. This chapter sets aside that set of issues. For one thing, defending the claim requires defending a semantics of evaluative terms such as 'better' and 'worse', and explicating the necessary uptake conditions of confronting the evaluative properties corresponding to those terms, all of which is well beyond the scope of this chapter. Fortunately, the issue is separable from the present topic, which concerns the possibility of asymmetrical practical justification. One can defend the existence and independent instantiation of commendatory force without (yet) claiming that it admits of degrees or otherwise normatively orders options.

This more moderate view is also, I take it, the more common platform for a deontic view of reasons, tacitly functioning as something like orthodoxy. Of course, the fact that a position occupies pride of place does not mean that place is well earned. In the remainder of this article, I'll argue that the extent to which the moderate deontic view is accepted, and its rejection viewed as mysterious or worse, far outstrips adequate argumentation.

I want to begin by looking at Raz's own theory, for Raz is a particularly striking example of a moderate deontic theorist. As we have seen, Raz is concerned to recover a more robust place for latitude in life. Latitude is far more pervasive, and agency within latitude far richer, than the rationalist thinks. Much if not most of agency, he urges, is about what we have called meaningful choice within latitude—the ability to choose, not just pick, an option despite the fact that it wouldn't be wrong not to do.

Looking for models that underwrite this picture, Raz considers the possibility that some reasons are not deontic, but ends up instead defending latitude by appeal to the concept of incommensurability (1999: chs. 3 and 5; see also 1989: ch. 13). Latitude in the face of reasons, Raz argues, is wide and rich because the world of reasons is rife with incommensurability—considerations that are neither better than, less than, nor equal to one another. When such reasons compete with and oppose one another, they not only provide reason to do their endorsed action, they, as it were, trade exculpatory favours. Providing counter-balance to each other's deontic challenge, their presence provides adequate justification for not following the other's direction. Because they are incommensurable, though, none emerge as dominant. Since none is defeated, each is still available as a robustly intelligible basis for acting, notwithstanding the attractiveness of the others.

The latitude we enjoy is more interesting than the latitude of mere indifference, then, since the reasons that clear the way for one another provide meaningfully different commendatory bases with which agency can engage. Still, to have latitude with respect to a reason, one needs to earn it by finding a reason that offers sufficient opposition to it. Latitude is not about some reasons having a less insistent nature; it must be achieved by the courtesy of other reasons extinguishing the original reason's deontic threat. Latitude in the face of a reason to act is a function of non-dominant opposition.

For all of his emphasis on the intelligibility of the will, then, Raz adheres to a deontic view of reasons. Reasons play what I have here called a commendatory function; that having been said, the will has purview to play with that aspect of reasons only when the deontic drama between reasons' peremptory force has run its course. Given the rich, incommensurable nature of reasons and values, it turns out that meeting this criterion often leaves us with a multitude of eligible options; and the will is now able to run creatively with the baton it has been handed. Still, that optionality is achieved only by first successfully meeting the deontic vulnerability that every favouring reason brings with it.

Raz's invocation of widespread incommensurability has generated controversy of its own (see, e.g., Chang 1997; Gert 2004: 102–5). For our purposes, though, the question is what was so wrong with that first option. As Raz himself pointed out, one way to account for the extensive scope of meaningful latitude is to posit what he calls 'enticing' reasons—in our language, non-peremptory reasons, which can render actions rational without carrying any deontic implication for not acting on their basis (1999: 101–2). One way of accounting for meaningful latitude, that is, is to think that reasons come with different personalities: some, like saving another's life, carry deontic implication in their wake, but others, like the coziness and adventurousness of an evening's plans, are content only to commend. Why not take this route?

It's a question that is particularly appropriate given our preceding discussion. The whole point of highlighting the limitations of the rationalist picture is to underscore the plausibility and importance of acknowledging a non-deontic mode in which reasons can render action intelligible. Having done the work of recovering commendatory force as a fully respectable basis of intelligibility, why think it always comes packaged with peremptory force? Why not think that it sometimes travels solo?

Raz's (1999: 101) own reasons for rejecting the idea, it must be said, are hardly persuasive. He first raises the concern that one and the same consideration might seem enticing in one context yet strike us as requiring or peremptory in another; or again, that a reason that seems enticing when it appears alone might seem peremptory when combined with enough others. As Dancy (2004: 94–5) points out, though, these are not problems that should concern the defender of enticing reasons. The claim does not have to be that one and the same consideration always serves as an enticing reason, but that considerations can favour in two different ways. Which favouring relation—enticing or peremptory—a given consideration carries could be subject to interaction effects, be an emergent property of its membership in a given set of considerations, or be a deeply contextual matter (we can guess which Dancy would choose).

Of course, at the end of the day, we will want a background theory of what it is in virtue of which a consideration favours in one way rather than another. But this isn't a surprise. Anyone who posits reasons—whether of one or of two types—owes a story, at the end of the day, about when, and in virtue of what, *facts* turn into *reasons*. Those who posit two kinds of reasons will have a richer such story. But the resources for filling it in are as varied as they are for a monistic theory: there can be as many answers as there are theories of practical reason.

Raz (1999: 102) next asks us to consider Mary, who is faced with a purportedly enticing reason to go to a play and a familiar peremptory reason to pay a visit to her mother some time that week. She decides to go to the play. Raz agrees that this choice is justified, but says that, on a view that endorses enticing reasons, it looks like an enticing reason is defeating a peremptory reason—a prospect that strikes him as implausible.

But whatever one might say about whether enticing reasons can provide exculpatory justification against peremptory ones, the example does not set up such a conflict. As Dancy (2004: 100) points out, to say that one has a duty to visit one's mother sometime that week does not mean that one has a duty to visit her that evening. The fact that one must ϕ sometime does not mean one must ϕ at a given time. So long as one has a clear sense that there will be other opportunities, one can perfectly sensibly go to the play—or indeed just stay home, one's duty to visit notwithstanding.

These sorts of concerns, then, are hardly compelling, based on misunderstanding of the nature and structure of the proposal. If we are to find the source of resistance, we must go deeper.

5. Deontic reasons, the structure of decision, and asymmetric justification

In the preceding section, we have seen how Raz's own arguments against non-deontic reasons are taken up with issues about the details of the proposal. But for many, rejection of non-deontic reasons is much more direct, for it is based on completely formal considerations. For many, there is something about the very idea of confronting a reason—one version focusing around the structure of decision, another around the concept of normative support—that shows the idea of non-deontic reasons as mysterious at best, incoherent at worst. Widespread as these views are, I think both are deeply mistaken.

Let's start with the argument about the structure of decision. The argument goes something like this. Sitting on the couch, I am faced with a reason to get up: the yummy chocolate in the cupboard. If I decide not to get up and eat the chocolate, then I seem to be deciding to do something else—if only the passive action of staying comfortably on the couch. That action itself, of course, has to be supported by adequate reason—if I have no reason at all to stay on the couch, it is irrational for me to do so. But this point generalizes: it is true of *whatever* I decide to do in lieu of getting the chocolate, whether it is going for a walk to get the chocolate off my mind or gearing up to do some work instead. Having confronted a reason, one is, as Christine Korsgaard (2012) puts it, 'condemned to act'.[7] But this means that unless I have adequate or better reason to do something else, I am irrational not to get the chocolate, for I haven't earned the rationality of its alternative.

We can put the challenge more formally.[8] If I confront a reason to ϕ and decide not to, then I am perforce performing the action of not-ϕ-ing. But I need adequate reason to not-ϕ, on pain of irrationality; ergo I must be in possession of an opposing reason not to act on the first reason. It turns out that it is irrational not to act on an unopposed reason, not because the first reason cares so very much, as it were, but because doing so will mean that one is doing something—not-ϕ-ing—for which one has no adequate basis.

If this is right, then a deontic view of reasons for action follows as a matter of logic from the very structure of decision. But it isn't right. For it ignores the possibility that one might confront a reason to ϕ and decide not to act at all.

---

[7] Her book opens with: 'Human beings are *condemned* to choice and action. Maybe you think you can avoid it, by resolutely standing still, refusing to act, refusing to move. But it's no use, for that will be something you have chosen to do, and then you will have acted after all. Choosing not to act makes not acting a kind of action, makes it something that you do.' My thanks to Ben Bagley for pointing out the passage and for helpful discussion on this issue.

[8] My thanks to Marc Lange for doing so.

It is a familiar point that action is more than mere behaviour. There are many views about how best to capture that difference, but one fundamental point of agreement is that for self-movement to count as action, it must be governed by some degree of counterfactual orientation to an end or goal, however modest or localized it might be. To borrow the language of one approach, in adopting an intention or decision to act, you set yourself to 'see to it that' (STIT) with respect to some goal (originally presented in Belnap and Perloff 1988). The goal can be positively demarcated, with success conditions of the action given by achievement of a state of affairs ('steal the money'), or negatively demarcated, with success conditions being avoidance of one ('don't get caught'). The means, in turn, can be active or passive; and the strength and scope of one's commitment, of course, can vary widely. But whatever those details, to act involves adoption of at least some minimal specific counterfactual commitment or STIT orientation toward a goal.

With this in mind, consider my position on the couch before I raised that important question of chocolate. My being on the couch may well be a piece of intentional (if passive) action. But it might not. Perhaps I went over to the couch on automatic drive; or I accidentally fell asleep there and have just woken up. In order for my being on the couch to count as an action, I have to be there as part of some counterfactual commitment or STIT orientation, and if there by automaticity or accident, my being there is not based on the execution of any such orientation.

Not every moment of an agent's waking life is performance of an intentional action. Sometimes, we are, as it were, simply behaving.[9] This is no disrespect to our life as agents: the capacity to act does not need to be exercised at every moment for it to be valued. Indeed, I might realize upon waking that I am not right now doing anything and continue in that state, declining yet to consolidate possibilities into an intention or decision about what next to do. I may simply remain, as it were, in behaviour land.

If we can be in behaviour land in general, we can also stay there following contemplation or consideration of a reason to act. Certainly it is true that often, in deciding not to take one course of action, I do so in favour of some other action. Having thought about the delights of getting the chocolate, I consider the alternative delights of spending more time on the comfy

---

[9] For support, see Velleman (1996).

couch and decide to stay there to relax for a while. Here, I have taken on at least something of a commitment to the lounging. I change my counterfactual baseline with respect to being there, resisting other temptations, following instrumental reasoning with things that would help its achievement, etc. Or again, in thinking about the chocolate, I might decide that my consumption has grown too high, that it is time to pull back, and resolve to stay on the couch as a way of avoiding that cupboard—and the chocolate in it.

But it is also possible that, having contemplated the idea of getting the chocolate, I decline to do so without declining in favour of *doing* anything else—either achievement- or avoidance-based. I do not adopt the STIT of getting chocolate, but nor do I adopt any new STIT at all. Having thus declined to get the chocolate, I will still be on the couch, with all prior STITs in place and no new ones added. One needn't decide to do something else in deciding not to do this; one simply declines to leave behaviour land. Of course, if one *does* decide to do something else, one needs adequate justification. But that just follows from the boundary condition of counting as an action, not from anything about having declined to adopt the STIT of the first reason.

Even if we believe that agents are always performing some actions if 'action' is broadly enough construed (e.g. I am right now dispositionally avoiding driving without a seatbelt), it does not mean that one is perforce performing a new action—adopting a new specific STIT—in the aftermath of every reason one encounters. Not every decision to decline is a decision to act.

Properly conceived, then, there is nothing in the structure of deciding that inherently pushes us toward a deontic view of reasons. Encountering a reason, one can decline not only to act on its behalf, but decline to pursue any new course of action at all.

The second argument focuses on the concept of normative support. For some, there is something about the *asymmetry* of enticing reasons—the very generosity that marks such reasons—that is basis for suspicion. Enticing or non-peremptory reasons are said to offer normative support for an option without placing one in need of any support not to follow its guidance. But this, it is said, is an inherently odd idea (see, e.g., Kagan 1989)—a form of having one's normative cake and eating it, too. How can a reason be said to offer normative support if one needs no reason to, as it were, ignore that support?

In fact, though, the idea of asymmetrical normative support is a familiar one elsewhere in the normative arena. It is a truism, for instance, in the emotions literature. As many in that literature have pointed out, part of what it means to be an emotion as opposed to a raw feeling is to be the sort of affective state that is susceptible to norms of aptness, reasonability, and justification. Feeling anger at someone who is two minutes late is unjustified; feeling anger when one has been stabbed is not. Sometimes, when judging a given emotion to be justified, we point to considerations that in fact make it problematic *not* to feel as specified. What justifies one's anger is, metaphorically, something that 'calls' for anger: one who does not experience it is failing to fully appreciate or mark the meaning of the situation. Such emotional responsiveness is especially important in the moral life: *pro tanto*, one is wrong not to feel appalled at news of genocide, sorrow at terrible tragedy, remorse over one's serious transgressions. These are peremptory reasons for having an emotion.[10]

But we also sometimes judge an emotion as an apt, justified, normatively appropriate reaction to a situation while seeing nothing wrong, even *pro tanto*, with one who does not respond to it in that manner. A slight or insult may render anger reasonable without rising to the level of mandating it. The situation is such that being angry is fully *consistent* with what a properly functioning emotional agent might feel without being *necessary* to what a properly functioning emotional agent feels. The fact that I am justified in feeling angry does not always mean that I need justification not to feel it. Instead, it is, we might put it, a reasonable emotion to feel: the emotion is based on something that makes it intelligible, and is consistent with what a well-functioning emotional agent might feel, but one is not required, even *pro tanto*, to experience it.

Many reasons for emotion, in short, are non-peremptory: they are sufficient to render an emotion normatively intelligible—moving them from the umbrella of mere sensation to emotion, and an emotion *pro tanto*

---

[10] Some will question whether emotions are the sorts of things it can be wrong not to feel. Those who believe that deontic reasons should be reserved for instances in which the will can immediately exercise control will talk of reasons for emotion as intelligibility-making rather than wrong-making, reserving the latter for the actions of indirect control—cultivation and the like—that the will itself can take. Even if one believes this, note, it affirms the idea that there are modes of intelligibility beyond deontic ones, and affirms the idea that normative support is often and unproblematically asymmetrical. The fact that the will can be subject to deontic modes does not mean it cannot be engaged with non-deontic ones.

consistent with what a well-functioning agent might feel in that circumstance—without placing one in need of justification not to experience or cultivate it.

The present suggestion is that some reasons for action similarly offer asymmetrical justification. I care about my garden; this gives me reason to weed it. On occasions when I do not have other claims on my time, it would be perfectly intelligible and consistent with well-functioning agency to go out and put in a good half hour. But this does not mean I need to justify every waking moment not spent weeding. Not only may I decline to weed if I find sufficient reason to pursue some other worthy action, I may decline action altogether, remaining permissibly in behaviour land.

Or again, I love my partner; the fact that I do makes it intelligible at any number of moments to stop and do something sweet for him. But it does not, one might hope, place me in the position of needing to justify every occasion that I don't. The fact that the world is saturated with possibilities to do him sweet favours—actions that would be utterly intelligible should I decide to pursue them—does not mean that the permissibility of my staying in behaviour land or pursing other options is under question in a correspondingly saturated way.

In short, there is nothing in the generic idea of normative support that inherently presses toward a deontic view of reasons. The idea of non-deontic reasons, at a minimum, is a cogent one, rather than something that inherently involves some formal or conceptual fallacy. If one contends that all reasons for action are deontic, one is advancing a substantive claim, and defending it requires arguments that treat it as such.

Distinguishing between action and behaviour, on the one hand, and symmetrical versus asymmetrical normative support, on the other, can help us articulate the difference between the two forms of reasons for action. In the face of a peremptory reason to ϕ (whether ϕ-ing is active or passive, positively or negatively demarcated), one needs to defend not acting as it directs. Absent adequate exculpatory justification, one needs to adopt the STIT that the reason outlines. In the absence of said justification, peremptory reasons defeat the permissibility of remaining in behaviour land, and defeat the permissibility of following the lead of lesser other favouring reasons. Peremptory reasons also carry commendatory force—the presence of commendatory force, I have suggested, is a defining mark of reasons rather than rules; but it rides atop its peremptory cousin.

Non-peremptory reasons, in contrast, are comprised exclusively of commendatory force. They render an action reasonable, providing a basis that is sufficient, if deployed, to put self-movement undertaken on its behalf under the umbrella of intentional action, and intentional action that is *pro tanto* consistent with what a well-functioning agent might do in that circumstance, without placing one in need of exculpatory justification not to act on their basis. In this way, such reasons serve only to expand one's agential possibilities. If I face a non-deontic reason, I have a new possibility opened to me—a new action I could reasonably perform. But it does not thereby threaten the permissibility of anything else—the innocence of staying in behaviour land, the permissibility of continuing what I am doing, or the permissibility of choosing an action that is different from the one it suggests. If two such reasons compete, as often happens, they each offer an intelligible basis for action, but neither minds the other's deontic business.[11] Deliberation is possible with respect to such reasons; but it takes the form of exploring the reasons' natures and consequences, not searching out the action they determine or testing their ability to satisfy more general or higher-order rationalizing desiderata. One has multiple options; the space of agency allows one to decide which reason, if either, to engage.

Non-peremptory reasons, as we might put it, justify one action without unjustifying anything else, whether that be doing nothing, doing exactly what you had been doing before this reason happened by, or pursuing an action that is supported by a different reason. They invite, as it were, rather than tell you what to do.

In the final section, I want to take seriously this metaphor, and in doing so, increase the pressure against the deontic view of reasons. Allusions to speech acts actually help remind us, I'll argue, that the idea of confronting commendatory force without peremptory ballast is in fact eminently familiar in the realm of action—if we know where to look.

---

[11] Crucially, they may mind one another's evaluative business. Depending on whether one thinks that commendatory force is able to order actions normatively, the presence of a competing non-peremptory reason may make the decision to follow another one unwise, foolish, or bad. The present chapter does not take on this issue.

What happens if a peremptory reason competes with a non-peremptory reason? The answer depends on one's view of whether non-deontic reasons can play the function of providing exculpatory justification, an issue I do not take up in this chapter. For a defence of the idea that reasons may offer exculpatory justification out of proportion to the degree to which they offer positive justification, see Gert (2004).

6. Requests and invitations

When we think about what can put us into normative positions with respect to actions, we often think first of the abstract world of reasons and rules. That having been said, there is another important source—the world of speech acts, where others with standing exercise their ability to issue illocutionary force.

Take, for instance, the familiar example of demands and orders. When issued by one with requisite authority over another, demands and orders place their recipient into a new normative position—she would now be wrong to do nothing, and wrong to do something other than this, absent compelling exculpatory justification. The recipient is required, *pro tanto*, to do as directed. The *tanto* might be *pro*'d, of course; one might face a competing obligation or countermanding order, say. Still, in the absence of such exculpatory factors, one would be wrong not to comply: one would be wrong to do nothing, and wrong to do something other than this, absent compelling justification.

Yet not all speech acts direct others in such a pushy way. Some function to give us *pro tanto* justification to take an action without placing us in need of justification to decline.

Consider requests. Less discussed in ethics than demands, they are nonetheless an important staple in speech-act theory. And as those who have explored them note, there is an important sense in which the making of a request, where legitimate, itself gives the one so requested a reason or *pro tanto* basis of intelligibility for action. As David Enoch (2011) puts it, a request does not just point to the merits for doing the requested action, though it is a presuppositional feature or felicity condition of the speech act that such merits exist. Nor, we might point out, does it simply function to give permission for the recipient to help, though it does this as well. To issue a request is not simply to declare: 'Your ϕ-ing would help me and you may do so.' To issue a request, as Darwall puts it, is to exercise a form of standing to interpersonally insert oneself into the other's normative considerations.[12] Depending on who is asking (stranger, neighbour, colleague) and what is being asked (directions

---

[12] 'Even a bare request addresses a second-personal reason that is additional to any non-second-personal reasons that might stand behind it, since it presupposes the normative standing to make the request' (Darwall 2006: 257).

for the best way to the theatre; helping at the 4th of July parade; reading a draft), the making of the request can itself give the one requested a reason to act that is over and above the reasons the request might reference or release.

If asked by a colleague whether you would take on chairing a committee she is organizing, you might decide to accept because it would be fun (!), or because of the good the committee could accomplish. But you might also think the merits vanishingly modest yet agree on the very grounds that she legitimately asked it of you. One decides, as it were, to do it for her, and doing it for her not just in the sense that she wants you to do it, but that she *asked* it of you. Requests, where legitimate, do not merely point to or highlight already extant reasons for action; nor do they simply provide permissions or consent to provide the assistance sought. Where legitimate, they themselves give their recipient a reason to act.

For all that, it would get things badly wrong to think that the reasons such requests give rise to are *peremptory*. Your neighbor asks if you would be willing to help at the 4th of July parade. Coming from one's neighbor, it is, we will imagine, a perfectly legitimate request; and you may well decide to say yes precisely because it was she who asked. Still, that does not mean you need to provide justification to decline. In the usual event, of course, your neighbor will hope that you say yes; more than that, it is the internal aim of this type of speech act (that is, the aim by which we understand its success as a type, whatever the token intention of the speaker issuing it) that the request be granted. But for all that, the request does not give you an assignment, even a *pro tanto* one. It, as it were, hopes rather than tells you what to do. Expressions of regret in declining are appropriate as a way of registering the legitimacy of the request and the merits for which it may be advocating, but no parade of excuses, real or imagined, is owed. You may well *want* to give mitigating circumstances if you decline—as a way, for instance, to demonstrate your general willingness to help despite here declining. The point is that the illocutionary force of the speech act itself does not place you in need of doing so.[13]

---

[13] In *The Morality of Freedom*, Raz seems to regard both requests and demands as deontic, locating the difference between them in the fact that the latter, but not the former, impose an exclusionary structure on what counts as justification to decline. Demands, as we might put it, carry *imperatival*, not just peremptory, force.

I certainly agree that there are deontic directives that do not impose or reflect any exclusionary structure. To give an example from epistemology, evidence does not impose an exclusionary structure: it is a paradigmatic example of merits and demerits whose reason-giving nature is weighed and otherwise

Requests, by their nature, are something that 'permit of refusal' (Searle 1969). One owes an answer, but 'yes' and 'no' are both fully acceptable answers as a response to the normative import of the speech act. Other things may contingently make it wrong to decline (or for that matter, wrong to accept): perhaps the request brings to light (and provides permission to address) a need that is itself peremptory for you to meet.[14] In the usual case, though, the illocutionary force of the request itself does not place one in need of exculpatory justification to decline, even as it gives one an intelligible basis for acceding. Not every 'no' needs justification, even when the request to which it counts as response is an independently intelligible basis for 'yes'. If full uptake of a demand or order involves performing the action unless one has adequate justification to decline, the uptake of a request is to 'accept or decline; but let the person know'.

For another example, we can turn to another speech act expert—Miss Manners. Miss Manners often has occasion to explain to her readers just what the illocutionary force of an invitation is—and what it isn't (Martin 2005). Sometimes, of course, invitations are best read simply as proposals for coordinating an enjoyable event, with perhaps an offer to host.[15] But other invitations are more like a specific species of request, in which what is requested is the pleasure of your company against a presupposition of mutual enjoyment. Depending, as always, on legitimacy—on who is asking what (neighbor or stranger; dinner or marriage), such invitations can also give one a reason to do something. If your neighbor invites you to dinner

---

compared, not excluded. Still, when evidence reaches a certain threshold of compellingness, one is *pro tanto* wrong not to follow its lead: such evidence precisely places you in the position of needing exculpatory reason not to adjust your beliefs.

But I do not agree that this is the right account of requests. There is a core distinction between asking and telling someone to do something. Tellings are deontic directives: where legitimate, they make it *pro tanto* wrong not to do something. The fact that the *pro tanto* structure of some tellings is non-exclusionary does not change their nature as tellings. To return to the epistemology example, compelling evidence doesn't request that one believe; it *tells* one *pro tanto* what to believe.

[14] Or again, cases in which the making of a request of you by S triggers and specifies a background imperfect duty to S.

[15] Or again, sometimes, as with broadcast invitations to a charity gala, they function simply to call your attention to an event and its merits and give the permission needed to participate.

on Saturday, one might accept not just because the food will be delicious (and after all it might not), but for the very reason that you were asked for the pleasure of your company.

Yet for all that, invitations do not place on their recipient the need to justify declining. As Miss Manners puts it, in the usual case, those who issue an invitation do not have an entitlement, even *pro tanto*, that the invited shows up. Once again, it might for other reasons be wrong not to accept (perhaps you know that she is feeling down and would be sensitive to rejection). But the speech act does not serve to hand out an assignment whose discharge one can get out of only if one has sufficient counter-veiling justification. Indeed, to think it does goes precisely contrary to the internal aim of invitations, which is to provide an opportunity, not an assignment. Issuing an invitation itself constitutes a new reason for action; but being in receipt of an invitation, in the usual case at least, does not place me in possession of needing justification to stay home. The proper uptake of an invitation is an RSVP: declining with regret rather than defence is consistent with full uptake of the invitation's illocutionary force.

The structure of requests and invitations, then, is different from that governing demands and orders. Requests and invitations are not deontic directives, even as they provide an intelligible basis for action. Relative to the force issued by these normative entities, I am in a fortunate position: I am in possession of justification to act, but there is nothing in that reason that imposes deontic vulnerability.[16]

Far from odd or alien, the idea of encountering a reason for acting that does not travel by way of imposing deontic vulnerability is eminently familiar when we look to the rich world of speech acts. It is a richness that those who look to speech acts for insight on reasons would do well to remember. As Dancy points out, many have a tendency to use demands as a

---

[16] If there is a tendency to overlook this in discussions of reasons for action, it is perhaps due to confusion about the concept of a 'directive'. In its broadest sense (Austin's and Searle's), a directive is any speech act whose illocutionary aim is to get you to do something. Understood in this sense, it includes requests, invitations, advice, urgings, and suggestings. In a narrower sense, directives are speech acts whose defining uptake involves following the direction or presenting adequate exculpatory justification for refusing. These latter are deontic—and include demands and orders that assign actions and tell us what to do. This is clearly the sense Dancy is talking about when he says that '[t]he notion of a directive, like that of the mandatory, is deontic' (2004: 106). The former, though, are not, and can, for all that, constitute rational bases for action. My thanks to Coleen Macnamara for outlining this distinction.

model or metaphor for the normative force of reasons. This tendency, we can now appreciate, stacks the deck in favour of the deontic theory of reasons. For demands, as we have seen, are paradigmatic examples of peremptory force: if one thinks of reasons on their model, the deontic theory of reasons will feel irresistible.

Indeed, doing so will press one back in the direction of the reductive version of the deontic theory. For the illocutionary force of demands and orders, like the normative force of rules, is *purely* peremptory. A demand whose deontic sting has been removed has no directive force left. For those dissatisfied with a reductive deontic theory, demands are the last place to look for a model for reasons.

At any rate, we need not think of demands as the sole model or metaphor for reasons. Reasons can also place us in the form of asymmetrical justification that requests and invitations provide. To play with the presuppositional aspects of their respective illocutionary forces, we might say that the chocolate in my cupboard invites me to eat it, and my garden requests that I weed it. Details aside, the point is to remind us of the range of normative positions we can be in with respect to actions.

Such reminders are useful for another reason. Those who endorse a deontic view of reasons are often drawn to a kind of monism about reasons: if some reasons are acknowledged to be peremptory—as e.g. saving lives of others clearly are—then all must be peremptory. But reflection on speech acts reminds us of the pluralism of the normative landscape. Many things can provide entrance tickets to rational action: reasons, rules, demands, invitations. Some of those also place their recipient in need of exculpatory justification: rules, demands, orders, and peremptory reasons. But some do not: aspirations, requests, and invitations—and, on the present suggestion, non-deontic reasons.[17]

---

[17] Early versions of this chapter benefited greatly from discussion with audiences at the Royal Conference at the University of Texas, Austin; the University of North Carolina at Chapel Hill; and the University of Reading at a day honoring Jonathan Dancy's retirement from that institution. Thanks, too, for discussions with Jonathan, the Dancy family, Susan Wolf, Walter Sinnot-Armstrong, Kelly Heuer, Doug Wolf, Ben Bagley, and Marcus Hedahl, and for comments from Sarah Buss, David Bakhurst, and Coleen Macnamara. Particular thanks go to Coleen; this chapter draws on our co-authored work as well as many long and deeply helpful discussions.

References

Austin, J. L. (1965) *How To Do Things with Words* (New York: Oxford University Press).

Belnap, N. and Perloff, M. (1988) 'Seeing To It That: A Canonical Form for Agentives', *Theoria*, 54: 175–99.

Chang, R. (1997) 'Introduction', in R. Chang (ed.), *Incommensurability, Incomparability, and Practical Reason* (Cambridge, MA: Harvard University Press), 1–34.

Cupit, G. (1994) 'How Requests (and Promises) Create Obligations', *Philosophical Quarterly*, 44: 439–55.

Dancy, J. (2004) 'Enticing Reasons', in R. J. Wallace, P. Pettit, S. Scheffler, and M. Smith (eds.), *Reason and Value: Themes from the Moral Philosophy of Joseph Raz* (Oxford: Clarendon Press), 91–118.

Darwall, S. (2006) *The Second-Person Standpoint: Morality, Respect, and Accountability* (Cambridge, MA: Harvard University Press).

Enoch, D. (2011) 'Giving Practical Reasons', *Philosophers' Imprint*, 11: 1–21.

Gert, J. (2004) *Brute Rationality* (Cambridge: Cambridge University Press).

Hampton, J. (1998) *The Authority of Reason* (Cambridge, MA: Cambridge University Press).

Kagan, S. (1989) *The Limits of Morality* (Oxford: Clarendon Press).

Korsgaard, C. (2009) *Self-Constitution: Agency, Identity, and Integrity* (Oxford: Oxford University Press).

Martin, J. (2005) *Miss Manners Guide to Excruciatingly Correct Manners: Freshly Updated* (New York: Norton Publishing).

Nagel, T. (1970) *The Possibility of Altruism* (Princeton, NJ: Princeton University Press).

Raz, J. (1986) *The Morality of Freedom* (Oxford: Oxford University Press).

—— (1990) *Practical Reason and Norms* (Princeton, NJ: Princeton University Press).

—— (1999) *Engaging Reason: On the Theory of Value and Action* (Oxford: Oxford University Press).

Scanlon, T. M. (1998) *What We Owe to Each Other* (Cambridge, MA: Harvard University Press).

Searle, J. (1969) *Speech Acts: An Essay in the Philosophy of Language* (Cambridge: Cambridge University Press).

—— and Vanderveken, D. (1985) *Foundations of Illocutionary Logic* (Cambridge: Cambridge University Press).

Velleman, D. (1996) 'The Possibility of Practical Reason', *Ethics*, 106: 694–726.

7

The Deontic Structure of Morality

R. JAY WALLACE

Morality presents itself as a source of practical necessities. It is not merely a domain of normative reasons, in the familiar sense of considerations that count in favour of the ways of action morality happens to recommend. It makes demands on us, ones that it is not open to us to neglect or ignore in deliberating about our options for action. What accounts for this dimension of moral thought? How can we make sense of the idea that morality is a source of rational requirements or demands?

In this chapter I want to address one important aspect of this complex problem. To set the terms for the discussion to follow, it will help to begin by distinguishing between three potentially distinct things that might be meant when reference is made to the necessity of the demands that morality makes on action. First, it might be meant that moral considerations are normative reasons for all agents or persons, without reference to the contingencies of taste, preference, or interest that distinguish some individuals from others. Call this the dimension of inescapability. Second, moral reasons might be said to be especially weighty, insofar as they trump or override any competing normative considerations with which they might potentially come into conflict. Call this the dimension of importance. Third, morality strikes us within deliberation as a source of normative requirements, in an elusive way that cannot be traced to the first two factors I have already identified. Moral reasons enter the deliberative field, as it were, in the guise of considerations that we lack discretion to ignore, structuring our practical reflection in a distinctively peremptory style that contrasts with the contribution made by other kinds of normative consideration. Call this the dimension of deontic structure.

My aim will be to explore the idea that there is a distinctively deontic style of normativity that moral considerations in particular might be said to exhibit. This seems to me a fitting theme for a contribution to a volume of essays in honour of Jonathan Dancy, whose work over the years has done so much to alert contemporary philosophers to neglected complexities in the structures that constitute the normative domain.[1] Dancy himself has proposed a distinction between two styles of normativity that is in the general ballpark of the distinction that interests me in this chapter. I offer some critical remarks about Dancy's distinction in the course of my argument. But I have been inspired by his close attention to the diversity that prevails within the broader category of normative reasons, and hope that my discussion can be understood as a way of honouring his example.

The chapter begins with some non-moral cases that illustrate the intuitive difference between deontic and what I call aspirational normativity. Discussion of these examples in sections 1 and 2 will reveal that there are different kinds of factor that can lend to normative reasons the character of requirements. Sometimes this character will be a reflection of the systematic importance of the reasons in question; but there is a distinct source of deontic structure that is seemingly independent from considerations about normative importance. In section 3 I propose an account of this elusive further source of deontic normativity. My thesis will be that a kind of deontic structure is implicit in cases in which reasons come embedded within essentially relational structures; reasons that are bound up in a nexus of directional normativity are ones that we lack discretion to ignore or to discount in deliberation, insofar as our failure to take them properly into account affects our normative relations to other people. In section 4 I connect this discussion of deontic structure to the moral case. In particular, I distinguish between two familiar ways of thinking about morality and its normative significance, the consequentialist and the relational, and argue that only the relational approach has the resources to accommodate the thought that morality exhibits the elusive kind of deontic structure that it will be my aim in this chapter to elucidate. If this is correct, then whether morality in fact structures deliberation in the distinctively deontic style will

---

[1] See, e.g., the illuminating distinction between favouring and enabling reasons (and between normative intensifiers and attenuators) in Dancy (2004a: ch. 3).

1. Deontic structure: an elusive idea

Let us begin by thinking about the following three deliberative situations:

Movie. Suppose that you are considering what to do after dinner tonight. It has been a long and trying week, and you are feeling in the mood for something that will be a change of pace, and take your mind off the difficult issues you have been grappling with at work. To simplify matters let us assume that your options are basically twofold. You could stay home and finish the moderately entertaining but forgettable thriller you started the other day. Or you could drive down to the local arts cinema, which is showing on its large screen *Rocco and his Brothers*, a classic film that you have never seen, and may never again have the opportunity to see under such favourable viewing conditions. Here it would seem plausible to say that you have conclusive reason to choose the film over the novel, taking everything into account. And yet we would probably be reluctant to conclude that this is something you are strictly required to do. You might be foolish or lazy or unwise to stay home and read your book, as you yourself would presumably agree; but it is not clear that there is enough here to support the idea that the considerations that speak in favour of going to the movie have the shape or force of requirements. The reasons at issue exhibit what we might refer to as an aspirational character, insofar as they count in favour of the actions they recommend in a way that leaves the deliberating agent with some discretion to ignore or to discount their claims.

Small Loan. You have taken out a small loan from an electronics shop, with the help of which you have paid for a new television set. The loan agreement you signed upon purchasing the TV called for you to pay it off in a number of equal instalments, each of which is due by the 5th of the month. Here it seems more natural than in the previous case to say that you are obligated to make the payments. You have obligated yourself precisely by taking out the loan. Thus the fact that a new payment is due by the 5th of the month is not merely a consideration that recommends or speaks in favour of making the payment, in a way analogous to the attractions of seeing *Rocco and his Brothers*. Its claims on your deliberative attention seem more insistent, leaving you without the kind of discretion to reject them that appears to be in place in the scenario in which you are deliberating about what recreational activity to plump for this evening.

Distraught Friend. Consider next a situation that involves a valuable form of personal relationship. A good friend of yours calls up late at night, and you immediately notice from his tone of voice that he is distraught. He tells you that something horrible has come up at work that he does not know how to handle, and he asks if you could possibly get together with him for lunch the next day to talk about the situation and his options for dealing with it. You already have a lot on your plate for the next day, and had been planning as a result to work through lunch. But you feel that your friend really needs you, and this consideration strikes you as one that has a special kind of deliberative force. The fact that your friend is in a bad way is not merely something that speaks in favour of helping him out. Rather it presents itself as a kind of requirement, one that it would be an especially serious kind of mistake to ignore or discount. Once again, it is natural to put the point in the language of discretion, saying that you do not have the same kind of liberty to reject the claims of friendship that you seemed to have in the case in which you are deliberating about whether to go to the Visconti film.

My presentation of these three cases suggests that there is a difference in normative force between the reasons involved in Movie, and those at issue in Small Loan and Distraught Friend. The former are aspirational, as I put it, whereas the latter seem more in the nature of requirements; they exhibit what we might provisionally refer to as deontic structure. But what exactly does this difference in normative force involve?

Jonathan Dancy (2004b) has offered a framework that appears tailor-made to help us answer this question. Specifically, he suggests that practical deliberation can be framed in terms of two different practical questions. There is, first of all, the question 'What is the thing to do?', a question that is answered (in effect) by determining that X is something that one ought to do. But there is also a different question we can pose in deliberation, namely 'What shall I do?', and this question invites us to consider our options for action in rather different terms. Dancy's strategy is to explain the contrast between something like deontic and aspirational normativity by situating the two kinds of reasons in relation to these different practical questions.

Thus, what I have been calling deontic reasons are to be understood in relation to conclusions about what an agent ought to do. They may not alone succeed in grounding a true claim of this kind, insofar as they are not always conclusive reasons for action. But ought-judgments are the kind of practical claims that deontic reasons tend to support, and their counting in favour of such claims is what is distinctive about their normative significance. Aspirational reasons, by contrast, take us to 'bests' rather than 'oughts'; they thus exhibit a different kind of normativity from the deontic, insofar as the practical conclusions they tend to support are claims about what it would be best to do. Dancy proposes that we can make sense of the idea that we have discretion to ignore or discount aspirational considerations (or 'enticing reasons', as he calls them) against the background of this explanation of their distinctive normative significance. The ought-judgments that deontic reasons tend to support are to be understood in relation to the practical question, 'What is the thing to do?' But the nature of this relation is such that a determination that one ought to do, say, X, is already a conclusive answer to the question 'What is the thing to do?' Agents who judge that they ought to X, but who fail to act on that judgment, are therefore peculiarly at odds with themselves; they have posed a practical question, arrived at what they acknowledge to be a conclusive answer to that question, and then ignored their own answer in deciding what to do. By contrast, agents who conclude that X would be the best thing to do have not already thereby answered the practical question from which they set out. The judgment that X-ing would be best, though relevant to the question 'What shall I do?', is not itself a conclusive answer to that question. One can therefore fail to do what one judges it would be best to do without being at odds with oneself, insofar as the question from which one's deliberation began has not in this case already been given a conclusive answer through one's own practical judgment. It is in this sense, Dancy suggests, that we have a kind of latitude to go against aspirational reasons that is not present in cases of deontic normativity.

This strategy attempts to preserve the normativity of both aspirational and deontic considerations, while doing justice to the intuition that there is a significant difference in the way in which the two kinds of reasons count in favour of the actions they support. But the device that is hit on for achieving this end—namely the distinction between two different practical questions to which normative reflection might be a response—strikes me as artificial. There are no doubt differences of nuance between the questions 'What is the thing to do?' and 'What shall I do?', but it is doubtful that these differences provide a consistent principle for sorting normative reasons into two fundamentally different categories. Thus deontic considerations are at least sometimes relevant to reflection about what I shall do, while aspirational reasons can bear on reflection about what the thing to do might be. In Movie, for instance, I might conclude that heading out to the cinema is the thing to do, just because it is the option that would be best under the prevailing circumstances. If this is right, however, then we cannot understand the idea of discretion by appeal to the distinctive question to which aspirational reasons are presumptively relevant; reasons of this kind can equally be brought to bear in deliberation about what the thing to do would be, and in this context it would seem that we have no discretion of the kind Dancy has suggested to ignore their claims. By the same token, I might take into account considerations about what I ought to do in reflection that sets out from the question, 'What shall I do?' But in this context, Dancy maintains, we precisely have scope for ignoring our own practical conclusions in practice without our judgment thereby being at odds with itself. If deontic considerations take us to 'oughts', as Dancy suggests, we would therefore seem to have discretion to ignore them in at least some deliberative situations.

In the end, I believe we should resist the fragmentation of practical reason that is implicit in Dancy's approach. Deliberation begins from a practical question about what to do, a question that can be variously formulated depending on the context that is to hand, but to which reasons of any kind are at least potentially relevant. The problem, in these terms, is to make sense of the different ways in which deontic and aspirational considerations count in favour of the actions they support, without resorting to an artificial multiplication of practical perspectives.

2. The weight of reasons and the structure of deliberation

The most natural way to distinguish between different normative considerations, within the context of a unified conception of practical reason, would be to appeal to differences in weight or significance. But no simple appeal to differences of this kind can account for the distinction that seems to be present between the three cases I have described. In Movie, for instance, I suggested that the aspirational considerations that would recommend the Visconti film are conclusive reasons for action; what you have most reason to do, taking everything into account, is to see the film rather than to stay home to read your novel.[2] And yet in this situation we are precisely not tempted to think of the reasons as in the nature of requirements. It follows that the distinction between aspirational and deontic reasons cannot be understood simply by looking to the output side of practical deliberation, and considering whether a given consideration is or is not conclusive in determining what the agent finally ought to do.

A different strategy would be to attend to the ways in which normative considerations structure deliberation in the practical thought of those agents who are taking them correctly into account. Thus Joseph Raz (1990) has noted that some normative considerations amount to what he calls exclusionary reasons. The distinctive feature of such reasons is that their obtaining functions to block the normative force of potential competitors. Thus, in Small Loan, the fact that your payment is due by the 5th of the month is not merely a consideration that is to be set over against the attractions of the other things you might do with the same sum of money. Rather it silences those considerations, giving you second-order reasons not to act on them, even though they would be perfectly respectable reasons in contexts in which you had not thus committed yourself to making the payment. Similarly, John Broome (2004) has proposed that we can distinguish between reasons that do and reasons that do not enter into 'weighing explanations' of normative facts (such as the fact that a given agent ought to do X), where a weighing explanation in turn involves the aggregation and combination of different kinds of consideration. In this vein, we might say that the fact that payment is due on the loan determines the normative fact that you ought to arrange for timely transfer of funds to the creditor, without reliance on the kind of comparison, aggregation, or combination of considerations that would give the metaphor of 'weighing' a point in this context.

I find promising the suggestion that the difference between aspirational and deontic reasons has to do with the role of normative considerations in structuring deliberation. But it is not clear to me that deontic structure is correctly analysed in terms of the notions of exclusion or weighing. For one thing, considerations can exhibit the kind of deontic structure I am trying to

---

[2] The case, in this way, seems different from one in which there is, what we might call, genuine or full deliberative discretion. This would be a situation, for instance, in which the options of the movie and the novel are roughly on a par as solutions to the practical problem of what would make for a diverting evening. In a situation of this kind, neither choice that an agent might make would seem to involve a deliberative error or to be criticizable from the agent's own point of view.

capture without necessarily being conclusive in relation to the output of deliberation. In Small Loan, for instance, we can imagine circumstances, such as a medical emergency, in which the claims of your creditor are trumped by competing considerations. If there are unanticipated medical needs, and limited financial resources available with which to address them, then it might well be best on the whole to forego the payment in the month in which the emergency occurs, and to accept the consequences. If this is right, however, then we cannot understand deontic structure simply by appeal to the notions of exclusion or weighing. There may be situations in which deontic reasons do not exclude or negate the normative force of considerations with which they might compete, and determining whether such circumstances obtain will require something like weighing, comparison, and combination of the different kinds of reasons on each side of the issue.[3]

Furthermore, even to the extent exclusion and absence of weighing may be characteristic of deontic reasons, it is not clear that these are the features that render those reasons distinctively deontic. We might, after all, treat just about any reason as an exclusionary consideration, taking it to determine directly what we ought to do without reliance on the kind of comparison of normative considerations involved in weighing different kinds of reason in a balance. With deontic reasons, by contrast, it is very tempting to think that there is something else about them that makes it the case that it is ordinarily correct to accommodate them in these distinctive ways within practical reflection. It is *because* the claims at issue in Distraught Friend are deontic rather than aspirational in nature, one wants to say, that it is fitting to structure one's deliberations so that the reasons function to exclude other kinds of consideration from entering the deliberative field.[4] It remains to say what this further feature of deontic normativity might consist in.

---

[3] Raz would presumably appeal to considerations of scope to accommodate some examples of this kind, noting that a consideration could function to exclude acting on some first-order reasons, without functioning in this way in regard to others (see 1990: 40). But in the example I am considering, it seems that the loan contract gives one an obligation of some kind to make the payment, even if it is on-balance better not to do so. If we wish to make sense of this notion of obligation in terms of exclusion, then we cannot say that the reasons the contract gives us do not exclude from consideration first-order reasons of medical exigency, since that would entail that they are no longer obligations of any kind.

[4] Raz would agree, appealing in this connection to 'indirect' considerations about the degree to which acceptance of exclusionary reasons would enhance one's ability over time to conform to such first-order reasons as one has (see 1990: 194–9). This idea, which is of course crucial to Raz's accounts of legal authority and promissory commitment, seems less promising as an account of the more general phenomenon of deontic structure that is my quarry.

To make progress in understanding better what this feature might be, it will help to return to the original contrast I have drawn between the aspirational and the deontic. I have characterized aspirational normativity, to this point, in terms of the notion of deliberative discretion. In Movie, you seem to have a certain leeway to ignore or discount the considerations that speak in favour of seeing the Visconti film. With deontic reasons, by contrast, this kind of discretion seems lacking. If we can make sense of the lack of discretion that sets deontic reasons apart from aspirational ones, we might be closer to understanding what it is about them that renders it fitting that they should ordinarily structure our deliberations so as to silence other kinds of normative consideration, and to determine what we ought to do without reliance on procedures that weigh competing reasons and values against one another.

A natural way to approach the notion of discretion at issue here would be to focus on the consequences that attend the failure to act on aspirational and deontic reasons. Thus it might be said that we open ourselves to strong rational criticism if we do not comply with our deontic reasons; we are irrational from our own point of view if we agree that a consideration of this kind obtains, but do not succeed in acting on it. In the aspirational cases, by contrast, no such consequences may seem to follow from the failure to act on our reasons. Our discretion to ignore aspirational reasons might thus be traced to the fact that we can deliberately flout them without opening ourselves to criticism as irrational.[5]

This suggestion cannot be accepted as it stands, however. For one thing, it is not obviously the case that we open ourselves to rational criticism whenever we fail to act on reasons that exhibit deontic structure. This possibility has already been illustrated by the earlier reflections on Small Loan. If a medical emergency arises, it might well be rational to miss a payment on the consumer loan, and yet the fact that the payment is due continues to have a residual (if admittedly elusive) deontic character. But the suggestion under consideration seems equally problematic with regard to the aspirational side of the contrast that I have been gesturing toward.

---

[5] For this suggestion, see Gert (2005). A similar approach is taken by Patricia S. Greenspan in her recent work on reasons and morality (e.g. 2005 and 2007). The latter paper develops her position in a direction that converges to some extent on the position I shall eventually defend, tracing normative requirements to criticisms that are relational, insofar as they are grounded specifically in the standpoint of another agent.

Aspirational considerations, such as the attractions of the classic film in Movie, may well be considerations that we have a certain latitude to ignore. But this idea cannot plausibly be fleshed out in terms of the notion of rational criticism, for the simple reason that we often *are* irrational insofar as we fail to act on aspirational considerations of this kind. In Movie as I have described it, for instance, the agent who acknowledges the force of the argument in favour of seeing *Rocco and His Brothers* may well be subject to regret if they fail to act in accordance with that argument. The natural expression of this regret will be the thought that they have done something stupid or squandered a rare opportunity, and in the present context thoughts of this kind amount to acknowledgements of one's own irrationality. To deny that aspirational reasons ground rational criticism in this way, it seems to me, is in effect to deprive them of normative force. They become considerations that render options eligible for agents to pursue, but without really counting in favour of such pursuit in the perspective of practical deliberation.[6] If we want to hold onto this dimension of aspirational considerations, and with it the idea that they are a species of reason for action, then we need to allow that a failure to comply with aspirational considerations can ground rational criticism of the agent.[7]

Granting this point, however, it might be suggested that the considerations at issue in Movie do not exhibit deontic structure only because they are not compelling enough. They are (by hypothesis) conclusive under the circumstances described; but as presented, the case is something of a close call, with reasons on the other side that are also not negligible, and that would indeed render intelligible the decision to stay home and read the novel rather than go to the film. If we vary the case, however, then the same features that speak in favour of the movie option might appear to acquire the character that I have attributed to deontic reasons. Suppose, for instance, that there is virtually nothing to be said for the alternative of staying home:

---

[6] This conclusion is affirmed explicitly by Greenspan (2005: 391–2), who denies the normativity of the kind of reasons I have called aspirational.

[7] One might, I suppose, attempt to distinguish between two different kinds of normativity in this connection, holding that some reasons are such as to render options eligible for pursuit, while others count positively in favor of such pursuit by the agent. But this sounds forced to my ear: ordinarily options are rendered eligible for pursuit by the fact that there is something to be said in favor of such pursuit, perhaps because it would be valuable along some dimension or other. Furthermore, to distinguish in this way between two different kinds of normativity would threaten a problematic bifurcation of practical reason, of the kind I discuss in section 1 of this chapter.

the novel you have been reading is both lousy and a bore, your neighbors are having a boisterous party with music that drives you crazy, and anyway you are strongly in the mood to get out of the house.[8] Under these altered circumstances, the attractions of going out to see the Visconti film appear much more compelling. They *dominate* the other main option, to a degree that makes it natural to say that you lack discretion to ignore or to discount them in the situation at hand. (To fail to act on the reasons in favour of the movie option, under these circumstances, would be not merely irrational but virtually unintelligible, and if this is the cost of ignoring or discounting them then these strategies are ones we lack discretion to go in for.) If lack of discretion is in turn criterial for deontic structure, then we would appear to have normative reasons that exhibit this feature in the revised Movie case.

Of course, the considerations that speak in favour of seeing the Visconti movie are of a kind that do not *routinely* dominate competing reasons in this way. They are dominant under the revised circumstances just described, but in many other deliberative situations they would easily be outweighed by reasons on the other side. For instance, the admitted attractions of seeing the movie would hardly be conclusive—never mind dominant—if it were showing on an evening when you have promised to attend your nephew's performance in the school play, or when there is work that needs to be done on a paper you are writing if you are to meet an imminent deadline. This feature of the reasons in question would make it inappropriate to structure your deliberations in such a way that they function as exclusionary considerations, regularly silencing potential competitors that would otherwise have significance for your deliberations about what to do. Perhaps this is what makes us reluctant to classify the attractions of the movie as deontic in character, despite the fact that we sometimes lack discretion to ignore or discount them in deliberation.

If this is the crux, however, then we can easily imagine other kinds of considerations that routinely function as the attractions of the Visconti film do in the revised Movie case, dominating the reasons on the other side with which they might potentially come into conflict. Consider, in this connection, the reasons that stem from our deepest personal projects and ambitions, or considerations related to our health and survival. As typically understood, these are reasons whose importance is such that they dominate potential

---

[8] I am indebted to Sharon Street for suggesting this variation.

competitors across a wide range and variety of deliberative contexts, determining decisively what we have most reason to do in those contexts. Insofar as this is the case, it might seem that the reasons in question are ones that we regularly lack discretion to ignore or to discount in deliberation; this in turn would make it fitting to allow them to function as exclusionary reasons, of the kind that are routinely insulated from competition in reflection about what to do. Deontic structure, as I have been calling it, would on this account reduce to a kind of deliberative importance.

I am happy to concede that normative considerations that are important in this way have the character of requirements, ones that we lack discretion to ignore or discount in our deliberations about action. Furthermore, since friendship is among the things that have this kind of importance for most people, the account on offer might explain our sense that the reasons at issue in Distraught Friend have the character of requirements. The difference between this case and the original Movie, we could say, is the difference between considerations that routinely dominate the reasons with which they might potentially compete, and considerations that, in the case at hand, outweigh by a fairly close margin the reasons on the other side. Aspirational normativity turns into deontic structure, on this picture, once it crosses a threshold of sufficient systematic importance.

But what about Small Loan? This, by hypothesis, is not a case in which the normative factors at issue are presumptively important in relation to other kinds of normative consideration. And yet, I maintain, it seems to us that we lack discretion to ignore or discount the reasons in this case too, in a way that makes it natural to think of them as requirements. (Thus we speak of contractual commitments of this kind as obligations, referring e.g. to a person's 'financial obligations'.) This suggests that there can be different explanations for the phenomenon of lack of deliberative discretion, and correspondingly different senses in which normative considerations can be said to take on the character of requirements. I want to explore the question of what this further sense might amount to. Doing so, I conjecture, may eventually reveal something else that is going on in a case such as Distraught Friend, opening our eyes to a way in which considerations can be deontically significant that is potentially independent from questions about deliberative importance.

One reason in particular for pursuing this line of enquiry is the following. On the account currently under consideration, normative reasons are considerations that we lack discretion to discount or ignore when they systematically dominate the other reasons with which they might potentially come into conflict. A reason could satisfy this condition, however, without being dominant in all conceivable conflict situations, and in fact the kinds of reasons that are routinely dominant in this way sometimes do not dominate their competitors. This can happen, for instance, when they end up conflicting with each other, as in a case in which the demands of a personal project interfere with the things that need to be done within an important personal relationship. A situation of this kind will have the character of a hard choice, precisely because it involves a clash of normative considerations that are in the nature of requirements. This conclusion will not be available to us, however, if we think of deontic normativity simply in terms of the notion of rational dominance, for it is precisely characteristic of a hard choice that neither of the alternatives at issue dominates the other. Something else must be at issue in cases of this kind, something that leads us to think of the normative considerations in conflict as requirements despite the fact that, under the circumstances, they are not rationally dominant in relation to the other factors that are at issue.

Practical conflict of this kind is a complicated phenomenon, and I cannot hope to provide a comprehensive treatment of it within the scope of this essay.[9] But some light might be shed on the phenomenon if we can get clear about the kind of deontic structure apparently at issue in Small Loan, in which there seem to be normative requirements whose standing as such is independent from questions of systematic rational dominance. One thing that is noteworthy about the kind of normativity exhibited by this case is that the considerations at issue enter the deliberative field from the start, as it were, in the modality of requirements. Their having this standing does not depend on the relation that ends up holding between them and their potential competitors in the situation at hand. Rather, even before considering what other reasons and values might be in play, they present themselves to us in an insistent voice, as considerations that we lack leeway to disregard. Their deontic standing seems not only independent from issues about importance, but also endemic. Why these reasons should have this

---

[9] One implication of the account I shall eventually offer is that the normative considerations involved in the most serious practical conflicts should be thought of as having a relational aspect (which might include, in the case of personal projects, something in the way of an obligation to one's future self to be true to the project undertaken). But I will not be able to develop this suggestion here.

character is something that we have not yet succeeded in explaining; but if their deontic appearance can be made sense of, we would thereby have identified a different way in which reasons might be said to qualify as requirements.

In what follows I shall adopt a more restrictive terminology, using the expression deontic structure to pick out the elusive kind of normativity that seems to be at issue in Small Loan. My suggestion will be that this distinctive kind of normativity, once we see what it involves, will also turn out to play a role in Distraught Friend, contributing something important to our sense that the reasons in that case are in the nature of requirements. This in turn will have ramifications for our understanding of the special character of the reasons at the centre of morality.

3. Relational normativity

The approaches to deontic structure considered in the preceding section have one striking feature in common. They are all attempts to distinguish between different kinds of normative force by attending solely to the deliberative perspective of a single agent. I now want to suggest that this focus on the agent in isolation may be obscuring our view of an important potential source of normative requirements. To make sense of the kind of deontic structure that is distinct from the phenomenon of rational dominance, we need to consider the essentially interpersonal framework within which the individual's deliberation takes place.

Thus in Small Loan, there is a distinctive institutional context to the contractual agreement between the consumer and the creditor. If you fail to make a payment on the loan by the 5th of the month, then the contract itself, or the framework of consumer law within which it is embedded, will presumably specify that certain penalties are going to be imposed. You will incur special punitive fees, and perhaps become subject to a different and higher rate of interest on the balance of the loan; in addition your credit rating may suffer, in ways that will disadvantage you when you attempt to engage in other consumer transactions in the future. Nothing like this network of social sanctions is ordinarily present in a case such as Movie.

This suggests a sanction-based explanation of the difference between deontic and aspirational reasons. The comparative leeway we have to ignore or discount the considerations that speak in favour of seeing the Visconti film might be traced to the absence of clear institutional sanctions for doing so, of the sort that seem to be present in Small Loan. Furthermore, this difference in respect of discretion would seem to illuminate the distinctive role that deontic reasons typically play within practical deliberation. The fact that financial sanctions would attend a failure to make a payment on one's loan, for instance, makes it reasonable to structure one's deliberations so that other consumer pleasures that might be purchased with the same resources do not even enter into one's calculations, as considerations to be weighed against the advantages of making the payment. Lack of discretion, interpreted in this way, thus promises to explain the characteristic role of deontic reasons within practical deliberation.

At the same time, lack of discretion, on this account of it, is not simply identical with these structural features of practical reflection; the sanction-based account thus leaves room for the possibility that reasons might be deontic in nature even when they are not conclusive in relation to the output of deliberation. Consider, again, the variant of Small Loan that involves a medical emergency, in which it would be best on the whole to forego the monthly payment on your consumer loan. Insofar as the institutional sanctions remain in place, we would not say that you had discretion to ignore or to discount the fact that the payment was due in deliberating about action. As long as the loan agreement remains in force, failure to make the specified payment by the 5th of the month will incur the sorts of penalties already mentioned, and this in turn gives a sense to the idea that you lack discretion to neglect the terms of the loan in deliberation. By contrast, in Movie we have a reason that is conclusive, on the output side, but that precisely leaves you with discretion to ignore its claims, insofar as no similar network of sanctioning responses is in place.

Attention to the context of deliberation thus suggests a new account of the elusive normative distinction that has been our quarry in this chapter. The explanation offered so far, however, still seems inadequate in important respects. Most significantly, it ties deontic force too closely to the literal application of sanctions. Thus, the credit institution in Small Loan might decide, in its mysterious wisdom, not to impose the prescribed financial penalties when you fail to make your monthly payment. Perhaps they send you a letter reminding you of your financial obligation, but announcing that they will waive the penalty for this first infraction if payment is received in the next five days. In this situation it seems to me that their action does not retroactively nullify the obligation you were under to make a timely payment, or modify its original normative force. Yet if deontic structure were understood strictly in terms of the application of penalties and sanctions, this is what we would have to say. At the time, you may have taken yourself to lack discretion to make your payment, but as it happens you were mistaken about the matter, since the anticipated penalties were not in fact imposed.

Furthermore, aspirational reasons are not turned into deontic ones simply through the imposition of arbitrary sanctions or penalties in the event of noncompliance. In Movie, for instance, an acquaintance of yours might issue a credible threat to post an embarrassing picture of you to their Facebook wall if you fail to take advantage of the opportunity to see the Visconti film. This odd intervention into your deliberative space would plausibly alter the normative situation in some way or other, adding (perhaps) a new reason to see the movie that you did not have before. But it would not transform your aspirational reason into a deontic one, making it the case that you now lack discretion to act on the reason to see the film. The idea of discretion that we are trying to pin down thus cannot be interpreted simply in terms of freedom from social sanctions or penalties.

To see how we might improve on the preceding account, let us return to the case of Small Loan. The initial suggestion is that you lack discretion to ignore the reason to repay your creditor, insofar as failure to make a payment will eventuate in certain sanctions or penalties. But what if the bank decides to waive the prescribed penalty in a given case? Even if it makes this decision, it remains true that the bank was legally *entitled* to impose a penalty on you for nonpayment. Your reason for payment is not a free-standing normative consideration, but part of a nexus linking you and your creditor. Your creditor has a claim against you for payment, and the fact that it has this claim is constitutively connected to the fact that you have a reason to make the payment; you would not have the same reason to pay the instalment if the creditor were not also entitled to the payment. It is further characteristic of the normative relations that are in play here that your obligation to pay is specifically an obligation to the creditor, who—as I have said—has a claim *against you* for payment. If you fail to act on your reason, there is a sense, fixed by the conventions of contract law, in which you may be said to have injured or wronged the creditor, in a way that you will not have injured or wronged an uninvolved third party. Your reason in this case is thus grounded in legal principles that structure your relationship with your creditor, specifying corresponding claims or entitlements to performance on the creditor's part.

It is the role of reasons in structuring relations of this kind, I now want to suggest, that is the key to understanding the elusive dimension of deontic normativity that we are after. Reasons exhibit deontic structure when they are constitutively implicated in complexes of relational (or 'bipolar') normativity.[10] Thus in Small Loan it is the fact that you have entered into a valid consumer contract that gives you reason to make the payment; but this very same fact gives your creditor a special claim against you that payment be made. This normative complex remains intact even if your creditor should decide, for whatever reason, to forego the penalty that would ordinarily be imposed in the event of failure to perform. A decision of this kind would amount to the renunciation by the credit institution of something that they were entitled to, as a matter of contract law, and it is this normative relation between you and the bank that gives content to the vague idea that you lack discretion to ignore your reason in this case. Even if that reason should be outweighed by competing normative considerations (as in the variant of Small Loan involving a medical emergency), it remains the case that payment is due to your creditor, and this is reflected in the fact that you will injure or wrong them through your failure to pay, leaving undischarged a legal obligation you owe specifically to them.

In Movie, by contrast, relational normative structures of this kind are not in play. Your reason in this case is provided by the value of seeing *Rocco and His Brothers* on a big screen, where this is connected to the aesthetic pleasure of experiencing the film under excellent viewing conditions, and to the intellectual and emotional interest of the various things that contribute to its cinematic quality (the cinematography, performances, atmosphere and mood, and so on). Values of these kinds make it the case that going to the

---

[10] On 'bipolar' normativity, see Thompson (2004); also relevant is Darwall (2006). I have profited from both Thompson's and Darwall's writings on this general topic, though I disagree with their interpretations of what I call relational normativity in various respects. (Darwall's second-personal reasons, for instance, seem to me to run together a relational conception of normativity such as I have described, and a distinct voluntarist conception of reasons as deriving from authoritative commands; see Wallace 2007.)

film is the option you have most reason to choose under the circumstances, where it is a question of what would make for a rewarding break from your daily routine at the office. But these same considerations do not ground claims on the part of other agents to performance of the valuable action. The cinematic qualities that make going to the film the best option under the circumstances do not also make it the case that others are entitled to have you choose that option, nor would a failure on your part to do so wrong or injure anyone else in particular. This remains the case even in the variant of Movie in which the reasons in favour of seeing the Visconti film are postulated to dominate the deliberative field, insofar as there is nothing significant to be said on the other side. Nor is the situation altered by the supposition that an acquaintance of yours has taken a spectator's interest in your cinematic education, or bizarrely threatened to douse you with water if you fail to take advantage of your opportunity to see the movie under such favourable viewing conditions. Under these circumstances we would not say that your acquaintance is entitled to performance on your part, or vulnerable to being wronged specifically by you in case you decide not to see the film; your reason for seeing the film does not implicate you in a normative nexus with your acquaintance, however interested they may be in your exposure to classics of the genre. This in turn gives a distinctive content to the idea that you have discretion to ignore the reason at issue in this case, of a kind you lack in Small Loan. Your discretion consists in the fact that failure to act on the reason will not itself injure or wrong another person, depriving them of something that is theirs as a matter of right or entitlement.

But what exactly is it for a nexus of this kind to obtain, such that certain actions that are open to you would count as things that wrong or injure another party? The intuitive idea would seem to be that the other party would be in a privileged position to complain or object if you choose the options in question. In the legal case we have been considering, the 'complaint' would presumably take the form of the imposition of a financial penalty by the credit institution, and the idea that they are in a 'privileged position' to react in this way is given content by the framework of consumer law, which authorizes or entitles the institution to impose the penalties at issue in the event of nonpayment. So we have the idea of a response that can be said to be expressive of a complaint, together with the idea that the institution is entitled to adopt such a response. These ideas alone, however, do not quite capture the suggestion that there is a nexus linking the creditor specifically to the consumer. In the United States, for instance, creditors may be 'entitled' to impose punitive interest rates on consumers who default even on loans taken out with other credit institutions, insofar as such actions affect the consumer's credit rating. And yet we would not think that the act of default itself constituted a wrong or an injury in any sense to the parties who are thus legally authorized to impose the penalties. The missing element, it would seem, is the further idea that the very considerations that give the consumer reason to pay the original loan should *themselves* give certain parties a privileged basis for complaint. In the case at issue, of course, this link is effected through the contract linking the consumer and the original creditor; it is the fact that you have signed such an agreement that 'obligates' you (as we say) to keep its terms, and that same fact grounds the credit institution's entitlement to impose penalties in the event of default.

The case of financial obligation, however, has certain artificial features, which make it of dubious value as a general paradigm for understanding deontic structure. For one thing, there are not many situations in which our sense that we have been wronged or injured by someone will connect with an entitlement to complain through the imposition of a financial penalty. For another, the entitlements and reasons that are at issue here are defined largely through legal institutions and arrangements, in ways that lack application to many ordinary interactions between individuals. If relational normativity is to be helpful in understanding the deontic character of ordinary reasons (both within and outside morality), then we will need a less artificial way of understanding the key elements that it involves.

At this point, I would suggest that we consider in more detail the structure of a case such as Distraught Friend. Within the context of a genuine friendship, the fact that one's friend is in a bad way may be counted as a normative reason to help out if one can. It is constitutive of friendship, we might say, that friends have special reasons of this kind to attend to each other's needs and interests (cf. Kolodny 2003). To the extent this is the case, we cannot grant that someone has an obligation of friendship to provide assistance, but question whether that obligation counts as a genuine reason for action. It is built into the idea of friendship that friends have normative reasons to help each other out, so that the fact that my friend is in a bad way itself counts in favour of my doing what I can to relieve the friend's distress.

Reasons of this kind, however, are not merely free-standing normative considerations. Rather they are parts of relational normative structures, analogous to the contractual glue that links creditor and debtor in Small Loan. It is not exactly that your friend has a right or entitlement to your assistance in a time of need; this legalistic language seems inappropriate to the intimate context that is constituted by a relationship between friends. But the friend does have a kind of claim on you to attend to their interests and crises, and a special vulnerability to being injured or wronged if you should fail to take these considerations into proper account in deliberating about what to do. The friendship that grounds your special reason to look out for the needs and interests of your friend equally grounds an expectation or demand on the part of the friend that you will be ready to provide aid and comfort when you can, and be willing to put up with some inconvenience when you are in a privileged position to help them out of a jam.

These connected reasons and claims in turn give a content to the idea that your friend has a special basis for complaint in the event you neglect their needs. Thus your failure to act on your reason to help your friend will give the friend a reason to adjust their attitudes toward you, of a kind that is not shared by uninvolved third parties. Only your friend is in a position to resent what you have done, or to experience feelings of personal disappointment or betrayal. This is because only a person who stands in a friendship relationship to you has the special claim to consideration and vulnerability to injury that is partly constitutive of friendship. The complaint that is at issue in this context will take the form of vulnerability to the kind of reactive sentiments that constitute relations of accountability. In general—or so I (1994) have elsewhere maintained—we hold people accountable when we hold them to expectations or demands, in a way that is connected essentially to reactive sentiments. But within the class of reactive emotions it seems that resentment has a special role to play in contexts of relational normativity. The natural thought is that only those who have themselves been wronged or injured normatively are entitled to react with this particular sentiment; it is not merely a reactive sentiment, but an essentially relational one. Such relational sentiments might accordingly be understood as the form of complaint that those who stand in a nexus of interpersonal normativity are in a privileged position to lodge.

Distraught Friend thus provides an attractive general model for understanding the kind of relational normativity that is also at issue in the legal context of Small Loan, and that contributes to our sense that the reasons in that case are in the nature of requirements. The basis for the nexus of reasons and claims in Distraught Friend, and the analogue of the contractual agreement in the legal case, is the value of a relationship of the kind that here obtains. It is this value that links your reason to respond to the crisis of your friend with the friend's expectation or demand that you should be willing to help out when they are in need. That expectation in turn involves a vulnerability to resentment on the part of the friend in the event that your reason to help should be neglected or ignored, giving content to the idea that the friend has a special claim against you to assistance.

If this is on the right lines, however, then the features I have identified may be part of what gives the reasons involved in Distraught Friend the character of requirements. We have in this case the kind of deontic structure that is implicit in situations of relational normativity, where a failure to acknowledge or act on your reasons will itself change your normative relation to someone else, and in that sense count as something that you lack discretion to do. We are inclined to suppose that people are subject to normative requirements to be loyal to their friends insofar as friendship is a source of especially important reasons, ones that weigh heavily across a wide range of deliberative contexts. There is no doubt something right in this idea, and it presumably contributes to our sense that these reasons are peculiarly insistent ones. But it does not by itself yield a complete account of the deontic character of the reasons at the core of friendship. A further and distinct contributing factor is the relational character of the normative considerations involved in a case such as Distraught Friend. The implication of your reason in a structure of this kind helps to give it the character of an obligation, a character that is very different from the free-standing forms of aspirational normativity at issue in a case such as Movie (in any of its variants). It means that, quite independently from considerations of systematic importance, there is a definite sense in which you lack discretion to ignore or discount the reasons at the core of friendship. This makes it fitting that you should ordinarily structure your deliberations in such a way that the claims of your friend function as Razian exclusionary reasons. Those claims enter practical reflection from the start as considerations that you lack leeway to disregard, and this makes sense in light of their imbeddedness within structures of relational normativity.

The implications of this for morality are significant. In Distraught Friend we are already very close to having a set of deontically-structured reasons that are moral in nature. The resentment that your friend would feel if you let them down belongs to a class of sentiments that we commonly think of as moral; by the same token, the wrong you would do to a friend whose plea for help you deliberately neglected is at least very similar in character to the actions that incur moral criticism and censure. The question is, can the account of deontic structure that we have extracted from this case be extended to the whole domain of morality, to yield a comprehensive framework for thinking about the deontic nature of the reasons that morality provides? That is the issue to which I now turn.

4. Two conceptions of morality

Moral philosophy in the English-language tradition has historically gravitated toward a consequentialist understanding of morality, treating moral rightness as the property of maximizing the impartial good. According to this approach, that action (or policy, institution, legislative determination, etc.) is morally right whose consequences would be best, by contrast with the consequences of the other actions (policies, institutions, legislative determinations, etc.) that are available in the situation. Consequences are here understood to include everything about the world that would be brought into existence if the actions under assessment were performed (including not only the distinct effects that the performance of the actions would cause to occur, but also the fact that the actions themselves are performed). And the value of the consequences is to be assessed from a suitably impartial point of view, taking into account the interests of all persons (and other sentient creatures) who would be affected by the actions under assessment, and treating equally the satisfactions of each of those persons (and other sentient creatures).

The advantages of this general approach to morality are both powerful and familiar. Among the most important of these advantages is that the approach promises to shed light on the normative significance of morality. Thus we might suppose that normative reasons are in general grounded in facts about value, in accordance with a basically teleological schema. Intrinsic value, on this way of thinking, inheres fundamentally in states of affairs, which may be ranked as better or worse in a way that reflects their overall comparative value, taking everything into account. Reasons may then be derived from values, insofar as various of the actions open to agents stand in a productive relation to the states of affairs that are bearers of intrinsic value. According to this teleological schema, what fundamentally recommends or speaks in favour of one's doing X is the fact that X-ing would bring about a valuable state of affairs. And one has most reason to do that action, from among the alternatives that are available, that would produce the best state of affairs overall, taking everything into account.[11]

If we assume that normativity has an essentially teleological structure of this kind, then the consequentialist approach to morality will not leave it an open question whether agents have reason to care about acting rightly. Actions will be morally right insofar as they produce the best consequences, from an impartial point of view, and according to the teleological conception of normativity this is already sufficient to establish that moral rightness is normatively significant. The consequentialist account of rightness thus aligns with the teleological conception of normativity, in a way that promises to make sense of the idea that morality is a distinctively normative domain. Moreover, a conception of normativity along these teleological lines seems independently attractive, defining a straightforward general framework for understanding reasons for action and their relation to values. Something like this framework seems implicit, for instance, in the maximizing conception of practical rationality that has found broad acceptance in modern economics and the social sciences. The fact that consequentialism makes moral reasons intelligible in terms of this influential conception of normativity has thus contributed to its philosophical appeal (cf. Scheffler 1998).

If the attractions of this general approach are familiar, however, its problems are as well. Most significant for my purposes is a difficulty that arises when we think about the distinctive character of moral reasons, as grounds of rational requirements on action. It has been an assumption of this chapter that the landscape of normative reasons is multiply diverse. Above all, there is a difference in the ways in which normative considerations impinge

---

[11] We might refer to this teleological conception as the Moorean schema, after the view about what we ought to do presented G. E. Moore's *Principia Ethica* (1903).

on deliberation, a difference that applies within both the moral and the non-moral domains, which I expressed as a contrast between aspirational and deontic normativity. The basic idea is that we have a certain latitude to ignore or discount aspirational reasons, of a kind we do not have when it comes to reasons that exhibit deontic structure. But this distinction seems to disappear on the teleological approach to normativity. If the fundamental normative relation is the productive relation that our potential actions stand in to valuable states of affairs, then it looks as if there is no room for differentiating between aspirational and deontic normativity. All reasons will derive from the value of states of affairs, via the role of our agency in bringing those states of affairs into existence. But this general schema seems fundamentally inimical to a distinction between different styles of normative relation.

The problem here is not that the teleological conception of normativity on which consequentialism relies cannot make any sense of the idea of a requirement. We may say, if we wish, that morality represents a set of normative requirements, insofar as agents are rationally required to maximize the good. But the same could apparently be said about any action that we have most reason to perform, on the teleological approach. If action X would produce the best consequences, taking everything into account, then X is the action the agent is required to perform. Conversely, we may allow that agents can have reasons for performing actions whose consequences would not be optimal on the whole, insofar as those consequences are valuable along some dimension or other. But these reasons will not be in the way of normative considerations that the agent has discretion either to act on or to ignore. To the extent that the action in question is non-optimal, it is something that the agent is rationally required not to perform. The result is that the distinction between aspirational and deontic normativity disappears from view.

A different way to make the same point is to note that consequentialism leaves no room for the category of the supererogatory: actions that we have some moral reason to perform, but that are not strictly obligatory. This is one of the familiar objections to consequentialism to which I referred above, and it brings out the difficulty that the view faces when it comes to making sense of the notion of moral obligation.[12] A second familiar

---

[12] Committed consequentialists could of course dig in their heels at this point, saying so much the worse for the notion of obligation (and the associated categories of the morally right, the permissible, and

objection, however, points the way to the solution. The objection is that consequentialism leaves it a mystery why there should be a presumptive connection between wrongness and reactions of moral opprobrium on the part of other people. Whether we have moral reason to blame someone who fails to maximize the good is a completely contingent matter, depending on whether our response is itself one whose consequences would be optimific (by comparison with the alternatives open to us). But ordinarily we think that the wrongness of an action is itself a basis for opprobrium toward the agent on the part of other people. This strongly suggests that morality has an inherently relational aspect, involving structures of reciprocal obligations and claims of precisely the kind that we saw to be constitutive of deontic structure in the preceding section. A philosophical account of morality will have to do justice to this relational aspect, as consequentialism fails to do, if it is to make sense of the connection between moral wrongs and our reactions to them. But this in turn should help us to understand the normative status of moral considerations, as grounds of genuine obligation.

The best way to develop a relational alternative to consequentialism, I believe, is to interpret moral rightness essentially by reference to a distinctive ideal of human relationship. There are different vocabularies available for talking about the kind of ideal that is suited to play this foundational role in morality; we might variously refer to it as the relationship of mutual regard, or mutual recognition, or mutual consideration and concern. The basic idea would be that morality fundamentally sets the terms for valuable relationships of this kind. Thus actions would be morally right if their performance is necessary for one to stand in relations of mutual recognition with all of one's fellow agents, and morally wrong if doing them would render one unable to enter into relationships of this kind with some other person. Actions might further be said to be morally permissible when their performance is neither right nor wrong in this sense, but compatible with maintaining relationships of the relevant kind with all other agents.

Among modern moral theories it is contractualism, in the version developed by T. M. Scanlon (1998), that perhaps most clearly illustrates the

---

the supererogatory); see, e.g., Norcross (2006). But I take it to be an important independent constraint on an account of morality that it should make sense of these deontic notions.

relational conception.[13] Scanlon holds that the demands of morality are defined by principles for the general regulation of behaviour that no one could reasonably reject, as a common basis for social life. Actions are morally right if they are required by such principles, wrong if such principles prohibit them, and permissible if their performance is neither required nor ruled out by the principles. According to this conception, morality is the condition for the possibility of a certain kind of relationship with other persons, a relationship in which one is able to justify oneself specifically to each of the people potentially affected by what one does. It is plausible to suppose that this capacity to justify one's actions to those affected by them, on grounds that it would be unreasonable for the affected persons to reject, is the condition that is crucially involved in relationships of mutual recognition and regard, and Scanlon himself appeals to the value of such relationships as providing the key to understanding the reason-giving force of morality (Scanlon 1998: ch. 4). We show proper regard for others precisely insofar as we strive to comply with principles that would enable us to justify our actions to them, and the value of relating in this way to our fellows helps to explain the normative significance of the moral realm.[14]

To this it will be objected that the appeal to the value of relationships appears to presuppose the teleological conception of normativity, rather than representing an alternative to it. If our reasons for caring about moral rightness derive from the value of the forms of relationship that right action makes possible, then it seems that we are still thinking about the actions morality recommends as standing in a productive relationship to valuable states of affairs. This suggestion fails to do full justice, however, to the relational aspect of the contractualist view. The point is that the valuable relationships at the heart of morality do not merely ground reasons for the agent considered in isolation; they represent structures of essentially relational normativity,

---

[13] There are recent defences of rule-consequentialism that appeal to a similar conception of what morality is fundamentally about, and that might therefore also be capable of acknowledging the relational dimension of moral obligation. See, in particular, Hooker (2000) and Parfit (2011: vol. 1, chs. 15–17).

[14] This leaves open the possibility, of course, that the principles that enable us to justify ourselves to others have the content of rule consequentialism, being principles whose general acceptance would maximize the impartial good; see Parfit (2011) for this suggestion. In that case, however, rule consequentialism would be a theorem of contractualism, not an independent account of the nature of moral reasons. What gives us reason to comply with the consequentialist principle, in other words, would not simply be the fact that doing so maximizes the good, but the different fact that doing so enables us to relate to other people on a basis of mutual consideration.

which can be understood very much by analogy with the norms at the heart of friendship. As we saw in the preceding section, the value of friendship that gives us special reasons to attend to the needs and interests of our friends also gives our friends special reasons to expect that we will be willing to help and comfort them if we are in a position to do so in a time of need. Our friends are vulnerable to being wronged by us if we fail to act on our own reasons of friendship, and they have a privileged basis for complaint in such cases. These expectations and vulnerabilities in turn provide the normative scaffolding for the specifically relational reactive attitudes to which the parties involved in a friendship are characteristically subject (such as the disappointment and resentment our friends feel when we let them down).

Similarly, on the contractualist view morality too defines a structure of reciprocal normative reasons and claims. The very considerations that give me reason to care about doing the right thing—namely the valuable forms of relationship that I am thereby able to enter into with other people—equally ground corresponding claims and expectations on the part of those who are affected by what I do. What makes an action of mine morally wrong is the fact that it cannot be justified to someone affected by it on terms that that person would be unreasonable to reject. In a situation in which I do something morally wrong, the person adversely affected will have been wronged by me, and have a privileged basis for moral complaint, resentment, and so on, precisely insofar as I have acted with indifference to the value of relating to them on a basis of mutual recognition and regard.[15] The very principles that specify what I have moral reason to do, on this relational conception, equally serve to specify normative expectations and entitlements on the part of others. Those principles are thus implicated in a directed normative nexus very like the one that defines the reciprocal reasons and expectations constitutive of a relationship of friendship. This

---

[15] A challenge for this approach is to develop a relational account of so-called imperfect duties, such as the duty of mutual aid, which do not appear to be grounded in the claims of individuals. A promising way of responding to the challenge would be to understand these duties to be grounded in claims that are held by all of the individuals in a position to be assisted. Thus, if I fail to do anything to alleviate the basic needs of those who are worst off in the world, then everyone in that class has a privileged basis for objecting to my behaviour, and I might be said to have wronged all of them. This ground for complaint is removed if I live up to the duty of mutual aid (by donating a large portion of my income to Oxfam, say), even if my doing so improves the lives of only a small subset of the people whose interests are at stake. Their claim against me is not that I help them in particular, but that I do something to help people who are in their position.

is a way of thinking about the normative significance of morality that is quite unlike the teleological conception upon which consequentialist approaches rely.[16]

With this relational conception of morality in place, however, we are in an improved position to make sense of the distinctively deontic structure of morality. In particular, we can explain why agents lack the kind of discretion to discount or to ignore their moral reasons that is present in cases of merely aspirational normativity. The sense in which this discretion is lacking is precisely given by the reciprocal normative complexes in which our moral reasons are constitutively involved, on the relational conception. If I discount or neglect my moral reason not to harm someone, for example, I will not merely have fallen short relative to a free-standing ideal of individual rationality. Rather, my neglect of my moral reason will itself give the agent who is harmed a special ground for complaint, and a corresponding normative basis for the reactive sentiment of resentment (see again Wallace, 1994). I will not merely have acted wrongly, by the terms of a normative standard that applies to my own conduct, but wronged the person I have harmed, insofar as my action will not be justifiable to that person on grounds that it would be reasonable for the person to accept. Neglecting my moral reason, on this way of thinking, changes my normative relations to other people, in ways that in turn ground alterations in their attitudes toward me. Nothing like this same complex of normative relations is implicated when we neglect or discount merely aspirational reasons (such as those at issue in Movie). The relational conception of moral normativity thus helps us to make sense of the intuitive idea that moral reasons enter the deliberative field in a distinctive normative key, structuring our reflection in the peremptory style of obligations or demands. It is fitting that they should structure our deliberations in this style, precisely insofar as a failure to act on

---

[16] We might put this by saying that valuable relationships of mutual regard are possible only if the agents involved in them do not view their reasons in standard teleological terms, but instead take themselves to be implicated in structures of reciprocal normativity. The consequentialist might reply that even if this is true, it is the value of states of affairs that include relationships of this kind that ultimately grounds the reasons in question. This would be an application of the familiar strategy whereby a consequentialist justification is provided for dispositions, practices, relationships, etc. that preclude agents from deliberating in consequentialist terms. Compare Pettit and Smith (2004). I agree with Bernard Williams (1973) in finding these 'self-effacing' forms of consequentialist justification problematic. On the contractualist approach, at any rate, the relational conception of moral reasons sketched in the text should be understood as the most fundamental account of the nature and source of moral reasons, an account that is not susceptible to a further 'justification' in non-relational terms.

them would change our normative standing with other people, in ways that would ground relational reactive sentiments on their part.

This is, to be sure, only a first step toward understanding the deontic character of morality. I have so far merely situated one aspect of deontic normativity in the context of larger debates about the nature of morality; I have not yet done anything to defend the relational conception of morality that is well-suited to render this phenomenon intelligible.[17] But even if a relational conception could be defended, there would still be outstanding issues to address.[18] The relational account attributes to morality a source of deontic structure that is independent from questions about the systematic importance of moral reasons. I have maintained that we cannot arrive at a complete understanding of moral requirements if we think of them solely in terms of the notion of importance. Insofar as the source of deontic structure I have identified is indeed independent from questions of importance, however, the possibility arises that moral considerations might exhibit the kind of deontic structure I have identified without being of compelling weight or significance in comparison to other kinds of normative reason. If that were the case, then we would no doubt feel that our picture of morality as a domain of special normative requirements had not fully been vindicated.

Questions of importance will thus have to be addressed on their own terms to arrive at a complete account of the standing of morality as a set of normative requirements on action. If a relational approach to morality is to provide the framework for this kind of investigation, then presumably what will need to be established is that the moral values that are implicated in an interpersonal normative nexus are also especially significant ones, such as to be capable of competing with the important values around which we

---

[17] One important challenge is presented by the fact that the value of mutual recognition functions very differently from the values that figure in the kinds of personal relationships that I have taken to be exemplary of the general phenomenon of relational normativity. Friends and family members have claims against each other in virtue of standing in ongoing historical relationships to each other. But what we owe to people morally is not in the same way dependent on the quality of the relationships that we already stand in to them. For discussion of this disanalogy, see Wallace (2010 and 2011).

[18] A further issue that would need to be considered is the following. Even if the relational conception is plausible, it might not provide a complete account of the entire moral domain. Some moral reasons might well be thought of in terms of relational normativity, while others resist treatment in these terms, exhibiting features that require to be understood within an essentially teleological framework. 'Morality', as we commonly understand it, would in that event not be a unified normative domain, but rather a collection of radically diverse normative considerations. If my suggestions about deontic structure are correct, it would follow that only some parts of morality might turn out to exhibit this kind of structure.

otherwise orient our lives. The value of relationships of mutual recognition, in other words, will have to be shown to be important in something like the way the values are that structure our projects and personal relationships. This is a difficult and elusive undertaking, which is beyond the scope of the present chapter.[19] But I hope to have paved the way for it by identifying and elucidating an independent source for the deontic character of the reasons at the heart of morality.[20]

References

Broome, J. (2004) 'Reasons', in Wallace, et al. (2004: 28–55).
Dancy, J. (2004a) *Ethics Without Principles* (Oxford: Oxford University Press).
—— (2004b) 'Enticing Reasons', in Wallace et al. (2004: 91–118).
Darwall, S. (2006) *The Second-Person Standpoint* (Cambridge, MA: Harvard University Press).
Gert, J. (2005) 'A Functional Role Analysis of Reasons', *Philosophical Studies*, 124: 553–78.
Greenspan, P. (2005) 'Asymmetrical Practical Reasons', in M. Reicher and J. Marek (eds.), *Experience and Analysis: Proceedings of the 27th International Wittgenstein Symposium* (Vienna: oebv-hpt), 387–94.
—— (2007) 'Practical Reasons and Moral "Ought"', in R. Schafer-Landau (ed.), *Oxford Studies in Metaethics* 2 (Oxford: Oxford University Press), 172–94.
Hooker, B. (2000) *Ideal Code, Real World: A Rule-Consequentialist Theory of Morality* (Oxford: Oxford University Press).
Kolodny, N. (2003) 'Love as Valuing a Relationship', *Philosophical Review*, 112: 135–89.
Moore, G. E. (1903) *Principia Ethica* (Cambridge: Cambridge University Press).

---

[19] I offer some suggestions about how to approach this issue in Wallace (2004).

[20] Earlier versions of this chapter were presented at the University of Canterbury, Christchurch (Erskine Lecture); the University of Maryland (conference on practical reason); the University of Sheffield; Harvard University; the University of Frankfurt; Princeton University; UC San Diego; the University of Vienna (conference on reasons and rationality); Reed College; the Analytic Legal Philosophy Conference (keynote lecture); the University of Oxford (Winchester Lecture); and the University of Saskatchewan. I am very grateful to the audiences on all of these occasions for helpful discussion and critical feedback. I owe a special debt to Simon Clarke, Patricia Greenspan, Brad Hooker, Niko Kolodny, Konstantin Pollok, Andrew Reisner, and Sharon Street, all of whom took the trouble to write up their incisive questions and comments; conversations with Jonathan Dancy during a visit to Oxford were also particularly helpful. Work on the chapter was generously supported by a Research Award from the Alexander von Humboldt Foundation, and by an Erskine Fellowship from the University of Canterbury, Christchurch.

Norcross, A. (2006) 'Reasons without Demands: Rethinking Rightness', in J. Dreier (ed.), *Contemporary Debates in Moral Theory* (Oxford: Blackwell), 38–53.

Parfit, D. (2011) *On What Matters*, 2 vols. (Oxford: Oxford University Press).

Pettit, P. and Smith, M. (2004) 'The Truth in Deontology', in Wallace et al. (2004: 153–75).

Raz, J. (1990) *Practical Reason and Norms*, 2nd edn (Princeton: Princeton University Press).

Scanlon, T. M. (1998) *What We Owe to Each Other* (Cambridge, MA: Harvard University Press).

Scheffler, S. (1998) 'Agent-Centered Restrictions, Rationality, and the Virtues', in his *Consequentialism and its Critics* (Oxford: Oxford University Press), 243–60.

Thompson, M. (2004) 'What is it to Wrong Someone? A Puzzle about Justice', in Wallace et al. (2004: 333–84).

Wallace, R. J. (1994) *Responsibility and the Moral Sentiments* (Cambridge, MA: Harvard University Press).

—— (2004) 'The Rightness of Acts and the Goodness of Lives', in Wallace et al. (2004: 385–411).

—— (2007) 'Reasons, Relations, and Commands: Reflections on Darwall', *Ethics*, 118: 24–36.

—— (2010) 'Hypocrisy, Moral Address, and the Equal Standing of Persons', *Philosophy & Public Affairs*, 38: 307–41.

—— (2011) 'Dispassionate Opprobrium: On Blame and the Reactive Sentiments', in R. J. Wallace, R. Kumar, and S. Freeman (eds.), *Reasons and Recognition: Essays on the Philosophy of T. M. Scanlon* (New York: Oxford University Press), 348–72.

——, Pettit, P., Scheffler, S., and Smith, M. (eds.) (2004) *Reason and Value: Themes from the Moral Philosophy of Joseph Raz* (Oxford: Oxford University Press).

Williams, B. (1973) 'A Critique of Utilitarianism', in J. J. C. Smart and B. Williams, *Utilitarianism: For and Against* (Cambridge: Cambridge University Press), 77–150.

8

Morality and Principle

STEPHEN DARWALL

Jonathan Dancy is largely responsible for the recent vigorous discussion of the position known as 'moral particularism' (see Dancy 1993, 2004, 2009; Hooker and Little 2000; McKeever and Ridge 2005, 2006; Lance and Little 2006). In his original *Mind* article, Dancy (1983) dubbed the view he there defended 'ethical particularism', but his focus was squarely on particularism about morality. As Dancy's thought has developed since then, however, it has mainly been driven by considerations about normative reasons in general, rather than anything specifically about morality.

In *Ethics Without Principles*, for example, although Dancy again defines particularism as the position that 'moral thought and judgment' do not require 'moral principles', what does the major work in his argument is a general view about normative reasons he calls 'holism'. Holism, as Dancy (2004: 7) defines it, is the thesis that a consideration can be a normative reason for something in one case, while no reason at all, or even a reason against it, in another. Dancy's diagnosis is that 'errors of generalism' (denying moral particularism) 'can mostly be traced back to errors in the theory of reasons' (p. 15). So Dancy first tries to show that normative reasons are holistic generally and then argues that, since there is no reason to think that moral reasons are any different, they are likely to be holistic also. Moral particularism is then claimed to follow more or less directly.

Dancy's arguments for holism are convincing and his observations about the complex relations between normative reasons persuasive. Not every consideration that is relevant to there being reason to have some attitude, or the attitude's being justified or an attitude one ought to have, is relevant in the same way. *Normative reasons* are considerations that count in *favour* or against an attitude. But considerations can also *defeat* or *enable* normative reasons, and so affect what attitudes we have reason, or ought, to have without being normative reasons themselves. For example, something's looking red can be a reason to believe that it is red. When, however, it becomes apparent that it looks red because a red light is shining on it, there is no longer any reason to think it actually is red. The fact that a red light is shining on the object is not, however, a reason to believe that the object is not red, or even not to believe that it is red, that is, a reason that weighs against and outweighs the earlier reason. It rather defeats the earlier fact's claim to be a reason. It shows that the fact that the object looks red is not, in fact, any reason to think it is red, and so affects what one should believe in a different way.

It is not difficult to find similar cases with normative reasons for action. If I promise to peel you a grape, that gives me a reason do so. Suppose that it is the only reason in the circumstances and therefore that peeling you a grape is what I ought overall to do. If you release me from my promise, then I no longer have reason to do what I promised. It is no longer true that peeling a grape is what I ought to do. But, usually anyway, that is not because your releasing me counts against my peeling you a grape, although there might be circumstances in which it would. It is rather because it defeats the earlier reason. It makes it the case that what was a reason in favour of an action is one no longer.

The existence of defeaters and enablers is sufficient to establish holism, as Dancy understands it. The fact that something looks red is sometimes, but not always, a reason to believe that it is red. The fact that one promised to do something is sometimes, but not always, a reason to do what one promised. Defeaters (and enablers) affect what attitude there is all things considered reason for one to have, but not by favouring or disfavouring attitudes or actions themselves. They are not themselves normative reasons, but help determine whether other considerations are.

Dancy canvasses other possibilities also. A fact might *intensify* a normative reason—give it more weight—without being itself a reason. Dancy gives the following example. The fact that someone needs help that I am in a position to give is a reason for me to help her. But the fact that I am the only person who can help seems to be, in itself, not so much an (additional) reason to help as something that intensifies the weight of the first reason (2004: 41). Likewise, if I am but one of a billion who can help, this seems not to be a reason not to help, but something that *attenuates* the weight of the reason to help consisting in the fact that someone needs help that I can give (p. 42).

Let us assume, therefore, that holism holds true in the theory of reasons. How does this bear on moral particularism? I believe we should also grant Dancy that holism holds true in the theory of *moral reasons* also, that is, reasons that favour or disfavour actions from the moral point of view and so bear on what one *morally ought* to do in the sense of being morally choice-worthy or best supported by moral reasons.[1] After all, all the examples of normative reasons for acting we have been considering seem to be moral reasons (p. 37).

It turns out, however, that, as Sean McKeever and Michael Ridge (2005, 2006) have argued, holism about moral reasons does not establish moral particularism. Dancy acknowledges this, moreover. We can see why with an example Dancy himself gives, one he takes to be in the spirit of McKeever and Ridge's point. That one's promise was extracted under duress, like being released from one's promise, can defeat the normative reason to do something that would otherwise be provided by the fact of one's promise. But it is entirely consistent with that, nonetheless, that the following general moral principle exists (Dancy calls it 'P1'): 'If you have promised, then you morally ought to do the promised act, unless your promise was given under duress' (Dancy 2004: 81). So holism about reasons—even holism about moral reasons—cannot entail moral particularism. As McKeever and Ridge point out, indeed, a general principle like P1 actually *presupposes* holism, as Dancy defines it. So moral reasons being holistic in Dancy's sense can hardly be incompatible with moral generalism.

P1 is no doubt too simple as it stands. Any plausible general principle about keeping promises would have to be much more complicated, including, for example, the absence of other defeaters such as having been released from one's promise. Taken by itself, however, holism in the theory of reasons, even of moral reasons, cannot establish that some such plausible generalist principles do not exist, as Dancy himself acknowledges (pp. 81–2).

Despite this, Dancy claims that an 'indirect' argument from holism to moral particularism can nonetheless be given. He grants that there are some areas, like mathematics, where we plausibly suppose that universal general principles hold despite the fact that there is a kind of holism there also:

---

[1] Or, as Dancy puts it, what one 'most morally ought' to do (2004: 31–7).

'dividing one number by another will not always yield a smaller number; sometimes it will, and sometimes it won't' (p. 82). But there is nothing, he claims, that could explain a similar supposition with respect to morality.

Now, as I have noted, Dancy defines 'particularism' and 'generalism' in such a way that they only concern moral principles, oughts, and reasons. But we can define other versions. A more general *normative particularism* would hold that the possibility of *normative* thought does not depend on the existence of general normative principles. *Normative generalism* would deny this, holding that normative principles are indeed necessary. And we might similarly define generalist and particularist positions within different specific normative domains.

Thus *epistemological generalism* would hold that the possibility of 'thought and judgment' about what there is reason to, or what one ought to, *believe* depends on the existence of general epistemic principles. And *epistemological particularism* would deny this. Similarly, *practical generalism* would hold that thinking or judging there to be things we have reason overall to *do*, and so ought overall to do, requires us to suppose that there exist general practical principles. And *practical particularism* would deny this. *Aesthetic generalism* would hold that aesthetic thought and judgement, say, that something has or lacks some aesthetic quality hence that there is reason, or that one ought, to have some aesthetic attitude toward that thing, requires us to think that there exist general aesthetic principles. *Aesthetic particularism* would deny this. And so on.

Now partly, I think, Dancy is relying on the fact that although his opponents deny moral particularism, they are much less likely to accept generalism about normative reasons across the board, that is, *normative generalism*, or generalism with respect to any practical reasons and oughts, *practical generalism*. He quotes Scanlon as saying that although principles have a 'significant role' in morality, there 'seems little work for principles to do' when it comes to thought and judgement about normative reasons generally (p. 132).

Dancy, however, denies that there is any relevant difference in this respect between morality and other normative domains. This is because he thinks that moral principles, were there any, would have to concern what we morally ought to do, or perhaps, what we morally ought most to do, in the sense mentioned earlier, namely, what moral reasons for action support, either *pro tanto* or all things considered. Moreover, he argues that oughts quite generally, and so moral oughts in particular, are better conceived in terms of normative reasons and moral reasons, respectively, than vice versa (p. 31). If what we morally ought to do is what the balance of moral reasons most favours, and if we have no need of principles to understand what it is for normative reasons in general or for moral reasons more specifically to favour an action, either *pro tanto* or all things considered, then why, he thinks, should we expect that principles are necessary for moral oughts? If moral oughts are no different from oughts of other kinds in their dependence on reasons, and principles are unnecessary for reasons, and therefore for oughts, of other kinds, wouldn't they also be unnecessary for moral oughts?

Dancy expresses some scepticism that the moral can relevantly be distinguished from the non-moral within the space of practical normative reasons (p. 132). If that were so, then moral particularism would simply follow, or perhaps be indistinguishable, from practical particularism. But Dancy's argument does not depend on this. We, might, for example, simply identify moral reasons by other-regarding content or through some characterization of the moral point of view, and that would not affect anything Dancy wants to say. He could still put his challenge in the following terms: if *oughtness* consists, quite generally, in the weight and force of normative reasons, and if principles are not required for the latter, then why should they be required *either* for oughts in general or for *moral* oughts more specifically? Even if moral oughts can be distinguished from oughts of other kinds by the content of, or point of view from which we accept, their supporting normative reasons, that wouldn't distinguish their normative character, weight, or force. If the normativity of the moral ought does not differ fundamentally from that of other oughts, and if principles are unnecessary for other oughts, then why should they be necessary for moral oughts?

My aim in what follows is to show that even if one were to concede every bit of Dancy's case for particularism deriving from the theory of reasons, including *almost* all of what he says about moral reasons and the moral ought, there would nonetheless remain a substantial case for generalism left standing that would have to be considered before particularism about morality could be established.[2] I shall argue, first, that Dancy's arguments leave

---

[2] I concede that 'morally ought' can be understood in terms of the weight of moral reasons, but I shall argue that moral obligation, moral duty, and moral wrong cannot. My argument will be that the latter

untouched a powerful rationale for thinking, as Scanlon says, that principles have a 'significant role' to play in morality. And second, I shall try to sketch that rationale, at least in broad outline. My conclusion will be that there is an important and promising line of thought leading to moral generalism that Dancy has failed to consider.

For purposes of my argument, we can simply stipulate that *normative particularism* and *practical particularism* are both true. So I shall assume that neither normative thought and judgement in general, nor thought about normative reasons for acting and so practical oughts more specifically, depend respectively upon *normative* principles in general or upon normative principles of *action* more specifically. And we can also stipulate that there is a *sense* of the moral 'ought', the one I take Dancy to have in mind, that may not require principles either.[3] This is the sense I mentioned before, namely, the one in which to say that someone morally ought to do something is to say that that action is supported by moral reasons, either *pro tanto* or overall, that is, that the action is morally *choiceworthy* in that sense.

My contention will be that conceding all of this does not yet touch anything a moral generalist should be, or, I think, that moral generalists primarily have been, concerned about. This is because the major rationale for being a generalist about morality is the thought that general principles, indeed general principles that can be assumed to be publicly formulable and available, are necessary for moral *obligations*. The concept of moral obligation has a special character that distinguishes it from that of what moral reasons favour or recommend, either *pro tanto* or overall. My argument will be that general principles are plausibly thought necessary in order for anything having this special character to exist, whether or not they are necessary for reasons and oughts generally, or for all *moral* reasons or oughts, more specifically.

---

have a special character and that there is reason to think that nothing having this character could exist without there being relevant general principles. If, as I shall argue, concepts with this special character, like that of moral obligation, are intrinsic to the concept of morality as we understand it, then moral particularism will not follow. It will also then be true that general principles are necessary for there to be moral reasons as well, since there can be no moral reasons without morality; moral obligations are necessary for that, and these cannot exist without general principles. If so, then though I can concede to Dancy that general principles might be unnecessary for *some* (non-obligating) moral reasons, they will nonetheless be necessary for moral obligations and therefore for there to be moral oughts and reasons at all.

[3] That is, as per the preceding note, its being the case that one morally ought to do *A* requires no general principle that in such and such circumstances, anyone morally ought to do *A*.

There are two main ideas underlying my approach. First, moral obligations are, as a conceptual matter, what we are morally responsible or *accountable* for doing. And second, when we hold people answerable for complying with moral demands, we have to assume that they can know that they are obligated, that they can regulate their conduct by this knowledge, *and* that this is all capable of being common public knowledge. I shall argue that this gives a role to publicly formulable principles in morality that principles need not have in other normative domains. Conditions like these seem to be no part whatsoever of the idea that a consideration is a reason for someone to do something. It seems to be enough that the consideration counts in favour of the action.

In this respect, morality, at least the part that concerns moral obligation, resembles law. Just as a connection to public reason and principle seem part of the very idea of law, so also, I shall argue, are these essential for moral obligation. We need not think, as we do with law, that moral obligations require the relevant public understandings actually to be in place, or that *de facto* attitudes and practices have the same power to constitute morality as they do to constitute law. Nonetheless, I shall argue, it is plausibly a constraint on moral obligation that the relevant public understandings at least be possible.

By contrast, it is clearly no part of the idea of normative reasons or oughts, whether moral or non-moral, that we are automatically answerable for complying with them. P's being a reason to do A just consists in p's counting in favour of A. And A's being something one ought to do, either *pro tanto* or overall, just consists in A's being supported by such reasons, either *pro tanto* or overall. Being answerable for doing A when p holds, if anyone *is* thus answerable, would seem to be an additional fact that is neither part of nor entailed by the simple fact that A is supported by the relevant reason, either *pro tanto* or overall. In many cases, in fact—for example, with garden-variety self-regarding reasons—we do not believe that people actually *are* answerable for complying with them. And in moral cases where the operative reasons support a moral obligation, the mere fact that moral reasons favour the choice, even overall, considered apart from the fact that they ground an action's being morally *obligatory*, neither involves nor entails answerability either.

1. Moral obligation as distinct from being favoured by moral reasons

Sometimes philosophers speak as though 'moral obligation' and 'moral duty' are simply synonyms for 'morally ought' in the sense of being an action moral reasons favour or favour most.[4] A moment's reflection is sufficient, however, to show that this is not so. By 'moral obligation' or 'moral duty', I mean here what we are morally *required* to do in the sense that failing so to act would be *morally wrong*. To see that being a moral obligation in this sense does not mean being favoured, or favoured most, by moral reasons, even by reasons that conclusively recommend the act from the moral point of view, all we need to notice is that whether there is such a thing as moral supererogation, that is an action's being 'beyond the call of duty', and something it would not be morally wrong to omit, is a substantive normative issue rather than a conceptual one.

Suppose someone puts forward the view that a certain action, say rescuing someone from a burning building, although it is conclusively recommended by moral reasons and clearly the morally best thing the agent could do, nonetheless is not, owing to the risks involved, morally obligatory or something it would be wrong for the agent to fail to attempt. The idea is not that the risks would be foolhardy for the agent to take, where this could constitute a moral reason that could weigh against trying to rescue the fire victim. Neither is the idea that the risks to the agent constitute an excuse for wrongly failing to attempt the rescue. Rather, the view is that the risks to the agent make an action, failing to rescue someone, that would otherwise be obligatory and wrong not to do, not wrong in this case. And this is so, even though the risks do not defeat the moral reasons for attempting to rescue the person. Were the person to enter the building and attempt the rescue, we might well regard her as a moral 'hero' in Urmson's sense, whether she was successful or not (Urmson 1958). But if she failed to do so, this would not be something she need excuse, since her failure would not have been wrong or the violation of a moral obligation.

Note also that the idea that the risks to the agent in this case defeat a moral obligation is not, or at least, not just, that it defeats a moral obligation *overall*

---

[4] Dancy's (2004: 31–7) discussion suggests this.

or all things considered. Rather, the thought is that the risks also defeat any *pro tanto* moral obligation that would otherwise exist, that is, if the risks to the agent were not so great.

Now whether any such view is true, it seems obvious that it is conceptually coherent. Someone could clearly hold such a view with full mastery of the concept of moral obligation and without contradicting herself. If, however, the concept of moral obligation were the same as that of the moral ought in Dancy's sense, that is, what moral reasons favour or most favour, however conclusively, then such a view would simply be conceptually incoherent. It would be like saying: 'Rescuing someone in such a situation is what moral reasons most favour, or favour conclusively, but such an action, nonetheless, would not be what moral reasons most favour, or favour conclusively.' The possibility of supererogation would be ruled out on conceptual grounds.

It seems clear, however, that this is not the case and that whether there is such a thing as supererogation is a substantive normative question rather than one that can be settled on conceptual grounds alone. And if that is so, then moral obligation must be a distinct concept from that being favoured most, or favoured conclusively, by moral reasons.

2. Moral obligation and accountability

Moral obligations are what morality *requires* or *demands*, not just what there are moral reasons for doing, however weighty or conclusive these reasons might be. But what is it for morality to require or demand something?

Plainly the idea of demand or requirement extends more widely than the moral. We speak also of requirements of reason or logical demands; for example, the demand not to have contradictory or incoherent beliefs or plans. But unlike demands of reason or logic, talk of moral demands is linked to accountability *conceptually*. What we are morally obligated to do is, as a conceptual matter, what we are morally answerable for doing.

There is thus an important difference between moral obligations and, for example, requirements that are imposed by logic. If I fail to act as I am morally required without adequate excuse, it simply follows straight away that what Strawson called 'reactive attitudes', like indignation, blame, and guilt, are thereby warranted (Strawson 1968). Responses like these seem appropriate to logical blunders, however, only in certain contexts, and even here what seems to be in question is a moral error of some kind (as when I have a special responsibility for reasoning properly). And though a connection to accountability is intrinsic to the concept of moral obligation, it is obviously no part whatsoever of the idea of a logical requirement or demand of reason.

Similarly, the idea of *excuse* is obviously also external to that of rational or logical requirements, though it is not to moral requirements or obligations. It is a conceptual truth that one is justifiably blamed for failing to comply with moral obligations unless one has some (adequate) excuse, though not that unexcused logical blunders are blameworthy.

Mill articulates this conceptual point when he says that 'we do not call an action wrong, unless we mean to imply that a person ought to be punished in some way or other for doing it' (Mill 1998: ch. 5). 'Punishment' may sound overly strong, but Mill includes under this heading blame and 'the reproaches of [the agent's] own conscience'. We do not impute wrongdoing unless we take ourselves to be in the range of the culpable, that is, unless the action is such that the agent is not just morally criticizable in some way or other, but aptly the object of some form of accountability-seeking reactive attitude such as moral blame if she lacks an adequate excuse. What it is, indeed, for an action to be morally obligatory and its omission morally wrong, is just for it to be an action the omission of which would warrant blame and feelings of guilt, were the agent to omit the action without excuse.[5]

In *The Second-Person Standpoint*, I defend this analysis of moral obligation as entailing accountability and argue that it reveals what I there call moral obligation's 'second-personal' character. Moral demands, I argue, are what we legitimately *demand* of one another and ourselves, where making such demands is invariably a second-personal matter, even when their object (and so addressee) is oneself, as in the emotion of guilt. Following Strawson, I argue that reactive attitudes have an essentially interpersonal (or, as I call it, second-personal) character since they implicitly put forward or address

---

[5] This claim is echoed in Baier (1966); Brandt (1979); Gibbard (1990: 42); Skorupski (1999: 29, 142); and Shafer-Landau (2003). Note that this still admits a distinction between wrongness—the violation of moral obligation, on the one hand, and blameworthiness, on the other. An action may be wrong, but not blameworthy, if the agent has an adequate excuse.

putatively legitimate demands to their objects and therefore presuppose, I argue, the authority to make them.

Because of this second-personal character, holding someone responsible through reactive attitudes inescapably involves what Gary Watson calls the 'constraints on moral address' (1987: 263, 264). In addressing putatively legitimate demands to someone, both addresser and addressee are committed to certain presuppositions as conditions of the reciprocal intelligibility of their interaction as second-personal address. Among these, I argue, is the addressee's competence to hold himself responsible by acknowledging the legitimacy of the demand and regulating his conduct by it.

My object here will be to argue that these presuppositions can be met only if what we hold people accountable for, moral obligations, are accessible to all, hence to those held accountable, as shared public knowledge. And practices of accountability must be able to be public also. Interpersonal answerability is public in its nature; justifying oneself to others is possible at all only within a shared space of public reasons. Since, moreover, people within a culture of mutual accountability must also be able to question claims of wrongdoing, much as participants in a legal order can contest charges of illegality, due process constraints would seem to be built into the very idea of a mutually accountable moral order no less than they are into that of a genuine legal order. And this, I shall argue, can give general principles a role in moral accountability, hence in moral obligation, that is similar to the role that rules and legal principles have in a valid system of law. It will follow that if the idea of moral obligation is essential to our concept of morality, as I shall argue it is, then morality will indeed depend upon general principles, and particularism about morality will be false.

It would be hubris to suppose that a fully convincing case for these claims can be offered in the space available here. I will be able to give only the barest sketch of an argument for general principles in morality that is broadly akin to one that is more familiar for principles in law. My hope, however, is to convince the reader that, when it comes to moral obligation, and therefore to morality, there are considerations that are relevant to whether principles have a 'critical role', in Scanlon's words, that simply are not present with respect to normative reasons and oughts more generally, including practical reasons or oughts, or even just any normative *moral* reason, that is, any consideration that might favour an action from the moral point of view. We are not, in these latter cases, forced by the very nature of our concepts to suppose that people to whom normative reasons and oughts apply are *accountable* for acting as the reasons recommend and therefore that the reasons and oughts must be able to be practically available as part of a shared public culture.

3. Accountability and 'constraints on moral address'

Before I begin to make this argument, I need first to say something about the Strawsonian picture of accountability and second-personal address on which my argument will draw.[6] In 'Freedom and Resentment', Strawson argues that consequentialist justifications for moral responsibility cannot provide 'the right sort of basis, for these practices as we understand them' (Strawson 1968). Whether holding someone responsible would be desirable or promote goods of any kind—whether personal or impersonal, moral or non-moral—is one thing; but whether the person's action was *culpable* and therefore warrants blame is quite another.

'Strawson's Point', as I call it, is an example of what philosophers call the 'wrong kind of reason problem' (see, e.g., Rabinowicz and Rønnow-Rasmussen 2004; Hieronymi 2005; Darwall 2006). For example, although there is perhaps a sense in which the fact that one will get a reward for believing *p* is a reason to believe *p*, this cannot possibly bear on whether *p* is *credible*. It is not a 'reason of the right kind' to believe *p* in the sense we usually have in mind. Similarly, the fact that holding someone responsible for an action would have good consequences, or even indeed that it would instantiate an intrinsically valuable state of affairs, though these can provide some reason *to desire* to hold him responsible and blame him, it cannot provide a reason of the right kind for our practices of accountability 'as we understand them', since it does not bear on the blameworthiness of his action.

To be a reason of the right kind a consideration must properly justify a *reactive attitude*. Strawson coined 'reactive attitudes' in 'Freedom and Resentment' to refer to mental states through which we hold people responsible, whether another person, as with indignation, resentment, or

---

[6] For a fuller development and defence, see Darwall (2006).

moral blame, or oneself, as in the emotion of guilt. Strawson didn't give a formal definition of these attitudes, but their central features are clear from the role they play in his argument about moral responsibility and freedom of the will. Strawson's central idea is that reactive attitudes involve a way of regarding the individuals who are their objects that commits the holder of the attitude to certain assumptions about the object individual and her capacities to regulate her will. Unlike 'objective attitudes', like disdain, disgust, and annoyance, reactive attitudes are essentially characterized by 'involvement or participation with others in interpersonal human relationships' (Strawson 1968). There is always an essentially 'interpersonal' or, as I prefer to put it, 'second-personal' element to reactive attitudes. Through the attitude we *hold* its object to something and thereby implicitly make a demand *of* (and so implicitly address it *to*) him or her (as it were, second-personally). As Strawson puts it, 'the making of the demand is the proneness to such attitudes' (Strawson 1968: 92–3). The reason that reactive attitudes distinctively implicate freedom of the will, then, is that we can intelligibly address a demand to someone to regulate her will appropriately only if we suppose that she can so regulate it as a result of recognizing our demand's legitimacy. The supposition is a 'constraint on moral address' (Watson 1987: 263, 264).

Consider the difference between disdain expressed by a put-down, like 'He's as thick as a post', and an attitude of indignation or moral blame. Unlike the latter, the former is unfettered by any constraints on address that inevitably arise when we take a second-person perspective toward someone. Disdain is not standardly addressed to its object at all; if it has an addressee, it is likelier to be others we think capable of appreciating why its object is a worthy target. When we blame someone for something, however, we implicitly make a demand *of him* to act differently and, if he has not, to take responsibility for not having done so, where taking responsibility is essentially an *interpersonal* matter (holding himself answerable to us—and, indeed, to himself—as representative persons). In so regarding him, we perforce see him, as someone, who is *competent* to take such an attitude toward himself and guide himself by it. We see him as capable of entering into reciprocal human relationships of mutual accountability.

Disdain involves no such assumptions. One can hardly imagine the disdainer in our example, believing his disdain's object to be too thick to appreciate how thick he is and unable to change his thick-headedness, withdrawing the put-down as not expressing a fully intelligible attitude. To the contrary, to such a person, such further 'thickness' would only seem to confirm the fittingness of the disdain. Moral blame, on the other hand, holds its object to a demanded standard and to its object's holding himself to that standard by making himself answerable for compliance. So it is not fully intelligible, or, at least, it is unwarranted in its own terms and not just unfair, when its object is someone who is known to lack the psychic capacities or knowledge necessary to do this. It just doesn't make sense to blame someone for dull-wittedness, unless one is under some illusion about the human ability to take responsibility for mental endowments. But no matter how regrettable or unfair, disdain for dull-wittedness is clearly an intelligible attitude.

Strawson makes an important distinction *within* reactive attitudes between 'personal' and 'impersonal' ones. This can be confusing, since it is possible to lose track of the fact that Strawson holds that *all* reactive attitudes, even impersonal ones, are 'interpersonal' (or 'second-personal'). 'Personal' reactive attitudes are those, like resentment and guilt, that are felt as if from the perspective of a participant in the events that give rise to it, whereas 'impersonal' reactive attitudes, like indignation or moral blame, are felt as if from a 'third party's' point of view. One cannot resent or forgive injuries to people with whom one lacks some personal connection, but this is no impediment to moral blame or disapproval. Nonetheless, however 'impersonal' blame is in Strawson's sense, it is not an attitude Strawson characterizes as 'objective'. It is just as 'interpersonal' or 'second-personal' as personal reactive attitudes like resentment or guilt.[7] Thus although impersonal reactive attitudes are as if from the perspective of a 'third-party', they are not 'third-personal' attitudes in the usual sense; they involve the same second-personal element of implicit address as do personal ones, only as if from the perspective of a representative person rather than any individual's standpoint.[8]

---

[7] 'The same abnormal light which shows the agent to us as one in respect of whom the personal attitudes, the personal demand, are to be suspended, shows him to us also as one in respect of whom the impersonal attitudes, the generalized demand, are to be suspended' (Strawson 1968: 87).

[8] Similarly, *second personal* does not imply *second party*. Guilt, like any reactive attitude is second personal, since it involves implicit address, but it clearly is not a second party attitude. In feeling guilt, one implicitly addresses a demand to oneself. Finally, any second-personal attitude is also first personal. Address, whether implicit or explicit is always from someone (an individual (I) or a collective (we)), but it clearly is not a second party attitude.

The difference between *warranted* personal and impersonal reactive attitudes tracks a distinction between an *individual authority* we presuppose when we implicitly address putatively legitimate 'personal' demands that others not treat *us* in certain ways and a *representative authority* we assume when we implicitly address 'impersonal' demands as representative persons in moral blame. Personal reactive attitudes and individual authority are conceptually implicated in moral claim *rights* and correlative 'bipolar' obligations that those against whom the right is held have *to* the right holder. For example, a right not to be harmed or coerced entails a correlative obligation others have *to him* not to harm him. And this involves, as a conceptual matter, others being distinctively accountable *to him* for respecting the right and his individual authority to hold them thus accountable, or, indeed not to, at his discretion. Thus in US civil law, for example, it is up to victims whether or not to seek compensation for a violation of their rights, as it is morally, whether to forgive or to resent. Only the victim, or perhaps those personally related to him, has or have the standing to do either.

When, however, it comes to the responsibility involved in moral obligations *period*, as we might call them (that is, wrongful conduct rather than the wronging *of someone* that consists in the violation of a bipolar obligation *to him*),[9] accountability is not distinctively to the victim, but to everyone, including the victim *and* the violator, as representative persons. It is, again, a conceptual truth that violations of moral obligation warrant the impersonal reactive attitude of moral blame when they are unexcused. It is a reflection of this that whereas it is up to the victim to seek compensation for violations of rights through the law of torts, it is up to the people and its representatives, e.g. public prosecutors, to decide whether and how to hold people responsible for violations of criminal law.

The line of thought I wish to consider for moral generalism derives from the second-personal character of moral accountability, and hence, moral obligation. When we address a moral demand to someone, whether to others or ourselves, we take up a second-person standpoint with respect to them. We 'regard' them, as Strawson says, 'interpersonal[ly]'. And this makes us subject to 'constraints on moral address', namely presuppositions of the intelligibility of so understanding ourselves. In *The Second-Person Standpoint*, I sum these into what I call 'Pufendorf's Point': We can intelligibly hold

---

[9] Of course, these may be the very same action.

someone responsible only if we regard her as capable of holding herself responsible. Genuinely to conceive ourselves as under *obligation*, rather than just obliged by force or having incentives to avoid unwelcome sanctions, we must be capable of blaming ourselves for failing to comply.[10] A being subject to obligation must be capable of being 'forced', not externally, but 'of itself to weigh its own actions, and to judge itself worthy of some censure unless it conforms to a prescribed rule' (Pufendorf 1934: 91). As I would put the point, we can intelligibly regard someone as under a moral obligation and hold her accountable, only if we regard her as able to take up the impartial (Strawson's 'impersonal') second-person standpoint of a representative person on herself, recognize the legitimacy of the moral demand, and make the demand of herself from this perspective.

4. General principles, and accountability, legal and moral

It is uncontroversial that generally formulable rules or principles are intrinsic to the rule of law in a way they are not, say, to rule by decree. This is common ground between legal positivists and their critics, the main issue between them being whether the existence of rule-structured practices, including perhaps second-order rules, such as Hart's 'rule of recognition', is sufficient for a legal order, as the positivists suppose, or whether, as Dworkin argues, appeal to general moral principles are also necessary (Hart 1961; Dworkin 1978: 23ff.).[11] Whether conventional rules are sufficient or whether these must be supplemented by moral principles, it has seemed more or less obvious to philosophers of law that it is part of the very idea of a legal order that it involves regulation by standards that can be formulated in a general way and are not irreducibly particularistic. It is consistent with this, of course, that legal standards will involve concepts that take judgement to apply and that may not be able to be readily operationalized in empirical terms. For example, uses of force otherwise proscribed by law, are permitted in self-defence when they are 'reasonably' believed

---

[10] See also Hart's (1961: 6–8) distinction between being obligated and being obliged.
[11] Such as, 'no person should profit from wrongdoing', which, Dworkin argues, the US Supreme Court appealed to in deciding law in *Riggs v. Palmer*.

necessary to repel a threat to which they are 'proportionate' (Black 1999). Even so, it just seems essential to the rule of law that laws must be formulable in general terms that those subject to them can be expected to understand and regulate themselves by, despite differences in values, taste, and expertise.

It is widely accepted that law claims *authority* over and to *obligate* those subject to it, thereby making them accountable for compliance (e.g. Raz 1979). I take it that a central attraction of the rule of law, as opposed to rule by decree, is that a legal order's claims to obligate have a substantially better chance of actually being legitimate and obligating than would comparable claims of a regime that did not govern by rules and principles that can be formulated in general terms and that anyone subject to them can be expected to know, understand, and regulate themselves by.

There are certainly many areas of human life where we live happily and appropriately by particularistic judgements, for example, regarding aesthetic matters. Judgements about art, food, decor, music, and so on, seem irreducibly particularistic, and it would be foolhardy to try to systematize them, or even worse, to attempt to ground them, in general rules and principles. We need not think of these areas as any less serious or even, indeed, less objective, though general agreement or even understanding cannot be expected. As Louis Armstrong is reputed to have said about jazz music, 'if you have to ask what jazz is, you'll never know'. But the aesthetic differs from law and morality in not purporting to impose obligations. Artists may sensibly take themselves to be obligated to pursue their art in certain ways and not in others, of course. And outsiders may make these or similar judgements also. But the point remains that obligation-imposing purport is not intrinsic to aesthetic standards in the way it is to moral and legal requirements.

Because the aesthetic seems particularistic, and because law, by its nature, purports to obligate, legal requirements seeking to impose aesthetic standards would be not simply unjust, but downright ridiculous. Imagine a city ordinance outlawing kitsch, schlock, or the banal, even with restricted scope, say, in literature. What would make such a law ridiculous, I take it, is the manifest absurdity of purporting to hold people answerable for something they cannot be expected to be able hold themselves to in their own judgement, that is, the obvious violation of 'Pufendorf's Point'.

The difference between law and morality is that whereas legal requirements *purport* to obligate, moral requirements necessarily actually do. Clearly, laws can exist that do not impose genuine, that is, *de jure* obligations. Law necessarily *claims de jure* authority, and arguably it must have *de facto* authority to exist at all. But law need not actually have the *de jure* authority it claims in order to exist *de facto*. However, this cannot be true of moral obligations, at least as we are currently thinking of them. These are *de jure* in their nature; if they don't have the authority they claim, then they simply do not exist. They are merely putative and not actual moral obligations. 'Legal obligation', by contrast, can refer to something that has only *de facto* authority and none *de jure*.

If what we have said so far about the absurdity of legally mandating the aesthetic is correct, it follows even more strongly that morality could not include any such requirements either. 'Pufendorf's Point' implies that *de jure* obligations cannot possibly exist unless those subject to them can be intelligibly held answerable for complying with them.

We cannot, however, conclude moral generalism, or even moral-obligation generalism, straight away from this. The example of the aesthetic combines two different features, its particularistic character, on the one hand, and its relation to *expert* or even *esoteric* particularistic judgement, on the other. A putatively obligating standard that would require a particularistic expertise that only some can be expected ever to acquire would violate 'Pufendorf's Point', but that might be owing simply to its esoteric quality. Might moral judgement be particularistic but nonetheless sufficiently widely shareable to impose obligation?

The moral particularist can admit that *legal* obligation cannot be particularistic, since formulability as general rules and principles is part of the very idea of law. But why couldn't the moral order, even an order of moral obligations, differ from that of law in precisely this respect. Even if, 'no law without general rules and principles', expresses a central truth about the law, why suppose that 'no morality without general rules and principles' expresses a core theorem of morality?

The reason why generally formulable rules and principles are essential to the idea of law is that nothing counts as a legal order unless there is something publicly formulable and specifiable with which subjects are held responsible for complying. Locking someone up cannot count as holding him responsible for and enforcing compliance unless there is something that is publicly accessible to enforcer and enforced alike to which the enforcement can refer—for example, that one is not to do an action of kind *A* in circumstances *C*. Both '*A*' and '*C*' may be quite complicated, but not so complicated that no one could intelligibly expect those subject to the putative standard to understand and be able to regulate themselves by it.

But why must the same thing hold with morality? Might the truth about moral obligation be particularistic even if law cannot be? A particularistic moral order would not be fit to be a legal order, but perhaps it might become one by establishing legal institutions and promulgating the single law: 'Comply with your moral obligations.' Such a law would seem to be universal and general, even if the moral obligations with which citizens were legally obligated to comply were themselves particularistic. So even if law has to take a universal general form in order to impose obligations, it might be that morality and moral obligations do not.

While this seems right as far as it goes, it underrates accountability's role in morality. We can see this by considering some things Dancy says about the idea that morality is tied to the social or interpersonal in a similar, but nonetheless crucially different, way. Dancy considers the possibility that a rationale for moral generalism might be found in the thought that 'morality is essentially a system of social constraints' that is necessary to fix expectations in a socially beneficial way (2004: 83). He evidently has in mind a kind of indirect or rule-consequentialist approach like Brad Hooker's (2000). Dancy's reply is that such a view 'is a description of something like a set of traffic regulations' (2004: 83). 'Morality', Dancy continues, 'was not invented by a group of experts in council to serve the purposes of social control' (p. 83). Nor is morality necessary to fix expectation, since 'people are quite capable of judging how to behave case by case, in a way that would enable us to predict what they will in fact do' (p. 83).

Dancy is of course right that morality, unlike legal orders, is not invented. So a fortiori it is not invented for any purpose: not social control, not fixing expectations, nor any other. And as far as the point I currently want to make goes, we could even allow Dancy that it is frequently true that people are competent to judge 'how to behave case by case' in a way that enables us to predict what they are likely to do. Of course, this wouldn't yet enable us to *fix* expectations as we can through the rule-structured practices, like promising, that rule consequentialists frequently discuss. But the role that rule- and principled-structured practices, like those in which legal systems consist or the more informal 'moral' practices of indirect consequentialism, play in bringing about various beneficial consequences, such as stable expectations, are actually quite different from the kinds of considerations to which I have been adverting.

According to morality as accountability, rules and principles are essential not to bringing about valuable consequences, even of mutual accountability itself. Rather they must be in play in order for us to be morally accountable to one another, and to ourselves, as representative persons in the first place. The idea is not that general principles are somehow prior to moral accountability, or vice versa. Rather they come together as a package deal. Moral obligations entail moral accountability conceptually, and agents can intelligibly be held accountable only if there exist general rules and principles that are accessible to all who are morally bound as a matter of common public knowledge.

Above we considered the conceptual point that the very idea of enforcing law and holding people (legally) responsible for complying with it entails that there must be something publicly formulable and recognizable in which law itself consists. When someone is charged with breaking the law, there must be some way of formulating the law he is charged with breaking. It is no good to say just that he acted illegally; there must be a formulable rule or principle that he can be charged with breaking.

When we think about the conceptual relation between moral obligation and accountability, we can see that something similar must hold in the moral domain also. When we blame someone for having acted wrongly, to ourselves or others, we assume the burden of characterizing the putatively wrongful act in some way that goes beyond the judgement that the particular act's features simply combined holistically in the circumstances to make up a wrongful act. As with the law, there must be some more specific *charge*. Moreover, when we hold someone accountable, we put him in the position of *justifying* himself to us, either to us as individuals, as in the case of rights violations, or to us (and himself) as representative persons, as in moral blame. This means that any charge of wrongdoing has to be publicly contestable; it must be able to be put in terms that, in principle, anyone can assess, criticize, and emend. Moral blame must be embeddable in a shared public culture of accountability.

Consider: you are walking with a friend at dusk in the winter woods, and he falls and badly sprains his ankle, making it impossible for the two of you to get to warmth and safety before nightfall. There is a locked cabin with a fireplace nearby and wood stacked beside. You deliberate about what to do and decide to break in and start a fire in the fireplace so that you and your friend can be safe overnight before trying to get back to town the next day. Have you done wrong?

Note, first, that if anyone, including you yourself, were to charge you with wrongdoing, this charge would have to be put in some more specific way, like: 'You acted wrongly because you trespassed; you broke into someone else's property.' It is no good just to say: 'What you did Tuesday night at 5.30 p.m. in the woods was wrong.' Or even: 'The properties of your action on Tuesday night at 5.30 p.m. taken holistically amount to moral wrong.' To intelligibly hold you accountable, the person must be able to levee some more specific charge like: 'You broke into someone else's property, and that is wrong', implicitly assuming a general principle. It is then of course open to you to say: 'Yes, often, maybe usually, maybe even almost always, that is wrong, but not when it is necessary for safety and survival.' In so doing, you implicitly emend the proposed principle: 'It is wrong to trespass, except when this is necessary for safety and survival.'

A particularist might well reply that there is no reason to suppose that this emended principle holds without exception. No doubt, a fully acceptable principle would have to be significantly more complicated. But, however complicated, two points would nonetheless remain. First, it seems essential to interpersonal accountability (and, indeed to intrapersonal accountability) that criticism, because it is essentially second-personal, must be able to be put in terms that the person to whom it is addressed can understand, respond to, and contest. This means, second, that obligation- and wrong-making features are not just normative grounds (which might admit, as such, of being irreducibly holistic and particularistic). Any features that could make an action morally obligatory or wrong have to be able to mediate second-personal accountability. They must be able to be formulated in terms that can mediate a publicly sharable discussion about whether the conduct warrants accountability-seeking reactive attitudes, specifically, moral blame.[12] And if this is right, when it comes to moral obligation, particularism seems to be ruled out on conceptual grounds.

---

[12] I do not mean, of course, that the discussion or consideration must actually be public. More often than not, it will not be. The point is that its terms must be publicizable.

5. Moral generalism

The foregoing reflections are obviously too cursory to be fully convincing. I hope, however, that they show that there is a potential line of argument for generalism, and against particularism, regarding moral *obligation*, that Dancy has yet to deal with. In this last section, I wish briefly to indicate why, if this argument were to go through, generalism, and the denial of particularism, as Dancy understands these, would thereby be established.

In a well-known chapter of *Ethics and the Limits of Philosophy*, Bernard Williams (1985) dubbed morality 'the peculiar institution'. Williams's rhetorical point was to associate morality with a kind of slavery, their 'peculiar institution' being the terms in which whites in the antebellum South used to refer to the enslavement of African-Americans. What makes morality 'peculiar', in Williams's view, in other words, what is distinctive about it, is its characteristic notion of obligation (pp. 174–5). Williams's ambition there was neo-Nietzschean, to argue that the 'morality system' with its distinctive concept of moral obligation was an unhealthy set of concepts to live with, since it shackles individuals' pursuits of cherished projects from which they derive their very integrity and identity.

Though I certainly reject Williams's rhetorical and philosophical agenda, I accept his view that moral obligation is an ineliminable aspect of the concept of morality as it developed in early modern philosophy in the West from the 17th century on. The idea that obligation is central to the idea of morality, at least as it has been conceived in the modern period, is also the core of Elizabeth Anscombe's (1958) critique of 'modern moral philosophy' as essentially incoherent. The only way morality could be a coherent concept is if its putative obligations could derive from God's supremely authoritative command, but only few moderns accept the divine command theory.

Obviously, this is not the place to try to respond to Anscombe's critique.[13] My point here is that if she is right, as I think she and Williams are, in characterizing its target—the centrality of moral obligation to morality—then generalism about morality will follow from generalism regarding moral obligation. Assume, then, that there would be no such thing as morality unless there were moral obligations. And assume, as the argument of the last

---

[13] I attempt to do so in Darwall (2006).

section attempted to conclude, that moral obligations depend upon general principles. It follows from these two assumptions together that there can be such a thing as morality only if there are valid, obligation-creating general principles. So it would follow that particularism as Dancy defines it is false.

What, then, about the possibility of holistic moral oughts and reasons, and, therefore, of particularism about these? I said above that I can concede that there is a sense in which there might be non-obligating moral reasons and oughts that are particularistic. However, if what we have just said is correct, then there is also a sense in which the very existence of *moral* reasons and oughts depends on general principles too. Any non-obligating normative moral reason or ought need not itself depend on a general principle. However, a reason or ought can be a *moral* reason or ought only if there is such a thing as morality. And there can be such a thing as morality only if there are moral obligations. And *these* require, if the argument of the last section is correct, that valid general principles be in place. So there can be moral normative reasons and moral oughts at all, and any specific normative reason or ought can be a *moral* reason or ought, only if there are valid general principles.

I put forward this argument, again, not so much to establish its conclusion as to show that there is an argument for generalism that Dancy's formidable case for holism about normative reasons and oughts simply does not touch. If this argument is correct, though there are senses of 'ethics' in which 'ethics without principles' is clearly possible, then 'morality without principles' is not.

References

Anscombe, G. E. M. (1958) 'Modern Moral Philosophy', in R. Crisp and M. Slote (eds.), *Virtue Ethics* (Oxford: Oxford University Press, 1998), 26–44.
Baier, K. (1966) 'Moral Obligation', *American Philosophical Quarterly*, 3: 210–26.
Black, H. C. (1999) *Black's Law Dictionary* (Minneapolis, MN: West Group).
Brandt, R. (1979) *A Theory of the Good and the Right* (Oxford: Oxford University Press).
Dancy, J. (1983) 'Ethical Particularism and Morally Relevant Properties', *Mind*, 92: 530–47.
—— (1993) *Moral Reasons* (Oxford: Blackwell).
—— (2004) *Ethics Without Principles* (Oxford: Oxford University Press).

—— (2009) 'Moral Particularism', *Stanford Encyclopedia of Philosophy*, <http://plato.stanford.edu/entries/moral-particularism/> First published in 2001, revised in 2009. Last accessed November 2012.

Darwall, S. (2006) *The Second-Person Standpoint: Morality, Respect, and Accountability* (Cambridge, MA: Harvard University Press).

Dworkin, R. (1978) *Taking Rights Seriously* (Cambridge, MA: Harvard University Press).

Gibbard, A. (1990) *Wise Choices, Apt Feelings* (Cambridge, MA: Harvard University Press).

Hart, H. L. A. (1961) *The Concept of Law* (Oxford: Clarendon Press).

Hiernoymi, P. (2005) 'The Wrong Kind of Reason', *The Journal of Philosophy*, 102: 437–57.

Hooker, B. (2000) *Ideal Code, Real World: A Rule-Consequentialist Theory of Morality* (Oxford: Oxford University Press).

—— and Little, M. (eds.) (2000) *Moral Particularism* (Oxford: Oxford University Press).

Lance, M. and Little, M. (2006) 'Defending Moral Particularism', in J. Dreier (ed.), *Contemporary Debates in Moral Theory* (Oxford: Blackwell), 305–21.

McKeever, S. and Ridge, M. (2005) 'What Does Holism Have to Do with Moral Particularism?', *Ratio*, 18: 93–103.

—— (2006) *Principled Ethics: Generalism as a Regulative Ideal* (Oxford: Oxford University Press).

Mill, J. S. (1998) *Utilitarianism*, ed. R. Crisp (Oxford: Oxford University Press).

Pufendorf, S. (1934) *On the Law of Nature and Nations*, tr. C. H. Oldfather and W. A. Oldfather (Oxford: Clarendon Press).

Rabinowicz, W. and Rønnow-Rasmussen, T. (2004) 'The Strike of the Demon: On Fitting Pro-Attitudes and Value', *Ethics*, 114: 391–423.

Raz, J. (1979) *The Authority of Law* (Oxford: Oxford University Press).

Shafer-Landau, R. (2003) *Moral Realism: A Defense* (New York: Oxford University Press).

Skorupski, J. (1999) *Ethical Explorations* (Oxford: Oxford University Press).

Strawson, P. F. (1968) 'Freedom and Resentment', in P. F. Strawson (ed.), *Studies in the Philosophy of Thought and Action: British Academy Lectures by Gilbert Ryle and Others* (Oxford: Oxford University Press), 71–96.

Urmson, J. O. (1958) 'Saints and Heroes', in A. I. Melden (ed.), *Essays on Moral Philosophy* (Seattle, WA: Washington University Press), 198–216.

Watson, G. (1987) 'Responsibility and the Limits of Evil: Variations on a Strawsonian Theme', in F. D. Schoeman (ed.), *Responsibility, Character, and the Emotions: New Essays in Moral Psychology* (Cambridge: Cambridge University Press), 256–86.

Williams, B. (1985) *Ethics and the Limits of Philosophy* (Cambridge, MA: Harvard University Press).

9

Moral Particularism: Ethical Not Metaphysical?

DAVID BAKHURST

1. Sentimental prelude

Late one afternoon in October 1978, I climbed the back stairs of Keele Hall for the first time. I was a fresher beginning Keele University's then-renowned Foundation Year, and I had chosen philosophy as a 'sessional' I would study throughout the year. The lecturer to whom I had been assigned was one J. Dancy. I had met this Mr. Dancy before, thanks to a chance encounter in the university book shop. He had been kind to me as I had stumbled to make conversation, and I was looking forward to seeing him again. When I reached the attic, I finally found the door I was searching for. Behind it was a tiny room dominated by an impressive roll-top desk, and sitting in an armchair beside the desk was Jonathan, looking pretty much as he looks today. That term and the next, two other students and I shoe-horned ourselves into this room once a week, and with Jonathan's guidance, made our way through Salmon's *Logic* and Ayer's *The Problem of Knowledge*. This was a magical introduction to philosophy. Jonathan's intellect could be a tad intimidating, of course, but the great thing was that he took his students really seriously, making it clear to us that philosophy was the kind of subject where, if we had enough smarts and enough imagination, we might just be able to say something illuminating about something genuinely perplexing. By showing us that kind of respect, Jonathan inspired us. This was the real thing: intensely stimulating, astonishingly difficult, and tremendous fun. I was hooked.

Jonathan and I became friends, and over the next four years we spent a lot of time together in that little room discussing philosophy, sometimes joined by David McNaughton whose office was around the corner. Topics were many and varied, but as time went on metaethics and the theory of motivation became the principal focus. These were the formative years of what Maggie Little (1994) has called 'British Moral Realism'. David Wiggins had published 'Truth, Invention, and the Meaning of Life' in 1976, and John McDowell was busy producing his famous early essays on ethics. There was a sense that a new era was dawning. The self-confident non-cognitivism that had dominated for decades was being vanquished by something altogether more sophisticated. This was not so much a new theory as a different philosophical sensibility (it is notable that Wiggins and McDowell referred to their positions as 'anti-non-cognitivism', rather than something more affirmative). Suddenly it was possible to entertain the idea that moral judgements are accountable to the world and can be assessed as true or false; that an agent's beliefs might, *contra* the Humean orthodoxy, motivate her to act; that the fact that some practice rests upon shared human sensibilities does not entail that the normative standards that govern it are wanting in objectivity; that moral concepts can be illuminated only from *within* the moral point of view, and hence that there is no chance of seeing off moral sceptics by grounding morality from an external perceptive; that philosophy should not aspire to resolve moral problems but leave them to first-order moral enquiry by our best lights; that such enquiry involves the exercise of good judgement, a commodity that cannot be bottled by philosophers (or anybody else) because it is essentially uncodifiable. These ideas were refreshing and exciting, and we set out to make the best sense of them we could. All of them came to inform Jonathan's work in one way or another, but it was the uncodifiability of moral judgement that he made his own when he developed the position now associated with his name: ethical particularism.

After I left Keele for Moscow in 1982 my philosophical studies acquired a rather different focus, but the intellectual concerns I formed under Jonathan's influence have remained with me, and over the years I have written occasional essays on particularism (2000, 2005, 2007a, 2007b). In these papers, my principal aim has been to identify areas where I think particularists should have more to say, such as on matters of character, commitment, and moral education. I make this case not just in the interests of completeness, but because we particularists need to do a better job of explaining how our position genuinely illuminates moral life. It would be too bad if particularism entered the history books as merely a thought-provoking episode in analytic metaethics, when it is a view that promises to transform our conception of sound moral judgement and our understanding of ourselves as moral agents. I hope Jonathan will forgive my returning to this issue here.

2. Back to the source

Let us revisit one of particularism's primary inspirations: McDowell's papers 'Are Moral Requirements Hypothetical Imperatives?' (1978) and 'Virtue and Reason' (1979). In these essays, McDowell maintains that moral judgement—specifically judgement about what to do in some situation—demands sensitivity to the morally salient features of the case at hand. He portrays this sensitivity as 'a sort of perceptual capacity' (1979: 51) that cannot be codified into rules or principles:

> In moral upbringing what one learns is not to behave in conformity with rules of conduct, but to see situations in a special light, as constituting reasons for action; this perceptual capacity, once acquired, can be exercised in complex novel circumstances, not necessarily capable of being foreseen and legislated for by a codifier of the conduct required by virtue, however wise and thoughtful he might be.
>
> (1978: 85)

It is, McDowell maintains, 'quite implausible that any reasonably adult moral outlook admits of any such codification'. Such outlooks are 'not susceptible of capture in any universal formula' (1979: 57–8). Thus he concludes that '[o]ccasion by occasion, one knows what to do, if one does, not by applying universal principles but by being a certain kind of person: one who sees situations in a certain distinctive way' (p. 73).

McDowell invokes Wittgenstein's rule-following considerations to counter the objection that the deliverances of this perceptual capacity are insufficiently robust to ensure that an agent's moral judgements exhibit genuine consistency. Consistency in judgement, so the objection goes, is explicable only in terms of an agent's being guided by universal principles. McDowell maintains that the rule-following considerations show that even where judgement is governed by explicitly-formulated rules, such as in arithmetic, consistency nonetheless depends upon agents sharing sensibilities as members of a common form of life, sensibilities that cannot themselves be codified. Thus the rationality and objectivity of moral judgement is hardly impugned for resting on the uncodifiable, for the same is true of deductive argument, 'our paradigm of reason' (p. 71). What follows is that understanding a moral outlook essentially involves entering into the sensibilities on which it rests: 'The rationality of virtue', McDowell concludes, 'is not demonstrable from an external standpoint' but discernible only from 'within the practice itself' (p. 71; cf. 1978: 89–90).

It would be natural for someone attracted to McDowell's view of moral judgement to feel that it stands in need of development. Much of his argument in these essays is directed to readers antecedently sympathetic to the ideas he expounds. His aim is to make space for a certain kind of position, rather than to defend it against all comers, and he leaves many details undetermined. For example, it is unclear how radical McDowell intends the particularist elements of his thinking to be. Obviously, the rule-following considerations no more show that we can relinquish moral principles than that we can dispense with mathematical rules. McDowell vigorously attacks the idea of principles mechanically grinding out answers to moral problems, but he represents moral judgement as informed by a 'conception of how to live' that comprises, in part, a nexus of sensitivities and 'concerns'. The latter notion suggests that McDowell might find room for a renewed idea of moral principles compatible with the primacy of unregimentable judgement in particular cases. But this, and much else, is left undeveloped.

Dancy moves to supplement McDowell's view of moral judgement with a finely-wrought theory of reasons that he takes to provide the ultimate foundation for particularism.[1] Dancy defends a non-psychologistic view of reasons for action: reasons are not mental states of agents, but features of situations: *that I promised, that it's raining, that she would be embarrassed, that it*

---

[1] To portray Dancy as developing and defending the particularistic view of moral judgement sketched in McDowell (1978 and 1979) is of course only part of the story. A fuller account would acknowledge McDowell's influence on other components of Dancy's philosophy, such as the theory of motivation and ethical realism (Dancy's version being defined partly in contrast to the view in McDowell 1985), and non-McDowellian influences on Dancy's particularism, both positive (e.g. his interest in intuitionism) and negative (e.g. his dissatisfaction with the conceptions of reasons that dominated the scene during his formative years, such as R. M. Hare's). I say a little more about such matters in Bakhurst (2000: 60–5 and 2007a: 124–7), on which the present discussion draws.

would be ungenerous are all features that can figure as reasons in appropriate circumstances. Typically, there will be several such features operative in any case and our judgement of what we have overall most reason to do will involve appreciating what matters most and how—or seeing the 'moral shape' of the situation. Dancy holds there is an irreducible plurality of features potentially relevant to the moral assessment of actions. And he is a holist about moral relevance; that is, the moral significance of any particular feature of some case essentially depends on its relations to other features. A property that is morally relevant in one situation may fail to be so in another: it may, as Dancy puts it, change its 'polarity' or 'valence'. For example, in one situation the fact that an action causes pleasure may be a reason to do it; in another, it may be morally irrelevant; in yet another, it may serve to make the action worse. Dancy takes holism to apply to all properties, including so called 'thick' ethical concepts, such as cruelty or kindness. This undermines the possibility of establishing substantive moral principles that depend upon the 'generalist' thesis that properties make the same, or the same kind of, contribution to our reasons wherever they are present. Thus Dancy arrives at the view that 'moral judgement can get along perfectly well without any appeal to principles, indeed ... there is no essential link between being a full moral agent and having principles' (Dancy 2004: 1).

3. Dancy's metaphysical turn

In *Ethics Without Principles*, Dancy writes that while he first saw particularism as 'a position in moral epistemology', he now thinks 'the real battleground lies in moral metaphysics' (p. 140). That is, while he initially thought particularism followed from considerations about how we *detect* that an action is right or wrong, he now thinks it a consequence of how actions get to *be* right or wrong. It is important to appreciate how this 'metaphysical turn' represents a departure from McDowell's approach. Both Dancy and McDowell place at centre-stage the question of how to understand moral decision-making by individuals in particular cases, and they portray the requirements of morality as 'imposed by the circumstances of action, as they are viewed by agents' (McDowell 1978: 78). McDowell has a lot to say about the nature of moral requirements, but he is also focused on elucidating moral competence. His discussion, informed as it is by his reading of Aristotle, implies a good deal about the nature of moral agents and what they bring with them to moral situations. So questions of moral character and psychology, and issues of moral instruction and the cultivation of sensitivity are in view, or not far from view. In contrast, Dancy's vision has become increasingly world-centred, focused on understanding the character of moral situations by analysing the 'metaphysics' of the reasons they present to agents. His position is thus sometimes described as 'ontological particularism' (see Garfield 2000: 181). It is not that Dancy has nothing to say on matters of competence and character, but he tends to present them as secondary to the theory of reasons. If we can get the metaphysics right, then we can represent the morally competent agent as she who has whatever it takes to respond appropriately to moral reasons, given what we now know moral reasons to be (see Dancy 1993: 64).[2]

One consequence of this 'metaphysical turn' is that particularism can look like a very narrow and austere view—an obligation-centred moral philosophy that dispenses with most of the ideas philosophers have deployed to make sense of obligation (the moral law, principles, rules, etc.) and treats obligation in terms of responsiveness to reasons understood as features of situations (see Bakhurst 2005). The focus is on *reality* as practical, while the practice of agents is cast as a matter of conformity to reasons as they emerge from the kaleidoscope of potentially relevant factors in particular cases. This presents a rather thin view of moral life, one which grants only a subsidiary role to questions of what kind of person to be, or what kind of life to lead. The particularist seems to treat moral reality as an ontological given and the theory of reasons as akin to a subject like chemistry, exploring the properties and relations of reasons considered as features of the world. Such an account leaves little room for the idea of morality as an *expression* of our nature, or as

---

[2] One might question whether the very idea of the 'theory of reasons' is consistent with the ethos of McDowell's philosophy. Can McDowell, who is no friend of constructive philosophical theory-building, look kindly upon a project in moral metaphysics with revisionary intent? As Tim Thornton (2004: 19, 92–9) suggests, revision of our everyday conceptions certainly looks like the particularist's intention. But Dancy might counter that his metaphysics is descriptive rather than revisionary since, as he argues, 'our actual morality is unprincipled' (2004: 82). Moreover, Dancy's metaphysics is hardly in the service of the kind of substantive philosophy McDowell rejects. This issue warrants further consideration.

a social institution or common project.[3] Morality is all discovery and no invention: we bring nothing to its constitution, save perhaps conditions of its possibility.

Someone might respond that particularism's metaphysical turn has brought significant gains in theoretical intensity and rigour. Some issues may have slipped from view, but at least we now have *arguments* for particularism, and a better sense of what we are arguing for. This is true. But one might also regret that, analytic philosophy being what it is, the discussion has become ever more complex and the language of the theory of reasons increasingly technical and, one might say, 'objectified' ('valences', 'polarities', 'defaults', 'enablers', 'attenuators', 'disablers', etc.). This has led some commentators sympathetic to particularism to bemoan that Dancy's particularism is obscure. Andrew Gleeson, for example, complains that Dancy 'has diverted attention away from what really matters in our moral lives and funnelled it into a scholastic dead end' (2007: 368) so that particularism is built 'on a foundation of sand' (p. 377).[4] In the present context it would be unseemly to endorse this assessment, and I am pleased to say that I do not, but the fact that such complaints are made gives me pause. It suggests, as I have argued before, that we need to bring some neglected themes into the limelight and locate particularism within a broader vision of moral life. After all, that vision is needed to assess the plausibility of the metaphysical views on which particularism supposedly rests. For such views are hardly supported by knock-down a priori arguments. As Dancy perceptively observes in *Moral Reasons*, arguing for particularism is a matter of laying out the salient characteristics of the view in a compelling story that

---

[3] Dancy is scornful of the idea that morality is 'a human institution', complaining that it casts morality as akin to a system of traffic regulations (see 2004: 83, 133–4). Though I share his contempt for overtly functionalist accounts of morality, more subtle views of the social character of morality are available, as I hope my discussion will show.

[4] Gleeson argues that Dancy's holistic metaphysics of reasons is irrelevant because even if morality could be fully codified, it would be wrong for agents to allow their judgements in particular cases to be dictated by principles. Sound moral judgement, he argues, is always a matter of responsiveness to the character of the case at hand; to allow one's judgement to be determined by rules is to succumb to rule-fetishism. I cannot agree with Gleeson's central argument. If there were a fully codified system of moral principles that correctly determined the rightness and wrongness of actions, then I cannot see why acting in light of an understanding of those principles would amount to rule-fetishism. After all, if the system of principles were any good, that understanding would involve not just *what* acts are prohibited, permitted, encouraged, etc., but *why* they are so. Contra Gleeson, the real issue is not rule-fetishism (disagreeable though that is), but whether the wrongness of, say, lying in this case is to be explained by appeal to the kind of general considerations that underwrite the principles.

reveals the attractiveness of the position (p. 114). If that story is to succeed, issues of moral psychology and education, about the kind of lives to lead and the kind of people to be, have to be up front and centre.

4. A speculative anthropology of morals

In what follows, I aspire to provide a counterbalance to particularism's metaphysical turn. To this end, I think we particularists should engage in a little speculative anthropology of morals, not to characterize morality as if from outside, but to trace the sources of morality from within, reflecting on the origins of our ways of thinking. The aim is to disclose how moral reality has the form the particularist takes it to have while developing complementary accounts of moral agency and psychology, moral education and character formation, that bring into view morality as a social phenomenon. The hope is that, by placing particularist insights in this broader context, the position will emerge as a compelling vision of moral life. I also hope to shed light on a number of issues that have dogged particularism, such as the role particularists should accord moral principles and the vexed question of the status of seemingly absolute prohibitions. Of course, there is no guarantee that we can write an anthropology of morals consistent with particularism, let alone one that illuminates and vindicates it.

I propose we take our lead from another figure influential in the development of British Moral Realism: David Wiggins, especially his article 'A Sensible Subjectivism' (1987) and his book *Ethics* (2006). This proposal may seem controversial, as Wiggins is much influenced by Hume, a philosopher usually associated with views anathema to particularists. But I take heart from McDowell's 1987 Lindley Lecture, which acknowledges the attractiveness of the position at which Wiggins arrives in 'A Sensible Subjectivism'.

In this article, Wiggins (1987: 199) represents the discourse of moral evaluation as emerging in 'a long and complicated evolutionary process'. He invites us to suppose that, at the outset, human beings typically respond in certain characteristic ways to certain 'objects' (states of affairs, actions, ways of behaving, traits of character, etc.). Some regularly 'please, help, amuse' us, others regularly 'harm, annoy, vex us'. Objects then become grouped together under various categories because they evoke these characteristic responses and are described as 'funny', 'pleasant', 'delightful', 'consoling', 'shocking', 'appalling', etc. Now, the properties such terms stand for will not be specifiable without reference to the characteristic reactions evoked by the objects that fall under them. So the funny is understood as that which is amusing. At the same time, the characteristic responses will be understood with reference to the properties that engender them. There will be no purely phenomenological account of amusement, nor a naturalistic reduction of the funny to properties specifiable independently of the typical responses that funny things evoke. Property and response form a tightly-knit pair: they are 'made for one another' and mutually intelligible (p. 199). This is because once a property-response pair establishes itself, the response is seen as fit to the property and the property as *meriting* the response. The amusing is not that which provokes laughter, but that which makes laughter appropriate.

With this idea in play there is room for discussion about what is *really* funny, shocking, disgusting, etc. It becomes possible to argue about just what features render appropriate what reaction. Such discussion might be aimed at appraising or cultivating people's perceptions and responses, but whatever its objective, its effect will likely be the diversification and refinement of the system of property-response pairs. We come to see things as funny in different ways, ways that warrant different kinds of amusement. And so we can debate in what way something is funny and just what kind of response is appropriate to its being so, and similarly for other objects and responses.

Wiggins's position is 'subjectivist' in that evaluative properties are rendered intelligible by appeal to modes of response. Moreover, that we typically respond as we do is portrayed as an aspect of our nature, though one open to cultivation. At the same time, this is 'sensible' subjectivism because it is also a form of cognitivism: claims that an object is 'funny' or 'appalling' can admit of genuine truth or falsehood. This is the case even though Wiggins represents any relevant standard of assessment as 'essentially contestable and internal to the thought and practices it relates to—indeed all of a piece with the practice of criticism, and vulnerable to anything that that can establish' (p. 201). What the truth of cognitivism depends on is whether an object's being, say, disgusting or amusing can explain and justify the corresponding response (p. 200).

Wiggins takes these reflections to carry over to specifically moral evaluation: moral concepts are similarly response-involving (see 1990: 68–70). Out of the 'merely subjective' responses of natural beings there emerges a discourse that is object-directed and governed by objective standards.[5] The possibility of such discourse presupposes that, for the most part, human beings share the susceptibility to respond in like ways to like objects—they catch on to the same 'property-response associations'—but this is not to say that agreement in response makes it the case that the objects have the properties we take them to have. An action is, say, contemptible only if it is such as to merit the appropriate response in appropriately sensitive subjects. It is the nature of the object that constitutes its being contemptible, not agreement in subjects' responses or beliefs. Wiggins writes:

> You can say, if you like, that we create a form of life that invests certain features of people, acts and situations with the status of values. (Surely that is not false.) But this is not to say that *values* are created thereby. Rather values are discovered by those who live the form of life that is said to have been created.
>
> (1990: 79; see also 1987: 205).

5. Holism and principles

Wiggins's picture is certainly at odds with the suggestion that cognitivists treat moral reality as 'an ontological given', but it remains consistent with the view, endorsed by McDowell and Dancy, that moral values and reasons

---

[5] Wiggins's argument that moral judgements can admit of 'plain truth' is subtle. He first enumerates what he calls, following Frege, the marks of the concept *true* ('A mark of a concept F is a property that anything has if it falls under F' (1987: 142 n. 5)). These include (i) that if *p* is true it is consistent with all other truths, and (ii) if *p* is true it will, in favourable circumstances, command convergence of belief, the best explanation of which includes reference to the fact that *p*. It follows that moral cognitivists are committed to the claim that moral enquiry does, or at least could, issue in sufficient convergence of belief. Wiggins then treats this commitment, not as a claim that might be justified a priori, but as a 'form of speculative optimism'. The truth of cognitivism rests on our finding just enough of the marks of truth exhibited in moral discourse. The cognitivist's focus must therefore be on the nature and quality of first-order moral discourse, and the onus on the philosopher is not just to observe and describe this discourse but to contribute to it in a way that might strengthen its claims to be genuinely in pursuit of the truth (see Wiggins 1987: essay 4; 1990; and 2006: lecture 11). This speculative optimism has to be maintained notwithstanding the ubiquity of essential contestability: that 'with the valuational and the practical the determination of truth is a *dialectical* undertaking in which we have to be content for the objectively stronger to defeat the weaker consideration, but without indulging the hope that there is some way by which we can be assured that we have finally arrived at the strongest consideration in the comprehensively best framework' (1987: 318).

are autonomous—irreducible to non-moral considerations and intelligible only from within the moral point of view. The question, however, is whether Wiggins's position can be rendered consistent with particularism. If the property-response relation is that between *being morally bad/wrong* and *disapprobation*, then although the 'thin' moral properties of badness and wrongness always (or almost always) warrant just that response, it will also be that the feature or features that make an act bad or wrong in one situation (her embarrassing him, say), and hence warrant disapprobation there, may warrant a different response in different circumstances. This is the basic particularist insight. It might appear, however, that this cannot be true of 'thick' moral concepts such as generosity and cruelty. Here it can seem as if such properties are themselves intimately bound up with certain modes of response, so that properties and responses are 'made for one another', and this suggests a notion of general moral relevance at odds with the idea that the significance of any property is determined contextually case-by-case. If Wiggins is right, then where the property is present it cannot be an open question whether the corresponding response is warranted. Or can it?

But just how exactly *is* Wiggins's position to be extended to morality? What *are* the relevant property-response relations for something like generosity or cruelty? There are two ways to go. One is to say that thick moral properties are not paired with responses all their own. They each provoke the same kind of response: either moral approbation or disapprobation. Those responses are 'made for' the properties in question, but they lack the specificity relevant to determining the nature of, say, generous acts as a kind. The character of the response doesn't enter into our understanding of what the act is, except in so far as it is good or bad, right or wrong. So this loses much of the subtlety of Wiggins's account. More in keeping with his view would be to recognize that by the time thick moral properties are on the scene, the object-response relation exhibits a certain complexity. Our subjective responses to instances of disloyalty, say—feelings appropriate to having been betrayed or let down, felt on one's own account or vicariously in response to witnessing the betrayal of another—are consolidated into an *attitude*[6] to disloyal acts, an attitude which remains associated with certain

---

[6] Wiggins moves, without explanation, from talk of sentiments to talk of attitudes (at 1987: 198). Of course, the notion must be liberated from the narrow construal it has typically been given by non-cognitivists. As McDowell puts it, 'a remark that expresses an attitude can also affirm a truth' (1987: 153).

feelings (and 'reactive attitudes' in Strawson's sense, e.g., resentment, indignation, etc.). This attitude is not just one of general moral disapproval, though perhaps we can think of it as a modulation of such. It embodies a way of disliking a certain sort of object. To characterize this attitude, you have to focus on just what is bad about disloyalty—why certain instances are deplorable in the way that they are. So we have to explore *how* disloyalty harms its victim, how it diminishes the disloyal themselves: that in addition to whatever external harm it may do to its victim, disloyalty affronts or destroys the relationship on which legitimate expectations of loyalty have been founded, that it breaches trust, and so on. And this draws into play the kind of evaluative notions Wiggins does directly treat: the contemptible, the disappointing, and so on. But the idea is to preserve the thought that the evaluative concept, disloyalty, is tied to a 'response', in the form of an attitude and associated feelings, that is, as it were, all its own. And being party to the attitude is essential to understanding what disloyalty is; it 'conditions the sense' of the term, as Wiggins (1990: 74) puts it.

If this can be made out, then we can appeal to the paradigmatic association of moral properties with certain attitudes and responses to ground a picture of the general moral relevance of the property in question, of why, given the sort of thing disloyalty is, it is likely to matter to the moral significance of a particular situation that there is disloyalty in the picture. But from this it doesn't follow that the property's contribution to each situation will be invariant, and the measure of variation will be reflected in the character of the responses it provokes in particular cases.[7]

There is also no obstacle to admitting that there are cases where the property, though in the offing, is simply irrelevant to what one should do. Sometimes, that it would be the loyal thing to do is no reason to do it. There can be cases where loyalty is *misplaced*, and hence where being loyal would contribute no value to the situation or make matters worse (consider a case where one feels one must blow the whistle on a friend one discovers to be engaged in illegal activity). Our standing attitude to loyal acts has to be to cases where loyalty is appropriate. And we can grant that though in particular cases where loyalty is misplaced we can explain why it is, there will be no

---

[7] Of course we should not think that the property always brings the same amount of (dis)value to every situation, as if a trivial case of disloyalty was one where something really quite bad was made not so bad at all by what else was going on.

codifying a criterion that we can deploy across all cases to determine when it is.[8] We can even admit cases where the disloyal thing *is* the thing to do (imagine a case where soldiers betray a commander who has treated them monstrously). The test of whether our standing attitude to loyalty/disloyalty can accommodate such exceptions is not just whether good reasons can be given for them, but whether the cases provoke the sentiments and reactive attitudes normally associated with the property in question, and of course they typically do not.

These holistic considerations notwithstanding, we should expect the standing attitudes associated with thick moral properties to be given voice in expressions that have the look of principles (McDowell agrees; see his 1995: 53). We might hope that, by bringing such attitudes into view, we can make sense of concerns and commitments, general and specific (in the case of loyalty, e.g., a concern to respect and defend those people or institutions to whom or which one owes allegiance, or a commitment to, say, support some particular person(s) or institution(s) in some particular way). I think we need to get such commitments and concerns into the picture if we are to make sense of moral personhood. They are constitutive of what we might call one's 'moral identity': they determine, at least in part, what kind of person one is. With such notions in view we can begin to make sense of moral conviction and integrity, and recognize that living a moral life is not just a matter of responding to reasons as they present themselves, but actively endorsing, and self-consciously pursuing, a certain way of living.[9]

---

[8] We need to understand, for example, the special bonds that loyalty presupposes. I can be loyal only to that to which I owe allegiance of some kind—my spouse, my friend, my employer, my sports club, my university, and so on. Loyalty requires that I have a certain faith in the person or institution in question, in virtue of which I will defend, support, or protect her, him, or it. Loyalty requires that I 'think the best of' the person or institution, and give her/him/it the benefit of the doubt, that I look kindly upon shortcomings, forgive weaknesses and mistakes, and so on. But not come what may. A loyal person must have an honest understanding of the strengths and weaknesses of the object of her loyalty so that she can forgive the weaknesses in light of the strengths. If the weaknesses are too significant, they compromise or render irrelevant the strengths, and requirements of loyalty are diminished or cancelled. To bring this properly into focus, we need to reflect on cases, from life and literature, but it should already be clear that the prospects are remote of codifying, in an informative way, when considerations of loyalty are overridden or silenced.

[9] In a previous paper (2000), I said that we need to give sense to concerns and commitments to explain our attunement to what matters and our setting ourselves against or in favour of certain things. Here I have something broader in mind. Wiggins's reflections on the evolution of moral thinking suggest a process in which what begins as behaviour issuing from merely subjective responses evolves into action informed by a conception of how to live. This conception issues from consideration of how our responses are merited by the objects that engender them, consideration that refines our view of what

Dancy might counter that everything worth acknowledging here can be accommodated by his idea of 'default' values and reasons. A 'default reason' is 'a consideration which is reason-giving unless something prevents it from being so' (2004: 112) and features have 'default values' if they always 'bring a value with them' to the situation (p. 185), though the value they bring can be cancelled or reversed by the influence of other factors. So Dancy can say that disloyalty has a negative default value and that an action's being disloyal is a reason against doing it unless some other factor operates to cancel disloyalty's significance.[10] I have to confess an aversion to talk of 'defaults'. First, I am not sure what it would mean to say, of the case in question, that considerations of loyalty 'bring to the situation' value that favours certain courses of action, but that this contribution is 'switched off' by the presence of other factors. What makes it look as if this is explanatory is the terminology Dancy employs—which reflects the image of the theory of reasons as a kind of chemistry: it invites us to think of the reason-giving features of situations as ingredients about which we can ask: what characteristics do they have prior to entering the situation and what do they acquire in interaction with other features? This way of speaking 'ontologizes' the thought that although loyal acts are, as it were, of a kind that we commend, considerations of loyalty are here irrelevant. But it does not really explain how this is so. Or rather, it explains it only if we have in view the kind of account of how our first-order moral thinking operates that I have been trying to articulate with Wiggins's help. I prefer to affirm a thorough-going holism, but maintain that if we reflect with sensitivity and open-mindedness on our moral lives, we will find the resources to appreciate the complexity of such phenomena as loyalty and disloyalty and what they demand in attitude and response, both emotional and practical, in particular cases. Such reflection will bring home both the enduring moral significance of loyalty, and how, notwithstanding everything of a general nature that we can say about it (which will inevitably find expression in something like

---

the objects are and the character of our responses. Even though it cannot be codified, this conception sets a standard of conduct to which we have to hold ourselves. It stands in need of affirmation and endorsement, for the moral life is not the only one that can be lived. Moral agents must in some sense commit themselves to it and to the values it embodies. (Julia Annas discusses the idea that virtue involves a commitment to the good in her 2011: ch. 7.)

[10] Though Dancy (in 1999: 145) confessed a certain wariness about the notion of defaults, he now seems at ease with the idea (see 2004: 186, responding to Bakhurst 2000). I criticize defaults in my (2005: 278–79 n. 10). Stangl (2006: 215–28) scrutinizes the notion at length.

principles), discerning the relevance to action of loyalty in particular cases demands the exercise of judgement that cannot be decided by principles because how much loyalty matters, or whether it matters at all, depends on the configuration of the case at hand.

So the idea is that, once we attain an appreciation of the full range of moral considerations, and the complexity of moral life, it will be natural to embrace a particularist vision of moral judgement. This vision, though hostile to much that philosophers have made of moral principles, need not deny a role for principles in the expression of the enduring concerns constitutive of a moral point of view. Such principles cannot be invoked to grind out answers to moral problems, for their application demands the exercise of judgement informed by much inarticulable background knowledge. Particularism so conceived is consistent with Dancy's holistic theory of reasons, but I do not see it as primarily a view in moral metaphysics any more than it is primarily a position in moral epistemology. Indeed, one might say that the principal considerations that recommend it are ethical in nature. It carries conviction because we recognize it as a compelling account of the nature and character of moral judgement. Matters metaphysical, epistemological, and psychological can come into play in illuminating that account, but particularism must ultimately look for vindication to the character of ethical life itself.

6. Infinite ends

As an alternative to talk of defaults, I suggest deploying the notion of 'infinite ends'. In his account of action explanation, Sebastian Rödl contrasts finite and infinite ends (Rödl 2007: 34–8). A finite end is extinguished in the act of realizing it. If my end is to paint my study, then once I have done this, painting my study is no longer my end. An infinite end, in contrast, is not extinguished by its realization. Rödl's example is health. If my health is my end, it does not cease to be so if I attain it. A finite end explains an action as a part of the end: my action of buying paint is explained as a part of the action that is my end: painting my study. In contrast, an infinite end explains an action as a manifestation of the end. If I play soccer for the sake of my health, my playing is explained because it is a healthy thing to do. Rödl comments that '[t]his explains the infinity of infinite ends: while a whole is exhausted by its parts, what is manifest is not exhausted by its manifestations' (p. 37).[11]

What McDowell calls 'concerns' have the form of infinite ends. He gives as an example a concern for the welfare of one's friends. One might be moved to act on that concern when one recognizes that one's friend is in trouble, but securing her welfare in no way exhausts the end. One's friends' welfare continues to be one's end no matter how well they are doing. In like manner, the virtues of justice, truthfulness, generosity, courage, and so on, are manifested in the acts that express them, but not extinguished thereby.

Infinite ends have the kind of generality we need to make sense of moral convictions. As Rödl explains, infinite ends are 'time-general'. My love of justice may manifest itself in actions on different occasions, but it is not linked to a moment or a specific duration. This helps capture part of what agents bring to moral situations: knowledge of what is of value and commitment to its realization. It is thus natural that the expression of infinite ends with ethical content will take the form of moral principles.

One attraction is that the notion of infinite ends enables us to capture both the world-directed character of moral thought and the idea of agents creating themselves through their moral convictions. We can recognize that at least some infinite ends are adopted or endorsed by agents, and that living in accord with them expresses commitment to a way of living. Indeed, Rödl (inspired by Michael Thompson) argues that infinite ends form a unity in a *practical life-form*, a conception of how to live manifest in the life activity of an agent. At the same time, we can hold that which ends to adopt is a matter of objective import; that is, agents should endorse ends that are genuinely worthwhile. And we can ask whether there is one practical life-form or many: is there one or more than one way in which infinite ends can be coherently unified?

Rödl takes all this is to be compatible with a particularist view of moral judgement; indeed, he explicitly has McDowell in mind. To decide what to do, it does not suffice to determine that some action falls under a concept that expresses an infinite end because circumstances may necessitate an incompatible action. Suppose I am off to meet a friend when I encounter

---

[11] Many philosophers have noted such a category of ends. Michael Thompson, for example, calls them 'generic ends' (2008: 89 n. 7) and cites relevant passages in Anscombe.

an injured stranger. In this case, I have to determine whether to lend assistance and thereby let my friend down, or ignore the stranger and keep my appointment. This I cannot do merely by reflecting on general relations between my ends because they do not form a ranked system. Nor can I look to the practical life-form to provide an independent criterion of action, for the question what to do just is the question of what practical life form to exemplify. What I must do is attend to the details of the case to decide which considerations are salient here and how they make a difference for action. To decide which end prevails demands the exercise of judgement, as McDowell describes.

Rödl represents the case of the injured stranger as one in which two infinite ends are in play. However, he does not see this as a conflict between ends for, on Rödl's account, the unity of infinite ends entails that they cannot conflict.[12] This forces him to say that attention to the case discloses that only one end is actually relevant there. If I see I must help the stranger and forego meeting my friend, what I see is that the end of friendship 'does not bear on the situation', and hence I do not act contrary to friendship in standing up my friend (p. 42). This has the attraction of capturing the holistic insight that considerations of friendship can be rendered irrelevant by circumstances. But the notion of ends 'bearing on the situation' is vague. Considerations of friendship clearly *do* bear on the situation in the sense of forcing us to deliberate, even if deliberation reveals that we should ultimately accord them no weight. How otherwise are we to explain why I am required to apologize or make reparations to my friend?

But of course Rödl captures an important truth. If our ends are sound, they endure through cases where circumstances frustrate their realization. One might say that infinite ends are invariant qua concerns, but not invariant in their implications for action in particular cases. It is not that the ends of promise-keeping or friendship are undermined by my helping the stranger. My action does not somehow betray that I care less about my friends. It does not even show that my friend-directed concerns are qualified. Those concerns coexist with ends of benevolence and charity even if the world sometimes contrives to frustrate their joint realization. Consider a case where I can care for an elderly and infirm aunt only by inviting her to

---

[12] Rödl writes that 'an action cannot manifest one's being X and yet manifest one's failure to be Y, if X and Y are infinite ends' (2007: 42).

live with us at a cost to my children's well-being. If this is the right thing to do, it does not compromise my concern for my children's welfare. The decision does not mean that I accord my aunt's comfort more significance than their happiness. To show this position coherent is as much an ethical as a metaethical task. Recourse to the theory of reasons may assist in this, though we cannot but work in consort with our antecedent moral intuitions. The real question is an ethical one: how can I defend my decision to my children without hypocrisy? And that is best answered by reflection on how living in accord with such ends is fitting for a morally admirable agent, notwithstanding the necessity of the exercise of judgement in hard cases forced upon us by a recalcitrant world.

7. Wiggins's ethic of solidarity and reciprocity

I turn now to the rather more ambitious anthropology of morals presented in Wiggins's book, *Ethics*. This will help place talk of concerns, commitment, and infinite ends in the context of a broader understanding of morality. Here Wiggins continues his sympathetic modulation of Hume's philosophy. The result is an account of our present moral conceptions as comprising what he calls, with Philippa Foot in mind, an ethic of solidarity and reciprocity. In keeping with Wiggins's Humean genealogy, this ethic is seen as growing out of the exercise and expansion of the sentiment of benevolence and our capacity for sympathy, refined and channelled through the emergence of the objective viewpoint presupposed by a shared language of moral evaluation. Wiggins maintains that moral evaluation incorporates an extreme pluralism, arguing that a 'grown-up moral philosophy' must embrace 'the full gamut of moral predications, seeing them as mutually irreducible and mutually indispensable, allowing no primacy to character traits *or* virtues *or* practices *or* acts *or* states of affairs—or allowing primacy to all at once' (2006: 82).[13]

---

[13] It is as if each stage in the history of moral philosophy alights upon some critical dimension of moral evaluation and tries to construct an entire moral theory based upon it. Failure is the inevitable result of such ambitions, and so moral philosophy reconstitutes itself with another dimension taken as primary. Wiggins's strategy is to retrieve the insights of a variety of moral philosophies and incorporate them into a single multi-faceted vision. An adequate view of our moral conceptions must find room for Aristotelian ideas about the formation of moral character and human flourishing, Humean insights about the origins

Wiggins imposes order on this pluralism by placing the following thought at the centre of his ethic of solidarity: each person is owed, as Foot puts it, 'a kind of moral space, a space which others are not *allowed* to invade' (quoted in Wiggins 2006: 241).[14] This is something first recognized in personal morality—something fashioned out of reflective appreciation of the requirements of benevolence—but it becomes the foundation of a social morality that requires us to live out that recognition in solidarity with other beings, in a climate of mutual acknowledgement and joint participation. This insight becomes the core of a common commitment to the security and well-being of (in Hume's words) 'the party of humankind'. This social morality is then supplemented by, and finds further expression in, a range of 'artificial' virtues and requirements centered on the concept of justice. As the latter domain develops, so it modulates the sentiments of benevolence that initially gave life to the ethic of solidarity and engenders debate about just what we owe each other.

This tiny sketch cannot do justice to Wiggins's discussion. It is significant, however, that this is a rather different view of the social character of morality than Dancy considers and rejects. This is not a picture of morality 'as a sort of social device, a human institution that has got set up for a purpose, a bit like the National Trust or the World Bank' (Dancy 2004: 133). Indeed, Wiggins is sceptical about such functional accounts of morality.[15] Nevertheless, this is a vision of values, concerns, commitments, ideals ... as objects around which people can unite and live by with a view to enhancing their common well-being. What this asks of us is something

---

of morality in shared sentiment, Kantian concerns about autonomy and dignity, and utilitarian commitments to human well-being, happiness, and so on.

[14] We can acknowledge the significance of this thought without forsaking holism, for it does not follow that *no* circumstance can obtain in which it is legitimate to invade a person's moral space.

[15] Wiggins writes:

> In truth, the inner or enactable aim of morality, the real aim of morality, is inseparable from the everyday meaning of everyday life and its everyday extensions and elaborations. It is something practically apparent but apparent only within the business of life itself. There is everything to be said for starting, as Warnock and Mackie do, with some foundational purpose or purposes (countering the narrowness of human sympathies, say). But there is no question of advancing from these to the specification of an overall end that would be required for purposes of reconceiving morality as a means to that end. It begins to appear that the idea that morality is a *device* (or a means to an end) is either, as literally understood, false—or else, as charitably understood, uncomfortably close to vacuous. (2006: 329)

that cannot be legislated by philosophical theory, but must be worked out in the messy domain of first-order moral reflection. Importantly, Wiggins combines his thoughts on the social origins and purposes of morality with an argument for a kind of particularism. According to Wiggins's pluralistic vision, moral deliberation is answerable to considerations of a variety of kinds, relevant to the assessment of different aspects of the moral domain (actions, qualities of character, ways of living, states of affairs, etc.). These considerations cannot be corralled into a coherent theoretical system. We have to countenance the ways in which these notions are in play in ordinary moral discourse, and there is simply no saying how these contrasting considerations should be weighed against one another prior to and independently of the particular circumstances of judgement. Accordingly, Wiggins turns to Aristotle for an account of the qualities possessed by those capable of sound moral judgement. People who possess practical wisdom:

> [S]ee what to aim for in *this* situation or in *that*. The assertions of such people, taken in context, will help others to grasp what a practically wise person should be concerned with under these circumstances—what they should attempt when things are *like this*. With respect to this specific sort of circumstance, their claim is universal but not very general. These assertions do not constitute general instructions because they are made in a specific context *for* that context. From the midst of such a context, the things said by the practically wise and virtuous will indeed point towards a more general 'that for the sake of which'; but it is not by following verbal instructions so much as by living and doing and engaging with the practically wise and virtuous that anyone can enter into the whole spirit in which these precepts of experience are to be understood. (2006: 238)

So Wiggins returns us to a view of moral judgement reminiscent of McDowell's.

It is important that the ethic of solidarity and reciprocity embraces this particularist view of moral judgement while combining it with a fundamental sense of the unforsakeable and the utterly forbidden. What is unforsakeable is the ideal of solidarity, and accordingly, what is forbidden is that which arbitrarily invades the moral space of individuals or otherwise undermines the very basis of solidarity. Bringing this into view makes unmysterious invariant strictures against the wilful harming of innocents, the enslaving of persons, and so on. These strictures will naturally find expression as principles.[16] Understanding the significance of such categories, however they find expression, is an ineliminable ingredient of a recognizably moral point of view.

What have other particularists made of the unforesakeable and the forbidden? Some appear willing to renounce such ideas altogether, conceding that it is at least possible that there are circumstances in which, say, torturing children for fun would be morally acceptable. Witness Gregory Pappas, describing Dewey's contextualism:

> It does follow, according to Dewey's view, that it is possible for there to be a situation where torturing children for fun is morally permissible.... Is there any genuine doubt that the presumption against torturing children for fun is so strong that it is hardly ever the subject of conscious deliberation? That does not make it immune to criticism, nor does it suggest that its stability and validity are independent of particular situations. It can be subject to evaluation and doubt in a situation, no matter how unlikely this may seem. Although it is hard to imagine a situation where torturing children for fun is morally permissible, it is clear that a Deweyan fully committed to the openness entailed by contextualism, must bite the bullet and take this as evidence of the limits of our imagination. (2008: 57)

I think this is exactly what particularists should *not* say. It is not a failure of imagination to be unable to envisage circumstances in which torturing children for fun would be morally permissible. On the contrary, thinking one has successfully imagined such a thing would be to have lost one's moral bearings.

Dancy, of course, does not follow Pappas's strategy. He admits there are 'invariant reasons', but argues that invariance is 'not a matter of the logic of such a reason' for 'the invariance of a reason is an epistemic matter rather than what one might call a constitutive one' (2004: 78): 'Invariant reasons, should there be any, will be invariant not because they are reasons but because of their specific content' (p. 77). This argument may appear sophistical (see Gleeson 2007: 376). Dancy's point, however, is that there is nothing in the 'nature' or 'logic' of reasons from which it follows that some or all are invariant. If there are such reasons, it is a fact about moral

---

[16] Central to Wiggins's cognitivist framework is the idea that we can arrive at the judgement that *there is nothing else to think but that*, e.g., slavery is wrong. Such beliefs are obviously not restricted to pronouncements about what is right or wrong in particular cases. In Bakhurst (2005), I suggest that such principles should be seen as analogous to Wittgensteinian 'hinge' propositions.

reality as we find it that some considerations make the same contribution to the balance of reasons wherever they figure. We might grant, however, that invariance is in this sense an ethical not a metaphysical issue, but nonetheless maintain that the invariance of certain reasons is a 'constitutive matter' in a different sense: namely, that recognizing the invariant contribution of certain reason-giving considerations is constitutive of anything we can properly conceive to be a moral view. After all, we surely need to do more than affirm that torturing children for fun is invariantly wrong-making; we need to show that there are absolute prohibitions against such actions.

Dancy may reply that the example is misleading (see 1993: 227–30). What is really at issue is the status of *torture*. What we can say is that an action's being a torturing has a strongly negative default value providing a default reason against it. But by considering an example of the torturing of children (i.e. innocents) 'for fun', we are just ensuring that we have a case where the default status of torture is not overridden. So the idea that we have isolated an invariantly decisive reason is really an artefact of how the case is described: the wrongness is 'a structural feature, built into the description' (p. 229). This is a perceptive response, which works well for the case Dancy considers (killing the innocent and unwilling[17]), but there is something not quite right in its application to torture. It is not clear that we should think of the wrongness of torture as merely a default status. For a case where one has no recourse but to resort to torture surely presents as a tragic dilemma. The supposed default value of torture is hardly suspended by circumstance: what one has to do remains very bad and its badness speaks against doing it even if doing it is necessitated by the certainty of some other even worse outcome. So I do not think that the notion of a default is strong enough on its own to ground the notion of absolute prohibitions. We need in play a sense of how such acts threaten to diminish morality itself.

Wiggins's position suggests further ways in which particularists might need to accommodate principles. A social ethic of the kind Wiggins articulates presupposes and demands a universe of discourse where the participants

---

[17] Dancy writes:

Killing an innocent and unwilling being is always wrong—absolutely wrong—since there is a default position [against killing] against which we already know there is nothing to put in this case.... The wrongness of killing is not essential to it, even though an ordinary act of killing the innocent is absolutely and intrinsically wrong. (1993: 230)

can reflect upon and argue out moral issues. There are many dimensions to this, but some clearly require articulation in principles. For example, once the social ethic incorporates considerations of justice that find expression in policy and law, moral discourse cannot entirely eschew principles, or cast them merely in the role of rules of thumb. A law that forbids the possession of firearms by private individuals is not a moral principle, but it can naturally be seen as a manifestation of a society's moral commitments. It would be just as natural to express this in terms of a principle that it is (other things being equal) morally wrong for private individuals to possess lethal weapons. A good deal of moral thinking operates at this level. We ask: How do we cultivate and protect the kind of society we want to live in? What kind of people should we aspire to be? Discourse on such questions naturally finds expression in principles. Finally, it is incumbent upon those united around a social ethic of the kind Wiggins envisages to understand and articulate the preconditions of public debate on ethical issues—to address questions about freedom of speech and action, issues of participatory democracy, and so on. Once again, such questions, which lie squarely in the domain of the ethical, cannot be addressed without recourse to principle.[18]

These reflections may provoke a dismissive response. Even if it is necessary to have recourse to principles, or something akin to them, in the contexts that I have outlined, the result will not be a 'principled ethic' as Dancy (2004: 116–17) understands it. These are not principles that determine and explain the moral status of every action. They fall far short of that, as they must to be consistent with Wiggins's Aristotelian view of moral judgement. Dancy may therefore feel that, insofar as he has to take my reflections seriously, he can accommodate the various kinds of principle I envisage without compromising his style of particularism. My point, however, is that the issues I have sought to bring into the limelight are not just to be accommodated or explained away, but should be central to philosophical reflection on morality.

---

[18] Wiggins's discussion of situations of dire emergency, again influenced by Foot, is also thought-provoking. Such situations might seem ripe for austerely particularist treatment, as Dancy (1993: 227) suggests. But where one is forced to do things that are, or might otherwise be, appalling, it is important that one can explain how there was nothing else to do consistent with the integrity of morality, and this requires some kind of 'principled' sense of how what one is forced to do does not undermine the foundation of morality itself.

8. Conclusion

In this chapter, I began by arguing that Dancy's metaphysical turn has had the effect of narrowing the focus of the particularist's concerns. As an antidote, I tried to place particularist insights in a less austere context by engaging in what I called speculative anthropology of morals. I argued that Wiggins's genealogical reflections in 'A Sensible Subjectivism', supplemented by Rödl's treatment of infinite ends, and the ethics of solidarity and reciprocity sketched in Wiggins's later book *Ethics*, help us see how a particularist view of moral judgement, of the kind initially advanced by McDowell, can be combined with a view of moral agents whose lives are structured by enduring concerns constitutive of a conception of how to live, a conception that, in recognition of the significance that morality plays in our lives, acknowledges the fundamental ethical importance of the unforsakeable and the utterly forbidden.

In this way I have tried to supplement Dancy's metaphysical particularism with a richer vision of moral life.[19] I want to stress that I am talking about supplementation and enhancement, not displacement. Someone might respond to my argument by asking: Isn't the particularist view of moral judgement painted by McDowell and Wiggins particularism enough? Why don't we declare that particularism is ethical not metaphysical, and give up on the so-called theory of reasons? But this would be a mistake. In my view, what we need is the theory of reasons and Wigginsian reflection on the nature of morality as equal partners in the effort to elucidate ethical life. So the spirit of my remarks is friendly amendment, not refutation. The question posed in my title is to be answered with: ... ethical *and* metaphysical.

My basic thought is this: particularism offers us a conception of the moral agent and a conception of moral reality. The former embodies an ideal of what an excellent moral agent is like. If particularism is to be vindicated, we must be able to recognize ourselves in that conception of agency and find the ideal it embodies worthy of endorsement. That recognition may take the form of a discovery, but unless particularism offers us a compelling view

---

[19] Perhaps Dancy himself acknowledges the need for this when he writes in *Ethics Without Principles*, with a touch of chagrin, that he would have liked to have written a book about 'the subtleties of our moral thought and the actual complexities of life', but wrote instead a book that 'deals largely with *theories* about reasons rather than with life' (p. 2).

of the moral agent, then no amount of theorizing is going to persuade us that the overall position is true. And that is why I think that we particularists have to have a rich picture of ethical life, not just responsiveness to reasons in particular cases. Success in this endeavour would refute those who think that particularism, considered as an ethical view, is bad or corrupt. Dancy's response to such arguments is typically to show that particularists (a) avoid certain kinds of ethical failings (e.g. rule-fetishism), and (b) are not precluded by their particularism from making morally-correct decisions in particular cases (see, e.g., 1999: 154). But this fails to speak to the concern that motivates the objection. We need to show that particularism offers the most compelling picture of a morally admirable agent living a morally worthwhile life. In contrast to Jonathan, this is where I think 'the real battleground' lies.

But whatever the differences between Jonathan and me, they are differences between colleagues who share much common ground and are united in a common cause. For showing me the importance of this cause so long ago at Keele, and for much else besides, I owe Jonathan a huge debt of gratitude.

References

Annas, J. (2011) *Intelligent Virtue* (Oxford: Oxford University Press).
Bakhurst, D. (2000) 'Ethical Particularism in Context', in Hooker and Little (2000: 157–77).
—— (2005) 'Particularism and Moral Education', *Philosophical Explorations*, 8(3): 265–79.
—— (2007a) 'Pragmatism and Ethical Particularism', in C. Misak (ed.), *New Pragmatists* (Oxford: Oxford University Press), 122–41.
—— (2007b) 'Laughter and Moral Ambiguity', in M. Lance, M. Potrč, and V. Strahovnik (eds.), *Challenging Moral Particularism* (London: Routledge), 192–208.
Dancy, J. (1993) *Moral Reasons* (Oxford: Blackwell).
—— (1999) 'On The Logical and Moral Adequacy of Particularism', *Theoria*, LXV (2–3): 144–55.
—— (2004) *Ethics Without Principles* (Oxford: Oxford University Press).
Garfield, J. (2000) 'Particularity and Principle: The Structure of Moral Knowledge', in Hooker and Little (2000: 178–204).
Gleeson, A. (2007) 'Moral Particularism Reconfigured', *Philosophical Investigations*, 30(4): 363–80.

Hooker, B. and Little, M. (eds.) (2000) *Moral Particularism* (Oxford: Oxford University Press).

Little, M. (1994) 'Moral Realism II: Non-Naturalism', *Philosophical Books*, XXXV (4): 225–33.

McDowell, J. (1978) 'Are Moral Requirements Hypothetical Imperatives?', in McDowell (1998: 77–94). (Originally published in *Proceedings of the Aristotelian Society*, suppl. vol. 52: 13–29.)

—— (1979) 'Virtue and Reason', in McDowell (1998: 50–73). (Originally published in *The Monist*, 62: 331–50.)

—— (1985) 'Values and Secondary Qualities', in McDowell (1998: 131–50). (Originally published in T. Honderich (ed.), *Morality and Objectivity: A Tribute to J. L. Mackie* (London: Routledge and Kegan Paul), 110–29.)

—— (1987) 'Projection and Truth in Ethics', the 1987 Lindley Lecture at the University of Kansas, in McDowell (1998: 151–66).

—— (1995) 'Deliberation and Moral Development in Aristotle's Ethics', in his *The Engaged Intellect: Philosophical Essays* (Cambridge, MA: Harvard University Press, 2009), 41–58.

—— (1998) *Mind, Value, and Reality* (Cambridge, MA: Harvard University Press).

Pappas, G. (2008) *John Dewey's Ethics: Democracy as Experience* (Bloomington and Indianapolis, IN: Indiana University Press).

Rödl, S. (2007) *Self-Consciousness* (Cambridge, MA: Harvard University Press).

Stangl, R. (2006) 'Particularism and the Point of Moral Principles', *Ethical Theory and Moral Practice*, 9: 201–29.

Thompson, M. (2008) *Life and Action* (Cambridge, MA: Harvard University Press).

Thornton, T. (2004) *John McDowell* (Montreal & Kingston: McGill-Queen's Press).

Wiggins, D. (1987) 'A Sensible Subjectivism', in his *Needs, Values, Truth*. 2nd edn (Oxford: Blackwell, 1991), 185–214.

—— (1990) 'Moral Cognitivism, Moral Relativism, and Motivating Moral Beliefs', *Proceedings of the Aristotelian Society*, 91: 61–86.

—— (2006) *Ethics: Twelve Lectures on the Philosophy of Morality* (Cambridge, MA: Harvard University Press).

10

A Quietist Particularism

A. W. PRICE

1. Reasons, enablers, and intensifiers

Particularism should contrast with generalism. And yet it may be a kind of generality that makes plausible the holism about reasons for action that is Jonathan Dancy's starting-point. While labels shouldn't matter much, I propose in this section that a plausible particularism might better be termed 'variabilism'. In the second section, I further argue for a recognition of considerations, constituting not reasons but side-constraints, that are also general in content. In the third section, I reject the thesis that concrete reasons rest upon abstract groundings that it is a task of theory to bring to light. In my final section, I argue for a kind of modesty: what ethical theory may yet illuminate is the practice of giving reasons for action, but without invoking any metaphysical picture of a realm of reasons that was always waiting to be mapped.

Dancy holds that a fact that gives one a reason to ϕ—or, as he likes to put it, *favours* one's ϕ-ing—in certain situations may fail to give one a reason to ϕ—or even (reversing its valence) give one a reason not to ϕ—in others. Dancy takes this to ground a scepticism about the role of principles in moral thinking. Variable valence, where it obtains, excludes any universal principles, even if these are not prescriptive or proscriptive, defining ways of acting that are always right or wrong, but *pro tanto*, identifying ways of acting that are always good or bad in a way. It may be that there is still an important role to be played by prima facie principles that hold only presumptively, since they fail to apply in certain circumstances.

There are varieties of holism, modest or immodest. The claim may just be that variable valence is not excluded by the very concept of a reason. That would still be significant, but would leave open that certain facts about actions may have a content of such a kind that they cannot but yield a reason for or against, whatever the context; such reasons would be invariable. Thus perhaps there is always something to be said against 'the causing of gratuitous pain on unwilling victims' (Dancy 2004: 77), or torture, or cruelty. It would then be pertinent to consider what kinds of reason may be invariable, how often they apply, and what strength attaches to them.

A perspicuous form of words for ascribing to an agent a reason for acting is this: 'The fact that p, taken in context, gives A a reason to ϕ.'[1] The prevalence of variable valence is not to be gauged independently of a distinction that Dancy draws between a fact's being a *reason*, and its being a *condition* of another fact's being a reason. Most obviously, there are what I call 'basic enablers'.[2] The clearest example is its open to the agent to ϕ. Its being open to A to ϕ evidently gives him no reason to ϕ; rather, in its absence nothing is a reason for him to ϕ. Conversely, there are basic disablers: if A is unable to ϕ, facts that would otherwise be reasons for him to ϕ are no such reasons. Dancy writes (2004: 40):

> In the sort of sense that 'ought' implies 'can', we might also suppose that 'has a reason' implies 'can'—that one cannot have a reason to do an action that one is (in the relevant sense) incapable of doing. I have, perhaps, a reason to run as fast as I can but no reason to run faster than that.[3]

One might reply that, while its being open to A to ϕ is not itself a reason for him to ϕ, it is a component of any reason that he has to ϕ. But it would be cumbrous to claim that the content of every practical reason contains a 'can', and more intuitive to hold that the predicate 'has a reason' entails 'can'. We can say that most reasons for A to ϕ are more precisely reasons for

---

[1] I shall also speak of a fact's *being* a reason, or *counting as* a reason, for A to ϕ. When I ascribe a variable valence to a reason, what I have in mind is a fact that, in different contexts, may be a reason to ϕ, or no reason to ϕ, or even a reason not to ϕ.

[2] See Price (2008: 165 n. 38). Being persuaded by Bernard Williams that 'a statement about A's reasons' must be 'a distinctive kind of statement about, distinctively, A' (1995: 194), I there add as a second basic enabler that the reason must, in some appropriate manner, be accessible to the agent: he must be able to appreciate it, or to appreciate a benefit that comes from paying regard to it, or to come to such appreciations after conversion by experience; see Price (2008: ch. 4, §2), and cf. Väyrynen (2006: 715).

[3] It might be said against this that one can regret being unable to ϕ; but how can I regret this if I cannot regret not ϕ-ing, and how can I regret that if I have no reason to ϕ? But I can regret not ϕ-ing when it would be really good to ϕ, even if an inability to ϕ robs me of what would otherwise be reasons for me to ϕ.

him to ϕ *if he can*. Suppose that the fact that p is a reason for A to ϕ if he can. This leaves open whether he can ϕ. However, if we add to p that he can ϕ, then the fact that p becomes a reason for him to ϕ *simpliciter*.[4]

Basic enablers and disablers at once generate a universal variabilism that is too weak to be interesting: *any* consideration that would otherwise count as a reason may fail to do so simply through the absence of a basic enabler (or, equivalently, the presence of a basic disabler). More significant, therefore, are any variable enablers (or disablers) that are only relevant to certain acts, in certain contexts. Dancy (1993: 60) offers this example: someone's having stolen a book disables his having lent it to me from counting as a reason for me to return it to him, though this would normally have been a good reason. It is not that, in a commoner case, his *not* having stolen it is either a reason, or even part of a reason, to return it. What makes it plausible, at least within our social world, that his not being a thief constitutes rather the absence of a disabler than either a reason or part of a reason, is two things: the improbability of his being a thief, and the innumerability of other circumstances, probable or improbable, whose presence would also be disabling. For it would be an impossible task to specify all of these in order to incorporate their absence within the statement of an invariable reason.

However, such considerations are themselves variable and sensitive to contingency. If I live in a community where books are commonly stolen, but other relevant complications are rare, I might well identify as my reason for returning a book the more complex fact that it has been lent to me by an honest man. This might also be my reason for returning a book to one man, who is honest, rather than returning a different book to another whom I know to be a thief, when I am willing to do either but lack time to do both. More recently, Dancy (2007: 87–8) has virtually conceded this: a consideration that only *enables* a reason for ϕ-ing may itself count as a reason for, or favour, what he calls 'a rather peculiar object', ϕ-ing but not χ-ing (when these differ in respect of that consideration). Yet there is nothing peculiar about the act of ϕ-ing *rather than* χ-ing; certainly this may be a conscious object of choice, as when I decide to ϕ, but not because I prefer ϕ-ing to not ϕ-ing in the abstract, but because, in context, I have just two options, ϕ-ing and χ-ing, of which I prefer the first to the second.

---

[4] A reason *for which an agent acts* has an additional enabler, which is his belief that the fact in question obtains. It is rarely that this belief is itself a reason for action.

Dancy (2004: 41–2) also distinguishes from reasons what he calls 'intensifiers'. He gives this example:

(1) *B* is in trouble and needs help.
(2) *A* is the only other person around.
So, (3) *A* helps *B*.

He takes (1) to be already a reason for (3), and denies that (2) is 'another reason, on top of the first one'. Rather, he takes (2) 'to intensify the reason' given by (1). (2) makes the reason given by (1) 'stronger'; we should not suppose that it is 'part of a larger reason which includes [*B*'s] need for help'. He writes: 'The tendency to agglomerate favourer and intensifier is much less strong than the tendency to agglomerate favourer and enabler.' If this is true, it is because favourers *require* the presence of enablers, but only *invite* the presence of intensifiers. It is hard to see that this prohibits agglomeration: if '*B* is in trouble and needs help' is already a reason for *A* to act (which entails that *A* is able to help), why shouldn't '*B* is in trouble and needs help that only *A* can give' count as a stronger reason for *A* to act—one that might override, where (1) on its own would not, a significant counter-reason (such as *A*'s having a really pressing engagement)? However, even if we *may* say that, we can also capture the case by saying that, in certain circumstances, it is only in the presence of (2) that (1) gives *A* sufficient reason for (3).

More significant, but not an objection to Dancy, is that a consideration that only intensifies a reason for (3) may be essential to a reason for something different but related. Suppose that *B* is only one of two people whom *A* is in a position to help, but that the other person can be helped (and, let us suppose, will be helped) by someone else if not by *A*. Here (2), which intensified a reason for (3), becomes a necessary part of reason for the following, which is more complex:

So, (4) *A* helps *B* rather than *C*.

Hence we capture a distinction if we say (with Dancy) that (2) intensifies (1) as a reason for (3), but goes to constitute a more complex reason for (4).

What also stands is that, if (2) intensifies (1) as a reason for (3), (2) cannot serve as a reason for (3) on its own. Contrast a separate reason such as this:

(5) *A* has promised to help *B* (whether he is in need or not).

Here, (1) and (5) stand to (3) as distinct reasons, whose double presence counts for more than the presence of either of them taken on its own. However, conjoining (1) and (5) in order to form a single, complex reason would not be intelligible.[5]

Such variations are intriguing. What is most important, I think, is that Dancy's policy of setting aside certain considerations as enabling or intensifying a reason, rather than being themselves a reason, or even part of a reason, has the effect of ruling out what would otherwise be further specifications of reasons.[6] A corollary is to leave what is itself a reason more general, and less specific. This may be important for the variable valences, and (we may now add) degrees of valence, emphasized by the holist. If we were to build the presence of enablers, the absence of disablers, the presence of intensifiers, and (we may add) the absence of attenuators into the very content of a reason, it would become less plausible that *further* information may always cancel, reverse, intensify, or attenuate a given reason. Why should we suppose that our practical sensibilities are so indefinitely fine-grained that a further specification of the circumstances can always make a difference? Rather, variations in valence are a result of a certain generality in the contents of a reason. In this respect, 'variabilism' may be a more apt label than 'particularism': it is the typical *generality* of the facts that give reasons that make them liable to vary, in different contexts, between favouring or not favouring or disfavouring, and to variable degrees, the very same act.

---

[5] There are doubtless other possibilities. Suppose that (6) *A* has promised to help if (1) holds. Clearly (6) is not a reason for (3) that is additional to (1), since (1) is a condition of (6)'s applying. Yet (6) gives a reason for (3) that is additional to the considerations of benevolence that were doubtless implicit in Dancy's appeal to (1) as a reason for (3). (6) relates to (1) rather than as an intensifier; but that may not be the *mot juste* when different kinds of consideration are in question.

[6] Dancy (2004: 96) rightly distinguishes a fact's being a reason, and what (if anything) *explains* its being a reason, or even *guarantees* that it is a reason. Reasons are typically things *for* which an agent acts, and which he can state if he is asked for a reason. Our concept of practical reasons is one of facts of such a kind that agents (and not just theorists) can typically *act on* them, and *avow* them as their reasons. (This implies not that agents are always aware of their reasons, but that their not being so is a *failure*. This would be the contingent product of a lack of clear-headedness or of self-knowledge, and not the inevitable result of what is unsurveyably complex or unfathomably profound.) A complete explanation that specified everything whose presence or absence affects the valence of a certain reason in a given context would not be stating what could count as a reason *for* an agent.

2. 'One thought too many'

A need to distinguish reasons from considerations that connect with reasons but are not themselves reasons is also illustrated, I believe, by some reflections of Bernard Williams that have become celebrated under the label 'one thought too many'. I shall further argue that these considerations may rest upon the presence or absence of side-constraints whose content is essentially general.

Williams (1981a: 18) takes over from Charles Fried the following case: a man can save one, but not both, of two persons in equal peril, and one of them is his wife. If he is to save his wife, does this demand an ethical justification? (We can imagine that the other person is also someone's wife, and, say, with more or younger children.) Williams resists 'the idea that moral principle can legitimate his preference, yielding the conclusion that in situations of this kind it is at least all right (morally permissible) to save one's wife'. He objects to it as follows (p. 18):

> This construction provides the agent with one thought too many: it might have been hoped by some (for instance, by his wife) that his motivating thought, fully spelled out, would be the thought that it was his wife, not that it was his wife and that in situations of this kind it is permissible to save one's wife.

There is something right about this; but it needs care to identify Williams's target. It is evident, at least in context, that he is rejecting any demand for a *moral* justification—in some sense of the term 'moral'. One way of reading the passage is as an appeal to romance: perhaps 'It's my wife' here has the same force as 'It's the love of my life.' (If so, one should permit a similar appeal to Tristan on behalf of Isolde, though she was Marke's wife.) For the really romantic, it may then even be inessential that *he* is also the love of *her* life. On reflection, all this is rather shocking. Doesn't it make a difference that she is his *wife*? And a wife, though ideally the love of her husband's life, may not be: should his commitment be contingent upon the state of his feelings? (If Isolde had ceased to be the love of Marke's life—and Wagner's Marke appears to be more pained by his friend's betrayal than by his wife's—would that have left Marke free to save whomever he fancied?) In fact, there is no ground to read Williams so. No doubt he leaves the husband's motivations unspecified. Very likely (as Susan Wolf has suggested to me) they were overdetermined. We may suppose that his wife was indeed the love of his life; in any case, she was the recipient of his marriage vows.[7] In the absence of any contrary indication, we may take him to be motivated by both considerations. We might then say that his motivation was partly moral, and partly romantic. And yet we should surely allow that a commitment to another person whom one both knows and loves intimately, even without any exchange of vows, could only be viewed as ethically indifferent on a puritanical conception of the ethical. Of course, we are free (as Williams was) to associate a more specific conception of the *moral* with certain features of our ethics, and not the most appealing ones. But fidelity is surely an ethical virtue, though its sphere is not restricted to the connubial (or otherwise explicitly obligatory).[8]

What we should rather notice is Williams's refusal to appeal to 'moral principle'.[9] Indicative is an extended earlier passage which I can only quote in part (1981a: 16):

> Someone might be concerned about the interests of someone else, and even about carrying out promises he made to that person, while not very concerned about these things with other persons... [To some extent] the lover's relations will be examples of moral relations, or at least resemble them, but this does not have to be because they are *applications to this case* of relations which the lover, *qua* moral person, more generally enters into.

Crucial then is not whether the husband saves his wife for an ethical reason (even for one arising from a promise), but whether he derives this from a general principle that applies in a multitude of cases. It is *this* derivation that Williams will reject (two pages later) as 'one thought too many'. His agent's reasons must count as ethical on any adequate conception of the ethical; but they are essentially particular. His focal concern is what he *owes to her*, or has otherwise, in his heart of hearts, *to do for her*. And this, surely, is what is essential for the virtue of fidelity. What one friend owes another is not a

---

[7] As the bridegroom is asked in the 1928 Book of Common Prayer, 'Wilt thou love her, comfort her, honour, and keep her in sickness and in health; and, forsaking all others, keep thee only unto her, so long as ye both shall live?' An appeal to an exchange of vows imports a regard for *duties*. But that shouldn't be taken as equivalent to an embrace of Kantianism, or deontology, or any other structuring of ethics. If the particularist is unable to take duties on board, his barque must lack ballast.

[8] Thus we should not assimilate what Williams is saying here to what he is willing to say elsewhere (famously in the case of Gauguin; see Williams 1981b: 23–4) about the possible subordination of ethical to other considerations.

[9] I heard Dancy make just the point that follows in an illuminating discussion (at which Susan Wolf and Miranda Fricker were also present) that has nourished what I say here.

high, general valuation of the opportunities and obligations of friendship. The proof of friendship is an ability to detect the facts that give one reason to act on a friend's behalf, and a willingness to respond generously to them.

Such commitments might well be called 'particularist'. They differ from the general commitment that we may take to be implicit in Dancy's example where (I take it) *some woman or other* 'is in trouble and needs help' (2004: 41). The first connects with the second, but not through being subsumable under it. If A turns out to be a dependable friend of B though an undependable friend of C, and an unjust and unkind agent in many other contexts, this is likely to be through contingencies (which are also restrictions) that save his friendship for B from being put to the test. Yet if friendship is a field of choice for the exercise of many of the virtues, this is not because *there* we are more likely to respect what we recognize as our general obligations, but because an alertness to reasons there can fuel an alertness to similar reasons elsewhere. We learn to be kind to those who *need* our kindness through habits of kindness to those to whom we *want* to be kind.

Yet there are limits to the partialities of friendship. Williams well notes (1981a: 17) that it is not that 'if there is some friendship with which his life is much involved, then a man must prefer any possible demand of that over other, impartial, moral demands'. He comments, 'That would be absurd, and also a pathological kind of friendship, since both parties exist in the world and it is part of the sense of their friendship that it exists in the world.' We need to capture a duality of concern: what I do for my friend I do as owed *to him*, but what is owed to him cannot be identified in isolation from what I owe *to others*. 'It's my wife' is a sufficient reason for saving her rather than another (when I can save one but not both); it wouldn't be a good reason for giving her a job rather than another (when a public appointment is in my power). We surely want the thought 'It is impermissible' to play an *inhibiting* role, even if there is a *motivating* role that we don't want to be played by the thought 'It is permissible.' Whatever we may say about the predicate 'is a reason', we should grant that the predicate 'is (im)permissible' naturally attaches to *kinds* of act. And what here 'wears the trousers' (as J. L. Austin used to say) is surely the *impermissible*: the permissible is simply that which, though being of a general kind that is liable to be impermissible, isn't. It is not plausible to say, in the appointment case, that the agent intuits the absence of a reason—though any reason he has otherwise to forward his wife's prospects is indeed silenced. Nor is it simply that he detects a moral obstacle *in this particular case*. Rather, he is inhibited, if he is inhibited (as within some cultures husbands and fathers are not), by a general consideration: acting *in such a way* is nepotism, and so a form of injustice. Such a constraint is not just a presumption: it rules out even *considering* certain situations in certain ways. (It operates rather as blinkers than as spectacles.) Principles have distinctive and useful roles to play, whose distinctiveness and utility are obscured if we suppose that *every* reason depends upon a principle.

There is no need to extend our conception of what can constitute a reason, or an enabler, or an intensifier: in each case, it is a fact. Yet what explains why a fact plays this role in a context varies. This can be illustrated by comparing Dancy's example of whether to return a book that was stolen with my example of whether to appoint a candidate who is one's wife. In one context, what would otherwise define an act as just (that it would be returning what one has borrowed) has its valence neutralized by a further consideration (that the lender had no right to it); in another context, what would otherwise give one a reason (that this would be helping one's wife) has its valence reversed by a further consideration (it is a public appointment). In the book case, what looked like making an act just fails to do so: to return a book to the lender is usually to return it to the rightful owner, but not in this instance; so it will not achieve the agent's presumed purpose. (However, if his aim is to return it to someone who wants it back, or needs it more than he does, this may be achievable by returning it.) In the job case, what looked like an act of helping one's wife may indeed be so, but is excluded by justice: it is not permissible to help one's wife in such a way, even when it would succeed. In the one case, a particular end would be frustrated (since justice is not done); in the other, a general constraint would be flouted (for what is done is an injustice).

All these cases exemplify that reasons often have a wide degree of generality: returning what one has borrowed, and helping one's wife, are characterizations that apply to a wide range of acts, though whether they connect with a reason in any particular case is sensitive to circumstance. General principles may be citable in support, or devisable in thought, but with varying ease and point. When I return a book to its rightful owner, I achieve something worthwhile in a manner I wouldn't know precisely how to generalize. 'Return what one borrows' is a good general rule, but too indiscriminate and imprecise to define how and when one should act in a particular case. 'Respect ownership' is hardly deniable (unless one holds that property is theft); but it is one thing to accept it, and another to understand what it *is* to respect ownership. Such rules can still be useful as prompts, alerting us, as occasion arises, to the presence of a reason for doing *this now*. Yet they do not *ground* such reasons: it is not that we have to *test* a reason by trying to universalize it in order to be certain of its reality.[10] By contrast, when I decline to appoint my own wife to a job, I am inhibited from achieving something desirable (her having the job) by the general principle that public appointments be made impartially. Here the rule is active: it acts as a *side-constraint*, excluding from my range of options one that would otherwise appeal.

Two lessons emerge even from these cursory reflections upon a few cases. The first is that we do justice to Williams's intuition of 'one thought too many' not by setting aside any thought that 'in situations of this kind it is at least all right (morally permissible) to save one's wife' as wholly out of place, but by taking it to constitute not one of the agent's reasons for action (or even part of a reason), but rather as a consideration that excludes the presence of a disabler (that is, of there being a feature of the situation that precludes him from putting his wife first).[11] The second lesson is that what explains the absence of a disabler can be the inapplicability of any general prohibition. If this is right, it must hold, in other cases, that it is the applicability of such a prohibition that makes some feature of the situation a disabler. We must therefore avoid two opposed mistakes: one is to intrude disablers, or their grounds, into the content of reasons; the other is to exclude disablers from being grounded, in certain cases, upon general constraints.

---

[10] Cf. Dworkin (1995: §5). Entirely different is the role of universalization in Kant and R. M. Hare: it starts from a mere maxim (Kant) or preference (Hare), which needs to be tested by universalizing before—as we may put it—an ethical reason emerges. Dancy rather starts from the recognition of a value (or disvalue) in context. There is no question that values can be universalized: if ϕ-ing has a certain value in this situation, it must have the same value in any situation identical in kind. Universalizability is here a corollary, and not a test.

[11] By contrast, suppose that one is the captain of the ship, and can only save one's wife by directing a lifeboat towards one group at risk of drowning rather than another. This would seem to be a ground for a randomizing procedure, such as spinning a coin, that would otherwise count as heartless or neglectful.

3. Reasons and groundings

One stimulus to particularism was the thesis of the *uncodifiability* of the virtues. According to this, we cannot hope to define adequately in concrete terms what it is, say, to be brave. For one thing, there are too many and too varied ways of being brave, each corresponding to some different figuration of danger. Besides, we find that if we take what is generally a way of being brave, capturable in a simple and unitary phrase, it ceases to be brave in certain contexts, and may even become cowardly. (Thus it could show cowardice to keep one's place in the face of the enemy, and thereby fail to perform a tactical retreat.) This aspect of uncodifiability is an analogue of the thesis that, applied to reasons for action, I have termed variabilism.

A good test case is lying and truth-telling. Truthfulness perhaps hardly lends itself to actual reversal: is there any situation in which it is actually *un*truthful to tell the truth? There is plausibly too tight a connection between the virtue and a certain highly general mode of action. And yet a kind of variabilism seems integral to the very content of the virtue. Here, at least, a promising view seems to be one that has been worked out by Mark Lance and Maggie Little (2007). The default is that it is untruthful, and so bad in a way, to tell a lie. One tradition has even maintained that it is *always wrong* to do so. This may be doubly too strong: we may rather hold that there is *standardly something very bad* in telling a lie; for on occasion this may be bad but the lesser of evils, and still more rarely it may not be bad at all.[12] Even so, I take this default to be distinctive in having the generality, and some of the proscriptive force, of a side-constraint (like that on showing partiality in a public appointment): it does not merely generalize about the presence of a major disvalue, but actively rules out what might otherwise be options. Contexts in which the default holds are privileged, not simply in that they are statistically the most common, but in that they are central at once to our practices of assertion, and to our morality.[13] From other

---

[12] For a few references, see Price (2008: 172 n. 50).

[13] This *duality* of centrality may not be universal. Take another default: that pain is bad. This admits of exceptions—though fewer than is sometimes argued (see Price 2008: 181–3). Is this central to our concept of pain? Possibly it is, at least aetiologically, for Wittgensteinian reasons: the primitive expressions of pain, out of which the language of pain develops, express at once that pain is present, and that it is unwelcome. However, it is plainer, and sufficient, that the default disvalue of pain, and its converse, the default value of pleasure, are central to our conceptions of human values.

contexts, the default is not simply absent; rather, it takes effect either as a vestigial presumption, or by indirection. Thus, even in the course of the board game *Diplomacy*, tactical lying is possible only because a weak presumption against lying remains. (Without that presumption, how could anyone be taken in? How, indeed, could there be even a pretence of 'diplomacy'?) When a prisoner is being interrogated by an invading enemy, the absence of any possibility of cooperation within an accepted framework and towards an agreed end (of the kind that makes the defendant in a criminal trial still *one of us*, even if he has stepped out of line) permits him faultlessly to mirror, in the mismatch of his answers to the questions, the mismatch between his licit purposes and the illicit purposes of his interrogators. Here a contortion of what commonly counts as truthfulness is imposed by necessity.

Yet there may be alternatives. Pekka Väyrynen has attempted, in an impressively sustained series of papers, to impose an intelligible and well-motivated framework.[14] He takes principles such as 'Stand your ground in battle' or 'Do not lie' and notes that, as we ordinarily mean them, they are *not* equivalent to the universal and unacceptable rules '*Always* stand your ground in battle' or '*Never* tell a lie.' Rather, when we subscribe to such rules we do so with an implicit hedge. He supposes that such rules, and also weaker statements about an agent's having a reason to act, or not to act, in a certain way, rest upon an implicit *normative basis*, a phrase that he defines as follows (2009: 96): 'By "the normative basis", I mean that factor (property, relation, condition) because of which the fact is a reason for (or against) performing the action, and which thereby explains why it is that kind of a reason in this instance.' He justifies a confidence in the existence of normative bases as follows (p. 96): 'Justification in ethics would threaten to be arbitrary unless at least generally there were an explanation of why something is a moral reason for (or against) something when it is, and why it isn't a moral reason for (or against) something when it isn't.' Hedging a principle denies it application in cases where its underlying rationale fails to hold.

Thus, in the case of lying, Väyrynen conceives two 'toy theories', as he calls them, about why we generally have reason not to lie. Theory 1 says this: 'An action's being a lie is a reason against it when, and because, lying contributes to undermining such beneficial social practices as trusting other

---

[14] I am further indebted to him for friendly responses to a draft of this chapter (two of which I shall quote).

people's word' (p. 97). Theory 2 says this: 'An action's being a lie is a reason against it when, and because the addressee is owed the truth (or has a right to it, or lying violates her autonomy, or the like).' These theories will agree that we generally have reason not to lie, but disagree about *why* we do, and hence about *when* we do not. Väyrynen supposes that any such practice must have a *single* basis, though he allows that what is superficially a single practice might conceivably divide into a pair of practices: promising$_1$ might be grounded by a principle 'It would be irrational to break, for no good reason, a voluntarily undertaken commitment', but promising$_2$ by a principle 'The promisee has some such right as to determine that one do what one promised or to receive the fruits of the promise' (p. 112). If so, something would have to make it clear which kind of promising was going on. (Which is evidently false of us.)[15]

An intuitive aspect of his view, which gives it an advantage over certain alternatives, is that he allows us to treat a normative basis not as a more basic reason, but as 'a condition for other things to be reasons' (p. 101). Hence my reason for not asserting something may simply be that it would be a lie. This need not be denied by a theorist who underpins a general prohibition on lying by appeal to Kant's categorical imperative, or to contractualism (pp. 101–2). We remain free to count as the agent's reason some fact that he could well cite himself, even if a theorist would ground his reason through the unfamiliar elaboration of a philosophical grounding.

Yet Väyrynen allows that on occasion a fact may fail to function as a reason *even though* the normative basis is instantiated. He writes (p. 100):

> Suppose . . . that the normative basis of an action's being a lie as a reason not to do it is that being lied to undermines one's autonomy. Cases seem nonetheless possible where being lied to would undermine one's autonomy and yet the fact that the action would be a lie is no reason not to do it. One might sometimes deserve to be deceived in this way.

He can concede this by permitting an element of contextuality: in different conversational contexts, an explanation of why an agent has a reason may cite a grounding that is more *proximate*, or more *fundamental*. It may suffice

---

[15] However, in reply to me Väyrynen allows for a double grounding: a lie may be wrong because it is socially harmful, or because it undermines autonomy. If so, a lie that is perfectly alright must be subject to neither complaint.

for some present purpose to cite a grounding that is not defeated in context, which is proximate to the act-type and familiar to the hearer, without one's needing to plumb the depths of explanation and cite a grounding remoter from the act-type, and less familiar to the hearer, that allows of no exceptions. However, it remains a concern whether Väyrynen can hope to fill out his normative bases without the use of concepts that are as liable to variable valence in *this* role as particularists would take them to be within reasons. Where he cannot, variable valence has still to be grounded.

Also significant about his concession is that it appeals to what intuitively are two different groundings: autonomy, and desert. Any claim that there must always be a unique normative basis for any invocation of a hedged principle becomes stipulative if we are instructed to put diverse groundings together within a single *tutti-frutti* concoction. (In this case, Väyrynen might well have said that, if I deserve to be deceived, deceit does *not* undermine my autonomy. But we are likely enough to need recourse to groundings, conjunctive, or disjunctive, that are disparate and not of a piece.)

Väyrynen concedes that our grasp of normative bases is often imperfect: 'More typically our conception of what moral concerns or ideals underlie the principles we accept is inchoate or incomplete' (p. 119). He accommodates this with two 'even if's (pp. 119–20):

> Firstly, even if my grasp of the normative basis designated by a hedged principle . . . is incomplete, this isn't a kind of incompleteness which would leave the proposition expressed by the principle incomplete or indeterminate. The incompleteness lies mainly in one's grasp of what property realizes a normative role which is itself reasonably determinate. Secondly, even if my grasp of what property realizes the relevant normative role is inchoate or incomplete, it may still have enough content reliably to guide my judgments, at least within a certain range of cases.

This attempts to make the best of a mismatch between the understanding of agents, which is taken to be limited, and the reality of normative relations, which is taken to be determinate. The two are linked in that agents are supposed to be guided by an inchoate grasp of a systematic reality. This can only be speculative until it is explained how agents achieve what is best interpreted as an imperfect mastery of a structured theory. Otherwise, there would seem to be no a priori reason to expect that what appeals to *one* theorist as a rational morality should be able to explain *any and every* agent's grasp of moral reasons. (Even if *I* happen to be that theorist, what would justify me in claiming for my theory such an explanatory role? It looks presumptuous.[16]) The data on which this conception draws might be interpreted quite differently as evidencing not a nascent and splintered sense of what itself is determinate and unified, but varying degrees of capacity to detect and balance a multitude of practical considerations.

Though neither is intended to be more than illustrative, Väyrynen's two 'toy theories' are well contrasted in that the first is consequentialist, attending to bad effects that come of lying, the second deontological, focusing upon bad aspects that are integral to lying. Each is problematic. Theory 1 would not explain our conceiving of lying as typically being *inherently* bad. Acting in a way that undermines a beneficial social practice is bad for its consequences; and then it isn't clear that anything would be amiss if the liar *also* acted in such a way as to preclude any undermining. (He might *make* an example of himself before his lie could *set* an example.) Yet we would rather suppose that rendering a lie innocuous makes things less bad without making them perfectly alright.[17] Theory 2 seems more apt in attempting to capture something bad that typically inheres in lying. Väyrynen writes of 'failing to exhibit the kind of concern or respect which persons merit' (2008: 87). Yet this reads rather as an umbrella that covers a range of considerations than as an explanation that grounds them. To the extent that we do share a conception of what it is to *respect* a person, it is rather derivative from, than explanatory of, a sense of such things as how bad it is to lie.[18] If we are persuaded to qualify this, allowing that, on rare occasions, it may be not only permissible but perfectly alright to tell a lie, this is likely to come of an attention to special factors whose relevance is no

---

[16] I am reminded of Hare's engaging but surely eccentric confidence that he could identify what early Christians *really* believed by appeal to his own philosophy of religion. One wonders whether Väyrynen supposes his normative bases to be perennial, or products of history. To the extent that they are the latter, we cannot expect them to be fully transparent to philosophy.

[17] To say this is not to dismiss general reflections upon the utility of truthfulness. So Dr Johnson: 'Society is held together by communication and information; and I remember this remark of Sir Thomas Brown's, "Do the devils lie? No; for then Hell could not subsist"' (Boswell 1887: iii. 293, cf. 228–30). However, such thoughts do not define the badness of lying in such a manner as to identify the exceptional cases (if any) where lying is not wrong, and perhaps not bad at all.

[18] So Arrington (2002: 280): 'All one can say [to defend the assertion that lying is wrong] is that lying to others is treating them with disrespect, but this comes to little more than treating them in ways in which one ought not—i.e. Lying is wrong.'

more explicable by some *prior* conception of proper respect than is the general badness of lying.[19]

Notoriously resistant to a grounding explanation is the wrongness of murder. Väyrynen (2009: 98) offers the following: 'Accounts of why killing a person is wrong (or there is a moral reason not to do so, or the like) include that it *frustrates the victim's prudential interests*, that it *deprives the victim of future experiences that it would be valuable for her to have*, that it *manifests ill will*, and so on.' Perhaps any of these is less off-target than G. E. Moore's concern that 'if it [murder] were a common practice, the feeling of insecurity, thus caused, would absorb much time, which might be spent to better purpose' (1903: 156–7). Yet it is disconcerting that Väyrynen presents not less than three groundings, with an indefinite offer of more ('and so on'). And that they are no stronger.[20] (The first two apply to dying in general, and the last applies to many regrettable but non-criminal acts and omissions.) And yet that it is generally very bad, and indeed wrong, to kill a fellow human being is unquestionable—as it might not be if this really *depended* upon a 'normative basis' that had still to be identified.

A more realistic picture, as it seems to me, is that certain rules (and other things, such as values, and paradigms) *stand firm for us*. Though they are not of a kind to *look* fundamental to a philosophical theorist, ever in search of the abstract and universal and potentially axiomatic, they belong to the framework of our practical thinking. Though firm, they are not grounded; for we could not think of any grounding of which we are more certain than we are certain of these.[21] Plausible examples are indeed 'It is bad to lie

---

[19] The same problem arises with the concept of *well-being* that underlies the contrasted consequentialism of Theory 1. I doubt whether we have a sufficiently determinate conception of this that is *independent* of paradigmatic counsels of prudence; if so, the former cannot serve to ground the latter. Väyrynen writes (2006: 720): 'When C provides a prudential reason for doing something, this is because of some connection between C and the agent's well-being.' There may well be such a connection, but it is another question whether the nature of well-being *independently grounds* prudential reasons.

In other cases, an impact upon well-being is intrinsic to the act in question. Väyrynen (2008: 90) suggests that the wrongness of causing pain 'has got something to do with its making people worse off'. Which explains nothing. 'Being worse off' may be more general (in the sense of less specific) than suffering pain; but how could I share our conception of what it is for a human being to be worse off without *already* appreciating the typical intrinsic disvalue of pain? (It is not even the case that, when I learn more generally what it is to be 'worse off', I gain a *deeper* appreciation of that disvalue.)

[20] As one character says to another in Henry James's story 'Covering End': 'It is when reasons are bad that one needs so many!'

[21] Behind this, of course, lies Wittgenstein (1969). A succinct application of that to ethics is to be found (in German) in Müller (1997: §§3–5); see otherwise Arrington (2002: §§2–3). Müller remarks (p. 454) that one could not seriously imagine *grounding* a disapproval of lying upon Kant's categorical

(mostly)', and 'It is bad to kill a fellow human being (mostly).' *Given* these as defaults—*initially*, no doubt, as principles without exception, even if we replace 'bad' by 'wrong'—we begin to grasp some necessary conditions of social life. Each is like a ripple that spreads across a pond, or a magnet that influences the fields of other magnets in its vicinity.

Though such rules are ungrounded, it confirms them indirectly that they come to be of a piece with more sophisticated obligations and permissions that help to structure a civilized social life. Not that they stand in need of confirmation: that could only arise if it dawned on us that we might dispense with them, and we wondered whether we would then be better or worse off. But to live with a principle is also to become at home with its connections and ramifications. One may doubt whether any principles or conceptions of values can become dominant within a society without connecting to *some* degree with confirming experience. However, inequalities of power or status may privilege the experiences of some unjustly over the experiences of others. And it is easier to confirm the existence of *a* reason to act in some way than of a *requirement* to act so. Societal change may bring it about, or make it clear, that some value or principle is unsustainable (cf. Price 2000: 155–7). However, that lying and murder are generally very bad stands firm, though not *upon* any basis that grounds it.

It fits with this that the grounds of making an exception are various. In certain rare cases, principles that seemed firm come into conflict—either implying contradictory prescriptions (which is a danger with principles of 'right' and 'wrong'), or at least producing problematic tensions (as can happen even with applications of 'good' and 'bad'). A notorious instance is Kant's case of a man who can only save his father's life by lying to a would-be murderer about his whereabouts. It can be argued that he shouldn't lie, since the responsibility is entirely the murderer's if the lie is false, but becomes in part the liar's if the lie turns out to correspond to the truth (so that he plays the role of an unwitting accomplice).[22] But it is also an

---

imperative. If one really disapproved of it *because of* Kant's argument, this disapproval would have to be infected by any later doubts about that argument; which would be insane.

[22] See Kant (1996: 182–4 = AK 6:429–31). Cf. Dr Johnson, *Rasselas* (1759: ch. 34): 'When, in prospect of some good, whether natural or moral, we break the rules prescribed us, we withdraw from the direction of superior wisdom, and take all consequences upon ourselves.' Johnson agreed with Kant (p. 184) that a servant should not say that his master is 'not at home' to save him from being disturbed; Boswell cites this, and dissents (1887: i. 436).

intelligible view that, if murder is wrong, and *supremely* wrong, then it is wrong to abet murder, even by telling the truth. Whether, in accord with Väyrynen's various hypotheses, we are then to suppose that telling truths to murderers is not a beneficial social practice, or that the murderer's autonomy is not being undermined, or—as he also allows—that he deserves to be deceived; these are questions, no one of them privileged, that can arise within attempts to think through the possible ramifications of permitting an exception in this case. As in many attempts to achieve reflective equilibrium, reflection may proceed in a number of directions. Some (like Kant and Dr Johnson) will exclude any exceptions. Others will admit an exception, and may then wonder what philosophical theories (relating to utility or autonomy or desert) this might feed into. Others again will be uncertain whether to admit an exception, and may then confirm or correct this uncertainty by general reflection. Others will wait to take one line or another until a particular case arises, with no sense that this will either invite or demand generalization. Whether there is anything here to be *explained* philosophically is an open question. For many (perhaps most) of us, the situation is one not of sharing an intuition that calls for explanation and grounding, but of honestly not knowing what stance to take, and being very unsure what the implications would be of elaborating one in general terms. That there must be a *correct* line to follow, one that stretches out indefinitely but determinately, like an already laid but invisible railway-track, is a picture that lacks application.

4. Metaethical modesty

Even a discussion as cursory as this raises general questions about the proper ambitions of ethical theory. In broad terms, there are two contrasted points of view. We may call one 'realist', the other 'non-realist'.[23] Of the moral philosopher the first requires immodesty, whereas the second permits modesty (though it does not entail it).

On a realist conception, the reason-relation, which holds between facts and acts, exists independently, not of course of the existence of free agents,

---

[23] I do not use the term 'non-realism' to imply a general non-cognitivism. Rather, the contrast has something in common with that between Platonism and intuitionism in the philosophy of mathematics.

but of their conceptions of it. About this, Dancy and Väyrynen appear to agree. Dancy calls his particularism 'a view in moral metaphysics' (2004: 140), while Väyrynen calls his generalism 'a metaphysical view concerning particular moral facts or truths' (2006: 708). Human beings may yet aspire to acquire some understanding of the reason-relation, and its instantiations, if Aristotle was right to remark: 'Everyone has a natural aptitude for grasping truth' (*Eudemian Ethics* I 6, 1216b, 30–1). It may be supposed that success is achieved or missed from occasion to occasion. As Dancy once wrote (1993: 64): 'To be consistently successful, we need to have a broad range of sensitivities, so that no relevant feature escapes us, and we do not mistake its relevance either. But that is all there is to say on the matter.' Or else, as Väyrynen supposes, success comes of a grasp, sufficient for the occasion, of underlying and unifying principles that explain what kinds of fact generally provide reasons, and when they occasionally fail to do so. Such principles would be at once justificatory and explanatory, and any theory of them faces two tasks. On the one hand, it must provide groundings of general reasons, and occasional exceptions, that yield determinate and consistent results (at least in cases where we take there to be ethically correct answers—for some cases may be really irresoluble, or insignificant). On the other, it must help explain the discriminations that we actually make, ascribing to different agents varying but always plausible degrees of understanding of an underlying rationale. In particular, it needs to have things to say about *how* this rationale is implicitly taught, imperfectly but recognizably, to new members of the moral community.[24]

---

[24] Väyrynen comments as follows:

> Regarding toy theories. I have no adequate substantive first-order theories of the wrongness of killing or lying to offer. What I was after were simple theories to illustrate a structure. As simple theories, they are most probably quite clearly false; but greater complexity might not illustrate the structure as well. I'm inclined not to worry all that much about the substantive shortcomings of the simple candidate explanations which I use as illustrations. Nothing in that shows that something more adequate cannot be offered. That's the job for moral theorists.

Problematic here is a duality of role: adequate theories will have to be complex enough to track our best reflected judgements, and simple enough to have been plausibly internalized (if only imperfectly) by morally decent agents.

I take it that any morality has to be a popular morality, in the sense that ordinary people internalize it in ways broadly familiar to us. I doubt whether these could suffice even for an imperfect grasp of Väyrynen's normative bases. (Perhaps a population could be indoctrinated in an ethical theory like the North Koreans in the Juche Idea. It is worth wondering how much *less* than that could instil a shared set of normative bases.)

On a non-realist conception, we are free to turn our back on hopes of a unified theory, and attend instead to all the actual ways in which a young agent is taught to do *this* rather than *that*, and learns to apply past lessons to new situations. As his experience expands and his judgement sharpens, he learns how to make new discriminations with varying degrees of confidence. Sometimes, an element within the framework that helps constitute morality feeds into a simple and satisfactory assessment of what, in a particular case, is morally right or wrong, good or bad. Yet only in certain cases do we simply apply rules, for there are *innumerable* other ways of making decisions that are equally supplied by the framework.[25] As soon as we begin to reflect upon unfamiliar cases, we find ubiquitous what David Wiggins (2002: 124–32) has termed 'cognitive underdetermination'.[26] In very many cases we are far from being agreed which way to go. To the extent that we are aware of being fundamentally in agreement, we can speak of getting things right and wrong, and can apply concepts, thick or thin, in accordance with what can count as their meanings or senses. Yet even here we often take chances, applying a term in a way that retrospectively may count as correct if and only if others come to accept it. We can think of ourselves as *constructing* at once our abstract concept of a reason for action, and our concrete conceptions of reasons—so long as there is no implication of the Bauhaus rather than of the improvised, intuitive, and often provisional. Ethical construction is essentially the work of amateurs, who derive what confidence they can, not from claims to expertise, but from feelings of solidarity and hopes of consensus.[27]

---

[25] Dworkin (1995) usefully sketches a wide range of different ways in which we convey moral instruction and make moral discriminations. One recurrent recourse is to prototypes: often 'the meaning of a concept is determined by a cognitive schema or image, and speakers determine whether some new instance falls under the concept by judging the degree to which the new instance matches the prototypical schema or image' (§7). Väyrynen (2008: 96) cites empirical data that 'seem to suggest that moral judgments are typically caused by psychologically immediate unreflective evaluations (often fuelled by stereotypes or emotional reactions)'.

[26] Rather, as pacifists (as Elizabeth Anscombe complained) risk suggesting, by their rejection of any *jus in bello*, that ways of waging war are all of a piece, so non-cognitivists risk suggesting, by their rejection of ethical knowledge as such, that moralists are always at the same distance from truth. What makes ethical thinking vulnerable is rather how quickly, once we have left the beaten track, we find ourselves without clear paths to follow. Moral conflict is too often the product of an unhappy combination of underdetermination and bad manners.

[27] Väyrynen replies, via email, in a way that I think illumines what is at issue between us:
   Reasons can depend for their existence on principles, and be explained by such, even if we'd prefer a moral agent's psychology to be such that the recognition or representation of a reason

Much that I have been saying is intended, and may (I hope) be accepted by Dancy, as the support of an ally. However, the particularism (or variabilism) that I have learnt from him is metaphysically quietist: it tries to capture general features of our ways of thinking and speaking that are not justifiable, as it were, from *outside* (or, indeed, from *above*, within a different and idealizing constructivism, as aspirations towards some ideal of rationality). Tactically, my view is convenient: if we really thought, like the realist, that the moral world has its contours fixed independently of our ability to map them, it would be hard to be sure that Väyrynen's programme might not reveal its true topography, little though it connects with any common cognitive capacities of ours. The non-realist is immune to the fantasy of a fixed ethical world waiting to be captured by ethical systematization. A quietist particularism that discards any metaphysical or rationalist ambitions, and is content to analyse the actual ways in which we think without taking these to reflect either some pre-existent reality or some rational ideal, may be more secure, in its very modesty, against the over-reachings of generalist theorizing.

References

Arrington, R. (2002) 'A Wittgensteinian Approach to Ethical Intuitionism', in P. Stratton-Lake (ed.), *Ethical Intuitionism: Re-evaluations* (Oxford: Clarendon Press), 271–89.

Boswell, J. (1887) *Life of Johnson*, 6 vols, ed. G. Birkbeck Hill (Oxford: Clarendon Press).

Dancy, J. (1993) *Moral Reasons* (Oxford: Blackwell).

—— (2004) *Ethics Without Principles* (Oxford: Clarendon Press).

—— (2007) 'Defending the Right', *Journal of Moral Philosophy*, 4: 85–98.

Dworkin, G. (1995) 'Unprincipled Ethics', *Midwest Studies in Philosophy*, 20: 224–39.

Kant, I. (1996) *The Metaphysics of Morals*, tr. M. Gregor (Cambridge: Cambridge University Press).

---

doesn't depend on a recognition or representation of a principle (given the availability of other kinds of sensitivity to principles). As I read your discussion, it concerns the structure of a virtuous agent's psychology rather than the metaphysics of reasons.

I do not believe that there *is* a metaphysics of reasons (nor that the recognition of reasons always depends upon a sensitivity to principles).

Lance, M. and Little, M. (2007) 'Where the Laws Are', *Oxford Studies in Metaethics*, 2: 149–71.
Moore, G. E. (1903) *Principia Ethica* (Cambridge: Cambridge University Press).
Müller, A. (1997) 'Totale Toleranz in Sachen Singer?', *Zeitschrift für philosophische Forschung*, 51: 448–70.
Price, A. W. (2000) 'On Criticising Values', in A. O'Hear (ed.), *Philosophy, the Good, the True and the Beautiful*, Royal Institute of Philosophy Supplement, 47: 141–58.
—— (2008) *Contextuality in Practical Reason* (Oxford: Clarendon Press).
Väyrynen, P. (2006) 'Moral Generalism: Enjoy in Moderation', *Ethics*, 116: 707–41.
—— (2008) 'Usable Moral Principles', in M. Lance, M. Potrč, and V. Strahovnik (eds.), *Challenging Moral Particularism* (London: Routledge), 75–106.
—— (2009) 'A Theory of Hedged Moral Principles', *Oxford Studies in Metaethics*, 4: 91–132.
Wiggins, D. (2002) 'Truth, Invention, and the Meaning of Life', in his *Needs, Values, Truth*, 3rd edn, amended impression (Oxford: Clarendon Press), 87–137.
Williams, B. (1981a) 'Persons, Character and Morality', in his *Moral Luck: Philosophical Papers 1973–1980* (Cambridge: Cambridge University Press), 1–19.
—— (1981b) 'Moral Luck', in his *Moral Luck: Philosophical Papers 1973–1980* (Cambridge: Cambridge University Press), 20–39.
—— (1995) 'Replies', in J. E. J. Altham and R. Harrison (eds.), *World, Mind, and Ethics: Essays on the Ethical Philosophy of Bernard Williams* (Cambridge: Cambridge University Press), 185–224.
Wittgenstein, L. (1969) *On Certainty*, tr. D. Paul and G. E. M. Anscombe (Oxford: Blackwell).

11

Contours of the Practical Landscape

DAVID McNAUGHTON AND PIERS RAWLING

Preface (by David McNaughton)

While both Piers and I have learned much from Jonathan Dancy, I have had the privilege and pleasure of having Jonathan as a colleague and personal friend over many years. I was appointed as a lecturer at Keele in 1970 and Jonathan joined the department a year later. We were of an age, and quickly became friends and allies. From the outset, Jonathan was highly impressive. He was not only extremely clever and very quick thinking, but willing to challenge orthodoxy. Philosophical debates tend to be conducted on certain agreed assumptions in terms of which the problems, and their possible solutions, are structured. It was Jonathan's willingness to question such assumptions that made his thinking so innovative and stimulating. Conversations with him—of which there were a very large number—were thus always liable to take unexpected, and even slightly unsettling, turns.

Jonathan was a profound influence on my philosophical development in incalculably many ways, but I want here to mention two crucial respects in which I am deeply indebted to him. In my early years I was a convinced, if somewhat reluctant, ethical non-cognitivist, and a disciple of Richard Hare. Jonathan's incisive critique of the case for non-cognitivism persuaded me that moral realism was not only defensible but highly plausible—a position I have never since abandoned. For about ten years, he and I jointly taught an exciting and demanding final year course on metaethics and ethical theory. Jonathan's Socratic method of tutorial teaching kept everyone, including me, on our toes. I have rarely had to think so hard, nor enjoyed it more.

In those days, early publication was not especially encouraged, still less required, and we were given little by way of guidance on how to publish. My technique for writing papers—think of a philosophical problem I found deeply perplexing and try to solve it—was not a recipe for success. Indeed, I began to feel a failure and seriously considered leaving the profession. Jonathan, who had already published *An Introduction to Contemporary Epistemology*, as well as two ground-breaking articles on moral particularism, encouraged me to write an introductory book on ethics, based on the course we had jointly taught for many years. As very many of the ideas that had emerged from that teaching were primarily Jonathan's, this was a deeply generous gesture. Not only did he suggest the project, he read every draft of *Moral Vision* and made extensive and extraordinarily helpful suggestions for its improvement. His encouragement and guidance at this crucial stage changed the course of my professional life. It is the sort of debt that one cannot repay, but for which one can simply remain profoundly grateful.

1. Introduction

Jonathan Dancy is renowned both for his moral particularism and his reasons holism. Moral particularism, in its original formulation, is, roughly, the thesis that there are no moral principles that are true, finitely statable, and knowable. Moral reasons holism is the claim that any feature might count as a moral reason, and that (almost) any feature that can count as a moral reason in favour of (or against) an action that bears it might be morally irrelevant, or even count morally against (for), such action in other circumstances.

How are particularism and holism related? That depends, of course, on the details of specific versions of the doctrines. But here's the general idea. Particularists certainly reject strict principles—say: lying is never morally permissible. They also, however, reject weaker principles, such as: the fact that your utterance would be a lie always counts against it morally speaking (even in cases in which lying is morally permissible). (Dancy (1993: 61) gives the example of games in which lying is part of the fun.) Such weaker principles can be expressed in terms of reasons: the fact that your utterance would be a lie is always a moral reason not to utter it (even when this reason is outweighed by reasons on the other side). The moral-reasons-holist's denial of this is of a piece with the particularist's rejection of the weakened principle against lying. But aren't both these positions easily defanged? Even if the fact that an act would be a lie doesn't always count against it, perhaps this is true only under certain conditions. If we specify these conditions, we can then safely say that, in their absence, lying counts against. However, both the particularist and the holist might adhere to a doctrine of uncodifiability: such conditions can't be specified (at least, not non-normatively—see section 2).

Moral reasons are a type of practical reason, and holism can, of course, be extended to practical reasons generally. One of our concerns will be with the relation between such holism and what one might call the contours of the practical landscape. Like us, Dancy sees a potential difficulty here (2004: 111):

> Holism maintains that anything whatever might make a practical difference, or provide a reason, if the circumstances were suitable. It sees no difference, apparently, between such features as being very damaging to one's health and the number of leaves on a tree. It sees no difference between the causation of unwanted and undeserved pain and whether one sets out with the right foot or the left. If there are differences between these things, it can only be that one of them matters more often than the other. But we all think that this is not all there is to it. The stubborn intuition is that though holism may be right in stressing the possibility of exceptions to all moral rules, still there are rules, and there must be rules for there to be exceptions. What is more, the exceptions are not statistical exceptions but moral exceptions. These exceptions bear their exceptionality on their face, as one might put it.

In fact, holism, in a more sweeping form, not only maintains that 'anything whatever might... provide a reason', but also that any consideration, such as 'being very damaging to one's health', can switch 'valence', as it is sometimes put, in analogy to the chemical notion. That some act would severely damage your health is ordinarily a reason against performing it (negative valence); but the radical holist claims that there are circumstances where this consideration would be irrelevant (zero valence), or even a reason in favour (positive valence). For many considerations, the idea of switching valence raises no concerns: that it's cold outside is usually a reason for you to wear your coat, but if you're trying to impress your Muscovite hosts in midwinter it may be a reason not to. For others, though—the fact that an act would, say, inflict undeserved harm—the idea of variance may well seem problematic: inflicting undeserved harm, it might be thought, has invariantly negative valence.

One proposal to solve the contouring difficulty for the holist, then, is to limit the holism. This is one thing we have proposed in the past (McNaughton and Rawling 2000), and we'll revisit it here (section 2), in part to contrast it with Dancy's own proposal (section 3). But we shall also explore a somewhat different approach to structuring practical reason. In the case of valence switching, the strength of a reason switches from positive to negative as circumstances vary. Moving from positive to negative strength may, however, be viewed simply as a decline in 'reason strength' in which, as it were, the reason's strength passes through zero. But changes in the strength of a reason can, of course, occur in the absence of a switch in valence—more generally a reason's strength simply varies in magnitude as circumstances vary. In section 4 we explore the extent to which a systematic account of reason strength can be given by looking to the notions of welfare and value, and the distinction between them.

2. Universal reasons

Donald Davidson (1980) famously argues that practical reasons are mental states with causal powers. But we adopt a different usage, according to which practical reasons are facts—the fact that it's cold outside is a reason for you to wear your coat.

It's important to note that there are two facts lurking here. Your reason is the first: it's cold. But there is also a second: the fact that the first fact is a reason. We have, then, a two-tier view of practical reasons. At tier one are the reasons; at tier two are the facts that the tier one facts *are* reasons. Experience tells us that it's easy to muddle this distinction, so perhaps it helps to appreciate that the two tiers give rise to different possibilities of error: you might be mistaken about the weather (tier one error); or you might fail to realize that cold weather is reason to wear a coat (tier two error).

In some contexts 'reason' refers only to a cause, as in, 'metal fatigue was the main reason for the bridge's collapse'. For Davidson, 'reason' refers, in psychological contexts, to a cause that rationalizes. If, say, his reason for calling was that he wanted to persuade her to go, and he believed he could do so by calling her, then, according to Davidson, these mental states caused his calling. But they also rationalize his behaviour. And rationality, unlike causality, is a normative notion: *ceteris paribus*, we *should* be rational. Our notion of a reason is also normative: if it's cold, and this fact is a reason for you to wear your coat, then (roughly speaking), in the absence of countervailing reasons, you should wear your coat.

Rationality, and reason (in our sense), are part of a broader family of intertwined normative notions. What is normativity? We have no analysis of it in other terms (we take seriously Butler's dictum that 'everything is what it is, and not another thing' (1729: 14)); all we can do is give illustrations of normative notions, and their relations. On our usage, for example, a normative requirement is not made so by the fact that most people *do* heed it (if they do), but by the fact that they *should* heed it—they have overriding *reason* to heed it. Or consider another pair of normative notions: the evaluative and the moral. To say that a potential act of yours would make the world better is, on Scanlon's (1998) 'buck-passing' account of the good, to say that you have a reason of a certain kind to perform it. If an act would be morally wrong, then (on many views, at least—but see section 7 below) you have overriding reason not to perform it. The list of other normative notions includes harm, benefit, innocence, desert, justice, fidelity, gratitude, reparation; and these too are inter-related. W. D. Ross (1930: 21), for example, takes justice to be concerned with the distribution of benefits and harms in accord with desert; and desert, of course, is tied to innocence. The normative is also tied to the non-normative. Supervenience holds, for instance: innocence, say, cannot be lost without a change in non-normative circumstances. And there may be non-normative items on lists of benefits, harms, and valuable (or not) features of states of affairs. Not all such items are non-normative, however; and normativity also enters when we ask what unifies the lists.

According to what we'll call the 'simple view' of reasons, normative notions do not enter into their content. On this view practical reasons (tier one facts) are non-normative facts. It is tier two facts that are normative—i.e. have normative content. (Note that adverting to content is crucial here—normative facts can be *picked out* using non-normative vocabulary, at least on occasion: for instance, 'the first fact David thought of when waking today' might pick out the fact that he has reason to go into the office.) A practical reason (on this view) is not itself a normative fact; it is the fact that you have it that is normative.

But is this view correct? Suppose an act you're contemplating would cause someone else undeserved harm. This, we think, is a reason against performing it, the normativity of the notions of harm and desert notwithstanding. We reject, then, the simple view of reasons, and allow that there are normative tier one facts—i.e. what we call 'normative reasons' (usage varies). And these may help with the contouring difficulty: there are some normative reasons that count against in all circumstances, and some that count in favour in all circumstances. In our view, we've just seen one of the former: that your act would cause someone else undeserved harm counts against it in all circumstances.[1]

Our discussion so far, however, has neglected a logical possibility: that a reason might count both for and against the very same act—might have both positive and negative valence—in the very same circumstance. Then it might be true of some reason both that there is no circumstance in which it doesn't count against, say, and that there is a circumstance in which it also counts in favour. The standard holist response to any purported example of, say, a reason that always counts in favour, is to come up with a case in which it counts against. But, if a reason can count in both directions at once, then merely coming up with a case in which a reason counts against does not suffice to rule out its always counting in favour. So, are there any cases of reasons counting in two directions at once?

A previous example will serve.[2] You find yourself in Moscow. It's a cold winter's day. This is a reason to wear your coat. On the other hand, not wearing your coat on such a cold day would impress your hosts (something you have reason to do, let's say). Thus the fact that it's cold is, here, both a reason for and against wearing your coat. Now, of course, there's a story to be told—we've just told part of it—and it might be maintained that if we

---

[1] Rejecting the simple view means abandoning a simple account of the supervenience of practical reasons on the non-normative: on the simple view, there cannot be a change in what you have reason to do without a change in the non-normative facts because your reasons are among the non-normative facts. If we allow normative facts at tier one, this, obviously, no longer holds. However, supervenience still holds provided that, to take the current case as an illustration, harm and desert have non-normative supervenience bases—that is, there cannot be two cases that differ in terms of harm or desert without some non-normative difference. This seems to us obviously true.

[2] Fans of *Yes, Minister* will recall another possible case—Sir Humphrey's oft repeated response to the Minister's proposals: 'That would be very courageous, Minister.'

spell everything out we'll see that no *full* reasons count in two directions at once. On the one hand, that it's cold and not wearing your coat would be uncomfortable is a reason for you to wear it. On the other, that it's cold and not wearing your coat would impress your hosts with your endurance of discomfort is a reason for you not to wear it. But matters here are somewhat tricky.

Dancy (2004: 97–9; see also 123) criticizes attempts, by such authors as Bennett and Raz, to defend the notion of a 'complete' reason. If reasons are complete, holism is false, since the more you pack into the content of a reason, the more difficult it becomes to switch its valence. On Dancy's view (e.g. 2004: 38ff), reasons are to be distinguished from 'enabling' (and 'disabling') conditions. Reasons for Dancy, we'll say, are 'compact', and our previous example stands: the fact that it's cold is the reason; but it is differentially enabled. What enables it to be a reason to wear your coat? That doing so would prevent discomfort. What enables it also to be a reason against wearing your coat? That not wearing your coat would impress your hosts.

Here's how we see the logic of the situation. One component of a thoroughgoing holism is:

(H) For any possible fact F, act ϕ, circumstance C, and agent A:
If F is a reason favouring (against) A's ϕ-ing in C, then there is a circumstance C*, distinct from C, and an agent A* such that F is a reason against (favouring) A*'s ϕ-ing in C*.

But if the reasons are not 'restrained', they will 'swallow' the circumstances, rendering (H) false for, as it were, the wrong reasons: it would not be falsified by a reason that cannot switch valence, but by the fact that a reason F will include all its circumstances, so that wherever F holds, C obtains, and hence there is no C* distinct from C in which F holds. This route to falsifying (H) is blocked by taking a compact view of reasons. The compact view, however, also allows for reasons that count in both directions at once—so that (H) is not inconsistent with the claim that some reasons count in favour (or against) in all circumstances.

So now let's return to a reason that, we contend, counts against in all circumstances: the fact that your act would cause someone else undeserved harm. Are there cases where it also counts in favour? Suppose someone threatens that he will inflict undeserved harm on several people unless you inflict it on one (it doesn't matter what harm, or on whom—it just has to be unjustly inflicted). That your act would cause someone else undeserved harm now seems to be a reason in favour of performing it. But it also remains a reason against. There is, of course, a difference in the means-end status of the act when considered, as it were, from the two different directions. Avoiding the infliction of undeserved harm is always an end in itself. However, in this case, its infliction is also a means to preventing the infliction of even more of it, so that it counts here in both directions at once.

That your act would inflict undeserved harm is an example of what we'll call a 'universal' reason against—a universal reason being a reason that counts in one direction (but not necessarily in *only* one direction) in all circumstances.[3] There are other universal reasons; and all such, we think, are normative (but not all normative reasons are universal). How much, however, do these universal normative reasons really help with the contouring difficulty? One thought is that, in the case at least of moral reasons, there is always some universal reason present. Take lying, for example. It is not always the case that you have moral reason not to lie—we certainly agree with Dancy that there are circumstances in which the fact that your utterance would be a lie does not tell against uttering it morally speaking. But when you do have moral reason not to lie, then, the idea runs, the lie would fall under a normative description that points to a universal reason against it. For example, lies can harm innocents, or violate fidelity (cf. Ross 1930: 21). And the fact that your act would harm an innocent or violate fidelity is always a reason against it. When there is a moral reason not to lie, there is, then, we claim, some universal reason also operative—a normative reason that counts against in all circumstances. (It is, however, merely a contingent statistical fact about our world that most lies fall under such further normative descriptions.)

We have suggested a similar approach before (McNaughton and Rawling 2000), to which Dancy responds as follows (2004: 119):

---

[3] Perhaps the advocate of compact reasons would maintain that the reason here is only that your act would cause someone harm, with lack of desert featuring in a different role. But for simplicity we'll ignore this somewhat flexible boundary between reasons and other considerations from here on since it doesn't affect our line of argument—rather than 'universal reason', sticklers might prefer the term 'universal consideration'.

> I think it fair to say that McNaughton and Rawling never offer any reason for supposing that variance is impossible without invariance. This is, of course, what is really needed. Otherwise the dispute will descend to examples, when for the particularist the point really is why we need the invariant at all.

The particularist here is not quite the person we characterized in our opening paragraph—someone who denies that there are any moral principles—rather, she is an advocate of Dancy's updated version of the position, who claims that 'the possibility of moral thought and judgement does not depend on the provision of a suitable supply of moral principles' (2004: 7). This position can, of course, be extended to practical reasons generally: the transcendental holist, as we'll call her, maintains that the possibility of practical thought and judgement does not depend on there being any universal reasons. Do we have an argument against transcendental holism?

Well, following Wittgenstein (1953), we certainly don't think that appealing to rules is helpful in explicating normativity *per se*. And we don't have a sort of transcendental argument to the effect that variance is impossible without invariance—Dancy is correct in this. Do we, then, have any argument to the effect that invariance is 'needed'—or, to put it in our terms, that universal reasons are needed?

In short, no. That is because we do not think that universal reasons are needed for any purpose. For instance, we certainly don't adhere to a model of practical reasoning according to which you should reach conclusions about what to do by a process of syllogistic deduction, or some such, so universal reasons are not needed as premises in deductive arguments. Rather, we simply see universal reasons as an integral part of the practical landscape. Ultimately (as we'll shortly see) we see the strength of your reason to perform some act as dependent on the amount of value (good or bad), benefit and/or harm it would contribute—and, in the case of benefit and harm, to whom. And universal normative reasons are universal because they concern the ways in which your act would contribute in these respects. In the case of lying, for instance, we cited harm to innocents and fidelity. The first of these refers to harm directly—harm to an innocent, which is bad. And breaches of fidelity, we think, are harmful to the victim of the breach in a particular way. (There is an issue, we acknowledge, about how interesting these universal reasons are—we see it, for example, as built into the notion of fidelity that one always has reason not to breach it. However this, obviously, does not exhaust the content of the notion.)

In our view, then, reasons holism reaches its limit when confronting universal reasons, which allow for principles such as: breaches of fidelity always count against. This is not to deny, of course, that competing reasons might outweigh this consideration, so that you have more reason to breach than not. We'll return later to the topic of weighing reasons; we turn now to Dancy's own approach to the contouring difficulty.

3. Dancy's view

Whereas we propose that there are universal reasons, Dancy proposes instead that there are merely 'default reasons' (2004: 112–13), where:

> A default reason is a consideration which is reason-giving unless something prevents it from being so. The idea is that some features may be set up to be reasons, in advance as it were, although it is always possible for them on occasions to fail to give us the reasons they are set up to give. One can express this idea more or less metaphorically. More metaphorically, one could say that some considerations arrive switched on, though they may be switched off if the circumstances so conspire, while others arrive switched off but are switched on by appropriate contexts. Less metaphorically, one could say that if a default reason-giving feature does give us a reason in this context, there is nothing to explain; we only have something to explain when such a feature doesn't provide a reason. With other features it is the other way around; if they do provide reasons there is something to explain, and if they don't, there isn't.

In some ways this approach echoes that of W. D. Ross in the following passage (1930: 138):

> Pleasure seems, indeed, to have a property analogous to that which we have previously recognized under the name of conditional or *prima facie* rightness. An act of promise-keeping has the property, not necessarily of being right but of being something that is right if the act has no other morally significant characteristic (such as that of causing pain to another person). And similarly a state of pleasure has the property, not necessarily of being good, but of being something that is good if the state has no other characteristic that prevents it from being good. The two characteristics that may interfere with its being good are (a) that of being contrary to desert, and (b) that of being a state which is the realization of a bad disposition. Thus the pleasures of which we can say without doubt that they

are good are (i) the pleasures of non-moral beings (animals), (ii) the pleasures of moral beings that are deserved and are either the realizations of good moral dispositions or realizations of neutral capacities (such as the pleasures of the senses).

One difference, of course, is that Ross is speaking of rightness and goodness rather than reasons. And another is that, in his discussion here of the goodness of pleasure, Ross lists what he takes to be the characteristics that may 'disable' pleasure's goodness. Dancy, as we read him, would deny that any lists of enablers or disablers can be given in advance of consideration of particular cases (see, e.g., 2004: 122).

While we do not see the gulf between our view and Dancy's as that wide—he would seem to agree with us, for example, that certain normative reasons have a special status (when it comes to thick concepts, for example, he wants 'centrality', though not invariance: p. 122)—nevertheless we have some doubts about his view.

How is the remark that 'if a default reason-giving feature does give us a reason in this context, there is nothing to explain' to be interpreted? What if an enquirer falsely believes that a disabler is present (i.e. falsely believes that something is preventing the default reason from being a reason)? To such an enquirer, the fact that the default reason is, as it were, operative *does* require explanation. Dancy contends (p. 113), for example, that the fact that an act would be just is a default reason in favour of it. On his account, then, it is only in the presence of disablers that there is anything to explain concerning justice's valence: when justice counts in favour there is nothing to explain. But suppose you falsely believe that there is a disabler present. Then there *is* something to be explained to you—namely, that there is no disabler present, so that justice counts favourably here.

This difficulty might be avoided, of course, by appeal to an account of explanation that is not enquirer-relative. Dancy rejects (p. 46), however, one non-enquirer-relative account—what he dubs 'the completeness of a full explanation' view—in favour of a view that parallels his account of reasons and their enablers. On this view (pp. 45–9) the *explanans* explains the *explanandum* even though it would not do so were certain enabling conditions not met, where these conditions stand outside the explanation. Dancy suggests, for instance, that a 'full causal explanation of an event might be thought of as one that specifies a sufficient set of events as causes' (p. 46), with the relevant laws playing the role of enabling conditions for such an explanation as opposed to being a part of it. Or, in the case of explaining an action, your having the belief, say, that it's cold outside is part of what enables the fact that it *is* cold outside to explain your wearing your coat—your having the belief is not itself part of the explanation.[4]

How might this account of explanation be applied to the explanation of some fact's counting as a reason in favour of an act? Consider our case of its being cold outside favouring your wearing your coat. Perhaps part of the explanation of this case of favouring is the fact that your wearing your coat would prevent your discomfort—one of the facts, as we have seen, that enables the fact that it's cold to be a reason for you to wear your coat. If so, then an enabler of the reason contributes to explaining its reason-giving force. If Dancy's default reasons required no enablers, as suggested by his claim that a 'default reason is a consideration which is reason-giving unless something prevents it from being so' (p. 112), then there would be no enablers to explain the default reason's reason-giving force—just as expected if there is nothing to explain.

On Dancy's account, then, it looks as though the claim that there is nothing to explain when a default reason counts in the default direction might be equivalent to the claim that defaults require no enablers. But if so, trouble looms, since Dancy suggests that all reasons require enablers (pp. 38–40). For example, the fact that you are able to ϕ is a 'general enabler' (p. 40) of the reasons that favour ϕ-ing. One response to this might be to point out that ability doesn't help explain reason-giving force—it is not what we might call an 'explanatory enabler'. So it could be that default reasons are distinct in having no *explanatory* enablers. But this returns us to the lack with which we began: we need a non-enquirer-relative account of explanation to elucidate the notion of an explanatory enabler.

Dancy also discusses (pp. 113–17) an approach to the contouring difficulty developed by Mark Lance and Maggie Little (see their 2005, 2006) that looks to defeasible generalizations. But he remains unconvinced that their approach yields a 'way of moving beyond the notion of a default reason' (p. 117). At this point, then, rather than continuing to canvass sufficient conditions for a fact to be a practical reason, perhaps we should look for

---

[4] As Dancy acknowledges, his account here is 'highly contentious' (2004: 46). One obvious difficulty (which, to be fair, he does his best to address) is how the account is to cope with cases of false belief—e.g. explaining your wearing your coat on a hot day in the mistaken belief that it's cold: that it's a *hot* day appears unlikely to do the trick.

other ways of structuring the practical landscape. Can we formulate necessary conditions for something to be a reason? Can we classify reasons into types? What contributes to their strength?

4. Welfare and the good

Whereas, say, Bernard Williams (1981) explores the idea that among the necessary conditions of reasonhood are certain features of an agent's motivational psychology, we propose to look in a different direction—at the claim that, roughly, you have reason to perform some act only if benefit or good would ensue. If this is correct, then a universal practical question is: what benefit or good would my proposed act contribute (or what harm or bad would it prevent)? Of course, the notions of good and benefit, it might be said, are so close to the notion of a reason itself as to make all this rather uninteresting. But, if so, we will have succeeded in part of our enterprise, since this close relationship is part of what we hope to establish.

What about types of reasons? We see reasons as falling into three and only three categories—the personal, the special, and those associated with considerations of value. Roughly, 'personal reasons' are reasons you have to benefit yourself; 'special reasons' are reasons to benefit those to whom you stand in special relationships of various sorts; and 'value reasons' are reasons you have to promote the general good. The strength of your reason to perform some act, on our view, then, is a matter of how much so acting would benefit you or those to whom you stand in some special relationship, and/or how much good it would do. We turn now to look at some details, and some contrasting views.

In acting you modify the state of the world. Some states are better than others; and some states are better *for you* than others. The 'better than' relation ranks states in accord with their goodness or value; the 'better for A than' relation ranks states in accord with how beneficial they are to A— that is, in accord with A's level of well-being in them (we use 'benefit', 'well-being', and 'welfare' interchangeably). Terminology can be confusing here: some authors distinguish between impersonal and personal value, but as we use the term, value is always impersonal; it is welfare that is personal. Each is measured on an objective scale—it is not the case, for example, that

A's welfare scale varies in accord with the perspective of the evaluator. And care must be taken not to conflate welfare scales with the value scale.

Consider, for instance, the following case from Ross (1930: 34–5):

> Suppose... that the fulfillment of a promise to A would produce 1,000 units of good for him, but that by doing some other act I could produce 1,001 units of good for B, to whom I have made no promise, the other consequences of the two acts being of equal value.

Ross sees this case as a potential counterexample to the view that right acts are 'those productive of the best possible consequences' (p. 34)—i.e. consequentialism. The consequentialist, however, might reply by distinguishing between welfare and the good. Ross seems to suppose that providing x units of welfare to someone (i.e. x units of good *for* them) produces x units of good *simpliciter*. But the consequentialist can deny this and claim that units of welfare are independent of units of good. She might, for instance, hold the following view of the example: keeping the promise to A has value x; providing 1,000 units of welfare to A has value y; providing 1001 units of welfare to B has value z. She then asks which is greater: $x+y$ or z? And the answer is determined by the particulars of the case. (Ross's oversight is made explicit in his discussion (p. 35) of a variant of the above example, when he starts by speaking of a disparity in the provision of 'units of good for A', and ends by speaking of 'a disparity of good' *simpliciter*.)[5]

We are not consequentialists, but we think that consequentialism can cover more of the practical territory than some of its opponents suppose. According to what we'll call 'simple consequentialism', you only have reason to perform a particular act if doing so will produce a better state of the world than doing nothing (where the value of the act itself counts as part of the value produced by it); and what you have most reason to do is perform the act that will maximize value.[6] The content of your reasons,

---

[5] G. E. Moore is one of Ross's targets. Moore's theory, Ross claims, 'says, in effect, that the only morally significant relation in which my neighbours stand to me is that of being the possible beneficiaries of my action' (1930: 19). We're not sure that is the case. But even if it were, it does not follow that Moore has to equate the value of a state with the sum of the benefits it includes. And Moore does not do this (although he does not adopt the approach in our previous paragraph either: see, e.g., Moore 1903: 214 ff).

[6] This definition of simple consequentialism differs from earlier definitions we have proposed—e.g. in McNaughton and Rawling (2006). Also, it should be noted that we are setting aside recent moves to 'consequentialize' all moral theories. Consider, for example, Portmore (2009). His leading idea is that any theory that determines the deontic status of an act 'by how its outcome ranks relative to those of the available alternatives on *some* evaluative ranking' (p. 330; emphasis ours) is a form of consequentialism.

however, need not mention value—the simple consequentialist could adopt something akin to Scanlon's (1998) 'buck-passing' view, and claim that although value determines reason strength, it need not enter reason content. Your reason to put on your coat is that it's cold; the strength of this reason is a matter of the value of the act relative to other alternatives available to you. But what determines the value of an act?

The hedonistic utilitarian holds, perhaps, the simplest view: pleasure is the only good (and pain the only bad). This might be construed as denying that welfare is relevant to value. Alternatively, however, the claim that pleasure is the only good can be seen as emerging from the conjunction of: (1) pleasure is the only thing beneficial; and (2) welfare is the only good. In addition, on this approach, the hedonistic utilitarian holds that (3) pleasure is always beneficial, and welfare is always good.

The simple consequentialist need not, of course, be a hedonistic utilitarian. The latter has no room for the thought that one distribution of welfare is better than another; the simple consequentialist, on the other hand, can incorporate, say, the view that justice—in the sense of distributing welfare in accord with desert—is itself good (see, for instance, Ross 1930: 26–7, 138). This adds to the list of goods, of course, in denial of (2); and (3) fails also, since a benefit going to someone who deserves harm, for example, is bad. (In passing, we would note that is important for our purposes below, that in order even to *raise* the issue of whether one distribution is better than another, there must be something to be distributed—namely, welfare.)

Setting aside the issue of (1), let's turn to consider reason strength. According to simple consequentialism, since each of us only has reason to do things that increase the good, you only have reason to pursue a benefit (for yourself or others) if conferral of the benefit in question will increase the good; and the strength of your reason to act in pursuit of a benefit is proportional to the amount of good the act will produce. You might, say, have most reason to pursue your own welfare in some circumstance, on this

---

The evaluative ranking here can be, for example, egoist, so that egoism is a form of consequentialism on this account (pp. 334–5). For Portmore, the appeal of consequentialism, as he defines it, rests on the thought (roughly) that outcomes can be ranked in accord with what we have reason to prefer, and we should perform the act at the top of the ranking. Disputes then arise over what we in fact have reason to prefer—is it, for instance, what would be good for me, or what would be good *simpliciter*? For us, by contrast, the appeal of consequentialism, as we define it, is the thought that the good *simpliciter* plays a central role in practical reason.

view, but only if the state you produce in that pursuit is the best (in the sense of maximizing value) you can achieve.[7] Welfare is relevant to reasons here, but only indirectly: while welfare is relevant to the value of a state, the strength of your reason(s) to produce that state is proportional only to its value.

We now have three notions in play: value, welfare, and reason strength. As we have just seen, the simple consequentialist sees reason strength as a matter only of value. But, of course, there are other possibilities. According to the normative egoist, for instance, value is irrelevant to reason strength—rather, the strength of your reason to do something is a matter only of how much it would benefit you. We try to occupy an intermediate position between these two extremes. Like the advocate of egoism, we see welfare as playing a direct role in our practical reasons. And like simple consequentialism, we also see the good as playing such a role.

Here's one component of our position: you have reason to perform some act only if, in comparison to doing nothing, either so acting will give rise to benefit (for someone or something) or good, or both. If your contemplated act is of no benefit or good (relative to doing nothing), you have no reason to perform it.[8] And, *pace* simple consequentialism, we think that there are occasions on which you have more reason to perform an act that is worse (in terms of value) than some other; and you do not always have most reason to maximize the good.

---

[7] Note that on our account, consequentialism is not a doctrine solely concerned with what one is morally required to do—your reason to pursue your own welfare here, for example, need not be a moral one. Parfit attributes something like our view of consequentialism to Sidgwick—at least to the extent that he sees Sidgwick's version of consequentialism as concerned only with impartially assessed reasons. But Parfit then goes on to say that 'this kind of Consequentialism may be better regarded, not as a moral view, but as . . . an external rival to morality' (2011, vol. 1: 168). We disagree, but this is a result of many further differences between our view and his that we have not the space here to address.

[8] Two aspects of this claim might initially appear puzzling. First, why the comparison to doing nothing? This is to accommodate cases in which, if you act either harm or badness will result, but if you do nothing even more harm will arise, or things will go even worse. We do not want to rule out your having reason to act in such unfortunate circumstances. (Implicit in our view, then, is the thought that reducing harm counts as producing benefit; and reducing badness counts as producing good.) Of course, the notion of 'doing nothing' is tricky, and we certainly don't want to enter the debates about acts and omissions. What it would be to do nothing will, however (we hope), be clear in any given case. Second, why not strengthen the claim from 'only if' to 'if and only if'? Well, suppose you could benefit a justly imprisoned felon by helping him escape. His benefit notwithstanding, you may have no reason to. However, if an act would do some good (in comparison to doing nothing), then you do have some reason to perform it.

On our view, the strength of your personal and special reasons (respectively, reasons to benefit yourself and reasons to benefit those to whom you stand in some special relationship) may exceed whatever contribution the conferral of such benefits would make to the general good. You may have reason to benefit someone to whom you bear no special relationship, but the strength of such a reason, we claim, is a function only of how much good would be accomplished—when benefitting such people you should, other things being equal, distribute the benefits so as to do the most good. When it comes to personal and special reasons, however, we contend that their strength can outstrip value.

What are the special relationships we have in mind? On the one hand, there are the ties you have with your friends and family and so forth. On the other hand, there are the ties you can also have with strangers in virtue of such things as making promises,[9] accepting benefits, or inflicting harm (see Ross 1930: 21). Consider, for instance, Ross's 'duties of reparation'. In our framework, these become special reasons to benefit those whom you have unjustifiably harmed—that is, you may have a reason to benefit someone that you have unjustifiably harmed, the strength of which is greater than the value of the act of reparation would warrant. The simple consequentialist could incorporate reparational thoughts along the following lines: the world goes better if wrongdoers make reparation to their victims themselves. But we're not sure that this goes far enough—for example, it would require that if you could ensure more such reparation by failing to make reparation yourself, that is what you should do.

We see the simple consequentialist as confronting at least a prima facie dilemma (among other difficulties). Either she acknowledges the existence of benefits and harms or she doesn't. If she doesn't, she is in the position of having to deny even the possibility of a debate over distributional concerns (see above). If she does acknowledge their existence, she has to counteract

---

[9] Some might claim that you have reason to keep a promise even though it will benefit no one and not do any good (and the same might apply to refraining from stealing). If this is correct, it is a counterexample to our view. Consider, for instance, a confidential death-bed promise to do something posthumously for the promisee that, as things turn out, will dishonour the promisee's memory. Is there room on our view for the thought that, even if you have most reason not to keep the promise, nevertheless you do have some reason to do so? It is open to us to maintain that the very keeping of a promise, regardless of its consequences, can be either beneficial to the promisee or valuable or both. We're not sure about this. But in our view, of course, whether you do have some reason to keep the promise is precisely a matter of whether it will benefit anyone (or thing) or do some good.

the plausible thought that, on occasion at least, we have personal and special reasons the strength of which is disproportionate to the value of the acts in question. For instance, a state in which I benefit may well be equally valuable to one in which you do. Let us suppose it so. Then, as far as value goes, you have as much reason to benefit me as you do to benefit yourself. But does such parity of value rule out the possibility that you have more reason to benefit yourself than to benefit me? Or consider a case in which your receiving some benefit would make the world worse, might you not have some reason to pursue it? (Consider the escape of a justly imprisoned felon.)

5. Constraints

Vis-à-vis personal and special reasons, then, we disagree with the simple consequentialist. But what about those moral restrictions that are now standardly known as constraints—rejected by consequentialists but accepted by many traditional deontologists? (see, e.g., Alexander and Moore 2008) A constraint is a prohibition against harming people, even in pursuit of good ends—even, indeed, to prevent a greater amount of the very kind of harm that is prohibited by the constraint in question. Proponents of constraints differ in how stringent they take them to be. Some think them absolute: Roman Catholic moral theology, for example, has traditionally held that one may never intentionally kill an innocent person—even to prevent others killing many more innocents. Other deontologists have held that although constraints are always a significant consideration, they may be overridden, especially if that is the only way to avoid catastrophe. Constraints that are seen, in this latter fashion, as having some threshold beyond which the bad consequences of adhering to them dictate that we should violate them, are known as threshold constraints. How, if at all, do we accommodate constraints within our framework?

First, we need an account of constraints in terms of reasons. While, in our view, there is no sharp division of practical reasons into the moral and the non-moral, examples can be provided that are clearly on one side or the other. Your reason to choose a peach over an apple—that the former is sweeter—is non-moral. Your reason to give to Oxfam, on the other hand—that doing so will reduce innocent suffering—is moral. Or suppose that you promised to repay a debt on Thursday; this fact is a moral reason to do so. What about your reasons to favour your friends? Some object to the idea that any of these are moral on the grounds that there is something less than ideal about doing things for friends out of a sense of obligation. But that is to confuse the issue of reason with that of motivation: it's quite possible to act on a moral reason—to refuse to betray a friend, say—out of affection.

The moral reasons just mentioned fall within two categories: some are associated with promoting the good, and some with special ties. And some personal reasons may also be moral. But the advocate of constraints can be seen as claiming that there is a further category of moral reasons. Suppose, for instance, there was a constraint against killing the innocent. Then, whether this constraint is absolute or threshold, there would be at least one possible occasion on which the strength of your moral reason not to kill an innocent stranger would be greater than that which would correspond to the disvalue of the killing. On such occasions, your killing the innocent stranger would be bad, but not doing so would be worse (in the sense of being more disvaluable—more innocents would be killed by others, say); yet the constraint would dictate that you have more moral reason not to kill. So the strength of your moral reason not to kill an innocent stranger does not vary only with the badness of doing so—call such a reason a 'constraining reason'.

Our view is that the strength of your reason to perform a given act is a matter only of how much benefit or harm to yourself or those to whom you stand in special relations, and/or how much good or bad, would result.[10] Thus we leave no room for constraining reasons. The badness of harm cannot do the job: the constraint *violator* in the previous paragraph would ensure that less bad comes about. And special relations do not help either. Constraints are independent of relations such as friendship, and the only relation to strangers that might appear relevant is the tie that grounds reasons

---

[10] What is it for an act to be morally obligatory on our account? It's complicated, so for present purposes let's make the following unrealistic simplifying assumptions: the agent knows what her practical reasons are, what they are reason to do, whether or not they are moral reasons, and their relative strengths; and there's exactly one act that she has most reason to perform, and exactly one act that she has most moral reason to perform. We then tentatively suggest that you are morally required to ϕ if and only if:

(1) ϕ-ing is what you have most reason to do overall;
(2) the preponderance of your reasons to ϕ are moral; and
(3) you have more moral reason to ϕ than you have moral reason to do anything else.

for reparation. But that tie results from the infliction of *unjustified* harm. Even if you harm someone in the course of doing greater good, the advocate of constraints will still see this as unjustified. But that is to beg the question against the simple consequentialist (and us, in this case), who sees the doing of good as justifying the harm.[11]

Constraints, then, from our perspective, would require a further primitive concerning reason strength—they cannot be accommodated by appeal to welfare or value. We see little prospect of a plausible rationale for including such an added extra.[12] But arguing this case in detail here would take us too far afield.[13]

6. Weighing Reasons

We have been speaking of the determinants of reason strength, but have said neither how reasons are to be weighed against one another, nor how our views on reason strength relate to holism.

Concerning the determinants of reason strength, matters are notoriously complex, both epistemically and metaphysically. Is there, for instance, a fact of the matter concerning rankings of the options available to you in terms of value and welfare? If so, how do we know the rankings? How do the rankings relate to reason strength? Some cases are clear-cut—for instance, you have more reason than not to get your shoes wet in order to save an

---

[11] What about personal reasons? Admittedly, violating a constraint might harm the violator (consider the psychological trauma, for example). But such harms to the violator do not provide her with *moral* reasons not to violate, and thus are not, presumably, what the advocate of constraints has in mind as grounding them.

[12] In many ways our view is similar to that of Ross (1930, 1939). But there are also many points of difference. For example, we see practical matters in terms of reasons, moral and otherwise; Ross, by contrast, sees practical reason as comprising only moral obligations. This leads to many further differences—for example, Ross (1930: 24–6) claims that we have a 'duty to produce pleasure for ourselves'; we think only that you often have a reason to pursue your own pleasure. Constraints may constitute another point of difference. Ross speaks of the 'duty of non-maleficence' (pp. 21–2) in a way that may imply he thinks of it as (what we would now call) a constraint against injuring others. However, one of Ross's main concerns in contrasting non-maleficence with beneficence is to emphasize that the former is 'a duty of a more stringent character'; but this point can be accommodated without any appeal to constraints once we distinguish (as Ross does not do as sharply as he might: see section 4) between benefits and harms on the one hand and value on the other: the bad of injury outweighs the good of benefit.

[13] For instance, one of the issues that we lack the space to address here are arguments to the effect that admitting personal reasons without constraints yields counterintuitive results—see, e.g., Kagan (1984) and McNaughton and Rawling (2006).

infant. Other cases are much trickier: under what conditions, say, do you have more reason than not to sacrifice your own life? We haven't space to comment further on such issues here, however—rather, we'll return to holism.

Our view appears consistent with it: reasons have strength only within a context, since an agent's situation determines how beneficial and/or valuable an act would be relative to her other options. If the context varies, the reason strength may vary too—valence switching being an extreme case of this. However, Dancy takes the holistic conception of weighing reasons a step further. He considers (2004: 190) what he dubs the 'kitchen scales conceptions of rationality'. It makes two claims:

1. The weight of a rational element or reason is not affected by the weight, nor indeed even by the presence, of any other rational element.
2. Once one has assessed the separate weight of each element, evaluative judgement consists of adding up the pros and cons to see which side is weightier.

Dancy rejects both components. We agree with him vis-à-vis the first. Holism entails its denial (although one need not be a holist to reject it: merely acknowledging that a reason's strength can vary with circumstances suffices). But we're not inclined to abandon the second component. One might take the view that holism involves an interactive effect that rules out, in a given circumstance, separating the reasons from one another and assessing their weights individually. Alternatively, on what one might call a 'Moorean' holism about reasons (after Moore's approach to assessing the value of a whole—see, e.g., Moore 1903: 28), although the weights of reasons can be separately assessed, their overall weight is not the sum of their individual weights. Both these approaches entail the rejection of (2). But there is a third holist approach—the one we favour—that sits quite comfortably with accepting (2) while rejecting (1). The idea is simply that, although the strengths of reasons are influenced by their surroundings, nevertheless, in any given circumstance, one's reasons for action have strengths that can be (roughly, at least) summed and compared to yield verdicts about what one has most reason to do.

But here's a case that might tell against our account of holism in favour of the interactive view. People are often somewhat incredulous at the very idea of particularism—'I'll give you a moral principle: inflicting pain on babies for fun is wrong!'[14] We agree. Contrast this case with the following: driving your car for fun is wrong. Why? Because, it might be claimed, it harms the innocent by contributing to the pollution of the air they breathe. In each case the agent will derive enjoyment from his actions, and we'll suppose, for the sake of argument, that his enjoyment constitutes a benefit and a reason for him to act in both cases.[15] But each also has a reason not to act (whether or not he sees this): it'll harm the innocent. So what distinguishes the two cases? Aside from differences in how much harm each might involve, in the torture case the sadist takes enjoyment *in* inflicting the harm. In the car case, you can weigh the enjoyment on the one hand against the harm on the other—for a given level of harm, perhaps if the enjoyment is sufficiently great you have more reason to drive than not. But the torture case has a different structure: increasing the amount of enjoyment for a given level of harm *decreases* the strength of the reason for the sadist to torture—assuming that increasing the pleasure the sadist takes in inflicting the suffering makes the situation worse, and to such a degree that it outweighs the increased benefit of the extra pleasure. There is an interactive effect: the enjoyment cannot be considered independently of the harm.

So how can we reconcile this case with our non-interactive holism? Consider the reasons confronting the sadist. We're assuming that the sadist's benefit (in the form of enjoyment) weighs on one side of the reasons scale; and we claim that the sum of (1) the badness of the harm he inflicts, and (2) that of the enjoyment he takes in inflicting it, weighs on the other—the interactive effect is situated, as it were, *within* (2). But aren't we counting the enjoyment twice? Yes, but in different ways. It's important, as we've seen, to distinguish sharply between benefits and harms on the one hand, and value on the other. Here we have a case where benefit is weighed against badness on the reasons scale: whatever the benefit's reason-giving weight, it is far outweighed by the sum of (1) and (2) (and the greater the enjoyment, the larger the disparity).

---

[14] David Copp pointed out to us in conversation that the principle we have in mind might be more precisely worded as: inflicting pain on babies is wrong if the only potential reason in favour of doing so is your own enjoyment.

[15] Note that we are neither committed to the view that enjoyment is always beneficial, nor to the view that benefits always provide reasons.

7. Conclusion

All we have proposed in the latter part of the chapter is a framework for structuring the practical landscape. We have said, for example, little about what is valuable or beneficial, or about the details of weighing reasons. But the framework does have some bite. We categorize reasons, for instance. And our framework leaves out constraints. We also place further bounds on holism beyond our suggestions concerning universal reasons. Recall that '[h]olism maintains that anything whatever might make a practical difference, or provide a reason, if the circumstances were suitable' (Dancy 2004: 111). The circumstances being 'suitable', we claim, requires that the act in question be of benefit or value.

Our attempt to systematize practical reason succeeds, then, in some respects. But it is limited. No doubt Dancy will see our view as far too systematic. We see ourselves, however, as in sympathy with his general approach. And, more broadly, we take it that he shares with us a view of morality as always reason-giving, and thus rejects the view of morality implicit in the following passage from Singer (1999: 308–9):[16]

> [Nagel and I] were discussing 'Famine, affluence and morality', and Nagel was unable to accept that morality could be so demanding. But eventually it emerged that he was assuming that if morality did demand that we give so much to famine relief, then there must be overriding reason to do so. I was making no such assumption. On my view, I could recognize that if I were totally committed to doing what I ought to do, I would give away my wealth up to the point indicated in my article; but at the same time I may, without any irrationality, choose to be less than totally committed to doing what I ought to do. My own interests, or those of my family, may counteract the demands of morality to some degree, and I may think it reasonable to give in to them, while recognizing that it is morally wrong for me to do so. Once Nagel and I realized that we held these distinct understandings of morality, the practical difference between Nagel and myself over the demandingness of morality became less acute.

On Singer's view, then, morality and practical reasons are, to some extent at least, in different camps. Singer sees morality, perhaps, as akin in some respects to the law—it is true, for example, that you do not always have

---

[16] Thanks to Doug Portmore for alerting us to this passage.

overriding reason to obey the law of the land. Indeed, it may be asked whether you have any reason to do so, and Singer would seem to invite the general question, 'Do I have reason to be moral?'. Within our framework this question becomes, 'Do I have reason to do what I have moral reason to do?'—a non-question if there are moral reasons. So for us the real question here is: 'Are there any moral reasons?'—a different question from the first. For example, some Hobbesians might claim that, at least on occasion, we each have reason to be 'moral' because it is in our self-interest.[17] But they might deny that there are any moral reasons on the grounds that egoistic reasons to be moral are not moral reasons.

Dancy would join with us, we take it, both in rejecting the legal model of morality (see, e.g., 2004: 83), and affirming the existence of moral reasons.

References

Alexander, L. and Moore, M. (2008) 'Deontological Ethics', in E. N. Zalta (ed.), *The Stanford Encyclopedia of Philosophy* (Fall 2008 edn), <http://plato.stanford.edu/archives/fall2008/entries/ethics-deontological/>. Last accessed November 2012.

Butler, J. (1729) *Fifteen Sermons*, ed. T.A. Roberts, (London: SPCK, 1970).

Copp, D. (ed.) (2006) *Oxford Handbook of Ethical Theory* (Oxford: Oxford University Press).

Dancy, J. (1993) *Moral Reasons* (Oxford: Blackwell).

——(2004) *Ethics Without Principles* (Oxford: Clarendon Press).

Davidson, D. (1980) *Essays on Actions and Events* (Oxford: Clarendon Press).

Gauthier, D. (1967) 'Morality and Advantage', *Philosophical Review*, 76.4: 460–75.

Kagan, S. (1984) 'Does Consequentialism Demand Too Much?', *Philosophy and Public Affairs*, 13: 239–54.

Lance, M. and Little, M. (2005) 'Defending Moral Particularism', in J. Dreier (ed.), *Contemporary Debates in Moral Theory* (Oxford: Blackwell), 305–21.

Lance, M. and Little, M. (2006) 'Particularism and Anti-Theory', in Copp (2006: 567–94).

---

[17] Although the early Gauthier denies this: 'The individual who needs a reason for being moral which is not itself a moral reason cannot have it' (1967: 470).

McNaughton, D. and Rawling, P. (2000) 'Unprincipled Ethics', in B. Hooker and M. Little (eds.), *Moral Particularism* (Oxford: Oxford University Press), 256–75.

—— (2006) 'Deontology', in Copp (2006: 424–58).

Moore, G. E. (1903) *Principia Ethica* (Cambridge: Cambridge University Press, 1966).

Parfit, D. (2011) *On What Matters*, 2 vols. (Oxford: Oxford University Press).

Portmore, D. (2009) 'Consequentializing', *Philosophy Compass*, IV(2): 329–47.

Ross, W. D. (1930) *The Right and the Good* (Oxford: Clarendon Press).

—— (1939) *Foundations of Ethics* (Oxford: Clarendon Press).

Scanlon, T. M. (1998) *What We Owe to Each Other* (Cambridge, MA: Harvard University Press).

Singer, P. (1999) 'A Response', in D. Jamieson (ed.), *Singer and his Critics* (Oxford: Blackwell), 269–335.

Williams, B. (1981) 'Internal and External Reasons', in his *Moral Luck* (Cambridge: Cambridge University Press), 101–13.

Wittgenstein, L. (1953) *Philosophical Investigations*, ed. G. E. M. Anscombe and R. Rhees, tr. G. E. M. Anscombe (Oxford: Blackwell).

12

Why Holists Should Love Organic Unities

SEAN McKEEVER AND MICHAEL RIDGE

In his signature work, Jonathan Dancy has opened important philosophical vistas. Most notably, he has called our collective philosophical attention to the idea that reasons and values might be context-sensitive (a doctrine he calls 'holism') and the idea that normative thought and judgment might not depend on normative principles (a doctrine he calls 'particularism'). Moreover, his work has amply demonstrated not only the internal coherence of these ideas, but has also powerfully highlighted what is plausible about them, and how they challenge numerous dominant strands of philosophical theorizing. If we have been amongst Professor Dancy's most consistent and vocal critics, this is only because he first enriched our sense of the space of possibilities, thereby posing a powerful challenge to our own antecedent enthusiasm for rules and principles. Indeed we have maintained that enthusiasm in no small measure by developing a version of generalism ('generalism as a regulative ideal') that is indebted to many of Dancy's ideas, especially holism about reasons and values.

In this chapter we focus on holism, as opposed to particularism. The bulk of the critical discussion of holism in the literature to date has focused on whether holism is true and whether it entails or indirectly supports particularism. We set aside those longstanding debates here. To put our cards on the table, though, we think the answer to the first question is probably 'yes' but that the answer to the second question is 'no'.

Here, though, we consider the neglected question of how holism coheres with other structural views in axiology—views which we might broadly characterize as concerning the 'logic' of claims about reasons and values—

especially G. E. Moore's so-called 'doctrine of organic unities'. Very roughly (we are more precise below), Moore's idea is that the value of the whole need not be the same as the sum of the value of its parts. Moore's view, like Dancy's, promises to dislodge certain seemingly naïve assumptions about the logic of value. Dancy's holism blocks the inference from 'is a good-making feature here' to 'is a good-making feature anywhere', whereas Moore's doctrine bars us from inferring the value of a whole by adding up the values of its parts. Both holism and the doctrine of organic unities aim to capture a sense in which sound evaluative judgment will need to take account of context. Yet is far from clear whether these two views are independently plausible and complementary ways of capturing two important and distinct forms of context dependency or whether they are brooding rivals for how best to explicate context dependency.

One of the few to address this interesting question is Dancy himself who argues that holism and organic unities do not cohere well, and that Moore's doctrine of organic unities is anyway implausible and should be rejected (Dancy 2003, reprinted in Dancy 2004: ch. 10). If one accepts these arguments, then holism is the sole surviving framework for explicating context dependency. Given his longstanding defence of holism, it is not surprising that Dancy would welcome this conclusion. In another respect, however, it is incongruous. For the broader tenor of Dancy's work has so often been to expand our sense of the normative and evaluative possibilities.

Here, we argue against these conclusions and Dancy's arguments for them. More positively, we suggest that, properly understood, the doctrine of organic unities is extremely plausible. Furthermore, we contend that shorn of some of Moore's own peculiar further assumptions, there is no deep tension between holism and the doctrine of organic unities. Finally, we suggest that a plausible axiology should endorse both these doctrines, and that they actually fit well together. We endorse this combined view in a strong form, which allows not only that sometimes there are organic unities and sometimes there are holistic values, but that there can be values which are at one and the same time organic unities and holistic.

In arguing for these conclusions, we ourselves try to open up new vistas, and in that sense take ourselves (perhaps perversely) to be following in Professor Dancy's footsteps even as we argue against him. In a sense, we here argue that Dancy should be more true to his vista-opening self than he has been, and should embrace organic unities whole-heartedly.

We will, of course, understand if he does not find this appeal to his own potential greater self-actualization persuasive. Fortunately, we have arguments to offer.

1. Holism and organic unities

Holism in the theory of value holds that the intrinsic value of a thing can vary with context even where the intrinsic ground for that value remains the same (Dancy 2004: 176). Here Dancy draws on ideas that he has developed in detail in his defence of holism in the theory of reasons. There the idea is that a consideration which is a reason in one context need not be a reason with the same valence, or indeed a reason at all, in another context.[1]

These differences between context are not brute differences, though. They are explained by the presence or absence of 'enablers', 'defeaters', 'intensifiers', and 'diminishers'. To some extent, these labels are self-interpreting. An 'enabler' enables a given consideration to function as a reason without itself being part of the reason. For example, that it is not sadistic may enable the fact that it would be pleasant to function as a reason to perform the action. Non-sadism is an enabler. For the same reason, sadism is a defeater. Intensifiers can make a given reason's normative strength greater but again without becoming part of the reason. That a great deal hangs on it can, say, strengthen the force of the fact that I promised without becoming part of the reason. Diminishers work in the opposite way. That someone brought a problem on himself can diminish the normative force of the fact that performing a given action would help him solve this problem, yet not rob this fact of its normative force entirely.

Holism in the theory of value is structurally identical. A good-making feature in one context might be no good-making feature at all in another context. This will be explained in roughly the same way, by distinguishing

---

[1] In this chapter we will not be too fussy about whether we characterize reasons as facts (as we prefer) or as considerations, which is Dancy's usual formulation. It would be possible to reformulate Dancy's views in terms of facts, but because facts do not seem to be repeatable in the way that considerations do, we would then have to introduce the idea of 'facts of the same type' and have some way of privileging the relevant type(s). Still, the niceties of the ontology of reasons, while important in their own right, are not our topic here, and everything we say should be consistent with the best view of this matter.

good-making features from enablers, defeaters, and the like. Dancy focuses on intrinsic value because the very idea might seem to be problematic on his view, but his holism naturally extends to value more generally. For him, something has intrinsic value only when it has intrinsic properties which are good-making features. However, those very same intrinsic properties might not be good-making features at all in another context. This is different from a standard view, which Dancy argues against, according to which intrinsic value entails invariability. Moreover, this view seems to inherit some plausibility from holism in the theory of reasons, given that on many plausible views there are important conceptual links between certain value claims and claims about reasons for action. These connections must be handled delicately, though, and we argue below (in section 2) that Dancy's argument against organic unities relies on certain unargued and problematic assumptions about these connections.

The doctrine of organic unities is often characterized as the thesis that the value of a whole need not be identical to the sum of the value of its parts. Moore illustrates the power of this idea with a variety of examples in which it seems very plausible to say that some larger whole has more value than the sum of what we would naturally think of the value of its parts. Each of the tiny dabs of paint which make up a painting may have very little aesthetic value indeed—negligible, in fact. So the sum of those values might still be very small. Nonetheless, in the case of a beautiful painting, the value of the whole might be very great.

In fact, Moore presses his idea further, denying not only that the value of a whole is necessarily identical to the sum of the values of it parts but that the value of the whole 'bears no regular proportion to the sum' (Moore 1903: 79). Following Moore, we can characterize the doctrine of organic unities as claiming that no mathematical function is such that it necessarily takes us from the values of the parts to the value of the whole.

One tricky issue which arises here is how we think about parts. Given a complex whole there will be different ways of dividing it into parts. Some of these parts will be overlapping. If we take a maximally permissive view of 'parts' the doctrine of organic unities will be uncontroversially true but utterly uninteresting. Take a beautiful painting. One part of that painting will be the whole painting except for some specified perceptibly indiscernible part in one corner of the painting. Another part will be the whole painting except for another perceptibly indiscernible part of another corner, and so on. Each of these parts will be as valuable or almost as valuable as the whole itself, and so the sum of the value of these parts will *obviously* be greater than the value of the whole.

Moore, of course, would be unimpressed. Organic unities are supposed to tell us something interesting about how distinct parts can interact to generate value for a complex whole; they are not supposed to be a consequence of mere 'accounting tricks'.

We can tighten matters up by formulating the doctrine of organic unities in terms of sets of parts, and insisting that (a) the parts which make up a set must be *complete*, in that they do not leave any aspect of the whole out, perhaps apart from the arrangement of the parts (more on this below), and (b) these parts must be *non-overlapping*, in the sense that for any two numerically distinct parts x and y, there is no part z such that z is a part of x and z is a part of y.

Having regimented our conception of 'parts', we should note that the doctrine can now be formulated in two different ways, one more and one less ambitious. First, note that for any given complex whole there will be many sets of parts satisfying (a) and (b). Less ambitiously, then the doctrine might hold that there is no mathematical function M, such that for *any* way of specifying a set of parts which satisfies (a) and (b), M takes you from the sum of the values of the parts in the set to the value of the whole. More ambitiously, the doctrine might hold that for any way of individuating parts, there is no mathematical function M which takes you from the sum of the value of the parts to the value of the whole. This latter doctrine is more ambitious because it rules out even mathematical functions which are dependent on ways of individuating parts, as opposed to mathematical functions which apply regardless of the chosen scheme of individuation. For now we simply want to note this complexity, and put it to one side. For most of our discussion this distinction will not make a difference. However, at one crucial point, the distinction will matter, and we will return to it at that stage.

Before turning to what might be said for or against organic unities, we should pause briefly to canvas Dancy's own characterization since it departs importantly from our own. According to Dancy:

> [Moore's] theory of organic unities combines two claims:
> (1) Parts retain their intrinsic value regardless of variations in the context.

(2) Parts may contribute either more or less value to a whole than they themselves have there. (Dancy 2004: 176)

Since (1) trivially entails the rejection of holism, this characterization has the unfortunate consequence that holism and organic unities are defined as incompatible rivals from the outset. If one is wedded to holism, then one should reject organic unities so conceived simply on the strength of holism, and Dancy does precisely this.

It is true, of course, that Moore himself accepts (1); he insists that all judgments of intrinsic value are 'universal'. And it is Moore's view in particular that Dancy has in view in the passage just quoted. Moreover, Moore seems motivated to adopt the doctrine of organic unities at least in part to avoid what he sees as potentially unwelcome implications of his atomistic conception of intrinsic value. Even granting all this, however, in our view, even Moore does not *define* the doctrine of organic unities in terms of (1), and (2) is of independent interest. The very concept of an organic unity should not be loaded up with such contentious assumptions. Doing so risks obscuring the possibility that holism and organic unities might be able to live side by side.

With these definitional preliminaries to one side, we next turn to Dancy's main argument against the doctrine of organic unities, an argument which, if successful, would tell just as much against our own favoured formulation of the doctrine.

2. Organic unities, value, and reasons

Dancy's leading argument against the doctrine of organic unities is that it cannot adequately account for the way in which parts contribute to the value of the whole. Dancy first invokes the intuitive idea that there is some necessary connection between values and reasons. Necessarily, whenever there is value, there are corresponding reasons for positive responses. Here is Dancy on just this point:

> When I say it [Moore's position] 'severs the necessary connection between values and reasons', I am going to have to speak cautiously, because there are various conceptions of that connection, and the point that I want to make is intended not to depend on any particular one of them. The general idea is that where there is

value, there are reasons of certain sorts—reasons to promote, cherish, respect, tend, approve, defend, and so on. (Dancy 2004: 177)

Dancy argues that the doctrine of organic unities threatens the supposed necessary connection between values and reasons. The argument turns on the notion of 'contributory value'. As Dancy understands it, the proponent of organic unities denies that the value of the whole is a sum of the value of the parts, but also denies that the value of the whole is utterly *sui generis*. The value of the whole must be potentially explicable in terms of the 'contributions' made by its parts. Insofar as a part contributes value to the whole, though, this gives us reason to protect that part, and this reason presumably must be at least as great as the reasons associated with the value it contributes. This, in turn, is supposed to show both that the part has value, and that its value is at least as great as the value it contributes. This, in turn, entails that the value of the whole can be no greater than the sum of the value of its parts, contradicting a standard line on organic unities. Here is the crux of the argument as formulated by Dancy:

> So to say that a part with no value can contribute value that it has not got commits one to saying, it seems, that though there is no reason to preserve the part as a part, there is reason to protect the whole, and that reason derives from the presence of the part. Now this does sound incoherent. Surely we have reason to protect the part *here*, if it is contributing value. So its presence is a value, it would seem, on pain of breaching the link between value and reasons (p. 177)

This formulation of the argument focuses on the limiting case in which a part contributes value without itself having *any* value. But the argument can readily be extended to purported cases in which a part has some value but contributes more than it has.

A formal reconstruction of Dancy's argument may be helpful:

(1) If there could be organic unities in which the whole has more value than the sum of the value of its parts then there could be parts which contribute value which they do not have.
(2) If there could be parts which contribute value which they do not have then it would not be a necessary truth that having value entails reasons for suitable positive responses.
(3) Having value entails reasons for suitable positive responses.

(4) There cannot be organic unities in which the whole has more value than the sum of the value of its parts (from 1–3 by *reductio*).

Importantly, (4) is not inconsistent with another type of organic unity, one whose value is *less* value than the sum of its parts. On this matter, Dancy's view is more complicated and depends on the distinction between a good-making feature, which itself contributes value, and an 'enabler' which somehow explains how that good-making feature manages to contribute value. Though controversial, this distinction informs Dancy's view in the following way. He allows that insofar as enablers do play a sort of 'positive' role in the explanation of why something is valuable, they will themselves be valuable. Yet he is very clear that they do not themselves contribute value to the whole—enablers are not as such good-making features, and hence they do not, simply qua enablers, contribute value in Dancy's special sense of 'contribute'. Here it is crucial to remember that the truth of the counterfactual, 'G would be less good if it were not for F' is *not* sufficient for F to count as contributing to the value of G in Dancy's sense.

This leads Dancy to endorse the possibility of the following sort of organic unity: A whole may have *less* value than the sum of its parts. Here is Dancy:

> But it is also true that some features that have value in that context that do not contribute that value to the value of the whole. In that sense, the value of the whole is not identical to the sum of the values of all the parts. (Dancy 2004: 181)

If, however, we restrict our definition of parts to include only *contributors*, then the thesis of organic unities is simply false. This is because it is only those parts which have value but do not contribute it—the enablers—which make possible the sort of organic unity that Dancy allows is possible:

> But the value of the whole is identical to the sum of the value of the contributing parts, as we might put it. Any part, then, that contributes value must have that value to contribute; but some valuable parts do not contribute their value to the whole, even though their presence is necessary for the whole to have the value it does.
> (p. 181)

We now turn to ask whether Dancy has given good grounds for the holist to reject (some) organic unities.

3. Values without reasons and reasons without values

In this section we develop three objections to Dancy's argument against organic unities in which the whole has more value than the sum of the values of its parts. First, we cast doubt on the necessary connection that Dancy assumes to hold between values and reasons. Second, we argue that even if the assumption of a necessary connection is sound, parts could nevertheless contribute more value than they have. Third, we argue that if Dancy's argument succeeds, it succeeds too well and threatens his own considered view.

Our first objection is directed at Dancy's assumption of a necessary connection between values and reasons.

(3) Having value entails reasons for suitable positive responses.

Contrary to (3) however, there are true value claims which do not entail the corresponding claims about reasons. To see why, recall Peter Geach's distinction between predicative and attributive uses of a modifier (see Geach 1956). Take a locution of the form 'is an F G' where 'F' is the modifier of 'G' and 'G' is the relevant kind or sortal term. If a use of 'is an F G' entails both 'is F' and 'is G' then the use is predicative. Otherwise it is attributive.

Predicative uses of modifiers are fairly straightforward. For example, a use of 'is a round shape' entails both 'is round' and 'is a shape'. So a use of this phrase will be predicative. Similarly, a use of 'is a living housefly' will entail 'is living' and 'is a housefly', and so uses of this phrase too will be predicative. When modifiers are used attributively, by contrast, one of these two entailments breaks down. Sometimes it will not follow that the sortal term applies. For example, 'is a false foot' does not entail 'is a foot'—in fact, it entails the opposite. More important for present purposes the modifier term may not independently apply. So, for example, 'is a large housefly' does *not* (as typically used) entail 'is large'.

Importantly, the predicative/attributive distinction operates at the level of usage. Consider the phrase 'is a funny philosopher'. This might be used predicatively, as when someone is recommending that we get Sidney Morgenbasser to emcee an event. In that case 'is a funny philosopher' will entail 'is funny' and 'is a philosopher'. However, a use of the same phrase might also be used attributively in another sort of context. For example, a long-suffering spouse of a philosopher who is not too impressed by the standard quality of philosophers' sense of humour might use that phrase to mean 'a philosopher who is funny by the standards of philosophers', but where the speaker deems those standards to be bankrupt and so denies that the person is really funny at all.

Couching the distinction at the level of use is critical because it allows us to accept it without following Geach when he claims that *all* uses of value predicates like 'good' and 'bad' are attributive. In our view, this further claim is not persuasive, and we are sure Dancy will agree. It is difficult to deny, however, that at least *some* uses of value predicates are attributive. Moreover, some of these uses are directly relevant to Dancy's argument.

Consider some examples:

'is a good assassin'
'is a good torture device'
'is a good thief'

In each case, it is plausible to suppose that standard uses of these phrases do not entail 'is good', in which case these uses are attributive.

Now consider the implications of this distinction for Dancy's argument given his assumption that having value entails reasons for suitable positive responses (premise 3). We can read this premise in two ways. If 'having value' is read to include true attributive value claims, then the premise is unsound. Alternatively, we can read 'having value' to mean 'being good' in a predicative sense. In that case, the examples just cited pose no problem for the plausibility of the premise. The scope of Dancy's argument, however, is unfortunately restricted. For many of the best examples of organic unities are ones which are most naturally understood in terms of attributive value claims.

Gustatory values, for example, seem like good exemplars of organic unities. The gustatory value of a cup of coffee may be greater than the sum of the coffee, the soy milk and the hazelnut syrup which constitutes the cup. Someone who claims she just had a good cup of coffee is most plausibly using 'good' attributively. She might expect agreement from those who recognize the values internal to the practice of evaluating cups of coffee, even those who detest coffee themselves, for example an embittered former barista. This strongly suggests that no claim that coffee is good full stop is even on the table. What we note here about coffee seems likely to hold for a wide range of aesthetic examples as well.

So it would be unfortunate if Dancy's argument were restricted to predicative value claims. In fairness to Dancy, Moore himself was clearly interested in predicative uses of 'good'—this is, after all, what led Geach to deploy his distinction against Moore. Nonetheless, our interest here is in the broader notion of organic unities, and not Moore's particular conception of them. Moreover some of Moore's own best examples are perhaps best construed attributively anyway, in spite of Moore's own intentions.

Our second objection is as follows. Premise (2) of Dancy's argument, as we have reconstructed it, asserts that if parts could contribute value which they do not themselves have then the necessary link between value and reasons would be severed. Recall that this link, as characterized by Dancy, is that necessarily whenever there is value there are reasons for positive responses of various kinds: 'The general idea is that where there is value, there are reasons of certain sorts—reasons to promote, cherish, respect, tend, approve, defend, and so on' (Dancy 2004: 177).

As we shall argue, however plausible this claim may be, the entailment does not run in the direction Dancy needs. What is needed is an entailment that runs from reasons to values, but such a claim is highly controversial. Let us take these points in turn.

The connection Dancy asserts goes from value to reasons, rather than the other way around. That is, the connection has the logical form of a universally quantified conditional, the antecedent of which is that there is value, and the consequent of which is that there are reasons for suitable positive responses. This, though, is simply not the direction of entailment Dancy needs to make premise (2) plausible. Instead, what he really needs is the entailment from reasons for positive responses to value. Let us explain.

Premise (2) asserts that if parts could contribute value which they lack then the necessary connection he posits would be severed. Why? Here again is the crucial passage from Dancy:

> So to say that a part with no value can contribute value that it has not got commits one to saying, it seems, that though there is no reason to preserve the part as a part, there is reason to protect the whole, and that reason derives from the presence of the part. Now this does sound incoherent. Surely we have reason to protect the part

here, if it is contributing value. So its presence is a value, it would seem, on pain of breaching the link between value and reasons.   (p. 177)

Note the way the argument proceeds. Given that a part can contribute value without itself having any, it will follow from the necessary link from value to reasons that we have reason to protect the whole which is derived from the presence of the part. However, according to Dancy, it also follows that we will have no reason to preserve the part, given that it has no value, but he suggests that this is absurd. Note, though, how the last step of this argument goes: It goes from the fact that the part has no value to the conclusion that there is no reason to protect the part. That inference, from *no* value to *no* reasons for positive responses of the relevant kind, though, holds up only if we posit a necessary connection *in the other direction*—from reasons to value. The fact that value entails reasons itself does not entail that whenever there is no value there are no reasons of the relevant kind. Again, we get that result only if we endorse another necessary connection, according to which whenever there are reasons for positive responses there is value of the relevant kind. So the argument for premise (2) of the master argument is fallacious until a further necessary connection is posited.

The thesis that there is a necessary connection running from reasons to values is rightly much more controversial than the corresponding claim running from values to reasons. To be plausible, the thesis requires significant qualification. Unfortunately, the very qualifications that might secure the entailment from reasons to values turn out to undermine the force of Dancy's argument.

A standard challenge to theories which analyse value claims in terms of reasons for suitable responses is to distinguish the 'right' kind of reasons from the 'wrong' kinds. The idea is simple enough. For any positive response which might specify a kind of value, there can be reasons for that response which we would not render the object of that response valuable. For example, suppose an evil demon credibly threatens to kill me if I do not admire him. This might provide a reason for me to admire the demon. However, this is not sufficient for the demon's being admirable. Notice that the reasons in this case may be perfectly good reasons; the trouble is only that they do not seem to bear on the value of the demon. If, then, there is a necessary connection running from reasons to value, it must be restricted to the right kind of reasons.

It is a difficult question whether the 'right kind of reasons' can successfully be distinguished from the 'wrong' kind, and if so, how. What we wish to point out here is that it is not enough for the truth of (2) that right and wrong kinds of reasons be distinguished. It must also turn out that the reasons we have to preserve and protect the parts of organic unities fall on the 'right' side of this distinction. Only then will the parts themselves be valuable. So at the very least there is an important gap in the argument. Dancy needs some way of showing why there will always be not only a reason to preserve the relevant part, but a reason of the right kind. It is unclear to us just how this gap in the argument can plausibly be filled.

Furthermore, note that Dancy's argument is couched in terms of reasons to protect and preserve the object of evaluation. However, not all value is well understood in terms of these specific kinds of positive responses. Another sort of positive response presumably is aesthetic appreciation. Moreover, many of the most intuitive examples of organic unities are precisely objects of aesthetic value. The aesthetic value of the *Mona Lisa* is plausibly not equivalent to the sum of the aesthetic value of the relevant parts—the dabs of paint, say. This illustrates the problem with Dancy's argument. For if we individuate finely enough, then we may have no reason at all to respond with aesthetic appreciation to the proper parts of the object of evaluation even though the whole does warrant such a response.

Dancy might reply that we still at least have reason to preserve and protect the parts. Even this is not obvious, depending on how finely we individuate parts. For example, a single electron of the *Mona Lisa* at a given time is not obviously worthy of preservation. Nor, indeed, are objects of aesthetic value themselves always clearly worthy of protection or preservation, anyway. Perhaps a certain sort of life is aesthetically valuable precisely because of the way the person 'burns the candle at both ends' and lives in the moment. Arguably, to see this person's life as worthy of preservation is not to see its distinctive aesthetic value—which is not to deny that the person's life is in fact worthy of preservation, but this will be a different (presumably moral) mode of value from its distinctive aesthetic value.

Furthermore, even if it is always the case that objects of aesthetic value are worthy of preservation, this would not secure the conclusion Dancy needs. For the whole will now be valuable in two ways—it will be worthy of (a) preservation and protection, and (b) aesthetic appreciation. The parts, though, may only be valuable in one of these ways. So the whole can still come out as more valuable than the sum of the value of the parts, at least qua its warranting aesthetic appreciation.

Finally, there plausibly are objects of evaluation for which the very ideas of protecting and preserving make no sense, yet which intuitively exemplify organic unities. Perhaps unique or important events are like this. For example, perhaps the big bang is worthy of awe, which is a kind of positive response, yet the very idea of 'preserving' or 'protecting' the big bang makes no obvious sense. Moreover, perhaps the big bang does in a sense have parts, but the extent to which the whole warrants awe may be greater than the sum of the awe-worthiness of its parts. At least, this seems intelligible insofar as there is some sense in which the big bang has proper parts.

Perhaps the big bang is peculiar in ways that obscure our more general point. Take another example—the French Revolution. Understood as a historic event, this may well be worthy of study—it may have scholarly value of a kind, say. Perhaps the French Revolution's worthiness for study is greater than the sum of the study-worthiness of its proper parts, at least on some ways of individuating its parts.

The basic point can also be illustrated with abstract objects. Perhaps a certain mathematical proof or chess combination has aesthetic value. Intuitively, the aesthetic value of the whole in these kinds of cases may be greater than the sum of the aesthetic value of the parts. After all, it is the way that the different parts of the proof or combination 'fit together' which intuitively captures our imagination or impresses us, and it may do so in a way that none of its parts do. Here again, the idea of 'protecting' or 'preserving' the object of evaluation does not make any sense. It is not some token inscription of the proof or some token instantiation of the chess combination, but the proof itself, and the chess combination itself, understood as abstract objects, which are beautiful on our proposal. The very idea of 'protecting' or 'preserving' an abstract object, whose existence is presumably necessary, just does not make sense.

As presented, Dancy's argument assumes that whenever a part contributes value, there is reason to protect or preserve the part, and that this reason in turn entails that the part is valuable, and indeed that it is valuable in the same way as the whole of which it is a part. We have seen that this line of argument is problematic in several respects.

Our third objection to Dancy's argument is a straightforward 'internal' objection. His argument, if sound, seems to 'prove too much', and by Dancy's own lights. Dancy's development of holism, recall, relies on a deep distinction between enabling conditions and the values (or reasons) that are enabled. The argument against organic unities, however, threatens to undermine the significance of that very distinction. For his point is that because enablers are worthy of protection/preservation as a means to the value they enable, they therefore (given the value/reason link he is assuming) themselves contribute value. This, though, does not sit well with Dancy's general take on the distinction between enablers and that which they enable.

To see why this is so, let us begin with the clearer case of reasons for action. An enabling condition for something's being a reason need not itself be a reason at all. The fact that I can do something is a kind of generic enabling condition for there being any reason for or against my doing it, but my being able to do it is not (at least not typically) a reason to do it or a reason not to do it. So enablers for reasons need not themselves be reasons.

Analogously, an enabling condition for something's being valuable need not itself contribute value. Indeed, this seems like just what Dancy should say, especially given that reasons and values are intimately linked in some way. In the case of parts, however, Dancy claims that parts do contribute value (and clearly thinks a defender of organic unities must agree). This claim, however, seems to turn on the fact that the parts are a *means* to value. Since one can equally well say that enablers are a means to value, his argument here commits him to saying that whenever something enables something else to contribute value, that enabler itself *ipso facto* contributes value. That seems analogous to saying that whenever some consideration enables another consideration to favour some response (that is, to be a reason), that enabler itself favours that response (that is, is a reason in favour of it). That would be a very unfortunate result, in that it would commit Dancy to a very strange asymmetry between the structural relations between enablers and reasons, on the one hand, and enablers and values, on the other. Dancy seems willing to embrace this strange asymmetry, but in our view, this makes his view as a whole much less plausible and attractive.

Indeed, it may make it dialectically unstable. For once value enablers are admitted simply qua value enablers to also be value contributors, why should we not say that reason enablers are not themselves reasons, or at least part of a proper statement of the relevant 'full reason'? To be clear, we do not think that the appeal to 'full reasons' as such is a very powerful objection to Dancy's holism about reasons, though it is frequently pressed against him (see, e.g., Crisp 2000). Our point here is that the objection gains considerable plausibility in virtue of the commitments of Dancy's argument against organic unities.

Having pressed these three objections to Dancy's argument against organic unities, we are satisfied that he has not undermined the very idea of an organic unity. Insofar as there are intuitively plausible examples of organic unities, we should be open to there actually being such structures of value, for all Dancy has said so far. In the next and final section of our chapter, we go further, and argue that there are indeed organic unities, and that anyone sympathetic to Dancy's 'holism' should be happy to allow that there are. On our proposed view, then, there are both organic unities *and* context-sensitive ('holistic,' in Dancy's terms) values.

4. Organic unities *and* holism

In this section we argue that the doctrine of organic unities is not only plausible in its own right, but that when joined with holism yields an interesting combination. Indeed, we are tempted to suggest that the theoretical value of the doctrine of organic unities plus holism is itself an organic unity! Moreover, we argue that there is nothing in the arguments for holism or indeed particularism which counsels against this view. In so far as the 'spirit' of particularism is to always emphasize just how complex the normative and evaluative can be, we urge Dancy and other particularists to endorse this combination of views.

The plausibility of both holism and the doctrine of organic unities are best demonstrated through evocative examples that, following Dancy and Moore, we have already canvassed. To our mind, these various examples provide a prima facie case for what we might call the 'weak combination' of holism and organic unities, where the weak combination holds only that there are examples of holistic values and examples of values which are organic unities.

Here we want to go further, and argue for what we call the 'strong combination', according to which there are examples which are *both* holistic and organic. The clearest sorts of examples are organic unities such that the value of the whole is itself context-sensitive. Given certain actual contexts, the value of the whole is greater than the sum of the value of the parts, though in other contexts the value of the very same sort of whole might be less than the sum of the value of its parts.

Consider first matters of taste. A fine wine has a certain gustatory value, as does a well prepared bowl of pesto pasta. If the wine complements the food then the combination may be an organic unity. At the same time, the gustatory value of this organic unity may itself be context-sensitive. If, for example, the pasta and wine were accompanied by a salad then the gustatory value of that combination (of the pasta and the wine) might be more valuable than it would be if paired with a bowl of chips or with some pretzels. Note, by the way, that here again we have a sort of value which is not well understood in terms of reasons to preserve and protect. Indeed, with gustatory value we seem to have reason to do just the opposite, insofar as consuming entails destroying! Admittedly, we should presumably savour the tastes of such gustatory delights, but this does not seem like preserving and protecting them in the relevant sense.

The aesthetic value of a narrative offers another example. The aesthetic value of a story is plausibly an organic unity—the aesthetic value of a whole story can be greater than the value of each of the sentences of the story, say. Yet, aesthetic value is itself plausibly holistic in the case of at least some narratives. For example, sometimes, though not always, the value of a story depends in part on its truth.

Consider the tale of Maggie Dickson who was convicted of the crime of concealment of pregnancy, and sentenced to be hanged to death in Edinburgh in 1724. She was indeed hanged in the Grassmarket of Edinburgh that same year. After she was pronounced dead, her body was put onto a cart and she was taken to be buried, but en route the cart hit a big bump on one of Edinburgh's many cobbled streets, and the shock of the bump brought her back to life! The legal conundrum thus created was eventually resolved in her favour, the authorities deciding that the sentence had indeed been carried out already, and that to hang her again would be to punish her twice for the same crime. Maggie Dickson went on to lead a long and fulfilling life. We take this story to be excellent, even if our telling of it is not. The story would not be such a fine one, however, were it not substantially true. In our view, this is a good example of an organic unity which is holistic—the story as a whole has more narrative value than the sum of the narrative value of its parts, and the value of the whole is itself context-dependent, for its value varies depending on whether the story is true.

Last, and somewhat impishly, we cannot resist an example involving Dancy himself. Dancy's signature headwear is a beret. Now imagine that Dancy also has a taste for leather trousers.[2] To those of us who know and love Jonathan, such a vision has a certain kind of comedic value. For leather trousers seem somehow slightly out of keeping with Professor Dancy's somewhat reserved, stereotypically English character. The surprising juxtaposition of Dancy and leather trousers is both endearing and amusing. And while such a combination might be an organic unity in other contexts, we should like to express our doubt that anyone but Jonathan could pull it off with more value.

In the remainder of this section we explore some specific reasons why, given Dancy's broader project and commitments, he should not be hostile to organic unities of the sort we have canvassed—ones in which the value of the whole is *greater* than the value of the parts.

First, we briefly recall a point already made. By denying organic unities, Dancy is forced to allow that enablers as such contribute value. This is both implausible in its own right, and in tension with Dancy's broader account of the distinction between enablers and that which they enable.

One final point arises out of the idea that an arrangement of parts should not itself be understood as a part on pain of an infinite regress. Dancy himself discusses this point, which goes back to Plato, and agrees that we should not understand the arrangement of some set of parts as itself being a part. In that case, though, there seems to be nothing stopping the arrangement from contributing value. Dancy (2003: 637) discusses this idea and admits that he can see no way to argue against it, though he confesses 'to a sense of unease in the attribution of value to so abstract a thing as an arrangement'.

---

[2] Whether this vision is, like the tale of Maggie Dickson, more valuable for being true must depend upon the credibility one attaches to the stories one can hear on late night television shows such as the one hosted by Craig Ferguson.

If, though, arrangements can contribute value, then we have a ready explanation of how there can be wholes whose value is greater than the sum of the value of their parts. Strictly speaking, Dancy might allow this but insist that at least the value of the whole must not be greater than the sum of the value of the *value contributors*, where value contributors include not only parts, but arrangements. Indeed, on some readings, Dancy's main idea is really that the value of a whole cannot be greater than the sum of the value of the relevant contributors. Zimmerman (1999) develops and criticizes such a version of the doctrine, but characterizes it as a significant 'reformulation.'

This warrants three points. The first is that this concession seems seriously to diminish the disagreement between Dancy and the defender of the doctrine of organic unities—at least, once that doctrine is separated from certain Moorean assumptions about intrinsic value which Dancy must reject. For the doctrine of organic unities is, after all, traditionally formulated in terms of *parts*, and not in terms of Dancy's special notion of value contributors (Moore 1903: 27; Chisholm 1986; Hurka 1998; Lemos 1998).

Second, we do not share Dancy's unease at allowing something as abstract as an arrangement of parts to contribute value. Because we think abstract objects like mathematical proofs can have beauty, and that this is a kind of value, we are already committed to the possibility of abstract objects contributing value. Unless Dancy has some argument against these sorts of examples of aesthetic value, then we do not see much reason for his unease.

Admittedly, though, these examples are controversial (see Zangwill 1998), which brings us to our third point. For Dancy's own theoretical resources enable us to say that the arrangement does not *contribute* value. At least, those resources allow us to say this if we reject Dancy's claim (as we have argued we should anyway) that value enablers as such are value contributors. For in that case, we can hold that the arrangement of parts *enables* the relevant value without being a value *contributor*. We have already shown how this can be a theoretically stable view, Dancy's concerns about the links between values and reasons notwithstanding. We do not know if Dancy would be any less uneasy with something as abstract as an arrangement being an enabler than with its being a value contributor, where these are distinguished, but we thought this possibility at least worth putting 'on the table'.

One final reason to allow organic unities is that Dancy's position leads to a very odd and artificial view of the value of parts of certain seeming-organic unities. Consider a case in which the value of a whole depends on the presence of each of the relevant parts, so that without any one of those parts the whole would be worthless. It seems that in such a case Dancy should say that each part is as valuable as the whole itself, since we have as much reason to preserve each part as we do to preserve the whole. Dancy rightly resists this implausible result. Instead he holds that the value of the whole should be divided equally amongst the parts:

> even though each part is such that, without it, all the value would be lost, this does not mean that each contributes all the value. No: the loss of any one part means that all the other parts lose value, and the value lost is divided equally between them, according to their equal contribution. (Dancy 2004: 182)

This *ex post facto* assignment of values to parts is very ad hoc and artificial. Moreover, it does not square with Dancy's arguments against organic unities. For those arguments seem to assume that the value of something was a function of how much reason there was to respond positively to it in the relevant way (in particular, to preserve and protect it). Here, though, in the context of the whole being entirely present already, we have just as much reason to protect and preserve each part as we do to protect the whole. So Dancy's argument against organic unities seems to put some pressure on him to treat this example very differently, but in an even more implausible way.

Finally, it is not exactly clear how Dancy's positive proposal looks once we remember that parts can be individuated in many different ways. For now we may have to say that, on one scheme of individuation, parts 1 and 2 and 3 each contribute 1/3 of the value of the whole, while what is part 1 on this scheme of individuation may come out as contributing more or less value on other ways of individuating parts—on ways which keep part 1 the same but vary the size and number of the other parts, say.

Conclusion

Jonathan Dancy's important work has enlarged our sense of the possible in axiology and normative theory. In his discussion of the doctrine of organic unities, he somewhat uncharacteristically tries to shrink our sense of the possible. We have in this chapter argued that his reasons for this view are not sound, though the reasons his arguments go wrong are themselves interesting and instructive. More positively, we have argued that the doctrine of organic unities, once shorn of some of the Moorean baggage Dancy rightly criticizes, is both plausible in its own right and actually coheres quite nicely with holism. Furthermore, we have argued that the two views cohere well not only in that there are instances of holistic values and instances of organic unities, but that in fact there are plausible instances in which there are holistic organic unities. We therefore invite Dancy to be more true to his usual vista-enlarging instincts and embrace these axiological possibilities as well.

References

Chisholm, R. M. (1986) *Brentano and Intrinsic Value* (Cambridge: Cambridge University Press).

Crisp, R. (2000) 'Particularizing Particularism', in B. Hooker and M. Little (eds.), *Moral Particularism* (Oxford: Oxford University Press), 23–47.

Dancy, J. (2003) 'Are There Organic Unities?', *Ethics*, 113: 629–50.

—— (2004) *Ethics without Principles* (Oxford: Oxford University Press).

Geach, P. (1956) 'Good and Evil', *Analysis*, 17: 32–42.

Hurka, T. (1998) 'Two Kinds of Organic Unity', *Journal of Ethics*, 2(4): 299–320.

Lemos, N. (1998) 'Organic Unities', *Journal of Ethics*, 2(4): 321–37.

Moore, G. E. (1903/1993) *Principia Ethica* (Cambridge: Cambridge University Press).

Zangwill, N. (1998) 'Aesthetic/Sensory Dependence', *British Journal of Aesthetics*, 38: 66–81.

Zimmerman, M. (1999) 'Virtual Intrinsic Value and the Principle of Organic Unities', *Philosophy and Phenomenological Research*, 59(3): 653–66.

13

Practical Reasoning and Inference

JOHN BROOME

I have been thinking about reasoning—particularly practical reasoning—for many years. During that time I have often talked to Jonathan Dancy about the subject, with great enjoyment and benefit. Dancy has accurately criticized many of my arguments. Many of his criticisms appear in his paper 'From Thought to Action'. Because of them, and also because of criticisms I have received from other philosophers,[1] my views about reasoning have changed a lot. This chapter corrects the account of reasoning contained in my most recent paper on the subject, 'The unity of reasoning?' (Broome 2009).[2]

I hope Dancy will recognize that my account has improved, but I know he will still disagree with it. I think practical reasoning is much more like theoretical reasoning than he does. This chapter aims to bring out the parallels between these two types of reasoning.

I shall start by describing reasoning in general, but only briefly and without much argument. Then I shall go on to the question of correctness in reasoning. Some reasoning is correct and some incorrect: what makes the difference? There is where I think the disagreement between Dancy and me is sharpest. It will be the chapter's main focus.[3]

1. Theoretical reasoning

As I use the term, 'reasoning' refers to a process—specifically a mental process. I shall concentrate on conscious reasoning only. I dare say unconscious

---

[1] Particularly Michael Bratman (2009b) and Anthony Price (2007).
[2] For further developments, see Broome (2013).
[3] My thanks to Yair Levy for his helpful comments on this chapter.

reasoning exists, but in this chapter I shall ignore it. So 'reasoning' in this paper always refers to conscious reasoning.

I start my description of reasoning with an example of theoretical reasoning. Suppose you have a standing belief that mammals do not lay eggs. In particular, you believe that if platypuses lay eggs they are not mammals. Then suppose you come to believe that platypuses lay eggs; perhaps you see one doing so. And suppose that, either immediately or at some later time, these two beliefs cause you to acquire the third belief that platypuses are not mammals. This causal process may not be reasoning; all sorts of processes might cause you to acquire a new belief. However, if it satisfies some particular conditions, then it is reasoning. What are those conditions? In this section I shall present my own answer to this difficult question, but I shall not try to defend it.

First, if the process is to be conscious reasoning, you must be conscious of the contents of the beliefs involved in it. You may just happen to be conscious of them. But sometimes you bring these contents to your consciousness by a mental act; we have the ability to call to mind the contents of our beliefs.

Sometimes you do this using language, by saying to yourself sentences that denote the contents. In this case I say your reasoning is 'explicit'. Occasionally, you may even say the sentences out loud; usually you do it silently. In the example you might say to yourself:

Platypuses lay eggs.
If platypuses lay eggs, they are not mammals.
So platypuses are not mammals.

(The word 'so' indicates that the last sentence is the conclusion of reasoning.) I do not claim that conscious reasoning must be explicit. However, setting out sentences that denote the contents of your attitudes is sometimes a convenient method of describing a piece of reasoning. I shall sometimes use this method, but I do not thereby imply that the reasoning is necessarily explicit.

A second condition for the process to be reasoning is that you must *operate* in a particular way on the contents of your beliefs. The beliefs you start with cause the one you end up with, but when the process is reasoning there is more than a contingent, causal connection between these beliefs. There is also a semantic connection between their contents. The proposition that is the content of your concluding belief is derived in some way from the propositions that are the contents of your initial beliefs. You reason if you actually make the derivation.

In the example, your first premise—the proposition that platypuses lay eggs—is the antecedent of your second premise—the conditional proposition that if platypuses lay eggs they are not mammals. You operate on these two propositions by applying the modus ponens rule. This rule tells you to derive the proposition that is the consequent of the second premise: that platypuses are not mammals. You derive this consequent, and believe it.

Your operation is computational or algorithmic. These descriptions might suggest it is an operation on symbols that represent contents, but I do not mean that. You operate on meanings, not on representations. In the example, you operate on the propositions that are the contents of your beliefs.

Your operation applies some rule. The rule may be expressed by a schema. The rule for modus ponens reasoning is 'from p and (if p then q) derive q'. (This is a simplified version of the rule; it is stated more fully in section 2.) I assume in the example that you apply this rule, but you might alternatively apply the more specific rule 'from (platypuses F) and (if platypuses F they G) derive (platypuses G)', or some other rule. I shall ignore the well-known difficulties of identifying what rule you apply; I simply assume you apply one.

In order to apply a rule, you do not need to know explicitly what the rule is. You follow the rule, but you may do so in the way in which you often follow rules of grammar. You may compose grammatical sentences without knowing explicitly what grammatical rules you apply in doing so. Similarly, you may reason by modus ponens without knowing explicitly what the modus ponens rule is.

Nothing says that, if you are to reason, the rule you apply has to be correct or appropriate in some way. You can reason by applying a fallacious rule, such as 'from q and (if p then q) derive p'. Your reasoning will be incorrect, of course.

If a process whereby some of your beliefs cause you to acquire a new belief satisfies the first and second conditions I have mentioned, it is reasoning.

2. Practical reasoning

Reasoning in general is a process whereby some of your attitudes, which I call 'premise-attitudes', cause you to acquire a new attitude, which I call the 'conclusion-attitude'. We may classify types of reasoning according to the type of their conclusion-attitude. Reasoning that concludes in a belief, like the platypus example, is theoretical reasoning. I need to generalize my description of reasoning to include other types besides theoretical reasoning.

I call reasoning that concludes in an intention 'practical reasoning'. Here is an example of it. You intend to attend a particular conference. You learn that, to do so, you must register in advance. So you now believe that, if you do not register in advance, you will not attend the conference. This belief and your intention together cause you to acquire the intention of registering in advance. This causal process is reasoning, provided it satisfies some other conditions. What are those conditions?

They are generalized versions of the two conditions I specified for theoretical reasoning. I shall start with the second. For the process to be reasoning, as before it must be a rule-governed operation, but now the operation is not on contents alone.

The attitudes you reason with—beliefs and intentions for instance—are relations between a person (you) and a proposition. I shall call the proposition 'the propositional content' of the attitude. Attitudes of different types may have the same propositional content. For instance, if you intend to attend the conference, the propositional content of your intention is the proposition that you will attend the conference. If you believe you will attend the conference, the propositional content of your belief is that same proposition.

An intention to attend the conference and a belief that you will attend the conference obviously participate in your reasoning in different ways. For instance, reasoning that has the intention as a premise-attitude may arrive at a different conclusion from reasoning that has the belief as a premise-attitude. So when, in reasoning, you apply a rule, the rule must take account of the attitude's type as well as its propositional content. That is to say, it must take account of the pair consisting of the attitude's propositional content and its type. I shall write pairs of this sort using angle brackets. For example, the conference example involves the pair <I shall attend the conference; intention>. (I have expressed the propositional content as you would express it, in the first person.) The platypus example involves the pair <Platypuses lay eggs; belief>.

Reasoning is a rule-governed operation on pairs of this sort. If you are reasoning in the conference example, from <I shall attend the conference; intention> and <I shall not attend the conference unless I register in advance; belief> you derive <I shall register in advance; intention>. You are probably applying the rule 'from <p; intention> and <if p then q; belief> derive <q; intention>'. Alternatively, you may be applying the more specific rule 'from <I shall F; intention> and <if I shall F, I shall G; belief> derive <I shall G; intention>'.

For the same reasons, theoretical reasoning too must be an operation on pairs like this. For instance, the modus ponens rule must be understood as: 'from <p; belief> and <if p then q; belief> derive <q; belief>'. In section 1 I was considering only theoretical reasoning, so only beliefs were in play. In that context I was able to formulate the rule more simply, but this is the accurate formulation.

For a reason that will very soon appear, I call pairs of this sort the 'marked contents' of your attitudes. The 'mark' is the type of the attitude: intention, belief, or whatever it is. It is possible to think of the mark as part of the content, so that the content of an attitude is the propositional content together with the mark. But I prefer to think of the propositional content as the whole of the content, to which the mark is attached. It does not matter which notion of content we adopt. What matters is that reasoning operates on marked contents, rather than on propositional contents alone.

Now the first condition for a process to be reasoning. Remember I am concerned with conscious reasoning only. Since attitudes of different types participate differently in reasoning, to reason consciously with an attitude you must be conscious of the attitude's type as well as its propositional content. That is to say, you must be conscious of the pair consisting of the propositional content and the type. For example, in the platypus reasoning, you must be conscious of the pair <Platypuses lay eggs; belief>. More specifically, you must be conscious of the proposition that platypuses lay eggs *as* believed. I could alternatively say you must be conscious of the proposition in a believing way. In the conference example you must be conscious of the pair <I shall attend the conference; intention>. You must be conscious of the proposition that you will attend the conference *as* intended; you must be conscious of it in an intending way.

To summarize the conditions together: reasoning is a rule-governed operation on the conscious marked contents of your attitudes.

How can marked contents become conscious? Sometimes you call them to mind by a mental act, and sometimes you do this explicitly, using language. Although I do not claim that conscious reasoning is necessarily explicit, I need to explain how explicit reasoning is possible.

Our language is equipped to express marked contents. It does so by means of 'markers', as I shall call them. When you utter a sentence, you perform a speech-act of some sort. A marker is a linguistic item contained in the sentence that indicates what sort of speech-act you perform. When the speech-act is the act of expressing an attitude, the marker indirectly marks the sort of attitude you express. Indirectly, therefore, it denotes the mark.

Markers are often grammatical moods. The interrogative mood is the marker for the speech-act of asking a question, and the imperative mood the marker for the speech-act of commanding. The optative mood is a marker for expressing a desire. When Robert Browning said 'Oh to be in England now that April's there', he expressed a desire by using the optative mood (or the nearest approximation to the optative mood that English possesses). His sentence denotes the marked content <I am in England now that April is there; desire>.

The marker for expressing belief is the indicative mood. Unfortunately, the marker for expressing intention in English is often subtle or entirely silent. Some authors claim that using 'will' in the first person rather than 'shall' is a marker for intention (see Fowler and Fowler 1908: ch. 2). But in practice 'will' is rarely used for that purpose. In practice, we often express intentions using the very same indicative sentences as express beliefs. You would express your intention of attending the conference by saying 'I am going to attend the conference' or 'I shall attend the conference' or 'I will attend the conference'. Any of those sentences could equally well express a belief that you will attend the conference. So they could equally well denote the marked content <I shall attend the conference; intention> or <I shall attend the conference; belief>.

You may call to mind the marked content of an attitude by saying to yourself a sentence that denotes this marked content. You could call to mind your intention to attend the conference by saying to yourself the sentence 'I shall attend the conference'. Indeed, you could make the whole of your reasoning explicit, by saying to yourself:

I shall attend the conference.
If I do not register in advance, I shall not attend the conference.
So I shall register in advance.

The first and third of these sentences express intentions. They contain the silent marker for intention, but because the marker is silent they are indistinguishable from sentences that express beliefs. This leads to a puzzle, as I shall explain in section 9. But I do not claim that conscious practical reasoning is necessarily explicit, so I do not have to deal with the puzzle here.

3. Requirements of rationality

That concludes my brief description of reasoning. Now I move on to the question of what makes the difference between correct and incorrect reasoning. Reasoning is an operation governed by a rule. It is correct if and only if it is governed by a correct rule. The question is: what rules are correct?

For theoretical reasoning there is a natural answer: a rule is correct if and only if it is supported by a genuine inference. I use the word 'inference' to denote a relation among propositions, rather than among marked contents. It is the relation that holds among the propositions p, q, r, and so on, and the proposition t when t may be inferred from p and q and r and so on. Among genuine inferences I include deductive ones, by which I mean inferences where, necessarily, if p and q and r and so on, then t. Since I am not trying to give a full account of all sorts of correct theoretical reasoning, I can leave open the question of which other inferences are genuine. The list might include inductive inferences, inferences to the best explanation, and others.

That is a natural answer for theoretical reasoning, but I shall later explain that it is only approximately true. In any case, it is not available for reasoning with attitudes other than belief; inference among propositions obviously does not provide the criterion of correctness there. I believe that for these sorts of reasoning, the criterion must come from rationality. So I next need to describe rationality.

Rationality is one of a class of things that I do not know a proper generic name for; I call them 'sources of requirements'. Other members of the class are the law, convention, and morality. Each of these things makes requirements of you. The law requires you to pay your taxes; convention requires you to use your right hand for shaking hands; morality requires you to be kind to strangers, and so on. Rationality also makes requirements of you. Its requirements are to do with good order among your mental attitudes.

Here is an example of a requirement of rationality:

The instrumental requirement. Rationality requires of N that, if
(1) N intends at t that e, and if
(2) N believes at t that, if m were not so, because of that e would not be so, and if
(3) N believes at t that, if she herself were not then to intend m, because of that m would not be so, then
(4) N intends at t that m.

(where N is a person, t is a time, and e and m are propositions.) This requirement calls for elucidation. I can present it in a more friendly form by means of some devices. First, I define some expressions:

'm is a means implied by e' means that, were m not so, because of that e would not be so.

'm is up to N at t' means that, if N were not at t to intend m, because of that m would not be so.

These definitions give special meanings to the expressions 'means implied' and 'up to'. Nevertheless, I think the defined meanings are sufficiently close to the ordinary ones that they help to make the formula more transparent.

Second, I replace the person-letter 'N' by the less formal 'you', which is still meant to refer to a generic person. Third, I remove the references to the time t. They only serve to specify that all the attitudes are contemporaneous, and I can do that implicitly simply by using the present tense. I get:

The instrumental requirement, friendly formulation. Rationality requires of you that, if
(1) You intend e, and if
(2) You believe that m is a means implied by e, and if
(3) You believe that m is up to you yourself now, then
(4) You intend m.

This requirement is fairly widely applicable. It is much more so than Kant's formula: 'Who wills the end, wills (so far as reason has a decisive influence on his actions) also the means which [he believes] are indispensably necessary and in his power' (Kant 1948: 80–1). (I have inserted in square brackets words that Kant should have included; I assume he omitted them by accident.) Kant's formula applies to you only when you believe that the means is indispensably necessary to the end. You will rarely have such a strong belief. My formula applies when you believe that the means is implied by the end. You will have this weaker belief much more often than the strong one.

I recognize there are other requirements of instrumental rationality. For instance, there is no doubt a requirement to intend what you believe to be the best means to an end you intend. But I do not know how to formulate that requirement accurately,[4] whereas I believe my instrumental requirement is accurate.

4. Cognitivism

It is sometimes suggested that practical requirements of rationality can be derived from theoretical requirements. Michael Bratman calls this view 'cognitivism' (see, e.g., Bratman 1999, 2009b). The motivation for it appears to be simply the idea that rationality is ultimately a cognitive matter. I think everyone agrees it is a mental matter. That is to say, rationality supervenes on the mind, to use an expression I borrow from Ralph Wedgwood. If two people's minds have the same intrinsic properties (apart from their rationality) then those people are as rational as each other. Cognitivists go further, and assume that rationality supervenes on the mind's specifically cognitive properties.

Let us test out cognitivism on the instrumental requirement. Let us suppose you violate this requirement, and consider whether it follows that you also violate a theoretical requirement of rationality. If it does, that would give support to cognitivism. So let us suppose that:

(1) You intend e, and
(2) You believe that, if m were not so, because of that e would not be so, and

---

[4] I described the difficulties in Broome (2002).

(3) You believe that, if you yourself were not then to intend *m*, because of that *m* would not be so, but
(4) You do not intend *m*.

For the sake of argument, let us now make two hypotheses:

Hypothesis A: If you intend *e*, you believe you intend *e*, and if you do not intend *m*, you believe you do not intend *m*.

Hypothesis B: If you believe you intend *e*, you believe *e* is so.

From these and our initial suppositions, we may conclude that

(1) You believe that *e* is so, and
(2) You believe that, if *m* were not so, because of that *e* would not be so, and
(3) You believe that, if you were not then to intend *m*, because of that *m* would not be so, but
(4) You believe you do not intend *m*.

(2) and (3) say that you believe two complex conditional propositions. They are subjunctive conditionals with 'because' clauses added. But we may fairly assume they entail the corresponding simple indicative conditionals. We may assume that:

(1) You believe that *e* is so, and
(2) You believe that, if *m* is not so, *e* is not so, and
(3) You believe that, if you do not intend *m*, *m* is not so, but
(4) You believe you do not intend *m*.

If you are in this state, it is fair to conclude you are breaching some theoretical requirement of rationality. Your beliefs are mutually inconsistent, and it takes only two steps of modus ponens to reveal their inconsistency. Theoretical rationality must require you not to be in that state.

So if hypotheses A and B were necessarily true, there would be a case for thinking the instrumental requirement could be derived from theoretical requirements of rationality. I am willing to accept that hypothesis B is necessarily true, though many would not. I shall explain why in section 9. But hypothesis A is not necessarily true; you do not necessarily have correct second-order beliefs about all your intentions. Here is a counterexample. It is an elaboration of one of Michael Bratman's.[5]

You regularly shop on Fridays. However, you learn in July that the shops will be closed on the Friday of the last week in August, so you form the intention of shopping on Thursday that week. This intention will work as intentions usually do, to cause you to do what you intend. Early in the last week in August you will remember you are shopping on Thursday that week; you will draw up a shopping list on Wednesday evening and head for the shops on Thursday. Your intention is a particular sort of disposition to shop on Thursday that week, and that disposition is in place. However, by early August you temporarily forget that you have an unusual intention for that last week. Were you asked, you would say that you will shop on Friday that week, as usual. You believe you will shop on Friday that week, and you do not believe you will shop on Thursday that week. So you do not believe you have an intention you do have, and you believe you have an intention you do not have.

Since hypothesis A is not necessarily true; you may violate the instrumental requirement without violating any requirement of theoretical rationality.

A cognitivist may nevertheless defend her position. She may reject the instrumental requirement as I have formulated it. She might claim that rationality imposes requirements only on those of your intentions you have correct beliefs about. She would say my formulation of the requirement is too strong, because it applies even to intentions you do not believe you have.

Is her claim plausible? Cognitivists do not think that rationality imposes requirements only on those of your beliefs you have correct higher-order beliefs about. That would have the implausible consequence that there are no rational requirements on your top-level beliefs—those beliefs you have no higher-order beliefs about. Since cognitivists do not limit theoretical requirements of rationality to attitudes you have higher-order beliefs about, why should they limit practical requirements in this way? So far as I can see, doing so would be pure dogmatism, driven only by the view that rationality has to be a cognitive matter.

I shall therefore assume that cognitivism is false. I shall assume that practical rationality cannot be derived from theoretical rationality. In par-

---

[5] It is mentioned in Bratman (2009b).

ticular, I shall assume that the instrumental requirement is genuinely a requirement of rationality.

5. Quasi-inferences and the requirement theory of correctness

I call the instrumental requirement a 'material requirement' of rationality because it can be put in the form of a material conditional like this:

Rationality requires of N that, if
N has attitude A at t, and
N has attitude B at t, and
N has attitude C at t, ... then
N has attitude F at t.

For convenience, I make two innovations. First, I place no restriction on the number of antecedents in this formula, so I count a requirement as a material requirement even if it has no antecedents. Second, I count not having an attitude as a sort of attitude. If you do not believe the sea is wet, I say you have the attitude of non-belief towards the proposition that the sea is wet. I call attitudes of this sort 'negative'.

These innovations conveniently bring many requirements of rationality under the heading of material requirements. Among them is the requirement that you do not believe a contradiction—for instance that you do not believe the sea is wet and not wet. Another is the requirement that you do not have contradictory beliefs—for instance that if you believe the sea is wet, you do not also believe the sea is not wet.

Any material requirement generates something I call a 'quasi-inference'. When the requirement is put in the form I described, I say that the marked content of attitude F can be quasi-inferred from the marked contents of A, B, C, and so on.

Take the instrumental requirement from section 3 as an example. It determines that, from the marked contents

  $<e;$ intention$>$ and
  $<m$ is a means implied by $e;$ belief$>$ and
  $<m$ is up to me now; belief$>$

the marked content

<m; intention>

may be quasi-inferred. (I have expressed the propositional contents of your second belief in the first person. That is for a technical reason. In clause (3) of the instrumental requirement, 'you yourself' is a reflexive pronoun. It represents in indirect speech the pronoun 'me' in direct speech. It indicates that the propositional content of the belief described in (3) is *de se*. The easiest way to ensure the content is *de se* when it is expressed in direct rather than indirect speech is to put it in the first person.)

An inference is a relation among propositions that constitute the contents of attitudes. Correspondingly, a quasi-inference is a relation among the marked contents of attitudes.

Now I come back to the question of when reasoning is correct. I have described how material requirements of rationality generate quasi-inferences. Quasi-inferences might in turn provide a criterion of correctness for reasoning: that reasoning other than theoretical reasoning is correct if and only if the rule it follows is supported by a genuine quasi-inference. In this way, requirements of rationality would determine when reasoning is correct.

I call this 'the requirement theory of correctness'. It seems plausible at first. But it encounters two difficulties that will force us to abandon it.

6. Basing prohibitions of rationality

The first difficulty is that material requirements can be contraposed. For example, the instrumental requirement can be written in the form:

The instrumental requirement contraposed. Rationality requires of you that, if

(1) You intend e, and
(3) You believe that m is up to you yourself now, and
(4′) You do not intend m, then
(2′) You do not believe that m is a means implied by e.

So by my definition of a quasi-inference, from the marked contents

<e; intention> and
<m is up to me now; belief> and
<m; non-intention>

the marked content

<*m* is a means implied by *e*; non-belief>

may be quasi-inferred. According to the requirement theory, reasoning that followed this quasi-inference would be correct reasoning.

For instance, suppose you initially believe that registering in advance is a means implied by attending the conference. Suppose you intend to attend the conference. Suppose you believe that registering in advance is up to you, and you do not intend to register in advance. Now suppose that by reasoning on the basis of these last three attitudes, you bring yourself to drop your belief that registering in advance is a means implied by attending the conference. According to the requirement theory, your reasoning would be correct. That is absurd.

It is dubious anyway that you could possibly achieve this result by reasoning. Your reasoning would set out from the negative attitude of not intending something, and it would conclude in the negative attitude of not believing something. It is dubious that you can reason either from a negative attitude or to a negative attitude. But still, we should avoid a theory that implies this reasoning would be correct if it were possible.

My way of dealing with this difficulty clings on to the idea that correctness is determined by quasi-inferences. I restrict the notion of a quasi-inference. I start by recognizing that there are requirements of rationality of a sort I have not yet mentioned. I call them 'basing prohibitions'. A basing prohibition is a requirement not to have some attitude based on some other attitudes that you have. It has the form:

Rationality requires of N that it is not the case that
N has attitude A at some time and
N has attitude B at some time and
N has attitude C at some time ... and
N has attitude F at some time, and
Attitude F is based on attitude A and attitude B and attitude C ...

For example, rationality prohibits you from believing p on the basis of believing q and believing that if p then q. Rationality also prohibits you from not believing that registering in advance is a means implied by attending the conference, on the basis of intending to attend the conference, believing that registering in advance is up to you yourself now, and not intending to register in advance.

A basing prohibition does not prohibit the attitudes themselves. Rationality may permit you to believe p, even at the same time as you believe q and you believe that if p then q. But it prohibits you from having the first of these beliefs on the basis of the second and third.

What does it mean to say one attitude is based on others? For one thing, it means that the first was caused by the others. The causing of an attitude by others is an event, but the caused attitude's property of being based on the others persists after this event. The above formula for basing prohibitions does not restrict the times when the various attitudes may exist. In particular, unlike material requirements, basing prohibitions do not apply only to contemporaneous attitudes. However, N cannot fall foul of a basing prohibition unless she has each of her basing attitudes A, B, C, and so on at a time that is no later than a time when she has her based attitude F.

Not just any sort of causation is basing. Some attitudes of yours might cause you to have another attitude in all sorts of ways, and many of those ways are not basing. I am sorry to say I cannot give an analysis of basing; I shall have to take it as a primitive.[6]

However, I can give some examples of basing. Reasoning provides one: if an attitude has been derived from others by reasoning, then it is based on the others. But reasoning is not the only example. Sometimes basing happens automatically and unconsciously. Suppose you had always believed platypuses are mammals, but in some way you came to believe that platypuses are not mammals. Probably an automatic process caused you at the same time to stop believing platypuses are mammals; automatic processes normally prevent you from having contradictory beliefs. Then your non-belief in the proposition that platypuses are mammals is based on your belief in the proposition that platypuses are not mammals. Yet you did not acquire the non-belief by reasoning.

Once we have identified basing prohibitions, we can use them to restrict the notion of a quasi-inference. A quasi-inference is derived from a requirement of rationality in the way I described, but only if it is not contrary to a basing prohibition. This means that the instrumental requirement in its original form generates a quasi-inference, but not in its contraposed form. That removes the first difficulty.

---

[6] An idealized account appears in Wedgwood (2006: 662). I cannot use it because, as Wedgwood recognizes, it makes it impossible for one attitude to be based on others in a way that is rationally prohibited. It would consequently make basing prohibitions otiose.

7. Basing permissions of rationality

The second difficulty was first put to me by Geoffrey Brennan. Suppose you intend to attend the conference, and you believe that registering in advance is a means implied by this end. Suppose you believe that registering in advance is up to you. By that I mean you believe that, were you not at some time to intend to register in advance, because of that you would not register in advance. However, you do not believe that registering in advance is up to you *now*. That is to say, you do not believe that, were you not now to intend to register in advance, because of that you would not register in advance. Maybe you believe that just now you do not even need to think about means of attending the conference; you can leave that to another time.

Nevertheless, suppose you do happen to think about means. Then there is obviously some correct reasoning you could do that would bring you to intend to register in advance. Since you believe this is a means implied by your end, and you believe this means is up to you, of course it would be correct to arrive at the intention of doing it.

But this correct reasoning does not follow the quasi-inference I set out above. Nor does it follow a quasi-inference generated by any other requirement of rationality. You can be rational without now intending the means, so there can be no requirement of rationality that rules this out. It follows that there is something wrong with the requirement theory of correct reasoning. On that theory, correctness is generated by requirements of rationality. But in this case of correct reasoning, there is no relevant requirement.

This difficulty can be reinforced by a point made to me by Kieran Setiya. To continue the example, suppose you do not form the intention of registering in advance until a time arrives when you believe that registering in advance is up to you *then*. That is to say, you then believe that were you not then to intend to register in advance, you would not do so. Evidently you believe you have reached the last moment when you can register. At that time, your beliefs entail it is too late for you to reason your way to intending to register in advance. Reasoning takes time, so you would acquire the intention only later, whereas you believe you must have it then.

Indeed reasoning according to the quasi-inference generated by the instrumental requirement will always come too late. In order to satisfy the instrumental requirement by reasoning, you have to embark on the reasoning before the instrumental requirement bites. By the time it bites, it is too late to reason.

My solution to this difficulty is still to cling on to the idea that correctness is determined by quasi-inferences, but to put quasi-inferences on a different footing. I start from the idea of a basing permission. A basing permission is simply the negation of a basing prohibition. Rationality permits you to base an attitude F on attitudes A, B, C, and so on, if and only if it does not prohibit you from doing so. An example of a basing permission is that rationality permits you to intend m on the basis of intending e, believing that m is a means implied by e, and believing that m is up to you. Let us call this 'the instrumental permission'.

I now take it that *any* basing permission generates a quasi-inference, and that *all* quasi-inferences are generated by basing permissions. When, and only when, rationality permits you to base an attitude F on attitudes A, B, C, and so on, the marked content of F may be quasi-inferred from the marked contents of A, B, C, and so on.

The basing permission I mentioned gives us the quasi-inference from the marked contents

<e; intention> and
<m is a means implied by e; belief> and
<m is up to me; belief>

the marked content

<m; intention>

may be quasi-inferred. This quasi-inference differs in just one place from the one I derived in section 5 from the instrumental requirement: the formula contains no 'now'.

8. The permission theory of correctness

I continue to take it that reasoning is correct if and only if it follows a rule that is supported by a genuine quasi-inference. Since I now take quasi-inferences to arise from basing permissions rather than requirements, I have dropped the requirement theory of correctness and adopted a permission theory instead. This change deals with the first difficulty described in section 6, as well as the second described in section 7, since it entails that reasoning is not correct if it is opposed by a basing prohibition.

The permission theory covers theoretical reasoning as well as other sorts. Let the attitudes A, B, C, and so on be believing p, believing q, believing r, and so on, and let the attitude F be believing t. According to the permission theory, theoretical reasoning is correct if and only if rationality permits you to base a belief in t on beliefs in p, q, r, and so on, and your reasoning follows a rule that is supported by the quasi-inference that derives from this permission.

In section 3 I suggested that theoretical reasoning is correct if and only if it follows a rule that is supported by a genuine inference from p, q, r, and so on to t. At first this suggestion may seem to coincide with the permission theory. It is natural to think at first that rationality permits you to base a belief in t on beliefs in p, q, r, and so on if and only if there is a genuine inference from p, q, r, and so on to t.

But actually this is not so: 'only if' is right, but 'if' wrong. Suppose the Goldbach Conjecture can be inferred from the Peano Axioms of arithmetic. It is still not known whether this is so. Even if it is, rationality does not permit you (as you actually are) to believe the Goldbach Conjecture on the basis of believing the Peano Axioms, since you do not know that the Goldbach Conjecture can be inferred from the Peano Axioms. So not every genuine inference among propositions matches a quasi-inference among beliefs. The permission theory therefore passes fewer examples of theoretical reasoning as correct. It is intuitively right to do so. It would not be intuitively correct to reason directly from the Peano Axioms to the Goldbach Conjecture.[7] So this theory offers a better account of theoretical reasoning than my previous suggestion did.

The permission theory is therefore a nicely unified account of correctness for reasoning. It is intuitively satisfactory in other ways too. One is simply that, when your reasoning is correct, that intuitively means you are permitted to reason as you do. It does not intuitively mean you are required to. Second, the theory entails that correctness stems from *basing* permissions of rationality rather than *material* requirements or permissions of rationality. This too seems intuitively appropriate, since the effect of reasoning is to base the conclusion-attitude on the premise-attitudes.

---

[7] This point is made in Boghossian (2008: 269).

Indeed, the permission theory fits correct reasoning so closely that it may be criticized for lacking explanatory power. It says not much more than this: that a piece of reasoning is correct if and only if rationality permits you to reason that way. It says a little more than that, since the notion of a basing permission is broader than the notion of a permission to reason in a particular way. For example, rationality permits you to base a non-belief in a proposition on a belief in that proposition's negation, but you cannot reason from a belief in a proposition's negation to a non-belief in that proposition. Nevertheless, the permission theory will gain significant explanatory power only once it is supplemented by an account of basing permissions. It needs to be specified when and why it is permitted to base one attitude on others. Only then will we have a proper account of when and why particular patterns of reasoning are correct.

I have given some account of basing permissions for beliefs: these permissions derive from genuine inferences among propositions. But I have said that not all genuine inferences generate basing permissions, so I need to distinguish those that do from those that do not. That job remains to be done.

I have not given much of an account of basing permissions for attitudes other than beliefs, and I do not have much of an account to offer. However, I can say that basing permissions must be in some way closely related to requirements of rationality. Perhaps they are derived somehow from requirements.

For instance, the instrumental permission is very closely connected to the instrumental requirement. The quasi-inference that is derived from the permission is a slight generalization of the one I initially derived from the requirement. Moreover, I explained that the only way to satisfy the requirement is to reason according to the permission; if you do not at some time reason as the permission allows, you will not satisfy the requirement. This seems a plausible explanation of why rationality permits you to reason that way. If it is the right explanation, the requirement explains the permission.

In general, our activity of reasoning often improves our rationality. Indeed, that seems to be part of its purpose. To improve your rationality, you must do something that rationality requires of you, not something that it merely permits you to do. So correct reasoning, which is made correct by permissions, must often bring us to satisfy requirements. This suggests in general that requirements explain permissions.

That is as far as I have got in explaining correctness for practical reasoning.

9. Separating theoretical and practical reasoning

Now I return to my very first example of practical reasoning from section 2. You intend to attend the conference and you believe that, if you do not register in advance, you will not attend the conference. This belief and your intention together cause you to acquire the intention of registering in advance. Let us assume that this process satisfies the conditions I mentioned in section 2: it is a rule-governed operation on the conscious marked contents of your attitudes. So it is reasoning.

However, it is not correct reasoning. It does not follow a quasi-inference. The nearest quasi-inference is the one set out at the end of section 7. It shows that, if your reasoning is to be correct, you need stronger beliefs as premise-attitudes. You must believe, first, that registering in advance is a means implied by attending the conference and, second, that registering in advance is up to you.

These stronger beliefs are definitely needed. To see the need for the second one, suppose you intend to attend the conference and you believe that you will not attend it if you do not register in advance. But suppose you do not believe your registering in advance is up to you. Perhaps you have delegated your conference registration to your secretary, because it is beyond your own administrative ability. Then you could not correctly arrive by reasoning at an intention to register in advance.

To see the need for the first of those beliefs, suppose again that you intend to attend the conference, and you believe you will not attend it if you do not register in advance. But suppose you do not believe that registering in advance is a means implied by attending the conference. Suppose instead that you believe it will be a side-effect of some means that is implied by your attending the conference. For instance, suppose you believe you will get to the conference only by taking a lift with your colleague, and you believe that your colleague is an efficient type who will see to it that you register in advance. Then again, you could not correctly arrive by reasoning at an intention to register in advance.

So the piece of practical reasoning in section 2 is incorrect. At least, it is incorrect unless it is enthymematic. Some further premises need to be implicit.

This may seem puzzling. In section 2 I set out the reasoning in the sentences:

> I shall attend the conference.
> If I do not register in advance, I shall not attend the conference.
> So I shall register in advance.

Those sentences look as though they express a piece of correct reasoning by themselves, without needing any further premises. How can they not be?

They would indeed express correct reasoning in themselves if they all expressed beliefs. The three sentences would then express a correct piece of theoretical reasoning by modus ponens. This may explain why the practical reasoning looks correct: the sentences could express a piece of correct reasoning. But correct *practical* reasoning requires different premises.

That puzzle arises only from the expression of reasoning in language. Because the expression of an intention is also the expression of a belief, theoretical and practical reasoning can be confused.

There is a further puzzle that does not depend on language. Still, it is most easily appreciated by starting from the sentences set out above. When those sentences express practical reasoning, the first and third express intentions. But they also express beliefs. In section 2 I said they contain a silent marker that marks them as expressions of intention. Nevertheless, they are indicative sentences. Like most indicative sentences, they make assertions. Not all indicative sentences do that. At my school, a notice used to appear on the notice-board saying 'All gentlemen will take changed exercise this afternoon'. It was an instruction, and not an assertion. The context removed the sentence's assertoric force. But if you express an intention by saying 'I shall attend the conference', the assertoric force of the sentence is not removed. You assert that you will attend the conference. In general, indicative sentences that express intentions also make assertions. This means they also express beliefs.

How is this possible? How is it that, when you express an intention, you are even in a position to express a corresponding belief? Because of this principle:

Intention–Belief. Normally, if *N* intends at *t* that *p*, then *N* believes at *t* that *p*.

Normally, if you intend to do something, you believe you will do it. There are some exceptions. For instance, in section 4 I used the shopping example to explain that you may have an intention, but not believe you have it. In that case, you may not believe you will carry the intention out. This is an abnormal case.

Even with the qualification 'normally', the intention-belief principle is controversial (see Bratman 2009a). But it provides the best explanation of how the normal expression of an intention—an indicative sentence—can also express a belief. I accept it for that reason. Intention–belief is the true source of the puzzle I am describing. The puzzle does not depend on the expression of the attitudes in language. Now I can say what it is.

Suppose you intend to attend the conference and you believe you will not attend it if you do not register in advance. Since you intend to attend the conference and—let us assume—the case is normal, you believe you will. You are therefore apparently in a position to do the correct theoretical reasoning by modus ponens that can be expressed by the sentences above. So you are apparently in a position to arrive by theoretical reasoning at the belief that you will register in advance.

But this is puzzling. Suppose you believe that registering in advance is up to you now. In that case, you will not believe you will register in advance unless you believe you intend to register in advance. You will normally not believe you have this intention unless you do. You may be in a position to acquire the intention by practical reasoning, but you cannot acquire it by theoretical reasoning. Theoretical reasoning cannot possibly give you an intention. So in these circumstances, since theoretical reasoning cannot give you the intention of registering in advance, it cannot give you the belief that you will. Yet it seems that ordinary theoretical reasoning by modus ponens can lead you to this belief.

The solution to this puzzle is to realize that, even if a piece of reasoning would be correct were you to do it, you may not be able to do it. Take the platypus reasoning as an example:

Platypuses lay eggs.
If platypuses lay eggs, they are not mammals.
So platypuses are not mammals.

Suppose you believe the two premises. Then this piece of correct reasoning would bring you to believe the conclusion. But suppose you also believe that platypuses are mammals, and this belief is robust. It may prevent you from completing the reasoning. If it does, it will leave you with inconsistent beliefs, unless you drop one of your premise-beliefs. With luck, you may be able to do that by means of reasoning in reverse. But your forward reasoning is blocked, even thought it would be correct were you to complete it.

The case of theoretical reasoning about the conference is the same. Suppose again that you believe your registering in advance is up to you now. Suppose that at present you do not intend to register in advance. Even if you believe you will attend the conference, and you believe you will not attend the conference if you do not register in advance, theoretical reasoning by itself will not be able to bring you to believe that you will register in advance. That is so even though it would be correct reasoning if it did. It is blocked by your lack of an intention.

You may be able to acquire the belief in some other way. For instance, you may acquire the intention of registering in advance by practical reasoning. Then, by intention-belief you will believe you will register in advance. But theoretical reasoning cannot achieve this result.

10. Conclusions

Section 9 shows how careful we must be to separate practical reasoning from theoretical reasoning. But the main drift of this chapter has been to reveal parallels between the two. Both practical and theoretical reasoning, when they are conscious, are rule-governed operations on the conscious marked contents of attitudes. When they are correct, both are made correct by quasi-inferences. Quasi-inferences in turn are grounded in rationality, and specifically on basing permissions of rationality.

In 'From Thought to Action', Jonathan Dancy argues that practical reasoning is not inferential. Here are my conclusions about that. First, simply as a consequence of my terminology, neither theoretical nor practical reasoning is an inference. I use 'inference' to refer to a relation between propositions, whereas I use 'reasoning' to refer to a mental process.

However, theoretical reasoning does have a close link to inferences, since theoretical rationality is constrained by inferences. Rationality does not permit you to base one belief on others unless the content of the one may be inferred from the content of the others. Practical rationality has no parallel constraint.

Still, both practical and theoretical rationality are regulated by quasi-inferences. Although these are relations among marked contents rather than among propositions, it would not be unreasonable to use the term 'inference' for them, instead of 'quasi-inference'. If you use words that way, then you should recognize that both theoretical and practical reasoning is regulated by inferences. You should disagree with Dancy, therefore.

References

Boghossian, P. (2008) 'Blind Reasoning', in his *Content and Justification* (Oxford: Oxford University Press), 266–87.

Bratman, M. (1999) 'Cognitivism About Practical Reason', in his *Faces of Intention* (Cambridge: Cambridge University Press), 250–64.

—— (2009a) 'Intention, Belief, and Instrumental Rationality', in D. Sobel and S. Wall (eds.), *Reasons for Action* (Cambridge: Cambridge University Press), 13–36.

—— (2009b) 'Intention, Belief, Practical, Theoretical', in Robertson (2009: 29–61).

Broome, J. (2002) 'Practical Reasoning', in J. Bermùdez and A. Millar (eds.), *Reason and Nature: Essays in the Theory of Rationality* (Oxford: Oxford University Press), 85–111.

—— (2009) 'The Unity of Reasoning?', in Robertson (2009: 62–92).

—— (2013) *Rationality Through Reasoning* (Oxford: Wiley-Blackwell).

Dancy, J. 'From Thought to Action', forthcoming.

—— (2009) 'Reasons and Rationality', in Robertson (2009: 93–112).

Fowler, H. W. and Fowler, F. G. (1908) *The King's English*, 2nd edn. (Oxford: Oxford University Press).

Kant, I. (1948) *Groundwork of the Metaphysic of Morals*, tr. H. J. Paton under the title *The Moral Law* (London: Hutchinson).

Price, A. (2007) *Contextuality in Practical Reason* (Oxford: Oxford University Press).

Robertson, S. (ed.) (2009) *Spheres of Reason* (Oxford: Oxford University Press).

Wedgwood, R. (2006) 'The Normative Force of Reasoning', *Noûs*, 40: 660–86.

14

Why There Really Are No Irreducibly Normative Properties

BART STREUMER

Jonathan Dancy thinks that there are irreducibly normative properties.[1] Frank Jackson has given a well-known argument against this view, and I have elsewhere defended this argument against many objections, including one made by Dancy.[2] But Dancy remains unconvinced. In this chapter, I hope to convince him.

This chapter consists of eight sections. In section 1, I distinguish normative properties from descriptive properties. In section 2, I present Jackson's argument. In sections 3 to 6, I discuss four objections to the argument and, in doing so, put forward two new versions of the argument. In section 7, I discuss three reasons why Dancy may remain unconvinced. In section 8, I conclude that, despite this, the argument does show that there are no irreducibly normative properties.

1. Normative and descriptive properties

To distinguish normative properties from descriptive properties, we first need to distinguish normative predicates (such as 'is right', 'is good', and 'is a reason for') from descriptive predicates (such as 'is square', 'is yellow', or 'is larger than').[3] We can then say that

---

[1] See Dancy (1993, 2004a, 2004b, and esp. 2005).
[2] See Jackson (1998: 122–3, 2001: 655); and Streumer (2008). For Dancy's objection, see Dancy (2004a, 2004b: 63–7, and 2005).
[3] I here follow Jackson (1998: 120–1). Except in section 7 below, I use the term 'property' to cover both properties and relations.

A property is *normative* if and only if it can be ascribed with a normative predicate,

A property is *descriptive* if and only if it can be ascribed with a descriptive predicate,

and

A property is *irreducibly normative* if and only if it is a normative property that is not identical to a descriptive property.[4]

These claims are not definitions. They merely give necessary and sufficient conditions for a property's being normative, descriptive, or irreducibly normative.[5]

Some philosophers think that we should not call properties 'descriptive', either because properties do not describe anything, or because they think that normative predicates describe the world just as much as descriptive ones do.[6] But the term 'descriptive' is merely a label. We could instead use the term 'non-normative', and say that

A property is *non-normative* if and only if it can be ascribed with a predicate that is not normative.

But in that case a property could be both normative and non-normative, which would be confusing. I shall therefore continue to use the term 'descriptive'.

All philosophers who are realists about normative properties, including Dancy and Jackson, think that there are normative properties. But they disagree about whether there are irreducibly normative properties. According to non-reductive realists like Dancy, there are such properties. But according to reductive realists like Jackson, normative properties are identical to descriptive properties, which means that there are no irreducibly normative properties.

It may seem easy to show that there are no such properties. Suppose that, at time *t*, Fred is thinking about the normative property of rightness. In that case, we can denote the normative property of rightness with the descriptive

---

[4] It may be objected that some predicates (such as 'is courageous' or 'is just') are both normative and descriptive. If so, we should say either that these predicates are equivalent to conjunctions of normative and descriptive predicates, or that they ascribe normative properties.

[5] In Streumer (2008), I did present these claims as definitions. This was a mistake.

[6] The first claim is made by Suikkanen (2010: 88 n. 2), and the second claim has been made by Dancy in conversation. See also Dancy (2005: 142 n. 1).

phrase 'the property that Fred is thinking about at time t',[7] which means that we can ascribe the normative property of rightness with the descriptive predicate 'has the property that Fred is thinking about at time t'. But this does not show that there are no irreducibly normative properties. It merely shows that we should revise our claim about descriptive properties, and say that

> A property is *descriptive* if and only if it can be ascribed with a descriptive predicate that does not contain a descriptive phrase that denotes a normative property without ascribing this property.[8]

We should revise our claim about normative properties in a similar way. In what follows, I shall ignore these revisions, since they do not affect my arguments.

2. Jackson's argument

Inspired by a more general argument that was first given by Jaegwon Kim, Frank Jackson has given the following argument to show that there are no irreducibly normative properties.[9] Consider an action A_1 that has a certain normative property, such as the property of being right. Since anything that has normative properties also has descriptive properties, A_1 also has descriptive properties, which we can call $P_{A1-1}, P_{A1-2}\ldots$. And the objects $O_1, O_2, \ldots$ that are part of the same possible world as A_1 have descriptive properties as well, which for each object O_x we can call $P_{Ox-1}, P_{Ox-2}, \ldots$.[10] Action A_1 therefore satisfies the following predicate, which we can call predicate D_1:

> 'has descriptive properties $P_{A1-1}, P_{A1-2}, \ldots$ and is such that O_1 has descriptive properties $P_{O1-1}, P_{O1-2}, \ldots$, O_2 has descriptive properties $P_{O2-1}, P_{O2-2}, \ldots, \ldots$'.

---

[7] See Jackson (1998: 119 n. 10). A similar example is given by Williamson (2001: 629). See also Sturgeon (2009: 77 n. 46).

[8] I say 'without ascribing this property' because a phrase like 'the property that Fred is thinking about at time t' denotes a property without ascribing it, whereas phrases like 'is yellow' or 'is right' both ascribe and denote a property.

[9] See Jackson (1998: 122–3, and 2001: 655); and also Jackson and Pettit (1996: 84–5). For Kim's more general argument, see Kim (1993: 68–71, 149–55). For discussion of Jackson's argument, see van Roojen (1996); Williamson (2001); Shafer-Landau (2003: 89–98); McNaughton and Rawling (2003); Dancy (2004a and 2005); Majors (2005); FitzPatrick (2008: 198–201); Streumer (2008 and 2011); Kramer (2009: 207–12); Plantinga (2010); Suikkanen (2010); Brown (2011); and Enoch (2011: 137–40). My presentation of the argument in what follows assumes that the number of objects, properties, and actions in all possible worlds is countably infinite, but I take this to be merely a matter of presentation.

[10] I use the term 'object' to cover anything that has properties, including actions. Objects are part of the same possible world as A_1 if and only if they are actual in the possible world in which A_1 is performed.

Since a predicate that wholly consists of descriptive predicates is itself descriptive, predicate D_1 is a descriptive predicate.

Suppose next that actions $A_1, A_2, \ldots$ are all the right actions there are in all possible worlds.[11] Just as A_1 satisfies the descriptive predicate D_1, actions $A_2, A_3, \ldots$ satisfy similarly constructed descriptive predicates $D_2, D_3, \ldots$. These actions therefore all satisfy the following predicate, which we can call predicate D^*:

'satisfies either predicate D_1, or predicate D_2, or ...'.

As before, since a predicate that wholly consists of descriptive predicates is itself descriptive, predicate D^* is a descriptive predicate.

Now consider the following claim about supervenience:

(S) For all possible worlds W and W*, if the distribution of descriptive properties in W and W* is exactly the same, then the distribution of normative properties in W and W* is also exactly the same.[12]

If this claim is true, any object that satisfies predicate D^* also satisfies the predicate 'is right'. For otherwise there would be two possible worlds W and W* that have exactly the same distribution of descriptive properties but that do not have the same distribution of normative properties, which would contradict (S). And any object that satisfies the predicate 'is right' also satisfies predicate D^*. For objects $A_1, A_2, \ldots$ are all the right objects there are in all possible worlds, and these objects satisfy the predicates $D_1, D_2, \ldots$, which means that they satisfy predicate D^*.

This shows that the predicate 'is right' and predicate D^* are necessarily coextensive. Given that

(N) Necessarily coextensive predicates ascribe the same property,

---

[11] I assume for simplicity that only actions can be right.
[12] (S) is a claim about global supervenience. Williamson (2001: 627), Suikkanen (2010: 91 n. 6), and Brown (2011: 210 n. 10) suggest that Jackson's argument should instead appeal to the following claim about local supervenience: (S*) For all possible worlds W and W* and objects O and O*, if O in W and O* in W* have exactly the same descriptive properties, then O in W and O* in W* also have exactly the same normative properties. But as Jackson (2001: 655) points out, if we include the distribution of all descriptive properties in an object's possible world among this object's descriptive properties, as predicates $D_1, D_2, \ldots$ effectively do, we in effect turn (S*) into (S). Moreover, contrary to what Brown (2011) suggests, (S*) is then as uncontroversial as (S). For just as Dancy and other particularists do not deny (S), they also do not deny (S*) if we include the distribution of all descriptive properties in an object's possible world among this object's descriptive properties.

this means that the normative predicate 'is right' and the descriptive predicate D* ascribe the same property. It therefore means that the property of being right is not irreducibly normative. And since the argument can be repeated for any other normative predicate, it shows that no other property is irreducibly normative either.

Non-reductive realists have made many objections to this argument. They have objected that (N) is false; that predicate D* does not ascribe a property (either because there are no disjunctive properties, or because disjunctive predicates do not ascribe properties, or because infinitely disjunctive predicates do not ascribe properties, or because there are no infinitely disjunctive predicates); that predicate D* does not ascribe a descriptive property (either because its formulation presupposes the existence of normative properties, or because it is necessarily coextensive with a non-disjunctive normative property); that the argument supports reductionism about all supervenient properties; that the argument depends on implausible definitions of normative and descriptive properties; that the argument does not apply to natural properties; and that the argument does not apply to normative relations.[13] I have elsewhere defended the argument against all of these objections. In sections 4 and 7, I shall return to two of them. But I shall first discuss a new objection.

3. Two new versions of the argument

This objection has been made by Campbell Brown. Though Brown accepts the conclusion of Jackson's argument, he suspects that we cannot formulate predicate D* in English, since English does not seem to contain enough terms to name every object and property in every possible world.[14] In my

---

[13] For some of these objections, see Shafer-Landau (2003: 90–2); Dancy (2004a and 2004b: 63–7); and Majors (2005).

[14] See Brown (2011). More specifically, Brown claims that English may not be *descriptively complete*, where a language is descriptively complete if 'for any pair of worlds that are descriptively different, there is at least one descriptive sentence (of English) that is true in one world but not the other', and that English may not contain *maximally specific sentences*, where a sentence ψ is maximally specific if 'for any descriptive sentence χ, ψ entails either χ or its negation, $\sim\chi$, but not both' (Brown 2011: 207–8). For related worries about formulating (S) in terms of descriptive properties, see Sturgeon (2009: 75–8).

earlier defence of the argument, I suggested that we can avoid this problem by formulating predicate D* in a language that combines English with a 'Lagadonian' language in which all objects and properties that are not named by English are their own names instead (2008: 547). But I think we can also avoid it by formulating a version of Jackson's argument that does not rely on predicate D*. Brown himself presents one such version.[15] I shall now present two others.

The first is as follows. Suppose that the correct first-order view about rightness is a simple version of utilitarianism, according to which

> Necessarily, an action is right if and only if it maximizes preference satisfaction.

If this view is correct, the normative predicate 'is right' is necessarily coextensive with the descriptive predicate 'maximizes preference satisfaction'. If it is true that

> (N) Necessarily coextensive predicates ascribe the same property,

this means that these predicates ascribe the same property. It therefore means that the property of being right is identical to a descriptive property.

Suppose next that equally simple first-order views are correct about all other normative properties. These views may say, for example, that

> Necessarily, a consideration is a reason for action if and only if it increases the probability that this action will maximize preference satisfaction.
>
> Necessarily, a consideration is a reason for a belief if and only if it increases the probability that this belief is true.
>
> Necessarily, a state of affairs is good to the extent that it contains satisfied preferences.
>
> ... and so on.

If these simple first-order views are correct, all other normative predicates are also necessarily coextensive with descriptive predicates. If (N) is true, this means that each of these normative predicates also ascribes the same property as a descriptive predicate. This shows that

---

[15] Brown's version shows that irreducibly normative properties are what he calls *redundant*, in the sense that they 'do no work in distinguishing possibilities' (2011: 210). This only shows that there are no irreducibly normative properties if there are no properties that are redundant in this sense.

(F) If simple first-order normative views are correct, normative properties are identical to descriptive properties.

Now consider the following claim:

(W) Whether normative properties are identical to descriptive properties cannot depend on which first-order normative view is correct.

Of course, if normative properties are identical to descriptive properties, *which* descriptive properties they are identical to *does* depend on which first-order normative view is correct. For which descriptive properties normative properties are identical to depends on

(1) which objects have which normative properties

and on

(2) which descriptive properties these objects have,

and a first-order normative view is, in part, a view about (1) and (2). But (W) does not deny this. What (W) says is only that *whether* normative properties are identical to descriptive properties cannot depend on which first-order normative view is correct. That seems true, since whether normative properties are identical to descriptive properties seems to depend on the nature of these properties rather than on (1) and (2).

Suppose that normative properties would be identical to descriptive properties if simple first-order normative views were correct, but not if more complicated first-order normative views were correct. In that case, whether normative properties are identical to descriptive properties would depend on which first-order normative view is correct, which would contradict (W). This means that if (F) is true and if (W) is true as well, normative properties are identical to descriptive properties *whether or not* simple first-order normative views are correct. In other words, it means that if (F) and (W) are both true, there are no irreducibly normative properties.

Non-reductive realists may want to reject (F). But they cannot reject (F) by saying that we cannot formulate predicate D* in English, since this version of the argument does not rely on predicate D* or on any other infinitely disjunctive predicate. They also cannot reject (F) by rejecting (S), the claim about supervenience that Jackson's version of the argument appeals to, since this version of the argument does not appeal to (S) or to any other claim about supervenience.[16] They can only reject (F) by appealing to the other objections to Jackson's argument that I listed at the end of section 2, or to the new objections that I shall discuss in sections 5 and 6. But I argued in my earlier defence of the argument that these other objections fail, and I shall argue in sections 5 and 6 that these new objections fail as well.

Non-reductive realists may instead want to reject (W). They could say that (W) follows from a generalised version of the claim that

(W*) Which metaethical theory is true cannot depend on which first-order moral view is correct,

and they could point out that not all philosophers accept (W*). For example, Ronald Dworkin and others object to irrealist metaethical views that these views contradict uncontroversial first-order moral claims, such as the claim that torturing innocent children for fun is wrong.[17] Since this objection assumes that (W*) is false, it may also seem to assume that (W) is false.

In fact, however, the objection does not assume this. For (W) does not say that *which metaethical theory is true* cannot depend on which first-order normative view is correct. (W) only says that *whether normative properties are identical to descriptive properties* cannot depend on which first-order normative view is correct. And unlike irrealist metaethical views, neither the claim that

Normative properties are identical to descriptive properties

nor the claim that

Normative properties are not identical to descriptive properties

contradicts any first-order normative claim at all.

---

[16] Sturgeon (2009: 76–7) argues that claims about supervenience that are formulated in terms of descriptive properties are 'parochial', since it follows from some views about thick concepts that 'there are natural (or supernatural) properties for which we lack descriptive terminology, and they seem to be properties that make an evaluative difference'. I think we can defend (S) against such views by appealing to a language that combines English with a 'Lagadonian' language.

[17] See Dworkin (1996 and 2011). Similar views are defended by Nagel (1997) and Kramer (2009). For critical discussion of these views, see McPherson (2011) and Enoch (2011: 121–33). Dworkin, Nagel, and Kramer partly defend this objection by arguing that metaethical claims are disguised first-order moral claims, and that this allows us to reject metaethical views if they are incompatible with the most plausible first-order moral view.

Non-reductive realists may also want to say that, though they themselves accept (W), reductive realists cannot accept (W) and therefore cannot appeal to it in order to reject non-reductive realism. For non-reductive realists may say that they themselves accept (W) because they think it is a necessary truth that normative properties are not identical to descriptive properties, which is something that reductive realists deny. But this overlooks the fact that reductive realists can accept (W) because they think it is a necessary truth that normative properties *are* identical to descriptive properties. Moreover, reductive realists do not themselves have to accept (W) to put forward this version of Jackson's argument. For the argument only aims to show that non-reductive realism is false, and therefore only requires that *non-reductive realists* accept (W), not that reductive realists do so as well.

Non-reductive realists may still want to reject (W).[18] If so, we can turn to a second version of Jackson's argument that does not rely on predicate D*. Call normative truths that obtain independently of any descriptive truth *fundamental normative truths*.[19] Suppose that you are a non-reductive realist, and consider the complete list of what you take to be fundamental normative truths. Unless you are a particularist, this list will be finite. And if this list is finite, it will be possible to construct, for each normative predicate, a finitely disjunctive descriptive predicate that is coextensive with this normative predicate if the fundamental normative truths are as you take them to be.

Now consider again the claim that

> (S) For all possible worlds W and W*, if the distribution of descriptive properties in W and W* is exactly the same, then the distribution of normative properties in W and W* is also exactly the same.

If (S) is true, all fundamental normative truths are necessary truths.[20] For suppose that some were not. In that case, there would be at least two

---

[18] Oddie (2005: ch. 6) gives an argument for the existence of irreducibly normative properties that entails that (W) is false. But Oddie does not give an independent argument against (W), and (W) seems to me more secure than the premises of his argument (see Streumer 2008: 546–7 n. 20).

[19] As Enoch puts it (2011: 146 n. 32), to reach these fundamental normative truths (or, as he calls them, 'basic norms'), we 'backtrack, so to speak, practical syllogisms to their major premises, until we reach such a major premise that is not itself the conclusion of a practical syllogism, or that is (roughly speaking) free of empirical content'.

[20] Many non-reductive realists seem to agree that fundamental normative truths are necessary truths (see, e.g., McNaughton and Rawling 2003: 3; Parfit 2011: vol. 1, 129, and vol. 2, 307, 489–90, 747; and, more tentatively, Enoch 2011: 146). Dancy (2004b: 146–8) claims that what he calls 'basic normative facts' are contingent, but this is because he takes these facts to depend on descriptive truths. Dancy's basic normative facts are therefore not what I here call fundamental normative truths.

possible worlds that have different fundamental normative truths. If these worlds had the same distribution of descriptive properties, their different fundamental normative truths would make it the case that they had different distributions of normative properties, which would contradict (S). Different possible worlds could therefore only have different fundamental normative truths if they had different distributions of descriptive properties. But then these different normative truths would not obtain independently of any descriptive truth, and would therefore not really be fundamental.

If all fundamental normative truths are necessary truths and if the complete list of what you take to be fundamental normative truths is finite, it will be possible to construct, for each normative predicate, a finitely disjunctive descriptive predicate that is *necessarily* coextensive with this normative predicate if the fundamental normative truths are as you take them to be. If (N) is true, this commits you to the conclusion that there are no irreducibly normative properties. Particularists like Dancy can perhaps escape this conclusion by claiming that the complete list of fundamental normative truths is infinite. But other non-reductive realists cannot escape it so easily.

4. Do necessarily coextensive predicates ascribe the same property?

The three versions of Jackson's argument that I have now presented all assume that

(N) Necessarily coextensive predicates ascribe the same property.[21]

Non-reductive realists often claim that (N) is false. Many of them think that there are counterexamples to (N). Others think that (N) is only plausible if

---

[21] It may be thought that Brown's version of the argument does not assume that (N) is true. But it does assume that there are no properties that are redundant in Brown's sense (see n. 15), which entails that necessarily co-extensive predicates do not ascribe different properties. Brown defends this last claim by arguing that 'necessarily coextensive predicates...don't denote any properties at all' (2011: 216). But that cannot be true, since, e.g., the necessarily coextensive predicates 'is water' and 'is H_2O' clearly do ascribe at least one property. Brown will therefore have to defend the claim that necessarily coextensive predicates do not ascribe different properties by defending (N).

we take properties to be sets of possibilia.[22] Though I discussed this objection in my earlier defence of Jackson's argument, I shall now discuss it again. I shall argue that if we take properties to be real features of objects rather than meanings of predicates, all apparent counterexamples to (N) fail. If that is so, it shows both that (N) is true and that (N) is compatible with a wide range of views about properties.[23]

Since triangles have both three sides and three angles, one popular counterexample to (N) is that

> The predicates 'has three angles' and 'has three sides' are necessarily coextensive but ascribe different properties.

Though these predicates clearly ascribe different properties, they are not necessarily coextensive, since an open figure can have three sides but only two angles. The example should therefore be revised to:

> The predicates 'is a closed figure that has three sides' and 'is a closed figure that has three angles' are necessarily coextensive but ascribe different properties.[24]

But these predicates, I think, both ascribe the property of being a figure with the following kind of shape:

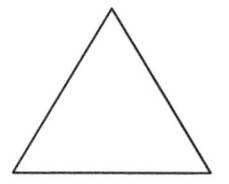

---

[22] See, e.g., McNaughton and Rawling (2003: 30). An account of properties as sets of possibilia is outlined by Lewis (1986: 50–69), though Lewis allows that there are also other conceptions of properties.

[23] Of course, it does not show that (N) is compatible with the view that properties are meanings of predicates. But the debate between reductive and non-reductive realists is not about whether sentences that contain normative predicates have the same *meaning* as certain sentences that only contain descriptive predicates, but about whether sentences that contain normative predicates have the same *truthmakers* as certain sentences that only contain descriptive predicates. Both sides in this debate therefore take properties to be real features of objects rather than meanings of predicates.

[24] Kramer (2009: 210–11) claims that the predicates 'has three sides' and 'has three angles' are necessarily coextensive but ascribe different properties when the class of things over which they range is implicitly narrowed to closed figures. However, if this class is implicitly narrowed in this way, it must be possible to make this narrowing explicit by reformulating these predicates as 'is a closed figure that has three sides' and 'is a closed figure that has three angles', which Kramer agrees ascribe the same property. This suggests that if this class is implicitly narrowed in this way, the predicates 'has three sides' and 'has three angles' do ascribe the same property. Of course, if this class is *not* implicitly narrowed in this way, these predicates ascribe different properties. But in that case, as I argued in Streumer (2008) and as Kramer agrees, these predicates are not necessarily coextensive.

For figures with this kind of shape also satisfy the predicate 'is a triangle'. And if the predicates 'is a closed figure that has three sides' and 'is a closed figure that has three angles' ascribed two different properties, why would the predicate 'is a triangle' not ascribe yet another different property? If we take properties to be real features of objects, these predicates clearly do not ascribe *three* different properties. But then the predicates 'is a closed figure that has three sides' and 'is a closed figure that has three angles' do not ascribe two different properties either.

Non-reductive realists may reply that the predicates 'is a closed figure that has three sides' and 'is a closed figures that has three angles' ascribe different properties because these properties consist of different parts: one consists of being a closed figure and having three sides, they may say, and the other consists of being a closed figure and having three angles. But this overlooks the fact that these predicates could both ascribe a single property that consists of the same three parts: being a closed figure, having three sides, and having three angles. Non-reductive realists who deny this seem to assume that we can read off the composition of a property from the composition of a predicate that ascribes it. If we could do this, the predicates 'is a closed figure that has three sides', 'is a closed figure that has three angles', and 'is a triangle' would again ascribe three different properties.

Non-reductive realists may also say that the predicates 'is a closed figure that has three angles' and 'is a triangle' ascribe the same property because these predicates are synonymous.[25] But suppose that we introduced a new predicate 'is a Δ', not by defining it but by pointing to a series of figures with the kind of shape that makes them satisfy the predicates 'is a closed figure that has three sides', 'is a closed figure that has three angles' and 'is a triangle'. Given how it was introduced, either the predicate 'is a Δ' is not synonymous with any of these other predicates, or it is synonymous with all of them. Suppose that it is not synonymous with any of the other predicates. In that case, if necessarily coextensive predicates that are not synonymous ascribe different properties, the predicate 'is a Δ' does not ascribe the same

---

[25] As Enoch (2011: 139 n. 13) writes, 'perhaps it makes sense to think of the property of being a triangle as identical by definition to one of the other two (say, that of having three angles), and then we only have here two properties after all'.

property as the predicate 'is a triangle', which is clearly false. Suppose next that the predicate 'is a △' is synonymous with all of these other predicates. In that case, if necessarily coextensive predicates that are synonymous ascribe the same property, these four predicates all ascribe the same property, which supports rather than undermines (N). I therefore think that this counterexample fails.

Another popular counterexample to (N) is that

> For any X, the predicates 'is X' and 'is X and is such that Socrates is identical to Socrates' are necessarily coextensive but ascribe different properties.

If we take properties to be real features of objects, however, the predicate 'is such that Socrates is identical to Socrates' does not ascribe a property. For being such that something else is identical to itself is clearly not a real feature of an object. This means that adding the phrase '... and is such that Socrates is identical to Socrates' to the predicate 'is X' does not affect which property this predicate ascribes. It therefore means that the predicates 'is X' and 'is X and is such that Socrates is identical to Socrates' ascribe the same property.

Non-reductive realists may reply that if the predicate 'is such that Socrates is identical to Socrates' does not ascribe a property, neither does the predicate 'is such that O_1 has descriptive properties $P_{O1-1}, P_{O1-2}, \ldots, O_2$ has descriptive properties $P_{O2-1}, P_{O2-2}, \ldots$', which is part of predicate D*. But Jackson's argument does not require that the predicate 'is such that O_1 has descriptive properties $P_{O1-1}, P_{O1-2}, \ldots, O_2$ has descriptive properties $P_{O2-1}, P_{O2-2}, \ldots$' *by itself* ascribes a property. All that needs to be true is that predicate D* *as a whole* ascribes a property. And the mere fact that a predicate that is part of a larger predicate does not by itself ascribe a property does not make it the case that this larger predicate as a whole does not ascribe a property, as is shown by the fact that the predicates 'is X' and 'is X and is such that Socrates is identical to Socrates' ascribe the same property. Moreover, the other two versions of Jackson's argument that I have presented do not rely on predicate D*. I therefore think that this counterexample fails too.

A third counterexample to (N), which has been given by Derek Parfit (2011: vol. 2, 296–7), is that

> The predicates 'is the only even prime number' and 'is the positive square root of four' are necessarily coextensive but ascribe different properties.

The sentence 'Two is the positive square root of four' does not ascribe a property to the number two, however, but instead says that the number two is *identical to* the positive square root of four. For we can reformulate this sentence as 'The positive square root of four is two', and we would normally formalise it as '$2 = \sqrt{4}$'. Moreover, suppose that this sentence did ascribe a property to the number two. Since Parfit admits that the phrases 'the positive square root of four' and 'the only even prime number' both refer to the number two, it is hard to see how he can deny that the predicate 'is the positive square root of four' ascribes the same property as the predicate 'is the only even prime number': namely, the property of being the number two. I therefore think that this counterexample fails as well.

A fourth and final counterexample to (N), which has been given by Alvin Plantinga (2010: 258–9, 262), is that

> If divine command theory is true, predicate D* and the predicate 'is such that God commands all persons to perform it' are necessarily coextensive but ascribe different properties.[26]

These predicates are only necessarily coextensive, however, if divine command theory says that God could not fail to exist and could not fail to command that all persons perform the actions that satisfy predicate D*. More fully stated, therefore, Plantinga's example is that

> Predicate D* and the predicate 'is such that a being who could not fail to exist and who could not fail to command that all persons perform the actions that satisfy predicate D* commands all persons to perform it' are necessarily coextensive but ascribe different properties.

Though I have great trouble imagining such a being, I am inclined to think that these predicates ascribe the same property. Of course, Plantinga (2010: 260, 264) disagrees. But this is because he accepts the following criterion of property identity:

---

[26] Plantinga gives this example in the course of arguing that Jackson's argument fails to show that normative properties are not supernatural properties, which Plantinga takes to be properties that involve God or beings like God. But Jackson clearly does not intend his argument to show this. He only intends it to show that there are no normative properties that are not identical to descriptive properties, and the property of being such that God commands all persons to perform it is a descriptive property.

If someone can believe that an object is F without believing that this object is G, the predicates 'is F' and 'is G' ascribe different properties.[27]

If this criterion were correct, Moore's open question argument would be sound.[28] Non-reductive realists could then demonstrate that their view is true simply by noting that someone who believes that an action is right can intelligibly ask, of any descriptive property, whether this action has this property. But if we take properties to be real features of objects, we should clearly reject this criterion of property identity. I therefore think that this counterexample fails too.

Non-reductive realists could say that merely showing that some counterexamples to (N) fail does not show that *all* counterexamples fail. But I think that at least one of the following claims will be true of any apparent counterexample to (N):

(1) There is a further predicate that is also necessarily coextensive with the predicates in the example but that clearly does not ascribe a further property.
(2) A phrase that is part of one of the predicates in the example does not affect which property this predicate ascribes.
(3) One of the phrases in the example does not ascribe a property, but is instead part of an identity statement.
(4) The example relies on a criterion of property identity that we should reject if we take properties to be real features of objects.

If that is so, the replies I have just given do show that all apparent counterexamples to (N) fail. And if these replies show this, they show both that (N) is true and that (N) is compatible with a wide range of views about properties.[29]

---

[27] Plantinga endorses what he calls the 'abundant' view of properties. He initially claims that defenders of this view will often accept this claim (2010: 260), but then goes on to treat this claim as part of the abundant view (p. 264).

[28] As Plantinga recognizes (2010: 265).

[29] Suikkanen (2010: 92) says that this defence of (N) leads to a 'stalemate', with both sides 'happy with their intuitions', and Enoch (2011: 139) similarly says that it leads to an 'impasse'. But if non-reductive realists want to say that the predicates 'is a closed figure that has three sides' and 'is a closed figure that has three angles' ascribe two different properties, as Suikkanen and Enoch apparently want to do, they will have to explain why this is so, in a way that does not entail that the predicates 'is a triangle' and 'is a △' ascribe a third and a fourth property. Enoch suggests that they can explain this by appealing to a general principle of parsimony (139 n. 13). But if so, why does this principle not also show that the predicates 'is a closed figure that has three sides' and 'is a closed figure that has three angles' ascribe the same property?

5. Can non-reductive realists appeal to Leibniz's law?

Non-reductive realists may now admit that (N) is true of descriptive properties, but deny that it is true of normative properties. They can only plausibly do this, however, if they can explain why (N) is not true of normative properties, in a way that is compatible with its being true of all other properties. I shall now discuss two new objections to Jackson's argument that can be seen as attempts to explain this.

The first objection, which makes use of Dancy's views, has been put forward by Jussi Suikkanen. Suikkanen thinks that non-reductive realists can explain why (N) is not true of normative properties by appealing to a version of

Leibniz's law: If there is a higher-order property that property p_1 has but property p_2 lacks, then p_1 and p_2 are not identical.[30]

As Suikkanen (2010: 101–3) notes, Dancy and other non-reductive realists endorse the following claims:

(1) Our knowledge that an action is right is normally a priori, but our knowledge that an action has the property that is ascribed by predicate D* is normally a posteriori.
(2) The property of being right is what Dancy calls *resultant*, in the sense that an action has this property in virtue of a subset of its descriptive properties, but the property that is ascribed by predicate D* is not resultant in this sense.
(3) The fact that an action is right has what, following Dancy, we can call *intrinsic practical relevance*, but the fact that this action has the property that is ascribed by predicate D* does not have this kind of relevance.[31]

---

[30] As Suikkanen points out, this version of Leibniz's law is the application to properties and higher-order properties of a consequence of the indiscernibility of identicals, which is the uncontroversial part of what is normally called 'Leibniz's law'.

[31] For Dancy's view that knowledge about normative properties is *a priori*, in the sense of not being grounded in knowledge of empirical facts, see Dancy (2004b: 146–8). For Dancy's notion of resultance, see Dancy (1993: 73–7, 2004b: 85–6, and 2005: 128). For Dancy's claims about the practical relevance of normative facts, see Dancy (2005: 136–7) (I call this relevance 'intrinsic' because Dancy thinks that the practical relevance of normative facts is not a further fact about these facts). Suikkanen also considers two other higher-order properties that the property of being right may be said to have but the property that is ascribed by predicate D* may be said to lack: being supervenient and having a unified 'shape'. But he rightly doubts that non-reductive realists can appeal to these properties to reject reductive realism.

If these claims are true, the property of being right and the descriptive property that is ascribed by predicate D* have different higher-order properties. If so, it follows from Leibniz's Law that these properties are not identical. And if similar claims are true about other normative properties, it follows that these other normative properties are not identical to descriptive properties either.

Suikkanen assumes that reductive realists can only answer this objection by denying that normative properties have the higher-order properties that (1), (2), and (3) say they have, and he notes, rightly, that this denial will be hard to defend. But he overlooks a different reply that reductive realists can give to this objection. They can make a distinction between two modes under which a property can be presented:

> A *normative* mode, under which a property is presented if it is ascribed with a normative predicate, such as the predicate 'is right',

and

> A descriptive *mode*, under which a property is presented if it is ascribed with a descriptive predicate, such as predicate D*.

And they can then say that

> (1*) Our knowledge that an action is right is normally a priori if this property is presented under the normative mode, but normally a posteriori if it is presented under the descriptive mode.
> (2*) The property of being right is resultant, but this is normally only clear to us if this property is presented under the normative mode.
> (3*) The fact that an object has the property of being right has intrinsic practical relevance, but this is normally only clear to us if this property is presented under the normative mode.

If these claims are true, the property of being right and the descriptive property that is ascribed by predicate D* do not have different higher-order properties. If so, it does not follow from Leibniz's Law that these properties are not identical.

This shows that if non-reductive realists want to appeal to Leibniz's Law to explain why (N) is not true of normative properties, they will need to explain why we should accept (1), (2), and (3) rather than (1*), (2*), and

(3*). One difference between these sets of claims is that whereas (1), (2), and (3) presuppose that the property of being right is not identical to the property that is ascribed by predicate D*, (1*), (2*), and (3*) presuppose that these properties are identical. But non-reductive realists cannot appeal to this difference to explain why we should accept (1), (2), and (3). For their explanation of why we should accept (1), (2), and (3) would then presuppose that (N) is not true of normative properties. And if their explanation of why we should accept (1), (2), and (3) presupposed this, they could not go on to appeal to (1), (2), and (3) to explain why (N) is not true of normative properties.

There are three other differences between these sets of claims that non-reductive realists could appeal to in order to explain why we should accept (1), (2), and (3). One is that (1*), (2*), and (3*) make assumptions about modes of presentation that are not made by (1), (2), and (3). But given that I have defined the normative and descriptive modes of presentation in terms of normative and descriptive predicates, these assumptions are very plausible. And non-reductive realists can only appeal to this difference between these sets of claims to explain why we should accept (1), (2), and (3) if they can show that these assumptions are implausible.

A second difference is that whereas (1*), (2*), and (3*) say that the property that is ascribed by predicate D* has the same higher-order properties as the property that is ascribed by the predicate 'is right', (1), (2), and (3) deny this. But it is hard to see how non-reductive realists can show that the property that is ascribed by predicate D* does not have these higher-order properties, other than by saying that this property is not identical to the property that is ascribed by the predicate 'is right'. As before, if they said this, they could not appeal to this difference to explain why we should accept (1), (2), and (3). For their explanation of why we should accept (1), (2), and (3) would then again presuppose that (N) is not true of normative properties.

A third and final difference is that whereas if (2*) is true, resultance is a form of entailment, (2) is compatible with resultance being what Suikkanen calls a 'metaphysically robust, worldly making-relation' (2010: 102).[32] But it is hard to see how non-reductive realists can show that resultance is such a worldly making-relation, other than by saying that normative properties are

---

[32] See also McNaughton and Rawling (2003: 32–3).

not identical to descriptive properties. Once again, if they said this, they could not appeal to this difference to explain why we should accept (1), (2), and (3). For their explanation of why we should accept (1), (2), and (3) would then again presuppose that (N) is not true of normative properties. I therefore think that Suikkanen's objection fails to explain why (N) is not true of normative properties.

6. Are irreducibly normative properties indispensible to deliberation?

A second objection to Jackson's argument that can be seen as an attempt to explain why (N) is not true of normative properties has been made by David Enoch (2011: 137–40; see esp. p. 140 n. 15). Enoch thinks that what underlies (N) is a

General principle of parsimony: We should not posit the existence of a property without sufficient reason.[33]

Many philosophers believe that if a property plays an ineliminable role in our best causal explanations, this is a sufficient reason for positing the existence of this property. Enoch argues that this belief is justified because

(1) This belief is indispensable to our project of *explaining the world*, in the sense that its falsity would undermine or greatly diminish our reason to engage in this project,

and because

(2) The project of explaining the world is non-optional for us, in the sense that we are rationally required to engage in it.

He then argues that the belief that there are irreducibly normative properties is justified for a similar reason. According to Enoch, this belief is justified because

---

[33] Enoch (2011) outlines this principle (which he calls a 'minimal parsimony requirement' and applies to ontological commitments generally) on pp. 53–4, and suggests that this principle underlies (N) on pp. 139–40. See also Enoch (2007).

(1*) This belief is indispensible to our project of *deliberating about what to do*, in the sense that its falsity would undermine or greatly diminish our reason to engage in this project,

and because

(2*) The project of deliberating about what to do is non-optional for us, in the sense that we are rationally required to engage in it.

He concludes that just as positing the existence of properties that play an ineliminable role in our best causal explanations does not violate the general principle of parsimony, positing the existence of irreducibly normative properties does not violate this principle either. And since Enoch thinks that this principle is what underlies (N), he thinks that this explains why (N) is not true of normative properties (Enoch 2011: 50–84, 137–40).

Some philosophers may object that what underlies (N) is not the general principle of parsimony, but a more specific

Causal principle of parsimony: We should only posit the existence of a property if this property plays an ineliminable role in our best causal explanations.[34]

But like Dancy and other non-reductive realists, Enoch rejects the causal principle of parsimony. This principle can only be justified, Enoch thinks, if (1) and (2) justify the belief that if a property plays an ineliminable role in our best causal explanations, this is a sufficient reason for positing the existence of this property. But if (1) and (2) justify this belief, he thinks, (1*) and (2*) similarly justify the belief that there are irreducibly normative properties. And in that case the causal principle of parsimony is false, since irreducibly normative properties are causally impotent.[35]

Whether Enoch's objection explains why (N) is not true of normative properties depends on whether (1*) is true. Enoch defends (1*) by claiming

---

[34] Enoch (2011: 53–4) (Enoch calls this principle the 'explanatory parsimony requirement'). (N) seems to be a consequence of the causal theory of properties defended by Shoemaker (1980) (see pp. 213–14), though Sober (1982) disputes this.

[35] Enoch (2011: 50–84). Clearly, whether this argument is sound depends on whether Enoch is right that the causal principle of parsimony can only be justified if (1) and (2) justify the belief that a property's playing an ineliminable role in our best causal explanations is a sufficient reason for positing its existence. If this belief can be justified in a different way, or if it does not stand in need of justification, Enoch cannot appeal to the similarity between (1) and (2) on the one hand and (1*) and (2*) on the other to argue that (1*) and (2*) justify the belief that there are irreducibly normative properties, and that we should therefore reject the causal principle of parsimony.

that deliberation about what to do 'is an attempt to eliminate arbitrariness by discovering (normative) reasons' which 'is impossible in a believed absence of such reasons to be discovered'; that such deliberation 'feels like trying to make the *right* choice'; and that its phenomenology is similar 'to that of trying to find an answer to a straightforwardly factual question' (Enoch 2011: 72–4). This may show that, when we deliberate about what to do, we form beliefs that ascribe normative properties. But it does not show that these beliefs ascribe *irreducibly* normative properties. Enoch argues that they ascribe such properties because we think that normative properties are too different from descriptive properties to be identical to them, a thought he calls the 'just-too-different intuition' (pp. 100–9).[36] But even if that is true, it does not show that engaging in deliberation commits us to the existence of irreducibly normative properties.[37] It merely shows that engaging in deliberation commits us to the existence of normative properties, and that we all happen to think that these properties are not identical to descriptive properties. That is not enough for Enoch's defence of (1*) to succeed.

Moreover, suppose that Enoch's defence of (1*) did succeed. In that case, engaging in our project of deliberating about what to do would commit us to the existence of irreducibly normative properties. But engaging in a different project, such as our project of explaining the world, may similarly commit us to the non-existence of these properties. For the concept of a property that we use in explaining the world may commit us to (N), and may thereby commit us to the claim that normative properties are identical to descriptive properties. If that were so, our concept of a normative property would be incoherent. We could then compare it to another concept that some philosophers think is incoherent: our concept of free will. Given that our concept of free will may be incoherent, we should not take the mere fact that engaging in deliberation commits us to the existence to free will to show that we actually have free will. Similarly, given that our concept of a normative property may be incoherent, we should not take the

---

[36] Enoch admits that reductive realists do not seem to have this intuition, which weakens this argument.

[37] I here use the term 'commit' in the sense outlined by Enoch (2011: 74). Enoch (pp. 100–9) also suggests that engaging in deliberation commits us to the existence of irreducibly normative properties because the questions we ask in deliberation cannot be answered with purely descriptive claims. But if so, that merely shows that deliberation commits us to the existence of properties that can be ascribed with normative predicates, which does not entail that these properties are irreducibly normative.

mere fact that engaging in deliberation commits us to the existence of irreducibly normative properties to show that there actually are such properties. I therefore think that, like Suikkanen's objection, Enoch's objection fails to explain why (N) is not true of normative properties. I conclude that (N) applies to all properties, including normative ones.

7. Why non-reductive realists are unmoved by the argument

Though Dancy is clearly sympathetic to Suikkanen's objection to Jackson's argument, his own objection is different: it is that the argument does not apply to normative relations, such as the relation of being-a-reason-for and the relation Dancy calls 'right-making'.[38] In my earlier defence of the argument, I tried to show that the argument does apply to these relations.[39] Consider a fact F_1 that is a reason for an action A_1, and which thereby stands in the normative relation of being-a-reason-for to an action A_1. Fact F_1 also has descriptive properties, which we can call P_{F1-1}, $P_{F1-2}, \ldots$, and action A_1 also has descriptive properties, which we can call P_{A1-1}, $P_{A1-2}, \ldots$. And the objects $O_1, O_2, \ldots$ that are part of the same possible world as fact F_1 and action A_1 have descriptive properties as well, which for each object O_x we

---

[38] See Dancy (2004a). Dancy actually says that 'there is a worry that Jackson will be unable to capture the notion of a reason' (p. 233), and that 'Jackson's descriptive metaphysics leaves him unable to capture the right-making relation' (p. 237). I take this to mean that he thinks that Jackson's argument does not show that the relations of being-a-reason-for and of right-making are identical to descriptive relations. Alternatively, he could mean to say that the conclusion of Jackson's argument is incompatible with the right-making relation being what Suikkanen calls a 'metaphysically robust, worldly making-relation', in which case his objection would be similar to Suikkanen's objection.

It may be thought that Dancy could also reject Jackson's argument by appealing to particularism. But though he can reject the second version of Jackson's argument that I presented in section 3 in this way, the two other versions of the argument do not make any assumptions that are incompatible with particularism. It may be thought that (S) is incompatible with particularism, since according to particularism two actions A_1 and A_2 can have the same descriptive properties but different normative properties. But (S) is only about the distributions of descriptive and normative properties in complete possible worlds, and therefore does not entail that two actions A_1 and A_2 that have the same descriptive properties must also have the same normative properties. Particularists can therefore accept (S), and Dancy does accept (S).

[39] As before, my presentation of the argument in what follows assumes that the number of objects, properties, relations, facts, and actions in all possible worlds is countably infinite, but I take this to be merely a matter of presentation.

can call P_{Ox-1}, P_{Ox-2}, ...[40] Fact F_1 and action A_1 therefore satisfy the following two-place predicate, which we can call predicate R_1:

'____ has descriptive properties P_{F1-1}, P_{F1-2}, ..., and ____ has descriptive properties P_{A1-1}, P_{A1-2}, ..., and both are such that O_1 has descriptive properties P_{O1-1}, P_{O1-2}, ..., that O_2 has descriptive properties P_{O2-1}, P_{O2-2} ..., ...'.

Suppose next that facts F_1, F_2, ... are all the facts that are reasons for action in all possible worlds, and that actions A_1, A_2, ... are all the actions that these facts are reasons for (with fact F_1 being a reason for action A_1, and so on).[41] Just as fact F_1 and action A_1 satisfy the descriptive two-place predicate R_1, facts F_2, F_3, ... and actions A_2, A_3, ... satisfy similarly constructed descriptive two-place predicates R_2, R_3, ... These facts and actions therefore all satisfy the following two-place predicate, which we can call predicate R^*:

'____ and ____ satisfy either the descriptive two-place predicate R_1, or the descriptive two-place predicate R_2, or...'.

We can use this predicate to formulate a version of Jackson's argument that shows that the predicate 'is a reason for' is not irreducibly normative.[42] And we can formulate a similar version of the argument to show that the right-making relation is not irreducibly normative either.

As I have said, this reply has failed to convince Dancy. More generally, in my experience, most non-reductive realists remain completely unmoved both by Jackson's argument and by replies to their objections to the argument. I can see at least three reasons for this lack of movement.

One is that many non-reductive realists seem, at least to some extent, to conflate properties with the meanings of the predicates that ascribe these properties. For example, Dancy writes that 'the naturalist idea has to be that the subject matter of the fact that this action would maximize welfare could be the same as that of the fact that it would make the action right', and that 'it just isn't true ... that the fact that this action maximizes welfare (say) has

---

[40] I use the term 'object' to cover anything that has properties or stands in relations, and I include the descriptive relations that these objects stand in to each other (and to F_1 and A_1) among P_{Ox-1}, P_{Ox-2}, ...

[41] Of course, many facts stand in the relation of being-a-reason-for to more than one action, and many actions are such that there is more than one fact that stands in the relation of being-a-reason-for to them. These facts and these actions are included more than once in F_1, F_2, ... and in A_1, A_2, ...

[42] Dancy (2004b: 65) objects to this that the relation of being-a-reason-for (or, as he calls it, the 'favouring relation') is necessarily asymmetrical, whereas the relation ascribed by predicate R^* is not. I reply to this objection in Streumer (2008: 556).

the same subject matter as the fact that that fact would make the action right' (2005: 140). These claims about the 'subject matter' of facts seem to me to conflate facts with meanings of sentences, and thereby seem to conflate properties with meanings of predicates. And Parfit writes that the phrases 'is the only even prime number' and 'is the positive square root of four' ascribe different properties because '[b]eing the only even prime number cannot be the *same* as being—or be *what it is* to be—the positive square root of 4' (2011: vol. 2, 297). This use of 'what it is to be' also seems to me to conflate properties with meanings of predicates.

A second reason why non-reductive realists remain unmoved may be that they think that Jackson's argument is meant to show that reductive realism is true. Jackson does sometimes give the impression that he takes the argument to show this. In fact, however, the argument only shows that there are no irreducibly normative properties. In other words, it only shows that

(1) If there are normative properties, these properties are identical to descriptive properties.

This conclusion is compatible with the falsity of reductive realism, since it is compatible with the claim that

(2) If there are normative properties, these properties are *not* identical to descriptive properties.

For (1) and (2) can both be true if their antecedents are false. The implausibility of reductive realism therefore should not stop Dancy and other non-reductive realists from accepting the conclusion of Jackson's argument.[43]

A third and final reason why non-reductive realists remain unmoved may be that they think that the most defensible alternative to non-reductive realism is an error theory according to which normative judgements ascribe non-existent properties, which is a view they cannot bring themselves to believe.[44] I agree that such an error theory is the most defensible alternative to non-reductive realism. But I do not believe this theory myself, and I do not think that anyone else should believe it either. For I have argued elsewhere that we cannot believe this error theory, and that there is

---

[43] I defend the claim that normative properties are not identical to descriptive properties in Streumer (2011).

[44] For the view that an error theory is the most plausible alternative to non-reductive realism, see, e.g., Enoch (2011: 115).

therefore no reason for us to believe it.[45] If that is so, non-reductive realists' inability to believe such an error theory should not stop them from accepting the conclusion of Jackson's argument either.

8. Conclusion

I have presented three versions of Jackson's argument against the existence of irreducibly normative properties, and I have argued that two existing objections and three new objections to the argument fail. I conclude, as before, that the argument shows that there are no irreducibly normative properties. I realise that Dancy may still not be convinced. But I hope he will at least agree that non-reductive realists have not yet come up with a wholly adequate response to the argument.[46]

References

Brown, C. (2011) 'A New and Improved Supervenience Argument for Ethical Descriptivism', in R. Shafer-Landau (ed.), *Oxford Studies in Metaethics*, vol. 6 (Oxford: Oxford University Press), 205–18.

Dancy, J. (1993) *Moral Reasons* (Oxford: Blackwell).

—— (2004a) 'On the importance of Making Things Right', *Ratio*, 17: 229–37.

—— (2004b) *Ethics Without Principles* (Oxford: Oxford University Press).

—— (2005) 'Non-naturalism', in D. Copp (ed.), *The Oxford Handbook of Ethical Theory* (Oxford: Oxford University Press), 122–45.

Dworkin, R. (1996) 'Objectivity and Truth: You'd Better Believe It', *Philosophy and Public Affairs*, 25: 87–139.

—— (2011) *Justice for Hedgehogs* (Cambridge, MA: Harvard University Press).

Enoch, D. (2007) 'An Outline of an Argument for Robust Metanormative Realism', in R. Shafer-Landau (ed.), *Oxford Studies in Metaethics*, vol. 2 (Oxford: Oxford University Press), 21–50.

---

[45] See Streumer (forthcoming).

[46] For comments on earlier drafts of this chapter, I am grateful to Campbell Brown, David Enoch, Margaret Little, and Jussi Suikkanen. I am also very grateful to Jonathan Dancy for helpful discussion of this argument over the years, and, more generally, for teaching me how to do philosophy when I was his PhD student at the University of Reading.

—— (2010) 'How Objectivity Matters', in R. Shafer-Landau (ed.), *Oxford Studies in Metaethics*, vol. 5 (Oxford: Oxford University Press), 111–52.
—— (2011) *Taking Morality Seriously* (Oxford: Oxford University Press).
FitzPatrick, W. (2008) 'Robust Ethical Realism, Non-Naturalism, and Normativity', in R. Shafer-Landau (ed.), *Oxford Studies in Metaethics*, vol. 3 (Oxford: Oxford University Press), 159–206.
Jackson, F. (1998) *From Metaphysics to Ethics* (Oxford: Oxford University Press).
—— (2001) 'Responses', *Philosophy and Phenomenological Research*, 62: 653–64.
—— and Pettit, P. (1996) 'Moral Functionalism, Supervenience and Reductionism', *Philosophical Quarterly*, 46: 82–6.
Kim, J. (1993) *Supervenience and Mind* (Cambridge: Cambridge University Press).
Kramer, M. (2009) *Moral Realism as a Moral Doctrine* (Oxford: Wiley-Blackwell).
Lewis, D. (1986) *On the Plurality of Worlds* (Oxford: Blackwell).
Majors, B. (2005) 'Moral Discourse and Descriptive Properties', *Philosophical Quarterly*, 55: 475–94.
McNaughton, D. and Rawling, P. (2003) 'Naturalism and Normativity', *Proceedings of the Aristotelian Society*, Supplementary Volume, 77: 23–45.
McPherson, T. (2011) 'Against Quietist Normative Realism', *Philosophical Studies*, 154: 223–40.
Nagel, T. (1997) *The Last Word* (Oxford: Oxford University Press).
Oddie, G. (2005) *Value, Reality, and Desire* (Oxford: Oxford University Press).
Parfit, D. (2011) *On What Matters*, 2 vols. (Oxford: Oxford University Press).
Plantinga, A. (2010) 'Naturalism, Theism, Obligation and Supervenience', *Faith and Philosophy*, 27: 247–72.
Shafer-Landau, R. (2003) *Moral Realism: A Defence* (Oxford: Clarendon Press).
Shoemaker, S. (1980) 'Causality and Properties', in his *Identity, Cause, and Mind* (expanded edition) (Oxford: Oxford University Press, 2003), 206–33.
Sober, E. (1982) 'Why Logically Equivalent Predicates May Pick Out Different Properties', *American Philosophical Quarterly*, 19: 183–9.
Streumer, B. (2008) 'Are there Irreducibly Normative Properties?', *Australasian Journal of Philosophy*, 86: 537–61.
—— (2011) 'Are Normative Properties Descriptive Properties?', *Philosophical Studies*, 154: 325–48.
—— (forthcoming) 'Can We Believe the Error Theory?', *Journal of Philosophy*.
Sturgeon, N. (2009) 'Doubts about the Supervenience of the Evaluative', in R. Shafer-Landau (ed.), *Oxford Studies in Metaethics*, vol. 4 (Oxford: Oxford University Press), 53–90.

Suikkanen, J. (2010) 'Non-Naturalism: The Jackson Challenge', in R. Shafer-Landau (ed.), *Oxford Studies in Metaethics,* vol. 5 (Oxford: Oxford University Press), 87–110.

van Roojen, M. (1996) 'Moral Functionalism and Moral Reductionism', *Philosophical Quarterly*, 46: 77–81.

Williamson, T. (2001) 'Ethics, Supervenience and Ramsey Sentences', *Philosophy and Phenomenological Research*, 62: 625–30.

Afterword

JONATHAN DANCY

I was drawn into philosophy kicking and screaming. Having done a little at school with my headmaster H. D. P. Lee, whose translation of Plato's *Republic* was the standard one for many years, I knew that philosophy was boring, and tried to persuade my tutors at Oxford to allow me to read Modern Greek instead. They resisted, and I meekly abandoned the idea, partly persuaded by Maurice Bowra, who said 'If you do it, you will regret it all your life'. Luckily I found philosophy much more interesting than it had been at school, but after a year my tutor J. O. Urmson, who died this year at the age of 96, was able to say truly that 'Mr Dancy and I meet for an hour each week to discuss philosophy, but no idea passes in either direction'. He knew that I was making an effort, but that the whole thing was as yet a mystery to me—a delightful mystery, after a while, but a mystery nonetheless. It was not until a few months before my Final Examinations that the light dawned and I began to feel at home in the subject.

Still, I went on to do graduate work (in the form of the two-year Oxford BPhil) not so much out of any passionate interest in philosophy as from a sense of the peculiarity of the Greats' 'syllabus'. In seven terms I had read Plato's *Republic*, Aristotle's *Nicomachean Ethics*, Locke, Hume, and Rousseau (but only on the Social Contract), some of Mill's *Utilitarianism*, Russell's 'On Denoting', and then pretty much everything written in Oxford in the 1950s. One could not but feel that this was a rather lop-sided menu, and my idea was to devote two years to filling in some of the gaps, and then become either a musician (more specifically a double-bass player), or a schoolteacher, or a civil servant. But by the end of the two years all such alternatives had ceased to appeal, and the course of my life was set.

Thinking about Reasons is apt as a title for this wonderful collection of papers, which has given me so much pleasure, and as a description of the main focus of my intellectual career. That focus emerged in a rather roundabout way. I was originally hired at Keele as a philosophical logician, but had always found that area incredibly difficult, and would have been drawn to moral philosophy had it not been for the deadening effect of R. M. Hare's dominance in that field, which tended to give the impression that everything had now been done and it was all sorted. How it came about I don't now know, but in the mid-1970s, some years after joining the profession, I found myself reading W. D. Ross's *The Right and the Good* with great admiration—and amazement that nobody in Oxford had ever even mentioned this book to me. And one of my first responses to Ross was to ask myself how he could be so sure that what was a prima facie duty in one case would necessarily be so in any other. (I was encouraged in this question by having pursued a similar line in a paper written as a BPhil student, in which I wondered why there could not be particular causal relations without benefit of causal laws.) Allowing that if a feature was a prima facie duty-maker in one case but not in another, there would have to be some explanation of that, which would probably consist in the presence of some further feature in one case that was absent in the other, I immediately found myself distinguishing between the reasons themselves and those features that are not reasons but whose presence or absence enables other features to act as reasons or prevents them from doing so. And this simple distinction was enough to set me off.

Another influential moment came when I drove down from Keele to Oxford once a week one summer term to attend Gareth Evans's class on deontic logic. I knew nothing about deontic logic at the time and it was not any particular interest in the subject that enticed me to make these trips, merely the excitement of seeing Gareth in action. One week he drew a distinction which has stayed with me ever since, between the epistemology of certain properties and their metaphysics. He claimed that chess experts can discern weakness in a position directly, without yet knowing what that weakness stems from. Though weakness is a resultant property (and this is a metaphysical matter), it can be directly discerned. And this means that the epistemology of moral properties need not match their metaphysics either.

Despite that, at this period I would have said, and did say, that my main interest was moral epistemology. This was partly because I was deeply into epistemology at that time anyway, and partly because the idea of a moral epistemology—of knowing the right—had been discredited by Hare, for whom all such issues made little sense; so it was fun to try to resuscitate it. And then there was the threatened naturalization of epistemology at the hands of W. V. Quine, to which the very idea of a moral epistemology was a rather satisfying antidote.

I fear that I then thought of moral philosophy as the study of reasons for believing actions to be right or wrong, rather than as the study of what makes an act right, or of how the things that do make actions right are able to do so, or more simply of what reasons there are to do the action. Nowadays I would distinguish fiercely between reasons for moral belief and moral reasons for action, and think of the latter as primary. In *Ethics Without Principles* I said that the epistemology should follow rather than precede the metaphysics, and if I had to choose between these, that does seem to me much more likely to be the right way round. But it too is a challengeable contrast, because the metaphysics of right-making, that is, an account of how it comes about that this action is right and that one wrong, is not obviously the same thing as an account of moral reasons for doing one thing rather than another. The favouring relation is what is involved in the latter, but it will not be involved in the former unless the properties of being right and being wrong are themselves to be understood in buck-passing terms, that is, as the properties of being that which there is most moral reason to do or not to do. I find myself tempted by such an account, despite significant difficulties. So I suppose I would say that my interests lie now not in the nature of moral enquiry (that is, moral epistemology) but in the nature of moral deliberation and its relation to action. Should I ever manage to find the time, I hope to write a very short book on this topic, and that this will be my last, to the relief of all concerned.

One of the penalties of propounding an iconoclastic position is that one is assailed on all sides. I am sure that I am not alone in finding this to be uncomfortable, though I know that there are some who positively enjoy it. David Gauthier would go hundreds of miles to hear himself criticized. He genuinely enjoyed the rough and tumble. My skin is not so thick, and one reason for this that has occurred to me is that (unlike in other areas of philosophy) a moral philosophy is often a cloaked account of the way in which the author finds it natural to think and behave. In this sense, a moral philosophy is often an account of the author, which has the implicit aim of showing, in each case, that it is alright to be me. It may be that we all live according to the precepts of our theoretical position, but if so, the reason might be, not that we are models of theoretical correctness and struggle courageously to live up to the positions we have reached on purely intellectual grounds, but that as moral philosophers we develop the intellectual positions which best fit our natural (and of course trained and developed) moral instincts. If that were so, it would explain both our tendency to instantiate our own theories, and, in this area at least, the sense that intellectual criticism is also personal, even when friendly. Those who work in other areas of philosophy do not have the same reason for finding attack uncomfortable. Whatever reason they have, we moral philosophers share. But we have another one as well.

The same is of course true in reverse. Particularism is an attack on those who feel the need for principles. That this attack hits a nerve I know, if only because of an extraordinary case in France quite recently in which someone was denied an interview for a position on the ground that nobody who was interested in particularism could be a suitable candidate for an appointment in higher education. This showed me that attempts to change aspects of people's basic moral perspective are themselves in danger of seeming not merely mistaken but immoral. Moral philosophy has its own risks.

Index

accountability 156
  and constraints on moral address 179–83
  and law 184
  and moral blame 181
  and morality 7, 8, 186, 187–8
    principles required for 187
  and moral obligations 174, 176–8
    moral blame 181, 182
    principles entailed by 187
    reactive attitudes 179–80, 181–2
    shared public culture 187–8
  and moral responsibility 179–80
Achinstein, Peter 34, 35
act-consequentialism 7
acting in the light of a fact 13–14, 25, 28
  and disjunctive approaches to experience 21–5
  and disjunctive approaches to rational intelligibility of actions 25–7
  and Hornsby's account 17–20
  and intelligibility of actions 17–18
  and practical reason 28
  weaknesses in Dancy's account 15–17
actions:
  act/agent distinction 106–7
  and beliefs 14–15, 39, 42, 52
  definition of 51
  and desires 52
  explanation of 3, 31, 33–7, 38, 39–42
  ideal 3, 66
  and reasons 33–4
aesthetic generalism 171
aesthetic particularism 171, 184, 185
aesthetic values 281–2
agency, rationalist conception of 116–21
agential reasons 3, 30, 32, 40
  constraints on 41
  disjunctive account of 30–1
  and explanation of actions 30–1, 33, 36–7, 38–9, 41, 42, 46
  and false beliefs 30–1
  and non-factivism 31, 46
  and non-psychologism 33
  and ontological concerns 43–6

Anscombe, G. E. M. (Elizabeth) 35n12, 189, 237n26
Aristotle 33, 197, 211, 236
Armstrong, Louis 184
aspirational reasons 6–7, 138
  consequences of failing to act on 145–6
  and deliberation 140, 141–3, 145
  and discretion 145, 151, 152, 153–4
  and social sanctions 152
asymmetric justification 127–9
attitudes and goodness 69
Austin, J. L. 225

balancing view of reasons 114–15
beliefs:
  and actions 14–15
  contrasted with believing/what is believed 45
  as dispositional states 52
  and experience 22, 23–4, 25, 26, 27
  and explanation of actions 39, 42
  and facts 16
  and false beliefs 2–3
  and rational intelligibility 25
  and reasoning 287–8
  warrant for 2
Belnap, Nuel 126
benefit, and reason strength 252–7
bipolar normativity 153
Black, H. C. 184
blameless wrong-doing 103–6
Bowra, Maurice 337
Bratman, Michael 294
Brennan, Geoffrey 301
Brentano, Franz 76
Broome, John 143
Brown, Campbell 314, 319n21
buck-passing 54, 244, 254
  and agent-neutral value 72, 73, 74
  and agent-relative value 72, 73, 74, 82–3
  and maximizing 87–9
  and caring about 77–8, 80, 92
  and consequentialism 69, 83–4, 85
  Dancy's objections to 66–74, 76, 95

buck-passing (*cont.*)
    resolving substantive questions by
        definition 83–7
    undermining distinction between
        moral rules 87–9
    and deontology 69, 83, 85
    and disputes in normative ethics 5
    and goodness 4, 67, 69–71, 78, 81, 84,
        89–90, 91–2
        fitting-attitude accounts of 78–9
    and intentional object constraint 77–80
    meaning of 76
    and polyadicity 89–94
    and pro-attitudes 70, 77, 79, 80, 86, 92, 94, 95
    and promise-keeping 72, 73, 84, 85, 88–9
    and reasons to act 79–80, 84, 92
    and rightness 4, 67–8, 69, 90–1
    and universality constraint 80–2
    and value 81
    and valuing something 80–1
Butler, Joseph 244

cognitive underdetermination 237
cognitivism 294–7
commendatory force of reasons 113–16,
    120–1, 122–3, 130
commitments 8, 148, 204, 210, 214, 225
consequentialism 253–4
    and benefits and harms 256–7
    and buck-passing 69, 83–4, 85
    and egoism 97–111
    and morality 158–61
    Parfit's theory of 103–6
    and reason strength 254–5
    and reparations 256
considerations 3, 41, 42, 45, 113, 123–4, 137,
    141–9, 168, 174, 179, 194–5, 218, 220
    and side-constraints 223, 227, 228
    those distinct from but connected with
        reasons 223–7
constraints 211–12, 257–9
    on moral address 179–83
    side-constraints 223, 227, 228
    and threshold constraints 257
context dependency 260, 266
    and holism 267
    and value 267–8
contractualism 7
    and morality 161–4
conversational implicatures 39
Copp, David 261n14
counterfactuals 41

Dancy, Jonathan:
    and agential reasons 30
    and buck-passing 54, 66–74, 95
        objections to 70–3, 76, 83–9
        resolving substantive questions by
            definition 83–7
        undermining distinction between
            moral rules 87–9
    and complete reasons 246
    contributions of 1
    and default values and reasons 205, 249–52
    and deliberation 140
    and disablers 198, 220, 246, 250
    and duty 72, 73
    and enablers 198, 220, 222, 246, 251, 279
    and enticing reasons 112–13
    and ethical particularism 193
    and *Ethics Without Principles* 168, 196
    and explanation of actions 34, 37, 38, 39,
        41–2, 250–1
    and goodness 67, 70–1, 89–90, 91–2
    and holism 168, 196, 241, 242, 262, 265
    and intensifiers 221, 222
    and invariant reasons 212–13
    and irreducibly normative
        properties 310, 331
    and morality 186
    and moral particularism 168, 216, 236,
        241, 248, 265
        metaphysical turn in 196–9
        obscurity of 198
    and *Moral Reasons* 198
    and motivating reasons 43
    and non-factivism 33, 35–6, 37, 39,
        40, 42–3
    and non-psychologism 30, 195–6
    and ontological particularism 197
    and organic unities 269–70
        argument against 270–2
        objection to argument
            against 273–80
    and Parfit:
        act/agent distinction 106–7
        consequentialism 103–6
        driver in the desert case 107–8
        indirect self-defeatingness 98, 99, 103,
            107, 108–11
        self-interest theory 98–103
    philosophical development and interests
        of 337–40
    and *Practical Reality* 2, 13, 29
        motivating-normative distinction 30

and principles 171–2, 196
  scepticism over role of 218
 and rightness 67–8, 69, 70, 90–1
 and weighing reasons 260
Darwall, Stephen 131, 153n10
Davidson, Donald 45, 51, 243–4
Davis, Wayne 33–4
 and motivating reasons 43–4
decision structure 125–7
default reasons and values 205, 249–52
defeaters 267
 and reasons 168–9
deliberation:
 and aspirational reasons 140, 141–3, 145
 and conflicting considerations 149
 Dancy's framing of 140
 and deontic reasons 140, 141–2, 144
 and discretion 145
 and institutional sanctions 150–2
 interpersonal framework of 150
 and irreducibly normative properties 328–31
 and morality 138–9, 164–5
 and normative considerations 159–60
 and relational normativity 150–8
 structure of 145–50
 and weight of reasons 143–4
demands and orders 131, 135
deontic normativity 138, 140
deontic reasons 6–7, 112–13, 140
 and balancing view of reasons 114–15
 and commendatory aspect of reasons 113–16, 122–3, 130
 and consequences of failing to act 145
 and deliberation 141–2, 143, 144
 and discretion 151–3
 and enticing reasons 5–6, 113, 123, 124
 and institutional sanctions 150–2
 and lack of discretion 145, 151
 and morality 137, 138, 140, 158, 164–5, 166
  elusive idea of deontic structure 139–43
  relational normativity 150–8
  structure of deliberation 144–50
  weight of reasons 143–4
 and non-peremptory reasons 123, 127, 130
 non-reductive view of 121–4
 and peremptory force of reasons 114, 115, 116, 120, 124, 129

and rationalist conception of agency 116–21
 reductive view of 113–21
 and rejection of non-deontic reasons 124–5
  asymmetric justification 127–9
  structure of decision 125–7
 relational nature of 7
 and relational normativity 150–8
 and structure of deliberation 145–50
deontology and buck-passing 69, 83, 85
desert 231, 235, 244, 245
desire 119–20
 as dispositional state 52
destitution 70–3, 74
Dickson, Maggie 281
diminishers 267
disablers 198, 219–20, 227, 246, 250
discretion:
 and aspirational reasons 145, 151, 152, 153–4
 and deontic reasons 151–3
disdain 180–1
disjunctive approaches to experience 25
disloyalty 202–6
Dolby, David 43n16
duty 72, 73, 83, 86
Dworkin, Ronald 183, 237n25, 317

egoism 5
 and consequentialism 97–111
 and paradox of hedonism 98
 and Parfit's self-interest theory 98–103
 and reason strength 255
emotions and asymmetrical justification 128–9
enablers 198, 267, 279
 and reasons 42, 168–9, 219–20, 222, 246, 251
Enoch, David 11, 131, 318n19, 321n25, 328, 329–31
enticing reasons 5–6, 113, 123, 124
 and asymmetry of 127
epistemological generalism 171
epistemological particularism 171
ethical particularism 193
ethics 8
 and act/agent distinction 106–7
 and ambitions of ethical theory 235
 non-realist conception 237

ethics (cont.)
    realist conception 235–7
    and indirectly self-defeating theories 98, 99, 103, 107, 108–11
    and Parfit's consequentialism 103–6
    and Parfit's self-interest theory 98–103
    as a practical matter 110
evaluative judgments 81
Evans, Gareth 338
Ewing, A. C. 69, 76
exclusionary reasons 143, 144
experience:
    and beliefs 22, 23–4, 25, 26, 27
    disjunctive approaches to 20, 21–5
    epistemological significance of 22–3
    and fallibility 22
    and justification of belief 22
    and knowledge 22–3
    rational significance of 25
explanation of actions 3, 31, 33–7, 38, 39–42, 250–1
    and agential reasons 30–1, 33, 36–7, 38–9, 41, 42, 46
    and beliefs 39, 42
    and borderline cases of action 53
    and Dancy's views 34, 38, 39, 41–2
    and false beliefs 31–2, 36, 46
    idealization approach 50, 51, 53, 54
    and infinite ends 206–9
    and instrumental rationality 52
    lowest-common-denominator approach to 50, 51, 52
    non-enquirer-relative account of 250
    and non-factivism 35–6, 37, 39, 40
    and non-ideal actions 66
    and psychological facts 41
    standard approach to 52, 53, 66
    and truth 31
expressive acts 62–3

facts:
    and beliefs 16
    normative 9
    and practical reason 243
    and reasons 2, 124, 169–70, 219
fallibility 22–3
false beliefs 2–3
    and agential reasons 30–1
    and explanation of actions 31–2, 36, 46
    and non-factivism 37
fidelity 224, 248

Foot, Philippa 209
Frege, Gottlob 30
Fried, Charles 223
friendship 140, 144, 148, 150, 224–5
    and relational normativity 155–7

Garfield, Jay 197
Gauthier, David 263n17, 339
Geach, Peter 273, 274, 275
Gleeson, Andrew 198
Glock, Hans-Johann 44–5
goodness 69–70, 76, 89–90
    and agent-relative value 82–3
    and attitudes 69
    and buck-passing 4, 67, 69, 70–1, 78–9, 81, 84, 91–2
    fitting-attitude accounts of 78–9, 94
    intrinsic 90
    polyadicity of 70, 89–94
    and reason strength 252–7
    and rightness 69
Greenspan, Patricia S. 145n5, 146n6
groundings, and reasons 228–35
gustatory values 274–5, 281

happiness, and paradox of hedonism 98
Hare, R. M. 195n1, 240, 338
harm 164, 182, 203, 248, 257, 258
    undeserved harm 9, 243, 245, 246–7, 259, 261
Hart, H. L. A. 183
hedonism 254
    and paradox of 98
Hempel, Carl G. 34, 51, 52
holism 10, 168, 196, 262, 265
    and defeaters and enablers 168–9
    limits of 243, 249
    meaning of 241, 267
    and moral particularism 170–1, 241–2
    and normative reasons 168
    and organic unities 266, 267–70, 280–4
    and practical reason 242
    and principles 201–6
    and reasons both for and against an act 245–6
    and reason strength 260
    and uncodifiability 242
    and valence switching 242–3, 246
    and value 267–8
    varieties of 218–19
    and weighing reasons 260
Hooker, Brad 186

INDEX

Hornsby, Jennifer 2, 13
   and acting in the light of a fact 17–20
Hume, David 51, 52, 199, 209
Hyman, John 38

impartial consequentialism 5
incommensurability 112, 122, 123
indifference 117, 118n4
indignation 180
inference 10–11, 292, 308–9
   quasi-inferences 297–8, 299, 301, 302, 305, 309
infinite ends 206–9
instrumental rationality 293–4
   and explanation of actions 52
intelligibility 19, 20, 25, 26, 117–18, 119, 120, 123
intensifiers 221, 222, 267
invariant reasons 212–13
invitations and speech acts 133–4
irreducibly normative properties 310
   conditions for 311
   and deliberation 328–31
   and descriptive properties 11
   distinguishing normative from descriptive properties 310–12
   Jackson's argument against 312–14
     necessarily coextensive predicates ascribe the same property 319–24
     new versions of 314–19
   and non-reductive realism 311
     appeal to Leibniz's law 325–8
     objections to Jackson's argument 314, 316–17, 318, 319–20, 331–4
   and reductive realism 311

Jackson, Frank 11, 310, 312–14
judgment-sensitive attitudes 59–60
justice 207, 210, 214, 226, 244, 250, 254
justification 229

Kagan, Shelley 112
Kant, Immanuel 234, 292–4
Kenny, Anthony 44n17
Kim, Jaegwon 312
knowledge and experience 22–3
Korsgaard, Christine 125
Kramer, Matthew H. 320n24

Lance, Mark 32n10, 228, 251
Latin grammar 45

latitude 7, 117, 122, 123
law:
   and accountability 184
   and general principles 183–4
     public knowledge of 185–6
   and morality 174, 262–3
     difference between 185
Lee, H. D. P. 337
Leibniz's Law 325–8
Lenman, James 32
Little, Margaret Olivia 193, 228, 251
loyalty 202–6
lying 228–33, 234–5, 241–2, 247

McDowell, John 30, 76, 193
   on concerns 207
   on moral decision-making 196–7
   on moral judgement 194–5
McKeever, Sean 170
McNaughton, David 193, 338
Mill, J. S. 177
modifiers, predictive and attributive use of 273–5
Moore, G. E. 10, 90, 233, 253n5, 260
   on organic unities 266, 268, 270
moral convictions and infinite ends 207
moral identity 204
morality 7
   and accountability 7, 8, 186, 187–8
     principles required for 187
     shared public culture of 187–8
   and ambitions of ethical theory 235
     non-realist conception 237
     realist conception 235–7
   and anthropology of morals 199–201
   consequentialist understanding of 158–61
   and constraints 211–12, 257–9
   and contractualism 161–4
   and deliberation 138–9, 164–5
   deontic structure of 137, 138, 140, 158, 164–5, 166
   as elusive idea 139–43
   relational conception of morality 161–5
   relational normativity 150–8
   structure of deliberation 144–50
   weight of reasons 143–4
   and ideal of human relationship 161, 162–3
   importance of 137, 165
   inescapability of 137
   and law 174, 262–3
     difference between 185

morality (*cont.*)
    and moral evaluation 199–201
        pluralism of 209–10
    and moral generalism 158–9, 170, 172, 173, 189–90
    and moral judgement 194–5, 206, 211
    and moral ought 78, 88, 106, 169, 170, 171–2, 173, 176
    necessity of the demands made by 137
    and normative requirements 160
    normative significance of 158–9, 164
    as 'peculiar institution' 189
    and principles 171–2, 173, 178, 213–14
        infinite ends 207
        objections to 194–5, 196
        required for accountability 187
    relational conception of 161–5
    as social phenomenon 199, 210–11
    and the unforsakeable and the forbidden 211–12
moral obligations 7–8, 73, 173, 258n10
    accessibility of 178, 187–8
    and accountability 174, 176–8
        entails principles 187
        moral blame 181, 182
        moral responsibility 179–80
        reactive attitudes 179–80, 181–2
        shared public culture of 187–8
    contrast with legal obligations 185
    definition of 175
    demands of 176
    as distinct from being favoured by moral reasons 175–6
    and general principles 178
    and moral generalism 189–90
    and moral ought 176
    and moral particularism 197
    second-personal character of 177–8, 182
moral particularism 8, 168, 185, 265
    and anthropology of morals 199–201
    and holism 170–1, 241–2
    and infinite ends 206–9
    meaning of 241, 248
    metaphysical turn in 196–9
    and moral agent 215–16
    and moral judgement 194–5, 206, 211
    and moral obligations 197
    obscurity of 198
    and principles 241–2
    and property-response relations 202–3
    and quietism 238

and uncodifiability 242
and the unforsakeable and the forbidden 211–12
motivating reasons 2, 43–4
    and agential reasons 30
    as intentional objects 43
    and normative reasons 29–30
Müller, Anselm 233n21
murder 233, 234–5

Nagel, Thomas 119
non-cognitivism 240
non-deontic reasons 5–6, 112–13, 123, 130
    rejection of 124–5
        asymmetric justification 127–9
        structure of decision 125–7
    and speech acts 134–5
        invitations 133–4
        requests 131–3
non-factivism 31, 33, 37, 42–3
    and agential reasons 31, 46
    and explanation of actions 35–6, 37, 39, 40
    and non-psychologism 32
    rejection of 32
non-peremptory reasons 123, 127, 130
non-psychologism 2–3, 30, 195–6
    and agential reasons 33
    and false beliefs 30–1
    and non-factivism 32
    objections to 32
normative bases 229, 230, 231
normative generalism 171
normative particularism 171, 173
normative properties, *see* irreducibly normative properties
normative reasons 2, 148–9, 168–9, 244, 245
    and aspirational reasons 138
    and deontic normativity 138
    and friendship 155–6
    and holism 168
    and morality 158–9
    and motivating reasons 29–30
    and practical reason 245
normative support 127–9
normativity:
    notions of 244
    and practical reason 244–5
    teleological conception of 159, 160
    and universal reasons 247, 248

obligations, *see* moral obligations
Oddie, Graham 318n18
ontological particularism 197
Oppenheim, Paul 34
organic unities 10, 266
  Dancy on 269–70
    argument against 270–2
  and holism 266, 267–70, 280–4
  meaning of 266, 268
  objections to Dancy's argument
    against 273–80
    connection between values and
      reasons 273–5
    contribution of parts to value 275–8
    internal objection 279–80
  and parts 268–9
  and value 268, 270–2
orthonomous actions 3, 54
  capacities required for 3–4
  circumstances of performance of 57–8
  criteria of correctness 55–6
  description of 56, 60–1, 64–6
  and non-ideal actions 66
  and reasons for action 59–61
    judgment-sensitive attitudes 59–60
  and reasons for desire 61–2, 64
    expressive acts 63
  and reasons for intention 61–4
    expressive acts 62–3
  sensitivity to how things are 54–5
  as two-track process 71

Pappas, Gregory 212
Parfit, Derek 77n6, 92, 322, 333
  and act/agent distinction 106–7
  and blameless wrong-doing 103–6
  and *Clare* 103–4
  and consequentialism 103–6
  and *Driver in the Desert* 107–8
  and egoism 97
  and indirect self-defeatingness 98, 99,
    103, 107, 108–11
  and *Kate* 101–3
  and *My Moral Corruption* 104–5
  and *Reasons and Persons* 97
  and *Schelling's Answer to Armed
    Robbery* 100–1
  and self-interest theory 98–103
particularism, *see* aesthetic particularism;
  epistemological particularism;
  ethical particularism; moral
  particularism; normative particularism;
  ontological particularism; practical
  particularism
peremptory force of reasons 114, 115, 116,
  120, 124, 129
Perloff, Michael 126
Pettit, Philip 54
Plantinga, Alvin 323–4
pleasure 249–50, 254
polyadicity and buck-passing 89–94
practical generalism 171
practical particularism 171, 173
practical reason(s) 9
  as both for and against an act 245–6
  and consequentialism 253–4
  and constraints 257–9
  and default reasons 249–52
  as facts 243
  and holism 242
  manifestation of 28
  as mental states 243
  and normative reasons 245
  and normativity 244–5
  and practical reasoning 11, 289–92
    consciousness of attitude type 290
    marked contents 290, 291–2
    meaning of 289
    rule-governed 289–90
    separating theoretical and practical
      reasoning 305–8
  and reason strength 243, 252–7, 258
    context 260
    determination of 259–60
  and relation of normative to
    non-normative 9
  as rule-governed operation 11
  two-tier view of 243
  and universal reasons 247, 248
  and valence switching 243
  and weighing reasons 259–61
principles 8, 9, 171–2
  and holism 201–6
  and infinite ends 207
  and law 183–4
    public knowledge of 185–6
  and morality 173, 178, 213–14
    not required for 194–5, 196
    required for accountability 187
  and moral particularism 241–2
Prior, A. N. 44n17
promise-keeping 72, 73, 84, 85, 88–9, 170, 230

psychological facts and explanation
    of actions 41
Pufendorf, Samuel 183–5

Quine, W. V. O. 44n17, 339

rationality 292–4
Raz, Joseph 112, 117, 120, 143, 144n3,
    144n4, 246
    and deontic reasons 122–4
reactive attitudes 179–80, 181–2
reasoning:
    and basing 300
    and basing permissions of rationality 301–2
    and basing prohibitions of
        rationality 298–300
    and cognitivism 294–7
    and conclusion-attitudes 289
    and conscious reasoning 286–7
    and explicit reasoning 287
    and inference 10–11, 292, 308–9
        quasi-inferences 297–8, 299, 301, 302,
            305, 309
    and modus ponens rule 288, 290
    operating on contents of beliefs 287–8
    and permission theory of
        correctness 302–5
    and practical reasoning 11, 289–92
        consciousness of attitude type 290
        marked contents 290, 291–2
        meaning of 289
        rule-governed 289–90
    and premise-attitudes 289
    and requirements of rationality 292–4
        instrumental rationality 293–4
    and requirement theory of correctness 298
    rules of 288
    separating theoretical and practical 305–8
    theoretical 10–11, 287–8
reasons:
    and actions 33–5
    balancing view of 114–15
    as both for and against an act 245–6
    categories of 252
    as cause that rationalizes 243–4
    commendatory aspect of 6, 113–16,
        120–1, 122–3, 130
    compact view of 246
    distinguished from considerations that
        connect with reason 223–7
    and enablers 42, 219–20, 222, 246, 251

and facts 2, 124, 169–70, 219
and groundings 228–35
and non-peremptory reasons 123,
    127, 130
normative force of 6
peremptory force of 114, 115, 116, 120,
    124, 129
and reasons 168–9
and rules 116
simple view of 244–5
strength of 243, 252–7, 258
    context 260
    determination of 259–60
universal 247, 248
and valence switching 219, 242–3
and values 10, 70, 270–1, 273–5
and weighing 259–61
see also agential reasons; aspirational
    reasons; deontic reasons; enticing
    reasons; motivating reasons; non-
    deontic reasons; normative reasons;
    practical reason(s)
reciprocity, ethic of 209–14
relational normativity 150–8
    and friendship 155–7
reparation, duties of 256
requests 6
    and speech acts 131–3
Ridge, Michael 170
rightness:
    and buck-passing 4, 67–8, 69, 90–1
    and goodness 69
    polyadicity of 70
Rödl, Sebastian 23n5, 206–8
Ross, W. D. 85, 86–7, 90, 94, 244, 249–50,
    253, 256, 259n12, 338
rules 7, 9, 87–9, 116, 186–7, 194–5, 227,
    229, 233–4, 248
    and reasoning 288–90
    and reasons 116

Scanlon, T. M.:
    and buck-passing 4, 76, 77, 80–1, 84,
        244, 254
    and judgment-sensitive attitudes 59–60
    and morality 161–2
    and principles 171, 173
    and reasons for action 60
    and value 80–1
Schroeder, Mark 77n6
self-interest theory 98–103

Setiya, Kieran 301
Singer, Peter 262–3
Skorupski, John 30n3
Smith, Michael 29n1, 41
solidarity, ethic of 209–14
speech acts 134–5
    demands and orders 131, 135
    invitations 133–4
    requests 131–3
Stalnaker, Robert 52
Strawson, P. F. 176–7
    on moral responsibility 179–80
    on reactive attitudes 179–80, 181
Sturgeon, Nicholas 317n16
Suikkanen, Jussi 11, 324n29, 325, 326, 327
supererogation 7–8, 115, 117, 160, 175, 176
supervenience 244

teleological approach to normativity 159, 160
Thompson, Michael 153n10, 207
Thomson, Judith Jarvis 60
torture 212–13, 260–1
truth and explanation 31
truth-telling 228–9, 234–5

uncodifiability 228, 242
universal reasons 247, 248
Urmson, J. O. 175, 337

valence switching 219, 242–3, 246
value 4, 76
    agent-neutral 5, 72, 73, 74
    agent-relative 4, 72, 73, 74, 82–3
        and maximizing 87–9
    and buck-passing 80–1
    enabling conditions of 10
    and holism 267–8
    and organic unities 268, 270–2

    objections to Dancy's argument
        against 273–80
    and reasons 10, 70, 270–1, 273–5
    and reason strength 252–7
variabilism 218, 222, 228, 238
Väyrynen, Pekka 9, 229–32,
    235, 236
virtues, uncodifiability of 228

Watson, Gary 178, 180
Wedgwood, Ralph 294
welfare and the good 252–7
well-being 233n19
White, Alan 30, 44, 45
Wiggins, David 8, 193, 199–201
    and autonomy of moral values and
        reasons 201–2
    and cognitive underdetermination 237
    and ethic of solidarity and
        reciprocity 209–14
    and *Ethics* 209
    and moral evaluation 199–201
        pluralism of 209–10
    and moral judgement 201n5, 211
    and principles 213–14
    and property-response relations 200–1,
        202–3
    and social origins and purposes of
        morality 210–11
will 117, 120
Williams, Bernard 109, 164n16, 189,
    219n2, 252
    and 'one thought too many' 223, 224,
        225, 227
Wittgenstein, Ludwig 30, 194, 248
Wolf, Susan 223

Zimmerman, Michael 283